It's So Much Work to Be Your Friend

HELPING THE
CHILD WITH LEARNING DISABILITIES
FIND SOCIAL SUCCESS

Richard Lavoie

A TOUCHSTONE BOOK
Published by Simon & Schuster

TOUCHSTONE
Rockefeller Center
1230 Avenue of the Americas
New York, NY 10020

Copyright © 2005 by Richard Lavoie
All rights reserved,
including the right of reproduction
in whole or in part in any form.

TOUCHSTONE and colophon are registered trademarks
of Simon & Schuster, Inc.

For information regarding special discounts for bulk purchases,
please contact Simon & Schuster Special Sales at 1-800-456-6798
or business@simonandschuster.com

Designed by Christine Weathersbee

Manufactured in the United States of America

10 9 8 7 6 5 4 3 2 1

Library of Congress Cataloging-in-Publication Data
Lavoie, Richard D.
    It's so much work to be your friend : helping the child with learning
disabilities find social success / Richard Lavoie.
        p.   cm.
    "A Touchstone book."
    Includes bibliographical references and index.
    1. Social skills in children.   2. Learning disabled children.   3. Social
acceptance in children.   4. Interpersonal relations in children.   I. Title.
HQ783.L38   2005
371.9—dc22   2005042461

ISBN-13: 978-0-7432-5463-2
ISBN-10:   0-7432-5463-5

The greatest gift that a mother can give
to her child is to have her face light up
whenever the child enters the room.

—Toni Morrison

To my mentor and partner, Janet . . .
whose face lights up for Kitt, Dan, and Megg.

And to my mother, Mary Kendall Lavoie . . .
whose face lit up for me for fifty-two years.

—RDL

Acknowledgments

My editor, Trish Todd, wrote me a kind and gracious letter upon reading the initial draft of this book. In the letter she generously stated, "I really do feel as if I have just read the results of a lifetime of professional experience."

As always, she was correct. This book reflects information, insights, and inspirations that I have received from countless colleagues, parents, and children who have crossed my path in the past thirty years. I am deeply indebted to them for their passion, patience, and persistence, which have contributed immeasurably to my career. Attempting to mention each individual by name would force me to rely on my carefully crafted journal (which I never kept) or my memory (which I am rapidly—but assuredly—losing). I would, undoubtedly, forget to include a name or two and that would cause me great angst in the future. So, rather than cite individuals, allow me to acknowledge groups of people whose fingerprints and footprints are all over this book.

To my undergraduate professors at Fitchburg State College in Massachusetts (1968–1972), some of whom recognized that—perhaps—I had the "soul" for special education and taught me the basics of the field that I love.

To the incomparable pioneers at Eagle Hill School in Hardwick (1972–1975), whose devotion and blind faith in the potential of special-needs kids allowed them to create miracles in the woods of central Massachusetts.

To my courageous comrades at Eagle Hill Schools in Greenwich, Connecticut, and Southport, Connecticut (1975–1990), whose friendship, guidance, wisdom, and creativity are within the pages of this book.

To the "Camelot Crew" at Riverview School (1990–2001), a group of believers who came together on Cape Cod to create a safe harbor for hundreds of children whose lives were changed forever. As Harry Potter's teacher Dumbledore said when he left Hogwarts School, "I will only *truly* have left this school when none there are loyal to me or believe as I believe."

To the extraordinary team at Touchstone/Fireside, particularly editor Trish Todd and copy editor Patty Romanowski Bashe, for their faith in this project.

To my colleagues and students at Simmons College in Boston, who accept my mentoring and mentor me in return.

To the countless colleagues and friends I have met on my travels, who continually confirm my belief that kids who struggle—and those who serve them—have a special place waiting for them in heaven.

To the individuals who had faith in my message long before others did: Beryl Kaufman, Jim Middleton, Bud and Jayne Schiff, Mel Levine, Dr. James Cavanaugh, Bruce Montgomery, Bob Brooks, Sister Carol Ann, Michael Held, Rick Goldman, Larry Lieberman, Sandy Gilligan, Carl Mores, Liza Dawson, and Noel Gunther.

To Kitt, Dan, and Meghan, who waited patiently while I dealt with the children of others.

To my brothers . . . who taught me that siblings can be best friends.

And to Janet . . . who has held my hand and my heart through all of the above.

I am indebted to all of you. Your friendship, loyalty, wisdom, faith, and love have made all the difference. God bless us . . . every one.

With every good wish,

—Rick

Contents

Getting in Good

"What do they all want from me?"
"What do I have to do so they'll like me?"
"Who do I have to be to be one of them?"
"Do I have the right stuff to satisfy and please them?"

They don't very often articulate these questions, but children and adolescents wrestle with these quandaries every day as they perform for diverse audiences: their peers, their parents, important grown-ups outside of their family (mostly their teachers), and their own self-assessments. They desperately want and need to get in good with these highly judgmental audiences. Some children are blessed in having what it takes to win rave reviews from all. They carry with them a widely coveted asset called *childhood versatility*, a packet of well-rounded abilities plus a keen sense of how and when to deploy them to please the outside world. Other kids are more narrowly specialized; their kinds of minds are calibrated to satisfy only certain highly specific demands. Many of them become remarkably productive adults—once they are permitted to practice their specialties. Their school years, on the other hand, may be punishing and arduous, sometimes so ego-lacerating that they are drained of ambition and left with enduring biographical scars. Adding to the damage, some of them experience rejection and isolation by their peers. Those who fail socially are especially at risk, and appropriately, they comprise the central focus of this book.

Proficiency within the social arena has two striking benefits: it is a source of fun and it makes you feel like a desirable person. When you're a child, other children are your yardsticks; you keep measuring yourself against them. And you hope they will come to perceive you as worthy of their companionship and admiration. For a child, few, if any, sensations compare with the ecstasy of social acceptance. The protected and connected feeling that comes with being sought after by peers pumps fuel into the engines of growing up. Intimacy and shared recreation provide positive stimulation and a much-desired feeling of belonging, thereby averting the dark shadows of loneliness. Every child needs to feel wanted. Exchanging instant messages at a rapid clip, having a cell phone that won't cease its melodic chirping, harvesting prestigious party invitations, and feeling you are in de-mand at a lunch table go far to make a kid feel validated. If others want you with them, you must be special.

But stringent admission requirements have to be met if a kid is to enter into the joys of interpersonal engagement. To get in good, she is obliged to prove her tastes are up to date. She must use well-crafted verbal and nonverbal communication, while projecting just the right public image. She is expected to exhibit well-calibrated body movements and facial expressions and implement ingratiating pat-terns of behavior. Throughout, she must be able to study her com-panions and monitor herself so as to keep delivering to others what they would like from her. She has to gauge the effects she is having on people around her; that way she can make on-the-spot adjust-ments of her behavior, speech, or conveyed impressions. She should be skilled at marketing herself—without boasting or aggressively overmarketing herself. It is helpful if she has some desirable products to offer, such as talent in sports, a sense of humor, video-game exper-tise, or good looks. She also must be a rapid and astute interpreter of social scripts and incidents. After all, how can you react appropriately to other peoples' actions when you misconstrue them? The presence or absence of such sophisticated interpersonal intelligence will either enable or disable the social life of a young child or teenager. And for most of them, nothing else matters as much.

Social success during childhood and beyond entails two central missions: friendship formation and reputation management. Inti-macy, shared pleasures, and privileged communication channels con-stitute the core ingredients of friendship. Close relationships bring out a child's altruism, collaboration skills, and empathy. Reputation, on the other hand, entails the cultivation and expression of an outer image, along with the political skills needed to satisfy the expectations of significant constituencies (fellow students, teachers, and others). Being well-thought-of demands affability and calls for the attainment of some performance and taste standards (possibly including overall "coolness"). Some children are triumphant; they establish and maintain rich friendships plus a laudable reputation. Others acquire decent reputations but forge no really close relationships. There are those who have friends without enjoying much popularity. And, very tragically, too many kids experience social success deprivation, a lack of success in both domains. They are rejected or neglected, and as a result, they suffer day after day in school. Often their woes are worsened as a result of cruel bullying and exclusion, artfully perpetuated by their more popular, socially deft classmates.

Adults who care for and about children need to reach out to kids who endure social impairments. They may be plagued by innate dysfunctions that impede their understanding of how relationships are supposed to work, thwart their processing of important social data, and prevent them from communicating and acting right with others—a collection of behavioral tools and sensitivities that are nearly instinctive to their classmates.

Not all children with learning differences suffer social injuries. It is common to hear a parent take pride in the fact that her child who seriously underachieves in the classroom possesses terrific "people skills." We should never underestimate the importance of this aptitude. In the long run, knowing how to form and sustain relationships is far more important than spelling accurately or mastering the intricacies of a foreign language's grammatical structures. People-skilled kids warrant our respect and they should be building on this important strength by developing their leadership skills. On the other hand, there are students who suffer from a condition I call "social intoxication." They obtain so much gratification from their peers that nothing else matters to them; their learning becomes mediocritized, and their family lives may be sacrificed for their social lives. They may abandon their uniqueness and personal strengths in an effort to do whatever it takes to win the adulation of their friends. A talented violist may quit the orchestra because his friends don't perceive that instrument as sufficiently "cool." This condition can be just as lethal as social rejection and isolation. Social intoxication is a bubble that may burst in early adulthood, if not sooner. There is a healthy zone between these extremes, an optimal level of interpersonal gratification. We need to help all kids strive toward this degree of social success.

Getting in good with peers is not the only social challenge children have to tackle. A child's acceptance by important adults is equally essential. Kids sense that even their parents have to be won over. For the most part, they know their parents love them. What they need to keep checking out is whether or not their parents respect them and boast about them to their colleagues at work and to neighbors and relatives. A child who grows up believing he is a disappointment to his parents is vulnerable to all sorts of lethal complications, including abysmal self-esteem and a hazardous depletion of motivation.

Children regard their teachers in part as evaluators and crave praise and acceptance from them. Those who can't seem to please their teachers question their overall intelligence and may come to believe that they were born to lose, in which case there is no point in trying. Others know what it takes to win over a teacher. They are able to read and meet her explicit as well as unspoken expectations. They sense, for instance, which teachers reward original thinking and which ones want you to stick to the facts and regurgitate small details on quizzes. They can predict what will be on an upcoming test because they have such keen insight into the workings of a particular teacher's thought processes. They may also be politically astute, knowing what they'll need to do or say to persuade a teacher to like them, a critical skill to cultivate, since today's teachers are tomorrow's bosses, immediate supervisors, and customers—it's definitely good to keep them feeling good about you. Such political insights and strategies are nearly automatic for some students, while others need coaching to analyze and implement positive relationships with grown-ups whose judgments can have such a durable influence over one's short- and long-term accomplishments and performance ratings.

The social issues I have mentioned are widely misunderstood by parents and by schools. As a result, vital social needs of young children and adolescents remain ignored or mismanaged. The public must be educated regarding this sorely neglected area of childhood striving. In *It's So Much Work to Be Your Friend,* Rick Lavoie has gone far toward filling the void by offering us a remarkably comprehensive view of the social stresses confronting so many struggling school children. He goes beyond theory to provide well-thought-out advice on helping kids surmount their social barriers. This book is also infused with valuable implications for students who are academically successful. All kids and parents need guidance on navigating the swift social and political currents of the school years. Rick Lavoie, relying on his many years of experience as a teacher, a leading educational administrator, and a dedicated parent, is an important voice, and he provides readily applicable suggestions on the ways in which parents can intervene in a sensitive manner to ensure that kids are getting in good in good ways. This book will most certainly enhance the parenting and schooling of a child of any age fortunate enough to have a parent or teacher who reads it.

—Dr. Mel Levine
The All Kinds of Minds Institute

Preface

As parents and people who care deeply about children, we believe that there is no responsibility more important than striving to give children the support and opportunities they need in order to grow up to be confident, happy, and healthy adults. In 1997 we started the I Am Your Child Foundation, and in 2004 we started the national advocacy organization Parents' Action for Children to raise awareness about the importance of a child's early years and to advance public policy through parental education and advocacy. Through the course of our work, we were very fortunate to meet Rick Lavoie and to learn about the valuable work he does. His profound understanding of the social and emotional needs of children with learning problems has come from his more than thirty years of experience working with children and parents, and this book reflects the best of his wisdom, compassion, and skill.

One of the most vital tasks of childhood is forming and maintaining friendships. Successful relationships with peers are known to have a significantly positive effect on a child's self-esteem and sense of well-being, in both the present and the future. The skills children learn through their friendships are ones that they will use throughout their lives. Friendships offer many opportunities for learning, growth, comfort, and pleasure. It is in the context of friendships that children learn how to understand and express their emotions and ideas, resolve conflict, tolerate frustration, learn healthy assertion, increase their appreciation for diversity, acquire leadership and cooperation skills, and develop empathy and humor.

All children have an innate need and desire to connect in meaningful ways with others. As Rick explains in this book, children with learning problems tend to struggle with social relationships. They often have a great deal of difficulty understanding social situations, and therefore are awkward in their attempts to make and maintain friendships. These children are frequently less accepted by peers and may often feel isolated and rejected. Because of their social difficulties, children with learning problems are less able to solve social problems, more likely to choose socially unacceptable behaviors in social situations, and, therefore, more likely to receive nonsupportive and negative responses from others. In addition to all of this, relationships with siblings and other family members can be very difficult and rocky, making home—a place that should be a child's safe haven—into yet another challenging and frustrating place to be. Of course, this also adds increased stress and difficulty to the lives of the parents of these children.

A lot of attention has been paid to addressing the academic needs of children with learning problems. As vitally important as this is, the reality is that children spend only about 20 percent of their time in school, meaning 80 percent of their time is spent in the community, on the playground, and at home with siblings and other family members. Rick reminds us that it is very important for adults to know that even if the six hours of a child's school day are going well, the remainder of his day may be extremely frustrating and demoralizing.

Think for a moment of how important friendships have been to you throughout your life. Some of the most meaningful, satisfying, and enjoyable moments in life happen in friendships. Think back to your childhood. It is likely that some of your happiest memories involve times of connection and friendship. Now imagine what childhood would have felt like without those moments. As adults, we know that there are many aspects to a productive and satisfying life. Certainly, finding work that is fulfilling and meaningful is important. But does life truly feel complete without friends and loved ones to share the successes and struggles? The relationship skills we learn in childhood are the very ones that serve us so well as we travel through the joys and challenges of our adult lives.

What would life be like if, in spite of your best efforts, you couldn't find ways to connect and join with others; if, in fact, you craved the companionship, trust, and rapport of a friend but instead found yourself shunned, rejected, and lonely? That is the experience for many children with learning problems. But it doesn't have to be. In this book, Rick explores the patterns that can emerge when a child with learning problems encounters social difficulties. Children who have no solid connections with friends often begin avoiding social situations, thus further increasing their sense of isolation and loneliness. What Rick has done so beautifully through his life's work, and now in his book, is to describe the ways we, as parents, can understand and help our children develop the skills that are so crucial to a happy, full, and productive life. This book is filled with warmth, wisdom, and stories that illustrate Rick's deep understanding of and empathy for children with learning problems and their families. His ideas are presented clearly and accessibly, giving parents and others who work with children the tools they need to actually teach the language of friendship to children.

In this book, Rick defines *social competence*. He explains that social competence is composed of a group of skills that a person knows how to use at the right time and place. These skills include knowing how to take turns in a conversation, expressing interest in another's point of view, appropriate ways to disagree, ways to enter a group, sensitivity, flexibility, and responsiveness. While many children may seem to pick up these skills naturally, this is not true for the child with learning problems. Rick explores a wide variety of learning difficulties and explores how each problem may be manifested in specific kinds of issues with social competence. He then goes on to offer practical and clear interventions and methods for each of the social issues. Rather than being a "one size fits all" solution, Rick's strategies differ depending on the particular learning problem. For example, Rick explains that a child with language difficulties may have particular challenges in regard to the "social side of language." Things such as taking turns in a conversation, maintaining eye contact, and adjusting tone of voice may need to be carefully taught and practiced. A child with auditory difficulties may have a very hard time understanding and remembering the information she hears. When this happens, the child can mistakenly appear to be rude, insensitive, or disobedient, thereby eliciting a negative response from peers and adults. The child with attention problems is going to have great difficulty with observing, understanding, and responding to the social world around him. Rick explores the social challenges that result from these difficulties, and offers approaches to teach these abilities directly.

One of the many strategies that Rick offers is called the Social Skill Autopsy. Using this innovative technique, an adult assists a child to improve social skills by analyzing social errors together and designing alternative strategies. This technique also works well in examining and identifying behaviors that contribute to positive social interaction. When children are helped to clearly understand what aspects of their behavior contribute to positive responses, they are more likely to use them again in other situations. Rick teaches the reader that this approach is successful because it provides the three things that children with learning disabilities need to develop and learn: immediate feedback, practice or drill, and positive reinforcement. This technique is a supportive, structured, constructive strategy to foster social competence. It uses problem solving to provide an opportunity for a child to actively participate in his or her learning process. Rick's book is filled with many such techniques to help foster the social skills that are so crucial to a happy childhood.

For parents of children with learning problems, the tasks of child rearing can be especially complicated and frustrating, leaving parents feeling overwhelmed and, at times, helpless. As parents who have children with learning difficulties know all too well, watching a loved child go through experiences of loneliness, confusion, and sadness is tremendously painful. However, Rick gives parents a more complete understanding of how to help their children learn the competence they need to form and maintain friendships. Using the information and tools that he offers, parents can help their children learn the skills they need to grow and flourish socially. What could be more joyous than watching your child's sense of self-worth blossom in the context of a meaningful friendship, all the while knowing that the skills being built and supported in these interactions are the very ones that will help carry your child through life? Rick's work has helped thousands of children and families greatly enhance the quality of their lives, and we are thrilled to support this wonderful book that will reach so many more.

—Rob and Michele Reiner
Santa Monica, California

"The Other Sixteen Hours"

I have been involved in the field of learning disabilities for more than thirty years. The majority of that time was spent as a teacher and administrator at residential schools for children with learning problems. During the early years of my career, I was very involved in the admissions process at these schools and, as a result, conducted hundreds of interviews with parents whose children were struggling in school.

I recall one interview vividly. A mother from Maryland was recounting her daughter's academic history and her struggles with reading. As she spoke, she was somewhat detached and spoke in a clipped, matter-of-fact fashion. She told me that her daughter was scheduled to enter fourth grade in the fall and that her family felt that she would not be able to succeed in that placement.

I asked whether her daughter agreed that an alternative placement was appropriate. With that, the mother's facial expression softened and tears began to well up in her eyes. She told me that the idea to change schools had actually *originated* with her daughter. She came home from school on the last day of classes and reported that her classmates, who had ignored or rejected her all year, had waited until the teacher left the room during the end-of-year party, picked her up, and placed her in the wastebasket. Sarah, the most popular girl in the class, announced, "You're garbage . . . and that's where garbage belongs."

The mother had been wringing her hands and looking down while she related this story. She then looked up and our eyes met. "Just one friend, Mr. Lavoie. Just one friend. That's all I want for my daughter."

In the 1970s, those who worked with learning disabled children believed that social rejection was a cruel *consequence* of a child's learning disorder. Conventional wisdom held that (a) the child had academic deficiencies, therefore (b) he failed in school, (c) this failure caused great embarrassment and humiliation that lowered his self-esteem, and therefore (d) he was reluctant to "join in" with his peers and was teased because of his inability to compete academically with his classmates.

If this theory were true, it would seem logical that once the academic failure was eliminated, the child would enjoy social success. Again, the conventional wisdom held that the learning disorder *caused* the academic failure, and the failure *caused* the social isolation and rejection.

However, my experiences with these children demonstrated that this cause-and-effect theory was greatly flawed. I watched as these children entered our school's highly individualized and noncompetitive classroom environment. Lessons were tailored to meet each child's unique needs. Success was an integral part of each child's program. Specialized teaching techniques were used to ensure mastery of the target concepts. For the first time in their academic careers, these children were experiencing genuine success in the classroom. As this success expanded, it seemed logical that their social skills and status would improve. But they did not.

This demonstrated to me a *direct* link between learning disorders and social incompetence. I have devoted my career to highlighting that link for parents and teachers and showing them how we can help children master the abilities they need to develop effective social skills.

I have served as an administrator in residential programs for kids with learning problems for more than twenty-five years. During that time, about two dozen parents have sat across my desk and sobbed, distraught over the difficulties that their children were experiencing. Not once—*not once*—were these parents crying because their children were unable to spell, read, or do the times tables. When a parent experiences that kind of pain, it is because of the social isolation, rejection, and humiliation that the child suffers every day—sitting alone on the school bus, hiding in the restroom during recess, eating lunch at an empty cafeteria table, waiting for the telephone to ring and the birthday invitations that never arrive.

Professionals have come to realize the critical fact that a child's social life—often referred to as "the other sixteen hours"—is immeasurably important to his happiness, health, and development. Most school systems now recognize that it is in the child's best interest— and, ultimately, in the community's best interest—to provide social skill instruction and remediation for school-age children who are not adjusting appropriately. Numerous formal studies have confirmed the wisdom of this. Children with learning disorders often have particular difficulty developing social competence. This creates a double whammy for them. They confront daily failure and frustration in *both* domains of school: academic and social.

The Keys to Understanding
Your Child's Behavior

The social competence of children with special needs has been the subject of extensive research and study in recent years. This research indicates several truths about the link between learning disabilities and social competence that will, doubtless, mirror your own experience with children who struggle in social environments.

Children with significant learning problems
- are more likely to choose socially unacceptable behaviors in social situations
- are less able to solve social problems
- are less able to predict consequences for their social behavior
- are less able to adjust to the reactions of their listeners in discussions or conversations
- are more likely to be rejected or isolated by their peers
- are more often the object of negative and nonsupportive statements, criticisms, and warnings from teachers
- are less adaptable to new social situations

- are more likely to be judged negatively by adults after informal observation
- receive less affection from parents and siblings
- have less tolerance for frustration and failure
- use oral language that is less mature, meaningful, and concise
- have difficulty interpreting or inferring the language of others
- are far more likely to be depressed
- are more likely to be ignored by peers when initiating verbal interactions
- tend to be involved in fewer extracurricular activities and have minimal social interactions with peers outside of school
- tend to have limited, repetitive, and immature vocabulary, use shorter sentences, and be less concise
- tend to have difficulty inferring the meanings of others in conversation, taking conversational turns, and seeing others' perspective
- have difficulty understanding humor, sarcasm, and ambiguities in oral language

When these facts are considered, it is little wonder that many children with learning disorders have significant difficulty functioning successfully in social situations.

It is a widely accepted fact that the *primary need* of the human being is to be liked and accepted by other human beings. Therefore, if a child is behaving in a way that causes others to *dislike* him, can we not assume that his behaviors are beyond his control? Why would a child intentionally behave in a manner that causes others to isolate and reject him? As parents and caregivers, we must remember that the social faux pas that these children make are, generally, beyond their control and are unintentional.

This is the key to understanding and remediating your child's social skill deficits. Once you accept the unintentional nature of these troubling behaviors, you will be able to cease "blaming the victim" and—most important—you will come to the realization that *punishing* the child for social errors is ineffective, unfair, and inappropriate. Punishing a child for having social skill deficits is akin to punishing him for being nearsighted or having the flu. The situation is beyond the child's control, so punishment simply won't work.

This book will provide analysis of and solutions to the most common social skill problems faced by school-age children. It is difficult to overstate the importance of a child's mastery of these basic social skills or the short-term and long-term consequences for the child who is unable to master them. Childhood provides a laboratory wherein the child uses trial-and-error to develop his repertoire of interactional social skills. The young person who enters adulthood without an effective repertoire of social skills will very likely experience significant difficulty in his home, workplace, and community environments.

Why Teach Social Skills?

Because inadequate social skills often result in peer rejection and unpopularity, they place a child at extraordinarily significant risk for aggression and other behavioral problems. Learning disabled (LD) children tend to have poorly developed problem-solving skills and, as a result, they tend to resolve conflicts by using aggression rather than negotiation.

Dorothy Crawford's classic study of the link between juvenile delinquency and learning disabilities has demonstrated that the LD adolescent confronts three significant risk factors in regard to delinquent behavior:

1. He is more likely to become involved in juvenile crime, due to his inability to secure meaningful employment.

2. He is more likely to be apprehended for his crimes, because of a failure to carefully plan and execute his actions. (Basically, he is bad at being bad.)

3. He is more likely to receive harsher court-ordered penalties than his nondisabled peers, because of this inability to successfully deal with the social demands of the judicial process

(e.g., meeting with attorneys, showing appropriate respect during proceedings).

Numerous studies clearly document the weak and inconsistent social competencies of adolescents with histories of delinquent behaviors. These behaviors are both the cause *and* consequence of a lack of social skills.

Mental health disorders (e.g., depression, anxiety) appear to be closely associated with—and often exacerbated by—social incompetence. The isolation and rejection children with poor social skills experience can create mental health problems and/or precipitate complications and worsening of existing problems.

The child with inadequate social skills has significant difficulty establishing and maintaining appropriate peer relationships. He is excluded from interactions and activities with other children and so misses the opportunity to learn and practice new social skills. In effect, a vicious cycle of social failure and skill deterioration results.

It is important that adults remain ever mindful of the fact that *children go to school for a living.* School represents their primary activity and purpose. If a child suffers from chronic rejection by and separation from his classmates, his ability to succeed in academic pursuits is greatly compromised.

It is in a school's best interest to provide social skill instruction and support for learning disabled children. This instruction has consistently resulted in improvement in children's behavior, acceptance, and academic performance. It also yields a decrease in antisocial, delinquent, and disruptive behavior. Everybody wins.

There are several additional reasons why we should provide direct instruction and guidance in the area of social skills.

1. *Social incompetence has a significant impact upon the family.*

I conduct a workshop entitled "On the Waterbed: The Learning Disabled Child at Home and in the Family." I use the term *waterbed* in reference to an analogy that I often make in the seminar: "A family of five is akin to five people lying side by side on a waterbed. When one person moves, everyone feels the ripple." So it is in a family. If one family member is experiencing difficulty of some sort, *all* family members inevitably feel the direct or indirect impact. If Mom or Dad is having trouble at work or if one of the children is struggling at school, everyone is affected in some way.

This is particularly true and noteworthy when a child in the family has social skill deficits. This child is frequently a source of embarrassment, puzzlement, and anxiety among his family members. His strange and inappropriate behavior is often disruptive to family outings or even the day-to-day interactions within the home and community. A child once told me, "It makes me sad and guilty when my friends say, 'Come over to our yard to play. But don't bring your brother. He's weird!'"

2. All environments are social.

Outside of school, your child can avoid confronting the majority of his academic deficiencies. If he cannot spell, he can play video games with his friends; you do not need effective spelling skills in order to play Sega. If she cannot read, she can spend her Saturdays playing soccer with the neighborhood children; reading is not a prerequisite for soccer.

But if your child has poor social skills, he simply cannot avoid situations that require these skills. Any and all activities that involve two or more people require the use of social skills. If you are alone on an elevator and the doors open for a second boarding passenger, that eight-foot-by-eight-foot chamber instantly becomes a social environment wherein you and your new social partner have defined rights, roles, and responsibilities. You need social skills to play video games or soccer. The child simply cannot avoid the use of social skills.

3. The child cannot compensate for his lack of social competence.

Thanks to numerous breakthroughs in assistive technology, a child can compensate for nearly any academic disability. The math-deficient child can use a calculator; the child who writes poorly can use a word processor; the nonspeller can use a spell check option on his personal computer.

When social competence is the problem, however, compensation is not possible. It is impossible for a parent to sit behind the child on the school bus and whisper suggestions for conversation starters or responses to him. When it comes to the use of social skills, the child is quite literally on his own.

4. *Social skills are the ultimate determining factor in the child's future success, happiness, and acceptance.*

The research here is overwhelming. The adult success of the person with learning disabilities is largely dependent upon his social-emotional relationship skills—not his academic skills.

Although most professionals recognize and acknowledge this fact, schools continue to invest the majority of their time and resources in the enhancement of *academic* skills, with minimal energy invested in the crucial social skills. I have often recommended that schools focus their energies equally in each of the *four* Rs: reading, 'riting, 'rithmetic, and *relationships*!

It is important to remember that children with learning problems often require intensive instruction, guidance, and assistance to master social skills. Most nondisabled children are able to learn these skills merely by observing the behaviors of adults and other children. They seem to learn these skills incidentally, almost through osmosis. Not so for the child with learning difficulties. To master social concepts, these children require instruction that is sequenced, direct, and carefully planned.

As we attempt to improve the child's social skills and enhance his social competence, we must understand that *social skills* and *manners* are not synonymous. Although the practice of accepted etiquette is an important part of social competence, appropriate manners alone will not improve a child's social status.

Abandoning Some Assumptions

Children with learning disabilities pose extraordinary challenges for the parents, caregivers, and professionals who wish to teach them social skills. The complexities of the child's disability cause myriad difficulties in several areas of development and behavior. The child simultaneously may be confronting problems in the areas of attention, memory, organization, language, and impulse control. Indeed, these children are fighting their battles on several fronts.

To teach and promote social competence to these children, we must consider the obstacles that they face, and that requires us to abandon some of the assumptions that generally underlie our relationships with others. For example, when we interact with others, we make the assumption that the person will listen to and be interested in what we have to say. This behavior is anticipated, as a sign of respect and a reflection of the person's desire to learn, grow, and cooperate. When this behavior is not present, we assume that the person is disinterested and inconsiderate. We respond with a negative, confrontational attitude.

We must understand that the distractibility and impulsivity of a child with learning disabilities may, at times, result in behaviors that seem inattentive and distracted. The adult must learn to take these behaviors *seriously*, but not personally.

Under most circumstances, we expect others to be consistent in their performance and behavior. Once a person demonstrates that he can do something, we make the understandable assumption that the behavior has been mastered and that the behavior will be performed consistently in the future. This is not a safe assumption when dealing with children with learning problems, whose performance is often characterized by significant inconsistency and irregular progress. This inconsistency is often misinterpreted as laziness, lack of motivation, or manipulation.

When dealing with another person, we assume that the person will be realistic and rational. When he fails to conduct himself in a rational manner, we have difficulty relating to him. Again, children with learning disorders have difficulty comprehending and responding to the reality of situations. As a result, they will often make statements or manifest behaviors that are in conflict with the reality of the situation. ("If I apologize to Bill for stealing and selling his bike, we can be best friends again.")

Another common assumption that we make with others is the belief that they will understand and accept *our* reality. For example, we anticipate that the child will understand and relate to our discomfort when he embarrasses us in front of our coworkers. However, children with learning problems have significant difficulty understanding the perspectives and feelings of others. This is often interpreted as selfishness or insensitivity. In actuality, it is neither. As you work to enhance the child's social competence, remember that the assumptions that we often make about people with whom we interact are neither appropriate nor valid when dealing with learning disabled children.

The Four Key Social Skills

To enjoy social success at home, in school, or in the community, the child must develop and master four basic skills that will allow him to interact positively with others. These fundamental skills are

1. ability to join or enter a group
2. ability to establish and maintain friendships
3. ability to resolve conflicts
4. ability to "tune in" to social skills

Ability to Join or Enter a Group

The strategies that a child utilizes to join a group of peers participating in an activity will largely determine whether he will be accepted or rejected by others.

Children with social problems have great difficulty in this area. Some will approach the group loudly with great fanfare, demanding that they be allowed to join the activity and insisting that the current rules and format of the game be changed. Others will stand quietly on the sidelines, hoping that their presence will be noticed and that they will be invited to participate.

The child's difficulty in joining a group reflects his inability to "read" social situations by interpreting the setting's various clues and cues. For example, if three children are huddled together and speaking in low voices, they are obviously involved in an intimate conversation that cannot and should not be interrupted. Failure to accurately interpret these clues and respond appropriately will result in social errors for which the child will be isolated or rejected.

Ability to Establish and Maintain Friendships

Unfortunately, many of the behaviors necessary to maintain a friendship are the precise skills that children with LD are lacking: sensitivity, ability to "read" body language, complex language skills, and so forth. Much of this book will be devoted to outlining these skills and teaching you how to foster them.

To make and keep friends, a child must demonstrate sensitivity, flexibility, and responsiveness. The attentional and behavioral difficulties manifested by children with LD often make it difficult for the child to put himself in another's shoes and understand the needs and desires of his peers. The child with LD is often viewed as insensitive, uncaring, immature, and self-absorbed. He is rarely aware of the negative impression that he presents to others and is puzzled by his inability to make social contacts and relationships.

Ability to Resolve Conflicts

Children with learning problems are often concrete in their thinking. Because they tend to be inflexible in their reasoning and view their world as black and white, with little tolerance for or understanding of shades of gray, it is difficult for them to compromise or negotiate. They feel that each conflict must yield a clear winner and a clear loser. They have difficulty understanding that both partners can be satisfied with a compromise.

This inability to resolve conflict without physical force or resorting to name-calling, threats, or disruptions is often cited by classmates as the reason for the child's lack of social acceptance.

Ability to "Tune In" to Social Skills

In order to explain this concept to your child, it may be useful to draw a comparison between social cues and radio waves. The air around you right now is filled with radio waves. You cannot see, feel, or hear them. However, if you turn on your radio, you will be able to hear those waves clearly, and as you move the dial to various frequencies, you tune in to still other waves.

Similarly, the child's daily home and school environments are filled with social cues. The child must learn to recognize and pay attention to these cues—tune them in—in order to gather the social information she needs to respond appropriately to the social environment. Again, the attentional and language problems experienced by children with learning disorders contribute to the child's inability to do this successfully.

Evaluating Children's Social Skills

A teacher or professional can use several methods and strategies to determine the social status of a child. This assessment will provide a valuable guide as you help the child improve his social competence. Currently, there is no widely accepted, standardized test or tool, but there are a number of ways to secure a "snapshot."

Sociometric Devices: These surveys are designed to evaluate an individual's relative popularity within a peer group. All members of a group are required to place the names of their colleagues in rank order based upon traits such as popularity and cooperation. In effect, a polling procedure determines the social acceptability of individuals within the group. While these devices generally provide a valid instrument for determining social competence, they tend to be somewhat reactive and often reflect the constantly changing school-age "in crowd/out crowd" dynamic.

Teacher-ranking Systems: Here, the teacher measures and records the frequency of each child's social interactions with classmates. Such systems can be valuable, but much like sociometric devices, they provide no diagnostic information about the quality of the interactions, only how often they occur.

Behavior-rating Scales: Parents, teachers, or peers complete these checklists, which measure a child's social behavior. They are valuable in determining the specific social skill deficits that require attention and remediation. They provide data for a comparison of a child's social skills in a variety of different settings (e.g., the home, the classroom, the playground).

Interviews: This type of assessment is often quite effective for students with learning disabilities, since it does not require extensive reading or writing skills. Because it encourages anecdotes and the citing of specific situations and incidents, it also allows for a more nuanced look at a child's social competence.

Observation Codes or Checklists: A more formalized, cut-and-dried observational approach depends on codes or checklists with which an examiner records the occurrence or absence of a specific, clearly defined set of behaviors (e.g., cooperation, self-talking, sharing). The examiner may observe the child in a structured social setting such as a reading group, Scout troop, or cafeteria and objectively record specific, predetermined, observable social behaviors of the child: for example, cooperation, self-talk, and sharing. These measures can be quite valuable in diagnosis of skill deficits as well as evaluation of training effectiveness.

Informal Social Skill Assessments for Parents

As a parent, you may want to informally and objectively assess your child's social competence. Unfortunately, the child himself may not be particularly helpful in such an assessment because he often misreads or mischaracterizes social interactions or may tend to exaggerate—"Billy *always* calls me names"—or minimize them—"I didn't do *anything* wrong and all the kids yelled at me!" The child may be confused or puzzled by the social situation and will, therefore, provide information that is inaccurate.

Your own observations are the most effective assessment tools. Carefully observe your child in numerous social settings to determine which of the primary social skills are lacking and require your attention.

Here are some key behaviors for you to watch for:

Handling Emotions and Social Challenges
- is unable to prioritize
- is unable to understand or react to nonverbal language

- is highly disorganized
- is indecisive
- shares private, confidential information inappropriately
- has low self-esteem
- has inconsistent motivation
- displays negative mood; complains often
- has a poor, undeveloped sense of humor
- loses belongings constantly
- is excessively shy
- is socially inept in many settings
- is a poor listener
- has difficulty understanding, identifying, or expressing his feelings
- has difficulty expressing affection
- is overly fearful
- has poor impulse control
- is easily embarrassed
- responds poorly to failure

Handling Peer Situations
- acts inappropriately in groups
- is overly aggressive
- reports that he is "lonely"
- has minimal empathy for others
- often misinterprets and overreacts to social situations
- prefers the company of much younger (or older) children wherein his role is well defined
- has poor relationships with siblings
- is excessively physical; pushes, shoves often
- seems to sabotage relationships
- bullies or is cruel to others
- is bossy, controlling, dominating
- has difficulty initiating and sustaining conversations
- seldom shares
- is ineffective at negotiation
- shows poor sportsmanship
- is highly susceptible to peer pressure

Handling Authority
- has difficulty understanding the link between behavior and consequences
- is excessively dependent on adults
- cheats; has difficulty following rules
- is often referred to as immature by adults
- has difficulty relating to authority figures
- asks for help ineffectively
- has difficulty following or giving direction

Handling Stress
- has difficulty dealing with transitions or changes in routine
- avoids new or novel social situations
- has marked difficulty making simple decisions
- is excessively silly in social situations
- has low tolerance for frustration
- often complains about his health
- responds poorly to failure
- worries excessively

If your child manifests many or most of these behaviors, she doubtless has significant difficulty with social competence.

Developing Children's Social Skills: Strategies and Methods That Don't Work . . . and One That Does

If your child is struggling in his academic subjects, he is probably experiencing difficulty in his social life too. In a recent government study, only 16 percent of children with learning problems reported that they had "normal social relationships."

This is understandable because learning disorders influence the way that a person perceives, interprets, processes, and explains his world. It is logical to assume that this pervasive disorder would have an impact as significantly on the child's sixteen-hour "social world" as it does on his eight-hour "classroom world."

We have come to recognize that social skill difficulties are a *direct*—not indirect—consequence of the learning problem. Even a child who is successful in his academics can have marked difficulty relating to peers, adults, and siblings. School failure is a consequence of the learning problem . . . but is not, necessarily, the cause of the social isolation and rejection.

Our collective recognition of the significance of social skill difficulties has given birth to a cottage industry of programs, strategies, and approaches designed to improve the social competencies of children. Many of these methods have met with limited and inconsistent results. Among these "questionable practices" are:

"The Deep End of the Pool": Some well-intentioned parents feel that the child will develop appropriate relationship skills if he is forced into social situations and left to fend for himself. The child is enrolled in a Scout troop, softball program, or community theater and is expected to develop the social competencies he needs in order to survive the experience.

This approach is generally unsuccessful and often results in public humiliation. This failure only enhances the child's reputation as an undesirable social partner. The overwhelming majority of children *want* to be accepted by their peers. If their behavior prevents this acceptance, it generally means that this behavior is beyond their control. *Forcing* the child to interact by way of this sink-or-swim approach will generally result in failure.

Incentives: Parents might offer rewards to the child if she improves her social skills: "If you behave appropriately at Aunt Paula's, we will get some ice cream on the way home." Perhaps the parent might take a behavior modification approach featuring checklists and scorecards that record the child's social performance. Positive social behavior results in rewards or privileges of some kind.

Again, this approach will doubtless fail. Any incentive program holds the belief that the child is *capable* of the target behavior (e.g., appropriate social behavior) and merely requires reminders and motivation in order to behave properly. This premise is greatly flawed when dealing with social competence. The child's inability to manifest appropriate social behavior is often caused by neurological difficulties that are beyond his control or influence.

Using behavior modification techniques to improve social competence is akin to using behavior modification to improve a child's eyesight, hearing, or growth. Incentives can actually *increase* the child's anxiety in social settings because of his inability to comprehend abstractions. For example, suppose you tell the child, "If you are good and act mature at the mall, we will go to the park this afternoon." Does he understand what "good" and "mature" actually mean? And if he does, has he acquired the skills to overcome his neurological difficulties and meet your expectations?

Teachers and parents must remember that there are a variety of reasons that a child may act in a socially inappropriate manner. Most of the time, these behaviors are unintentional. Therefore, *punishing* a child for being disruptive or inappropriate in a social setting is both unfair and ineffective.

There are widely accepted and effective principles of behavior management that should be followed when dealing with all children. Among these principles are:

- Behavior that receives attention and reinforcement is likely to be repeated.
- Positive feedback (praise, reward, privileges) *changes* behavior; negative feedback (punishment, scolding, loss of privileges) only *stops* behavior. You will not make meaningful, lasting changes in a child's behavior by punishing him.
- Children respond best to an environment that has clear expectations, rules, and limits. Establishment of a consistent, predictable, and structured approach is key.
- Providing children with viable and frequent choices can minimize power struggles.
- Effective behavior management depends largely on the adult's ability to be *pro*active rather than *re*active in regard to children's behavior.
- Behavior change is gradual, and each step toward the targeted behavior must be reinforced. Reward *direction,* not *perfection.*

- A well-managed learning environment is one where each child is successful and safe.
- An interesting, motivating, and engaging curriculum is the key to successful classroom management.

Often, a child's behavior is described as "attention seeking," and adults are encouraged to ignore the behavior. I have long felt that this is an inappropriate and insensitive approach. The child, through his behavior, is telling us that he *needs* attention . . . so *give him some!* You may choose to ignore the behavior, but you cannot and should not ignore the need. It is ironic that children send us such a clear message about their needs and we respond by giving them the opposite of what they require.

It is important to remember that, even though incentives rarely improve a child's social competencies, *reinforcers* can be extraordinarily effective. Incentives are outlined prior to a behavior. ("If you behave at the store, we will go to the arcade on the way home.") Reinforcers are unexpected and occur after the behavior. ("You were terrific at Uncle Jim's today. Thank you. Let's stop for an ice cream!") Reinforcement and praise are fundamental to the child's mastery of social skills. Parents must provide the child with the four Rs of social development:

1. *Reason:* Provide a reason for the rule.
2. *Rule:* State the rule.
3. *Reminder:* Provide the child with a hint or memory trigger of some kind.
4. *Reinforce:* Recognize and praise.

Examples:

On the ride to Grandma's
"Jamal, you know how proud Grandma is of her garden. The flowers are very delicate, so remember to stay away from that side of the yard. If you go past the toolshed, you are probably too close so stay in the front yard. You were so good at Grandma's last weekend. I am sure that you will be again."

Upon entering a restaurant

"Jen, this is a real fine restaurant where people come to enjoy a nice, quiet meal. Remember to talk quietly. You probably want to talk only to the person to your right or left. If your voice begins to get too loud, I will wink at you. That signal means to tone it down a bit, okay? I have been looking forward to taking you here. You'll love the lobster pie!"

Before religious services

"Benjy, today's synagogue ceremony is very important because we will be welcoming the new rabbi. We all need to remember that it is his day. Be sure to shake his hand and have a conversation with his son, who is about your age. Now, I know that you are excited about your upcoming Bar Mitzvah and you will want to talk to your friends about it, but remember—your ceremony should not be the focus of the day. The new rabbi is the reason for the gathering. If you start talking about your Bar Mitzvah too much, try to remember that, okay? I will be so proud to have you meet the new rabbi. From what I hear, he is a big Red Sox fan, too. I'm sure that he will enjoy talking to you about the Yankee series."

Ignoring: Several years ago, a technique known as *planned ignoring* became quite popular. This strategy was based on the premise that misbehavior is generally an attempt to get attention and that once the attention is removed, the behavior will cease.

This methodology has questionable effectiveness in behavior management and has virtually no positive impact upon a child's social development. In fact, quite the opposite occurs: by ignoring a behavior, the adult sends the message that the behavior is appropriate and acceptable. Suppose you were to begin to call your employer by his first name. He never corrects you or responds to this in any way. On your year-end evaluation, he gives you low marks in the category of Office Relationships and cites "inappropriate informality with superiors." You would make the argument that he never informed you that your behavior troubled him and so you considered your behavior acceptable and appropriate. So it is with children. If a child's social behavior is inappropriate, you must respond and react with guidance or instruction. Failure to do so sends the message that the behavior is appropriate. Ignoring the behavior will tend to routinize it and increase it, not eliminate it.

Social Skills Videos, Role Playing, Social Skill Groups: Most educational catalogues available today offer dozens of booklets, kits, videos, and DVDs designed to remediate social skill deficits. Although these materials can be somewhat useful and effective with some children, they will do little to impact a child's deep-rooted social competence problems.

Social skill groups provide instruction in interactional skills to small groups of children with social challenges. These groups are generally led or facilitated by a social worker, psychologist, or teacher. Many parents are disappointed in the results of these sessions.

Children with social skill deficits learn most efficiently in natural environments. So if you want to teach your child appropriate library behavior, conduct the lesson in the library. Clinical, contrived activities conducted in a classroom or office will not produce skills and competencies that will automatically transfer and generalize to the real world.

The effectiveness of a group approach will be enhanced if the group conducts occasional, well-planned field trips so that students can apply their newfound skills in natural settings. Do not expect that these sessions alone will have significant impact upon the child's social behavior. In order to maximize their impact, there should be consistent communication between the family and the facilitator so that the parents are aware of the specific skills that are being addressed in the sessions. The skills are more likely to be mastered if they are reviewed, reinforced, and practiced at home, at school, and elsewhere. As your piano teacher used to remind you, "The lessons aren't enough. You have to practice, practice, practice."

Among the most common social skill intervention is formal social skills training. A typical activity in a social skills curriculum consists of a discussion of a child's reaction to being excluded from a birthday party to which most of his classmates were invited. The students can generally develop dozens of effective and appropriate social responses to this situation (e.g., "I would ask the host politely if I could come," "I would ask one of my friends who *was* invited to ask the host to let me come," "I would ask my mom to call his mom"). Despite their ability to generate these solutions in a controlled, clinical classroom setting, it is doubtful that they will be able to spontaneously utilize these skills in a real-life social situation. The emotionality of the incident, coupled with the disinhibition and impulsivity that these children often experience, would generally result in a less appropriate response.

Another reason for the ineffectiveness of formal social skills training is the fact that morals are, for the most part, *situational*. That is, the daily moral decisions that we make are based largely on the *specific characteristics* of the social situation in which the incident occurs.

For example, suppose you went to your local post office to mail a letter. As you insert the letter into the mail slot, you notice a postcard protruding from under the mailbox. You pick the card up and note that it is stamped and ready for mailing. The card is a reminder of an upcoming meeting for an organization. Obviously, someone had been mailing a large number of postcards and dropped one.

Would you drop the card in the mail slot? Most people would.

Now suppose the postcard carried the return address of the Ku Klux Klan or the American Nazi Party. Would you drop *that* card in the slot? Most people would not.

This anecdote demonstrates the fact that the moral decisions that we make daily are often affected by the dynamics of the situation.

Social competence simply cannot be taught in a structured, artificial classroom setting. Teaching social skills in such an environment would be comparable to teaching tennis in a classroom. There are some tennis skills that one could learn in such a setting (e.g., scoring, regulations), but you will never become a skilled tennis player until you get out on the court and hit the ball around.

"One-shot" Interventions: Some professionals offer intense, focused instruction in social skill development that may require a child to attend a daylong seminar that covers the basic rules and conventions of

social interaction. Again, these interventions are likely to fail. Children who have poor social skills generally

- misread or fail to notice social cues
- have limited problem-solving and conflict-resolution capabilities
- have a low tolerance for frustration and failure.

These complex and intense problems will not be solved by a single intervention.

Some additional *Don'ts* related to social skill instruction include:

Don't necessarily discourage the child from establishing relationships with students who are a year or two younger than he is. He may be seeking his developmentally appropriate level. By befriending younger students, he may enjoy a degree of status and acceptance that he does not experience among his peers.

Don't force the child to participate in large groups if he is not willing or able. If the child responds well when working with another student, plan activities wherein he has ample opportunities to do so. Then add a third person to the group, then another, and so on, until the group approximates the entire class.

Don't place the child in highly charged competitive situations. These are often a source of great anxiety and failure for students with learning problems. Rather, focus upon participation, enjoyment, contribution, and satisfaction in competitive activities. Emphasis should be placed on the development of skills and strategies—not on winning or losing.

Don't assume that the child understood your oral directions or instructions just because he did not ask any questions. Ask him to repeat the instructions in his own words before beginning the activity: "What did you hear me say?"

Don't scold or reprimand the child when he tells you about social confrontations or difficulties that he has experienced.

He will respond by refusing to share these incidents with you. Rather, thank him for sharing the experience with you and discuss other strategies that he could have used.

Don't attempt to teach social skills at times of high stress. Rather, approach the child at a time when he is relaxed and receptive. For example, "Meghan, next week you will be going to Jilly's birthday party. Let's practice how you will hand her your gift and what you will say when she opens it and thanks you."

Don't view praise as the only verbal reinforcer—interest works, too! Expressing a genuine and sincere interest in a child can be as positive and motivating as praise. You might say, "I watched you playing soccer at recess, Adam. Do you play at home with your brothers?"

Don't encourage the frustrated child to relieve his stress by engaging in pointless physical activities (e.g., punching a pillow). Rather, teach him to relieve stress through an activity that has definable and observable goals (e.g., shoot ten baskets, run five laps, write a one-page letter).

Don't expect punishment or negative feedback to have a meaningful or lasting impact upon your child's social skill deficits. Punishment may stop specific behaviors in specific settings, but positive reinforcement is the only effective strategy for meaningful and lasting social skill improvement. Overuse of punishment is largely ineffective for the following reasons:

- It does not teach appropriate behavior. The child merely learns what he should *not* do.
- The child often becomes passive in the face of punishment and merely avoids situations similar to those in which he makes social errors (e.g., visiting grandmother, going to the store).
- The child may develop a concurrent set of inappropriate behaviors, such as lying, cheating, or blaming others, in order to avoid punishment.

- The child may adapt to punishment, which will require you to intensify the level and severity of the punishments.
- When the child is punished, the *message*—"We want you to improve your social skills"—is often lost in the resultant fear, anger, anxiety, stress, and tension.
- Children generally associate punishment with the *punisher,* not the offending behavior: "The coach yelled at me today," versus "I got in trouble today because I threw a volleyball at the scoreboard in the gym."
- Punishment is only effective as long as the threat of punishment exists.

We have reviewed the commonly used strategies that rarely improve social competence. What follows is an alternative technique that has been widely field-tested and has been quite successful in improving children's social skills in a wide variety of settings.

Social Skill Autopsies:
A Strategy to Promote and Develop Social Competencies

Janet and I were enjoying a wonderful dinner at the home of friends. The hosts, Jerry and Linda, were the parents of a terrific young girl who attended our school. Barbie, twelve years old, had significant learning and language problems, and these difficulties often caused social difficulties. Her impulsivity and her inability to monitor her language effectively often created embarrassing situations for Barbie and her family.

Barbie joined us for dinner, and the five of us were enjoying an exceptional meal and stimulating conversation. The discussion turned to automobiles. "We're going to get a new car next week! It's s-o-o-o-o beautiful and it has a CD player. It's very fancy . . . not a cheap car like yours!" Barbie blurted out, excitedly.

The table went silent. Jerry was humiliated. Linda was near tears. Barbie, unaware that her comments were offensive, continued her conversation.

Jerry erupted. "That is the rudest thing you have ever said, young lady! Leave the table right now and go to your room."

Confused, Barbie sheepishly left her seat and went to her bedroom, closing the door behind her.

The four of us quietly continued our meal under a pall of embarrassment. Jerry knows me well enough to recognize that I did not approve of his response. He finally broke the uncomfortable silence by saying, "Okay, Rick. I know that I blew that one. What did I do wrong? What should I have done?"

Reluctant to convert the meal into a consulting session, I replied, "We can talk later."

"No, really, Rick, I want to know. She's always doing that kind of thing. We punish her, but it doesn't seem to help."

"Jerry," I began, "you are wonderful with Barbie. You are her most effective teacher! What if you were trying to teach her the multiplication facts and she said that five times three equaled twenty. Would you have yelled at her and sent her to her room?"

"Of course not," Jerry responded. "I would have taught her the right answer so she would know it the next time."

"Exactly," I countered. "And that's what you need to do when she makes social errors, too."

This incident gave birth to the concept of the "Social Skill Autopsy." This technique is now used in schools and homes throughout North America and has been effective in improving the social competence of thousands of children. The strategy is based upon three basic tenets.

1. Most social skill errors are unintentional. It is universally accepted that a primary need of all human beings is to be liked and accepted by other human beings. Therefore, if a child conducts himself in a manner that causes others to dislike or

reject him, can we not assume that these behaviors are unintentional and far beyond the child's control? Why would a child purposefully defeat one of his primary needs?

2. If you accept the premise that the offending behavior is unintentional, it becomes obvious that *punishing* a child for social skill errors is unfair, inappropriate, and ineffective.

3. Traditional approaches to social skill remediation are not effective. These strategies—role-playing, demonstrations, videotaping, lectures, discussions—seldom have a positive impact on the development of children's social competence. They may have a temporary short-term effect, but the results are seldom lasting and do not often generalize to other settings.

The Autopsy approach provides the socially struggling child with an authentic real-life "laboratory" in which he can learn, develop, and apply effective social responses to actual social dilemmas. This authentic approach parallels the LD child's tendency to learn more effectively in *practical* situations. If you want to teach dining-out skills, conduct the lesson in a restaurant; teach bus etiquette on the bus; and so on.

Before outlining the process of the Social Skill Autopsy, it is useful to explain what this process is *not*. This technique is not intended to be a reprimand, a scolding, or a punishment. Neither should the Social Skill Autopsy be solely controlled by the adult, without input from the child. This strategy should not be viewed as a one-time intervention. Rather, the effectiveness of the Autopsy will be greatly enhanced if the strategy is used frequently. The technique will be ineffective if it is used in a hostile or angry manner. The child should feel secure and supported throughout the Autopsy process.

The Autopsy approach has been extremely effective in modifying and improving the social competence of children in a variety of settings. The technique is easy to learn and can be utilized by family members, babysitters, bus drivers, or coaches. By training *all* of the adults in the child's life, you ensure that he will be benefiting from dozens of Social Skill Autopsies each day. This intensive exposure will foster growth and generalization of the target skills.

The success of this strategy lies in the fact that it provides the child with the four basic steps in any effective learning experience:

- practice
- immediate feedback
- instruction
- positive reinforcement

Scolding, reprimanding, and punishing provide none of these elements. Barbie was sent away from the table for her inappropriate remark, but no teaching, learning, or reinforcement occurred. As a result, an important learning opportunity was lost. Nothing occurred to make the behavior less likely to be repeated in the future.

Another reason that the Social Skill Autopsy approach is so effective is that it enables the child to clearly see the cause-and-effect relationship between his social behavior and the responses and reactions of others. Children with social skill difficulties often are unable to recognize this relationship and are frequently mystified about the reactions of their classmates, teachers, siblings, and parents. As a child once told me, "People get mad at me all the time and I just don't know why."

The Social Skill Autopsy strategy can be a very effective and responsive technique if used properly. It is critical to be mindful that an Autopsy should be conducted as an instructional, supportive, and nonjudgmental intervention. It should be conducted as soon as possible following the offending behavior and should not be viewed—by the adult or the child—as a scolding or negative interaction.

Conceptually, the Social Skill Autopsy is based on the idea of a medical autopsy. Webster's dictionary defines *autopsy* as "the examination and analysis of a dead body to determine the cause of death, the amount of physical damage that occurred, and to learn about the causal factor(s) in order to prevent reoccurrence in the future." The working definition of a Social Skill Autopsy is "the examination and analysis of a *social error* to determine the *cause of the error,* the amount of damage that occurred, and to learn about the *causal factor(s)* in order to prevent reoccurrence in the future."

The basic principle is to assist the child in analyzing actual social errors that she has made and to discuss the behavioral options that the child *could* have utilized in order to have improved the situation.

In seminars, I often cite a classic Social Skill Autopsy that I conducted in a dormitory. I was walking the halls of the residence when I heard loud arguing in Tom and Chip's dorm room. I entered the room and inquired about the nature of the argument.

"It's Tom!" Chip bellowed. "Yesterday I bought a brand-new tube of toothpaste. Tonight, Tom borrowed it and lost it!"

I turned to Tom and said, "Let's autopsy this!" I began by asking Tom to tell me what had happened. He explained that he was unable to find his own toothpaste. He borrowed his roommate's tube, although he was unable to locate Chip in order to get his permission. He went down the hall to brush his teeth in the bathroom. As he was brushing, Jim (a mutual friend of Chip's and Tom's) entered the bathroom and asked Tom if *he* could borrow the toothpaste. Jim passed it on to yet another student and its current whereabouts was now unknown.

The following dialogue took place:

LAVOIE: "Okay, Tom, I understand what happened. What do you think your mistake was?"

TOM: "I know, Mr. Lavoie. I won't make that mistake again. I promise. I never should have borrowed Chip's toothpaste."

LAVOIE: "No, Tom, that *wasn't* your mistake. It's okay for you and Chip to borrow things from each other occasionally. You are roommates and friends. You borrow his stuff and he borrows yours. That's not a problem."

TOM: "Oh, okay. I've got it now. I know my mistake. I shouldn't have lent Jim the toothpaste. I should have told him, 'No.' "

LAVOIE: "Nope, that's not your mistake, either. Chip and Jim are good friends, too. Chip surely would not have minded you lending an inch of toothpaste to his friend Jim. Try again!"

TOM: "I've got it! I shouldn't have let go of the tube. I should have squeezed the toothpaste onto Jim's brush and then returned the tube to Chip!"

LAVOIE: "Bingo, Tom, you've got it! Our social lesson for the day is *not* 'Do not borrow,' it's not 'Do not lend.' Rather, our lesson is 'When you borrow something from someone, it is *your* responsibility to be sure that it is returned. You cannot give that responsibility to anyone else.' Got it?"

TOM: "Yup, I've got it!"

LAVOIE: "Okay, let's make sure. Suppose you stuck your head into my office and said, 'Mr. Lavoie, all the kids are playing catch and I don't have a baseball glove. Can I borrow the baseball glove that you keep in your closet?' I say 'yes' and toss you the glove. While you are playing catch, your dorm counselor comes over and tells you to return to the dorm to finish some chores. As you head off the field, one of the kids asks to borrow the glove because you won't be using it. What are you going to say?"

TOM: "I'd say, 'Sorry, but it's not my glove, so I can't lend it to you. It belongs to Mr. Lavoie. Why don't you come with me while I return it to his office? Then maybe you can ask him to borrow it.' "

LAVOIE: "Great! Now, Tom, I want to give you a little social homework. Today you learned that it is important to return what you borrow and that you can't give that responsibility to anyone else. Sometime this week, I want you to use that skill. I will check in with you on Friday and you can tell me how and when you did it!"

As you see, the Social Skill Autopsy has five basic and separate stages:

1. *Ask the child to explain what happened.* You will want to have him start at the beginning, if possible. However, some chil-

dren give a more accurate and complete accounting of an incident if encouraged to begin with the climax of the event and work backwards. Don't interrupt or be judgmental. You want *his* clear recollections.

2. *Ask the child to identify the mistake that he made.* This is an important and interesting part of the Autopsy process. Many times, the child will be unable to determine when and where the error occurred or his interpretation is inaccurate.

   Tom initially felt that borrowing the toothpaste was his error. It wasn't. Had I merely punished Tom ("Give Chip three dollars for a new tube of toothpaste"), Tom would have erroneously felt that his mistake involved borrowing the toothpaste.

   Often, a child will get in trouble with an authority figure, but the child will have no idea what he has done wrong. "I got in trouble at practice today." "What did you do?" "I dunno. But I got the coach mad!"

   How can a child stop repeating a social error if he is unable to determine or understand what the error is?

3. *Assist the child in determining the actual social error that he made.* Discuss the error and alternate social responses. At this point in the discussion, the adult should avoid using the word *should*. ("You *should* have waited your turn," "You *shouldn't* have asked the principal if he wears a toupee.") Rather, use the word *could*: "You *could* have asked if you could take your turn next because Mom was coming to pick you up early," "You *could* have asked the principal about his new car or complimented his ties." This strategy underscores the concept that children have options in social situations.

4. *The* scenario *is the part of the process wherein the adult creates a brief social story that has the same basic moral or goal as the social faux pas.* The scenario should have the same basic so-

lution as the incident. It should require the child to generate a response to the fabricated situation that demonstrates his ability to generalize and apply the target skill.

5. Social homework *is strongly recommended by Syracuse University psychologist Arnold Goldstein as a strategy to ensure the mastery and application of the target skill.* This step requires the child to use the target skill in another setting and report back to the adult when this had been done. This technique causes the child to seek out opportunities to apply the social skill that he has learned. In the toothpaste scenario, I assigned Tom the task of using the skill of appropriate borrowing. A few days later, he excitedly told me that the dormitory counselor had lent him her large snowman mug when the dorm students had cocoa on a wintry night. As Tom was rinsing out the mug, another student asked if he could borrow it. Tom told him that he was not at liberty to lend the mug, but encouraged his dormmate to ask the counselor if he could use it. Tom's application of the "borrowing concept" demonstrated that he is well on his way to mastering this skill.

Children respond very well to this strategy, and, if it is correctly applied, they do not view the technique as a scolding or a reprimand. On the contrary, they come to view the Autopsy as an intriguing and effective strategy designed to improve their social competence. Students actually *request* Autopsies when they are involved in a social interaction that they do not understand. A fourteen-year-old girl once entered my office and asked, "Mr. Lavoie, can you help me? Last night my sister called me from college and we ended up having a big argument. I know that I said *something* wrong that made her angry, but I don't know *what* I did. Can we do an Autopsy on the call?"

Remember the Autopsy is:
- a supportive, structured, constructive strategy to foster social competence
- a problem-solving technique

- an opportunity for the child to participate actively in the process
- conducted by any significant adult in the child's environment (teacher, parent, bus driver)
- conducted in a familiar, realistic, and natural setting
- most effective when conducted immediately after the social error

It is not:
- a punishment or scolding
- an investigation to assign blame
- controlled/conducted exclusively by an adult
- a one-time "cure" for teaching the targeted social skill

In the following chapters, you will learn the various symptoms of learning disorders and their impact on a child's social development. We will also explore numerous other strategies to foster a child's social confidence and competence. By understanding the unique way that the child views his social world, you will be better able to design effective strategies and interventions.

Author's note: The author and the publisher believe in and subscribe to the "Person First" movement, which recommends that people be referred to in a manner that places their handicapping condition after their name (e.g., "the girl with cerebral palsy" and not "the cerebral palsied girl"). This language reflects greater sensitivity and respect. However, this phrasing can be awkward when used repeatedly in an extensive text. As a result, the aforementioned phrasings are used interchangeably throughout this book.

PART ONE

Why Do They Do the Things They Do?

The Impact of Learning Disorders on the Development of Social Skills

> "Our explanation of behaviors leads directly to our response to them."
> —DR. ROSS GREENE

CHAPTER ONE

Children with Learning Disorders Are Wired Differently

It's All in Their Heads

Parents and professionals have many misconceptions about children with learning problems. Primary among these is a lack of understanding of the *pervasive* nature of learning disorders. As I often remind parents and teachers, a learning disability is not merely an academic problem—it is a life, language, and learning problem that affects every moment of the child's day. The child who has difficulty understanding and following directions in his fourth-period math class will doubtless have similar difficulty following the instructions in his Saturday-morning soccer practice or in his grandfather's workshop on Sunday afternoon. The neurologically based symptoms that plague him in school will also affect his ability to function at home and in the community.

An analogy: Every major metropolitan area has a discount furniture outlet whose advertising trumpets the fact that it sells "living room sets" that include a couch, loveseat, recliner, two end tables, two lamps, and a coffee table. These stores, as a matter of policy, will not sell you a single piece of furniture—you've got to buy the entire set!

3

So it is with a child's learning disorder. You must come to accept the fact that the learning problems will likely impact *all* areas of the child's development—academic, social, and emotional. It is unfair to accept *some* of these difficulties while refusing to tolerate others. I recall a dad saying to me, "I understand that Darren can't read very well, but I will not tolerate the fact that he interrupts me when I am trying to talk on the phone." Sorry, Dad! The neurological problems that cause Darren's reading problems also cause his poor impulse control. You *need* to understand *all* of the manifestations of learning disorder. You have to buy—and live with—the whole living room set.

Let's examine some of the most common symptoms of learning problems that affect academic progress and performance. As you will see, these difficulties can have a profound effect upon the development of a child's social skills as well.

The Child Who Misperceives

Many children who struggle academically have significant difficulty in the areas of *perception:* the way in which they organize and experience their environment through the five senses of hearing, vision, smell, taste, and touch. If a child is confident that his senses are providing him with accurate and dependable input, he will manifest confidence and self-assurance. If he has come to distrust the input that he receives from his senses, he will be hesitant and reluctant to interact with others. He may be plagued with self-doubt, feelings of inferiority, and lack of confidence.

One important perceptual skill involves visual/spatial abilities. These skills allow one to orient objects in space in reference to distance, size, position, and direction. Children with difficulties in this area may have trouble reading, often lose their place when reading, inadvertently skip over sections on workbooks or tests, or have highly disorganized writing skills. The *social* manifestations of visual/spatial problems are also significant. This child chronically misplaces things, is often unable to locate his belongings, has great difficulty following directions, and creates a cluttered environment in his room, on his desk, and inside his book bag. He often confuses left and right, and telling time may be a challenge for him. His poor sense of direction may cause him to become easily lost in the mall or the neighborhood.

Another visually oriented perceptual skill involves visual-motor coordination. This skill allows the child to coordinate his motor movements with his visual input. Deficiencies in this area can cause illegible handwriting and difficulty coloring, drawing, and so on. In the social arena, a child with this difficulty will often be clumsy and accident-prone. His athletic abilities may be limited, and his classmates and playmates may brand him a klutz. He may be an undesirable teammate because of his inability to perform well or consistently on motor tasks. One such child that I counseled was pointedly rejected by his sixth-grade classmates when, while playing soccer, he scored a goal for the opposing team by his uncontrolled, frenetic movement in front of the home team's net.

Auditory perceptive problems can also cause social difficulties for the child. Many children with learning disorders have difficulty processing and utilizing auditory input, even though their hearing (their ability to hear sounds) is normal and appropriate. A common difficulty for these children is in the area known as *figure/ground*, wherein the child is unable to screen out irrelevant auditory input (voices, sounds, noises) in order to focus upon the most important, primary auditory messages. It can be said that this child *over*hears more than he hears. This deficiency will have significant impact upon the child's social life. It may even affect his safety if, for instance, the child is focusing on a conversation he is having as he crosses the street and is unaware of the honking horn of an oncoming car. These children will have difficulty following conversations and classroom discussions, will often be confused and anxious in public settings, and may want to avoid these situations.

Children with auditory perception problems can become quite confused and intimidated by the rapid-fire give-and-take conversations of their peers. They will often respond "What?" when asked questions, which is frequently misinterpreted as some sort of hearing loss. Actually, the child is using this strategy to stall while he processes the auditory input that he has received. Such children are often mislabeled as inattentive and unmotivated because of their unfocused and unresponsive behavior. Again, the field has long recognized the significant impact that auditory processing can have upon the development of reading and language skills. We now recognize that difficulty in processing can have a lasting impact on social skill development as well.

The following are some social behaviors that may have their root cause in visual or auditory perceptual difficulties:

- Clumsiness or awkwardness in physical (gross motor) activities due to poor spatial orientation or perceptual problems.
- Inability to successfully participate in "small motor" activities. Perceptual problems may prevent a child from being successful at knitting, card playing, arts and crafts, even though the child may be quite athletic and skilled at gross motor skills.
- Poor observation skills. Because of a child's visual perception skills, she may not be very observant, and her failure to recognize—and comment upon—peers' clothing or appearance can be viewed as rude or self-absorbed.
- Poor response to visual input and aids. A child with difficulties in visual perception may be unable to learn material and concepts presented via video or class demonstration.
- Undeveloped sense of direction. A child with visual perception problems may become easily lost and may take an inordinate amount of time to become familiar with new settings.
- Significant organizational difficulties. Visual perceptual problems cause the child to lose things, maintain cluttered and disorganized environments, and fail to see "lost" items in plain sight.
- Difficulty judging distance and speed. A child with visual perception problems may have marked difficulty participating in playground or backyard games that require him to evaluate and respond to the distance and/or speed of a ball, teammates, or opposing players.
- Inappropriate volume in conversation. A child with auditory perception difficulties may be unable to modify the volume of his voice in response to the social setting, and his inappropriately loud voice is off-putting to peers and adults.

The Child Who Cannot Inhibit
His Behavior or Reactions

Another neurologically based cause for social rejection involves a child's inability to effectively *inhibit* behaviors, thoughts, or impulses. This *disinhibition* is relatively common among children with learning, social, or attentional problems.

Hundreds of times each day you have thoughts or impulses that you inhibit or hold in check. You may meet a former neighbor who has gained a significant amount of weight since the last time you saw him. You are unlikely to greet him by saying, "How wonderful to see you, Russ. Wow! Have *you* been packing on the pounds!" Such a response would be rude, inappropriate, and hurtful. So, although you have the thought, you do not express it. You inhibit it.

Suppose you stand behind a young woman in line at a grocery store. She is wearing a sweater made of soft, plush material. You may wonder what it feels like, but you would be very unlikely to reach out and stroke the material with your fingers. The social consequences for this behavior would be swift, embarrassing, and serious, so you inhibit your response.

Many socially deficient children have an ineffective neurological "braking system," and so they *do* (e.g., grabbing a French fry off of Grandpa's plate) or *say* (e.g., "Hi, Mr. Lavoie. Didn't get a chance to wash your hair this morning?") things that offend or disturb others.

The human brain has an amazing ability to filter out or ignore sensations or stimuli. For example, focus for a few minutes on the sensation of your clothes touching your body, or of your feet inside your shoes. After a few moments, these sensations become somewhat uncomfortable and disconcerting. These sensations have existed since you got dressed this morning, but your brain has been successfully filtering them out of your consciousness. However, when the sensations are called to your attention, you are able to feel them. After a minute or two, your brain will again focus out these sensations and the feelings of discomfort will vanish. Children with attentional disorders are often unable to filter out sensations, and they feel compelled to respond to them. As a result, they manifest behaviors that are viewed by others as intentional, and social rejection or isolation results.

It is extraordinarily difficult to remediate difficulties with disinhibition. Providing the child with an alternative behavior—"Nancy, do not reach out and grab the after-dinner mints at the restaurant's cash register; ask me for permission first"—is ineffective. That strategy would be comparable to telling an adult whose shoes are too tight to loosen his shirt collar to relieve his discomfort!

The Child Who Cannot Plan or Predict

Among the major neurologically based challenges faced by children with learning disorders is a deficit in *executive functioning*. This complex cognitive skill is critical to academic success, since it impacts such basic tasks as memorization, punctuality, perseverance, and emotional control. It is easy to understand the negative impact these weaknesses would have on the child's day-to-day performance at home or in the classroom.

Russell Barkley, author of the classic text *Taking Charge of ADHD*, defines executive functioning as those "actions we perform to ourselves and direct at ourselves in order to accomplish self-control, goal-oriented behavior, and the maximization of future outcomes." Basically, executive functioning is fundamental to the planning process. It is a necessary skill for short-term planning ("Should I do my math homework or my French homework first?") and long-term planning ("What will I need to bring and do before going to Aunt Mary Jo's house for the weekend?"). Executive functioning includes the subskills of prioritizing, sequencing, goal setting, self-monitoring, and self-correcting.

For example, suppose I have a significant amount of yard work to do. I enter my garage, and my executive functioning skills allow me to devise a viable plan for this activity. My thought process would be similar to this:

"I have a lot of leaves to rake, so I had better bring the bamboo rake. I will be raking for a long time, so I will need some gloves. The leaf pile will be a big one, so I ought to take a tarp so I can move the pile, and a wheelbarrow to get the leaves into the woods. In order to get the leaves onto the tarp, I will also need a shovel."

I don the gloves, put the tarp, rake, and shovel into the wheelbarrow, and head off to my task. If I were unable to do this preplanning, the activity would be replete with interruptions, complications, and stops-and-starts. Nearly every daily activity requires executive functioning skills (e.g., shopping, preparing for school, washing the dog). Children who do not possess these skills present a complex, puzzling profile for parents and professionals.

These executive functioning deficits often occur in children with high intellect and great potential. The inability of these children to effectively complete or plan simple daily tasks (e.g., completing homework, preparing for bed) is puzzling and frustrating for the adults in the child's life. Unfortunately, parents and teachers often view this behavior as willful, and the children are often incorrectly viewed as "passive aggressive." As a frustrated dad once told me, "Benjy is so bright. Why won't he take the time to plan his home study effectively? He is either stubborn or simply unmotivated." Perhaps Benjy was neither! Perhaps he had difficulty with executive functioning.

When the components of executive functioning are considered, it becomes obvious that weaknesses in these skills would have a profound negative impact on a child's social skill development. Among these components are:

- ability to internalize language: using "self-talk" to monitor and control one's behavior and plan upcoming actions
- problem-solving skills: the ability to analyze, deconstruct, and organize situations in order to solve problems
- emotional control: the ability to think reflectively *prior* to taking action; also, the ability to tolerate frustration and delay gratification
- recall and working memory: the ability to retrieve facts from long-term memory and to "hold" facts in your mind while manipulating information
- activation: the ability to initiate and start an activity
- arousal: the ability to pay sustained attention to a task or activity
- persistence: the ability to complete a task by maintaining effort and bringing closure

Students with executive functioning difficulties often have inconsistent memory functions. They are forgetful and have deficiencies in their long-term and short-term memories. The academic repercussions of these deficiencies are quite obvious, but consider the *social* impact of memory problems. These children will have marked difficulty following directions and summarizing or recalling past events. They may be viewed as spacey, disrespectful, or insolent by their teachers; they may be considered undesirable social partners by their peers because of their chronic confusion, forgetfulness, and disorganization.

The Child Who Is Inflexible

Another neurologically based symptom that is common among school-age children with learning disorders is *inflexibility*. These children can have significant difficulty adapting to changes in the home or school environment and are unable to handle transitions of any sort. One of my former students became so troubled by the disruption caused by the remodeling of his kitchen that his parents found it necessary to send him for a weeklong visit to his grandmother's until the work was completed. These children are often accused of "overreacting" to changes in the environment, but they are merely responding to their neurologically based need for continuity and sameness.

This inability to effectively "shift gears" causes the child to become easily overwhelmed by even routine daily events. As this feeling of powerlessness increases, his ability to analyze and solve the problem at hand is diminished. A vicious cycle is created, and the child may begin to avoid these situations by becoming increasingly isolated and solitary. The child's reactions to transitions—agitation, acting out, aggression—can cause social rejection.

These children develop a rigid and inflexible view of their world. They are intolerant of compromise or ambiguity and may attempt to apply oversimplified and rigid rules to social situations. ("That's *my* chair! I always sit there when I watch TV. Get out of *my* chair!") They often respond to social situations by attempting to impose their self-made rules on others and may have severe tantrums if their "rules" are not accepted or applied. Again, it is important to understand that the child is not merely being "selfish" or "demanding." Rather, this behavior is his inappropriate and ineffective response to a neurologically based inability to deal with ambiguity or transitions.

The behaviors of these children can be quite puzzling. The child may have serious "meltdowns" in response to simple and routine situations. We must remain mindful that these mundane situations can be extremely threatening and frustrating for the inflexible child. Because he has little faith in his ability to deal with the situation, he experiences great frustration and angst. In a moment of self-awareness, a student once asked me if I would give him "at least one week's notice" if I was going to change his lunch table assignment. "I will need at least a week to get used to the idea that I will be sitting in a different seat," he said.

Other Learning Disabilities and Behaviors

Below is a list of common areas of weakness and difficulty for children with learning problems. Accompanying each skill area are the academic *and social* ramifications of these skill deficits.

- *Dyslexia* (inability to read)
    - School problems: inability to complete reading assignments; difficulty comprehending written material.
    - Social problems: inability to read newspapers, directions, maps, movie subtitles, menus, brochures, and so forth.
- *Auditory memory* (inability to store and recall information received auditorily)
    - School problems: difficulty remembering information received in classroom lectures and discussion.
    - Social problems: difficulty remembering short-term instructions given by coaches, parents, or peers; inability to remember rules, regulations, and processes when playing games.
- *Auditory sequencing* (problems recalling sequences related to information received auditorily)
    - School problems: difficulty following sequences to solve math problems; significant spelling difficulties.

– Social problems: inability to recall sequential steps in sports activities; difficulty remembering basic rules and regulations for games.
- *Directional deficiencies* (inability to use directional skills efficiently or effectively)
    – School problems: drawing difficulties; inability to follow basic instruction (e.g., "Put your name in the left-hand corner of the paper and write the numbers 1 through 20 in the right-hand margin"); difficulty with number placements in math.
    – Social problems: great difficulty driving or steering a bicycle, skateboard, scooter, and so forth; becomes easily lost in public places; poor at dancing, exercising, sports, and other activities requiring gross motor skills.
- *Intersensory problems*
    – School problems: difficulty listening to lectures and taking notes at the same time; needs singular focus in order to write.
    – Social problems: unable to converse socially while simultaneously working on a task.
- *Short-term memory deficits:* inability to recall and utilize information even after a brief period of time
    – School problems: inability to apply instructive, corrective feedback given by teacher (e.g., "Taylor, go back to your seat and circle all of the capital letters on this worksheet").
    – Social problems: when playing games, unable to recall whose turn is next; constantly forgetting the score during a game or sport.
- *Visual coordination:* ability to track or pursue a moving object
    – School problems: reading difficulties; difficulty visually tracking teacher as she moves about the room.
    – Social problems: difficulty catching a thrown object; unable to track moving icons in video games.
- *Visual-motor problems:* inability to coordinate visual senses and motor system
    – School problems: poor handwriting, drawing skills.

– Social problems: difficulty with puzzles and games; great difficulty learning how to ride a bicycle or skateboard.

Soft Signs and Zero Order Skills

It has long been recognized that children with learning problems often manifest "soft neurological symptoms," and these behaviors are viewed as significant indicators of a child's learning capabilities and potential. A pediatrician or neurologist will generally evaluate these skills during an assessment. These seemingly innocuous diagnostic activities ("touch your nose with your index finger," "walk heel-to-toe along this line," "follow my hand with your eyes") can provide valuable insights into a child's progress and performance. A British study indicated that nearly half of the children who had observable soft signs at age five had been diagnosed with learning disabilities by age ten.

These soft neurological signs generally involve coordination and motor skills. These symptoms are readily observable and are often described as "dysmaturational" because they are behaviors that are common and normal among infants or young children, but are generally replaced by more mature behaviors in early childhood. These symptoms manifest themselves in the child's Zero Order Skills. This subset of skills is best defined as "skills that are only significant when they *fail to exist*." For example, a common soft sign is a child's inability to track with his eyes without moving his head. When you are having a conversation with others at the dinner table, you make eye contact with each person as he or she speaks. You establish eye contact by moving your head slightly and moving your eyes to meet the gaze of your conversation partner. Children with this soft sign may, instead, keep their eyes fixed and move their head in order to establish and maintain eye contact. As you can imagine, this behavior will be viewed as odd to onlookers. Although the behavior is normal for an infant, it is uncommon for a school-age child.

The ability to track during a conversation is a Zero Order Skill, noticeable only when it does not exist. It is highly unlikely that you would say, "I really like Frank. He's so social! He always makes eye contact during conversations without moving his head very much."

However, a comment like this is very likely: "What's the deal with Mark? Whenever the group of us has a conversation, his head jerks back and forth around the room like he's watching a tennis match. It makes me so uncomfortable."

Again, it is *assumed* that people will possess Zero Order Skills and it is noteworthy only when they do not.

Below is a list of the neurological soft signs that are commonly found in children with learning disorders and their corresponding Zero Order Skills.

SOFT SIGN	ZERO ORDER SKILL DEFICIT
Hyperreaction	high startle response; overreacts to sudden noises, touches, etc.
Hyporeaction	low startle response; fails to react to sensory input
Attentional dysfocus	short attention span; distractibility
Perseveration	constantly repeats a behavior (e.g., rocking, tapping) or "gets stuck" on a topic
Motor speed problems	hyperactive or hypoactive
Bimanual coordination problems	clumsy; poor fine motor skills, difficulty making hands work together in a coordinated manner
Balance problems	difficulty riding a bicycle, standing still, riding an escalator
Mirror movements	right hand (or foot) mirrors what the left hand is doing
Copying deficits	unable to copy off the board or copy letter forms
Echolalia (repetition of speech sounds)	mimics and repeats words said by others
Left/right disorientation	marked difficulty following directions and orienting self in space
Immature distance notion	difficulty determining or estimating distances; often bumps into objects or persons

Another soft sign that translates into a Zero Order Skill is a person's *standing face*. This is the most basic and common facial expression. The standing face is the neutral expression we use when watching a television show or listening to a lecture. In this facial posture, a person's eyes are open and looking forward, facial muscles are relaxed, and the mouth is closed. Many children with soft neurological signs have a standing face that features an open and slack-jawed mouth. This soft sign is very common among children with special needs. I recall observing a large group of special education students as they watched a movie and noting that nearly half of them sat with their mouths open during the activity. This behavior may be off-putting for people in the child's social environment. The child, of course, is generally unaware of his expression or the impression that it may make on his social partners.

If your child manifests any of these behaviors, it is in his best interest that you attempt to eliminate them. Discuss with him the fact that these behaviors exist and use photographs or a mirror to demonstrate this. You may want to arrange a signal system with him wherein you give him a nonverbal gesture (e.g., tug on your ear, flash a thumbs-up) to signal him that he is, for example, sitting with his mouth open. This strategy will eventually make him more aware of the frequency of these behaviors and, ideally, he will begin to monitor and self-correct these actions.

It is not only soft neurological signs that are included in Zero Order Skills. This skill subset includes any and all skills that are *expected* by others. Therefore, a person who possesses Zero Order Skills is not considered extraordinary or socially accomplished; rather the person is merely considered to be competent. Basic hygiene is considered a Zero Order Skill. If a person has no offensive body odor, it goes largely unnoticed. However, a person with obviously poor hygiene who emits a foul odor will be avoided and isolated by all. Again, it is unlikely that you would say, "I really like Ron; he never smells bad." Attention to basic hygiene is merely assumed and only its absence is noteworthy. You do not receive praise, compliments, or attention for possessing Zero Order Skills, but you can be rejected and isolated if you do not.

Zero Order Skills are generally performed automatically with minimal forethought or planning. They are learned quite naturally from childhood interactions with and observations of adults and peers in social settings. Children learn these behaviors by trial and error. Impromptu "lessons" in Zero Order Skills occur on a daily basis. Children soon learn how to adapt their verbal and nonverbal behavior in a way that makes them socially acceptable to others. However, children with learning and attentional difficulties often fail to master these skills through trial and error or observation. This contributes to their isolation, rejection, and difficulty establishing relationships. These children require direct, concentrated, focused instruction and guidance to master these critical skills.

Zero Order Skills are particularly important in regard to the routines and rituals of everyday life. These routines are established procedures that occur on a daily basis. They are mechanical and automatic. For instance, when a child encounters his parent in the kitchen at breakfast, it is expected that they will exchange a greeting of some sort. Failure to participate in this ritual is considered rude and inappropriate. Throughout the day, the child goes through countless such rituals and it is anticipated that he will comply. A child who complies is merely considered competent; failure to comply can result in isolation, rejection, or humiliation.

When one considers the nearly infinite number of Zero Order Skills that we apply in everyday life, it becomes obvious that instruction in these skills is a daunting and overwhelming task. The parent or teacher has two goals when providing instruction in Zero Order Skills:

1. to eliminate odd, deviant, or idiosyncratic behavior
    (e.g., picking one's nose, poor eye contact)
2. to assist the child in developing appropriate behaviors
    (e.g., proper use of a handkerchief, establishing appropriate eye contact)

Once again, if these thousands of skills are mastered, the social success of the child is not assured; however, the child is less likely to attract negative attention. It is insufficient and ineffective to merely eliminate a negative social behavior (e.g., cheating at games); you must also attempt to replace the negative behavior with effective social skills (e.g., following rules when game playing).

As an example, suppose that Joey has the soft sign of hyperreaction and has a high startle response. He becomes unduly upset at sudden noises (e.g., fire alarms), drastic changes in temperature (e.g., going outside for recess on a winter day), and touch (e.g., a classmate unintentionally bumping into him in the cafeteria line). These atypical and inappropriate behaviors cause him to be ridiculed by his peers, and some classmates may even purposely startle him in order to trigger strong reactions from Joey. Your two-pronged goal is to eliminate his overreactions and then replace his response with more reasonable, appropriate behaviors.

First, try to reduce the number of "sensory surprises" in his environment. Forewarn him of a fire drill, maintain a low level of noise in the class, and muffle the sound of the class bell in your room. Explain to him that his reactions to sudden sensory changes—although understandable—are viewed as immature by his peers, so it is in his best interest to modify them. Encourage him to reflect for a moment when startled and decide whether his response is an overreaction.

Teach Joey to minimize the impact of these "sensory overloads" by discretely covering his ears when a loud sound occurs, wearing proper outerwear, and avoiding crowded settings where he is likely to be pushed or shoved.

A further complication of this process is the fact that the child must not only learn *how* to use a particular social skill, but also *when* to use it. Dr. Don Deshler, of Kansas State University, draws an analogy between social skill mastery and driving skills. Suppose that a person has mastered the use of a car's brakes, directional lights, and dashboard CD player. It is also important for him to understand *when* each feature should be used. It would be inappropriate, for example, for the driver to respond to a child running across the street by inserting a CD in the player!

Similarly, children with social skill deficits often master specific social skills but fail to use them appropriately. One of my students, Craig, returned from a monthlong European trip with his mother. The boy and I had a long relationship; I was his tutor and his advisor for several years. Upon his return from his vacation, he dropped by my office to share his experiences. For over an hour, he regaled me with tales of his adventures. At the end of the meeting, he reached across my desk, shook my hand, and said, "It's been nice meeting you, Mr. Lavoie"!

For a month, Craig had observed as his very social mother met numerous strangers on buses, in restaurants, and aboard Eurorail. At the end of each of these encounters, Mom concluded the meeting by saying, "It's been nice meeting you." Craig recognized that this was a very appropriate remark to make, but he failed to realize that it was inappropriate to say this to a person whom he had known for several years.

When providing social skill instruction, we must provide the child with guidance in terms of *when, where, how,* and *with whom* the new social skill should be properly used.

Afterword

An interesting aspect of the "poor wiring" of children with learning and language problems is the phenomenon of *kinetic melodies*. The inability to consistently develop and utilize kinetic melodies can have a significant impact upon the child's ability to function at home, in school, or in the community. Kinetic melodies are stored patterns of muscular actions that have a specific sequence and rhythm. They are firmly established and automatized within a person by constant repetition.

Try an experiment. Take a pen and a piece of paper. Close your eyes tightly and write your signature. You will probably find that your signature is identical to the signature that you write with your eyes open. That is because your neurological mind has developed patterns or "melodies" for oft-repeated activities such as writing your signature. When you need to complete this activity, your brain and your motor system are nearly on automatic pilot; the established pattern is followed with little conscious thought to the action at hand. Many women find that it takes a degree of concentration to write their "new" signature when they adopt the husband's family name following their marriage. After years of signing and writing "Nancy Hunt," a woman's motor system has developed a set of established muscle patterns that are automatically followed when she writes her signature. Suddenly, a whole new set of muscle movements is required to write her married name, "Nancy Marshall." Because the previous motoric patterns were so firmly established, Nancy may find it difficult to adopt new ones. Who hasn't caught himself writing the old zip code after moving to a new home? How often do you throw on a light switch automatically, even when you know you are having a long-term power outage?

Your mind has developed kinetic melodies for hundreds of activities that you do every day or frequently. The next time you brush your teeth, for example, note that you follow the exact same motor pattern each time. You hold the brush in the same hand, squeeze the toothpaste in an identical manner, and brush your teeth in the same order and pattern that you follow each time. Your unique pattern may differ from your spouse's, but you follow your pattern consistently.

You have developed kinetic melodies for showering, starting your car, dressing, tying your tie, emptying the dishwasher, answering the telephone, washing your hair, and sweeping the kitchen floor. You are able to complete these daily tasks with little thought or concentration. In fact, you can complete these tasks while thinking about or even doing something else entirely. While brushing your teeth, you may also be rehearsing your presentation for your sales meeting that morning. While sweeping the kitchen floor, you may be simultaneously planning the menu for that weekend's dinner party. Established kinetic melodies do not require focused attention or concentration. They are automatic.

Many children with learning problems have considerable difficulty establishing kinetic melodies. As a result, they may perform a routine daily activity (e.g., brushing their teeth, making the bed) *as if they are doing it for the first time*. No motor patterns have been automatized or established. They complete the pattern in a different order each time. For this reason, repetitive and routine daily tasks require their focused attention and concentration. This causes them to take inordinate amounts of time to complete these daily tasks ("Bob, you've been making your bed for fifteen minutes!") or they complete the tasks inefficiently or incorrectly ("Bob, you didn't put the second sheet on your bed when you made it this morning"). The task is so mentally exhausting, it depletes the child's energy for the rest of the day.

Teachers, parents, and caregivers often find this lack of kinetic melodies to be baffling and frustrating. We would do well to reflect upon how frustrating it must be for the child.

RECOMMENDED RESOURCES

Educational Care, Mel Levine, MD (Cambridge, Mass.: Educator's Publishing Service, 2001).

Learning Disabilities A to Z, Corinne Smith, PhD (New York: The Free Press, 2001).

The Misunderstood Child, Larry Silver, MD (New York: McGraw-Hill, 1999).

The Myth of Laziness, Mel Levine, MD (New York: Simon & Schuster, 2003).

Taking Charge of ADHD: The Complete Authoritative Guide for Parents, Russell Barkley (New York: Guilford Press).

CHAPTER TWO

Anxiety

A Cause and Consequence of Social Isolation

During a newspaper interview, a reporter asked me an interesting and thought-provoking question: "If you could give America's parents one message, what would it be?" A provocative question, indeed.

I gave him an answer that, I believe, was an accurate and timely one. "We must always remember the simple but profound fact that kids go to school for a living—that's their job. They do it six hours a day." The repercussions of this deceptively simple statement are actually quite significant.

Suppose that you had a job wherein you failed at nearly every task you attempted; you were misunderstood and mistreated by your superiors and received little comfort or support from your peers. Your workday was a blur of failure, frustration, confusion, and humiliation. Surely you would respond to this situation by becoming moody, withdrawn, and uncommunicative. It would be difficult, indeed, for you to maintain a positive self-image, a happy home life, and an upbeat attitude in the face of this frustration and failure.

So it is with the child with learning and social problems. His day at school is a difficult one, and he is often unable to "leave the school day behind" when he returns home. The frustrations and emotional turmoil of his school day (his job!) often spill over into his home life.

21

• • •

Among the most serious of the common emotional reactions to school and social failure is *anxiety.* This is a greatly misunderstood emotional issue. *Anxiety* is often considered to be synonymous with *depression,* but in fact the two conditions are quite different. The difference between the two, as explained by Massachusetts anxiety expert Dr. Thomas Tokarz, is: "Depressed people worry about the past; anxious people worry about the future."

Children with anxiety disorders are obsessed with future events—real or imagined. They invest significant effort ruminating about events and incidents that will, almost certainly, never occur. These thought patterns are often referred to as "what if . . ." thinking. A teacher's announcement of an upcoming field trip to the zoo can send the anxious child off on an emotional "roller-coaster ride" of anxiety-ridden thoughts and questions.

> *"What if it rains? Will we still go?"*
> *"Should I bring a jacket?"*
> *"How much money will I need?"*
> *"Can I sit next to Timmy on the bus?"*
> *"Will we have homework that night?"*

This anxiety can be paralyzing, particularly during periods of transition or change.

Anxiety is a natural and unavoidable response to our daily lives. However, children with anxiety problems tend to experience nervousness more often and more intensely than do other children. They are highly susceptible and highly reactive to stress. This disorder can have a profound effect upon the child's ability to function every day and can cause significant difficulty with the child's ability to concentrate and focus. It can even result in chronic irritability.

Consider this analogy. Suppose there are two brothers, John and Charlie. They are approximately the same size and weight. John has severe hay fever; Charlie does not. They go for a walk in the woods on an early spring morning. They are breathing the same air; each is receiving an identical amount of pollen into his lungs.

However, John coughs and wheezes while Charlie continues to breathe normally. Why? Because John is physically sensitive to pollen and Charlie is not.

Now, turn the allergy into anxiety. Suppose that John has a severe anxiety problem. During their walk, they meet a mutual friend, Patrick. He invites them to his house to watch a video. Charlie responds positively to the invitation and accepts. John immediately begins to worry. What if Patrick has only Coca-Cola (John likes Pepsi)? What if they are late getting home for supper? What if the large, scary dog that lives in Patrick's neighborhood is off his leash? What if Patrick's dad gets angry because Patrick didn't ask permission to bring guests home? Why does John become involved in this "what if?" thinking while Charlie doesn't? Because John is susceptible to anxiety. Your anxious child will react atypically to even typical situations.

A good example of "what if . . ." or chain thinking is a story by humorist and philanthropist Danny Thomas. He tells of a man who has a flat tire on a lonely country road. While attempting to change the tire, he breaks his jack. Spotting a farmhouse in the far distance, he begins to walk in that direction in hopes of borrowing a jack from the farmer. As he walks, he engages in self-talk and chain thinking: "I'm sure that the farmer will have a jack that I can borrow. He probably won't charge me to use it, but I will give him five dollars anyway. Wait a minute . . . what if he realizes how badly I need the jack and charges me ten dollars to use it? Well, that's okay. It's worth ten bucks to get back on the road. But he will probably want twenty dollars or maybe even thirty. He's really got me over a barrel. I'm stuck here without the jack. I'll bet he'll charge me fifty dollars . . . the pirate! Maybe even one hundred dollars! Yeah, he thinks he's gonna get one hundred out of me! No doubt! And why would he stop at one hundred? He'll probably want two hundred because there's no other farm in sight. He's really got me where he wants me. Imagine, two hundred dollars to use a jack for ten minutes. I'm pretty well dressed today, so the farmer will know that I have money. He'll probably want three hundred dollars for the jack. Talk about highway robbery!"

Frustrated and angry, the man reaches the farmhouse and knocks on the door. An elderly gentleman opens the door and smiles at the stranger.

"KEEP YOUR DAMNED JACK!" the man yells and storms back to his car.

The impact of anxiety is often greatly underestimated. Children with anxiety problems are referred to as "high-strung" or "little old men." They are often simply told to "stop worrying"—as if that command could be easily followed. I once heard a psychologist minimize anxiety by referring to it as "the little brother of depression." Not true. An anxiety problem can be every bit as debilitating as depression. Anxiety problems compromise and complicate the lives of many children with learning problems.

Early in our evolution, anxiety helped us to survive and avoid danger. When early man heard the roar of a dangerous beast, he was curious and sought out the source of the sound. When he saw the beast and it pursued him, his body would have an immediate "fight or flight" response, including rapid heartbeat, adrenaline rush, and focused thinking. Thereafter, this stress reaction would occur whenever he heard the roar. Needless to say, our ancestors with the most effective "early warning systems" were the ones who survived and passed this anxiety reaction on to future generations.

Approximately 10 percent of human beings have defective anxiety systems that activate spontaneously in the absence of danger. As a result, the person is chronically and constantly fearful. A teacher once sarcastically told me, "Joey doesn't have an anxiety problem! He worries about nothing at all!" She unwittingly *defined* Joey's anxiety problems: fear in the absence of real danger.

The etiology (cause) of anxiety disorders has been researched extensively in recent years. Severe anxiety can occur in response to significant stresses that overwhelm the child's coping abilities. There is often a genetic predisposition to anxiety disorders, and half the children with this problem have parents with similar anxiety difficulties. It is important to remember that anxiety reactions are physiological in nature. That is, they have psychological *and* physical causes and consequences. During an anxiety episode, the child's brain actually functions abnormally to a degree that can be observed and measured on brain imaging.

Children with anxiety disorders often develop phobic reactions to incidents or situations. A phobia is described as a "fear that haunts." For example, an anxious child who is easily frightened by loud noises may become fearful when a fire alarm is sounded unexpectedly in a local mall. He may then generalize that fear reaction by becoming fearful of all malls.

Annie, a seven-year-old with an anxiety disorder, goes to her dad's office building to have lunch with her father. Her mom enters the elevator with her and they meet a young man with a small black dog on a leash. When Annie bends down to pet the dog, the animal lunges at her and bites her hand. Although her skin is unbroken, it is a painful and frightening experience.

Throughout the luncheon, Annie talks incessantly about the "bad dog"; she has difficulty sleeping that night, despite her parents' attempts to comfort her and their assurances that she is safe. The next day, Annie refuses to enter the elevator when her mom takes her to the doctor's for a checkup. When she returns home, she asks her sister to throw away the small black dog and small black cat that Annie has proudly displayed in her stuffed animal collection on her bed. She screams loudly when a woman walks her small black poodle in front of their house that evening. Annie's anxiety over the dog in the elevator is now generalizing to other settings and situations.

Anxiety reactions often create a cyclical pattern that can control the child's entire day. Because the child is anxious and fearful, he may purposely avoid situations that cause (or that he believes *may* cause) anxiety; this results in few relationships, family conflicts, and lower self-esteem. His lowered self-esteem causes him to avoid fearful situations, and on and on.

It is all but impossible to determine the root cause of these fears and phobias. It is often a mystery why these phobias develop. Our son Dan had an unrelenting fear of being locked in a store all night and was reluctant to go shopping during evening hours. Despite our explanations and attempts to assure him that this could not happen, he was plagued with this fear for several years. We were unable to determine the causal factor for this fear. It appeared to be random and irrational, but that fact did little to calm or comfort Dan.

Children with anxiety problems tend to have frequent authority conflicts. Upon consideration, it is easy to understand why. The child is secretly fearful of any changes in his environment and doubts his ability to effectively handle these transitions. As a result, he becomes defiant, resistive, and argumentative whenever he is asked to make transitions. It is important to remember that this behavior is not rooted in the child's stubbornness or rebelliousness. Rather, the behavior occurs because the child is genuinely fearful. This behavior represents his best strategy for coping with his anxiety.

Recognizing an Anxiety Disorder

A child's anxiety disorder can manifest itself in several different thought patterns that cause the child to view incidents and situations in a unique manner:

Arbitrary Inference. Interpreting events without factual evidence.

"The principal walked by me today and didn't say hello. He must be mad at me because he thinks I am the kid who broke the sink in the boys' room. He's probably gonna throw me out of school."

Selective Abstraction. Focusing on a detail (usually negative) taken out of context and ignoring all other salient features.

"Everyone applauded so loudly when I read my composition in class today. But Buddy didn't applaud at all. I must have done a lousy job on my essay."

Overgeneralization. "Black and white" thinking wherein broad conclusions are drawn from a single incident.

"I didn't score a goal today. I must stink at soccer and I always will!"

Minimization/magnification. Underestimation of positive factors (achievement, performance, ability) or gross overestimation (usually of an event) in which the person dwells on the worst possible outcome.

"I know there will be gangs of kids at the mall who are going to beat me up [magnification] and there is nothing I can do about it [minimizing one's ability to control]."

Dichotomous Thinking. Interpretation of events in absolute terms with no tolerance for ambiguity.

"Jim agreed with me in class, but Tom didn't. Therefore, Jim is my friend and Tom hates me!"

Personalization. Unsupported perception that an incident reflects directly on you.

"The principal was talking to my teacher in the hallway. They must be planning to make me stay in fifth grade for another year!"

Emotional Reasoning. Equating feelings with facts.

"I feel like a loser so I must *be* a loser!"

Control Fallacies. The belief that others are responsible for your problems, or that you are responsible for the problems of others.

"My mother forgot to wake me up on time" or "I heard my parents arguing last night. I'll bet it was my fault!"

Analyze your child's thought patterns and his reactions to everyday situations. You may find that his atypical responses are caused by severe anxiety.

Types of Anxiety Disorders

It is widely accepted that there are five basic types of anxiety disorders that affect children with learning and attentional problems. One of the most common is Separation Anxiety Disorder (SAD). Of course, it is normal and natural for an infant to experience and express anxiety when he is separated from his mother or caregivers. This anxiety reaction generally subsides by eighteen months of age. Therefore, it is unusual and significant when a school-age child experiences separation anxiety.

Besides experiencing great anxiety when not at home and/or when separated from the family, children with SAD may experience stress when separation is pending or even discussed. Their fears are often irrational (e.g., kidnapping, parent's death) but very, very real. The child may become fearful of sleep or school. Nightmares and psychosomatic complaints are also common. He can become distressingly "clingy" and demanding of parental time and attention.

Separation anxiety is relatively common among children with learning and attentional problems. Basically, the child views the pending activity (e.g., a sleepover at Grandma's) as both frightening and exciting. Often, the "fear factor" becomes greater than the excitement and the anxiety takes on a life of its own. The child is unable to cope with the fears, and the "what if . . ." thought processes begin to overwhelm him. What if Grandma's house is broken into? What if my dog gets hit by a car when I am gone? What if Grandma's neighbor yells at me? Though irrational, these fears are very real and tangible to the child. These feelings of dread and impending doom are often accompanied by physical symptoms of nausea, stomach cramping, excessive sweating, feeling faint, or headaches.

When a child is experiencing separation anxiety, allow and encourage him to verbalize his "what if . . ." fears and respond to each with a calm, reassuring answer. Do not minimize or dismiss his fears with a comment like, "It's just plain silly to worry about that. It could never happen." Rather, give him a reassuring and solution-focused answer: "Lots of people are afraid of big dogs like the one that Grandma's neighbor owns. Let's discuss this with Grandma. Maybe the neighbor could give Grandma a call and let her know when the dog will be taking his walk and you can stay inside during that time." Also ask the child to generate solutions. This will enable him to feel that he has some power and control over the dreaded situation.

When discussing "what if . . ." scenarios, help the child to view the situation more realistically by encouraging him to use "coping self-talk." Gently and supportively ask questions such as:

- How likely do you think it is that the dreaded event would occur?
- If it *did* occur, how bad would it be?
- Is there anything you could do to prevent it? If not, how can we prevent *thinking about it*?

You may want to have the child use the relaxed breathing techniques described on pages 34–35 during this discussion.

Provide the child with an informal agenda of the activities and the plans for the visit or trip that he will be taking. Focus on the activities that he will enjoy: "Did you know that the camp has a nature center where you can help take care of rabbits, ducks, and turtles? Remember how much you enjoyed watching the turtles in the zoo last month?"

If you anticipate that the child will be experiencing separation anxiety due to an upcoming trip or visit, ask her to assist you in preparing for the activity. Have her help with the planning, shopping, and packing. This will give her a sense of control and contribute to her feeling that the trip is being done *for* her and *by her* rather than *to* her.

Design a simple communication system for the child to use when he is separated from you. Establish a schedule that you will both agree to follow in order to assure the child that you will be able to maintain communication during his absence. "I will call you every Monday and Wednesday. You can call me on Saturday. I will e-mail you every day and your brother will send you three postcards every week." By doing this, the child is assured that he *will* be hearing from you. This also prevents him from attempting to call you several times a day. If the child uses his calls to outline a litany of complaints and laments, require him to also discuss the positive aspects of his experience. ("Ralphie, for every *complaint* you make about camp, you then have to tell me something that you did that you enjoyed!") If you respond passively to the complaints—but enthusiastically and animatedly about the enjoyable activities—the phone calls will eventually become more upbeat. As always, *behavior that is reinforced is replicated.*

Be sure to inform the adults who will be caring for the child about his high level of anxiety. Inform them of the communication plan and ask for their cooperation in ensuring that the child adheres to the schedule. Allow for some degree of flexibility by asking the adults to use their judgment in allowing extra calls on occasion. ("Mom! Guess what! I finished first in the swim meet this afternoon. My counselor told me that I could make a special call to tell you!") Or a cooperative adult might modify the arrangement: "Joey, I know you are scheduled to call your mom at 7:30, but you are pretty upset right now and the call won't go particularly well, will it? I will call her and tell her to expect your call at 9:00, after we watch the movie and you have calmed down a bit. This isn't a punishment, Joey. It just doesn't make a lot of sense to try to have a phone call when you are so upset."

Teachers and parents may find it useful to devise a graceful, unobtrusive "exit plan" for a child with severe anxiety difficulties. When he is feeling particularly overwhelmed or overcome by anxiety, he has "standing permission" to quietly leave the room and go to a predetermined place to calm himself by using some calming techniques. Of course, some children may overuse or abuse this special privilege, but most kids are greatly comforted by this option and use it only when it is truly necessary. The teacher or parent may also suggest or request that the child go to the "quiet place" if they feel that he is beginning to become anxious. The rule of thumb for this strategy is, When the child elects to go to his sanctuary, *he* decides when to return. If the adult initiates it, *the adult* determines when he should return to the activity. These departures should not be viewed as punitive; refer to them as "calm outs" or "calm downs." The child should not be penalized for classwork that he misses during the calm outs. One creative colleague referred to this as "R and R"—relax and return.

Anxious children benefit greatly from ritualized "check in/check out" activities at the beginning and end of each school day. A teacher can meet with the child at the beginning of the day to outline his schedule and give him reassurance. At the conclusion of the day, the teacher can have a second brief conversation, wherein she reviews his day, provides some reinforcement, and ensures that he has the books and assignments that he needs to successfully complete his homework.

Often, the source of a child's anxiety is unrelated to the activities or assignments in the classroom but, rather, is rooted in *nonclassroom settings* (e.g., restrooms, playground, school bus). These unstructured, unpredictable, and unmonitored environments can be very anxiety provoking. Provide him with the reassurance, strategies, and support that he may need to deal with this anxiety-ridden situation.

A second common anxiety disorder is known as *Generalized Anxiety Disorder* (GAD). For children with GAD, anxiety is their constant and unrelenting companion. They worry about their health, their safety, their families, and their friends. Their worries are often excessive and unrealistic (e.g., news of a tornado in Kansas causes anxiety for the child in New Jersey). They judge themselves harshly and are often dissatisfied with their own progress or performance. They need—and demand—constant reassurance from parents, teachers, or caregivers. It may seem that they are fishing for compliments, but caregivers must understand that these children need constant support and praise. Their problem is genuine and potentially debilitating.

Social Phobia is the third common anxiety disorder among children and is particularly common among students with social deficits. These children have an intense and debilitating fear of being embarrassed or humiliated. They may be extraordinarily shy, and their behaviors are often misinterpreted as oppositional because of their refusal to participate in activities such as class discussions and oral presentations. Again, it is important to remain mindful that this behavior is rooted in extreme and intense anxiety. Some children actually develop selective mutism, wherein they are unable to speak in social settings outside the home.

The fourth common anxiety disorder is referred to as *Obsessive-Compulsive Disorder* (OCD). This condition is often misdiagnosed and misunderstood. The OCD child's behavior is influenced and controlled by inappropriate and intrusive thoughts, impulses, and images. These result in inappropriate repetitive behaviors. For example, the child may have an irrational fear of gas leaks and so constantly, repeatedly checks the stove knobs to be certain that they are in the *off* position. The fear of gas is the obsession; the knob checking is the compulsion.

These children develop ritualistic behaviors that are troubling for their parents and off-putting to peers. They often have an unrelenting need for order and consistency in their environment and develop intense anxiety reactions about seemingly minor inconsistencies. A former student of mine would become hysterical if a family member were to move his bicycle from its designated location in the garage. His obsession with losing his bike created numerous compulsions about the bike's location and condition.

The final common anxiety malady is *Posttraumatic Stress Disorder* (PTSD). Previously, psychologists thought that PTSD could only be experienced by people who have experienced horrific and life-threatening incidents (e.g., plane crashes, automobile accidents, battlefield situations). We now realize that PTSD can be triggered by in-cidents that the victim *feels* are traumatic, although the situation may seem relatively insignificant to others. I know a child who suffered from classic PTSD symptoms following a difficult year in third grade. He was unable to forget about his conflicts with his third-grade teacher and often had flashbacks of particular negative incidents or situations. He developed the PTSD symptom of "hypervigilance," wherein he was constantly alert and had an exaggerated startle re-sponse to common stimuli.

Treatment and Coping Strategies for Anxiety Disorders

There are numerous medical interventions for the treatment of chil-dren with anxiety problems. These generally involve the use of med-ications that affect the child's serotonin levels. Clinical trials have demonstrated significant success with these drugs. Parents should consult with the child's pediatrician and psychologist regarding the use of medication.

In my experience, I have gained significant respect for and confi-dence in the use of *cognitive behavioral therapy* (CBT) with these children. CBT's effectiveness is rooted in one basic belief: you do not have "bad thoughts" because you feel badly. Rather, you feel badly be-cause you have bad thoughts. This therapy instructs the patient in specific strategies designed to identify, isolate, and derail the negative thought patterns. By eliminating these patterns, the patient's sense of well-being, safety, and confidence is greatly enhanced. When a pa-tient says to a cognitive behavioral therapist, "I can't stop thinking about it!" the therapist replies, "Oh yes you can!"

There are also many techniques that parents and teachers can use to bring relief to a child with anxiety problems. For example, use the same reassuring phrase to comfort him during periods of anxiety (e.g., "Things are getting better all the time" or "Let's not worry about that for a while"). This calming "mantra" will reduce the anxiety and bring comfort to the child.

Be careful not to ridicule or belittle the child's anxieties. These fears are very real to her and should be taken seriously. Telling the child "she has nothing to worry about" is ineffective. You may find that the anxious child is unable to pinpoint the specific source of his anxiety. Do not insist that she identify a reason for her nervousness. Some children experience unrooted, free-floating anxiety. Even if they do know the source, they may be too embarrassed to discuss it because they fear that you will consider it trivial.

When attempting to alleviate a child's anxiety, it is important to provide him with incentives for brave behavior. This may seem counterindicated, since anxiety is generally considered a "feeling," not a behavior. Incentives may not be effective in changing feelings. However, anxiety should be viewed as a behavior, or a way of thinking. Therefore, incentives or reinforcers are effective methods to modify the behaviors related to anxiety.

The anxious child responds well to praise and reinforcement. Parents and teachers should always be mindful of the wise adage, "Behavior that is reinforced is replicated." Conversely, punishment is relatively ineffective. Reinforce his "brave behaviors" (e.g., "I know that you were nervous about going to the grocery store with me and you should be proud of the way that you handled it. I am!").

You will also want to provide the child with a great deal of encouragement and assurance. Anxious children often feel that they are helpless, and they underestimate their ability to deal with the anxiety or to control the source of the tension they feel (e.g., "I know that the kids on the bus will make fun of me today and there's nothing I can do about it").

Assist the child in developing problem-solving skills. When he asks you what he should do in a specific situation, gently reverse the question and ask him what *he* thinks he should do. Enthusiastically praise and reinforce him if he generates an effective or workable solution, even if the solution is not the ideal one. Eventually, he will develop greater faith in his own ability to solve problems and create solutions.

In similar fashion, encourage the anxious child to self-evaluate. These children are often unable or unwilling to assess their own performance and they constantly seek reassurance from adults. ("Mrs. Flight, do you think this drawing is okay?") Encourage the child to develop an independent opinion of his performance. ("Well, Mac, what do *you* think about the drawing?") He will eventually develop greater faith in his own skills of self-assessment and become less dependent upon the opinions and input of others.

Do not instruct the child to "go into your room, relax, and calm down." This technique merely changes the location of his anxiety but does little to reduce or alleviate it. It may be useful to teach the child some simple but effective relaxation techniques.

Deep Breathing

Relax shoulders and arms.
Slowly circle head right, then left. Repeat several times.
Close eyes.
Take slow, deep breaths. Exhale. Repeat while concentrating on your breathing.

Six-second Quieting Response

Smile (to relax facial muscles).
Inhale. Imagine air flowing in through hands and feet.
Exhale. Let jaw, tongue, and shoulders go loose; "feel" warm air flow down from your chest and out through the feet.
Tell yourself that your body is calm.
Go back to what you were doing.

Progressive Muscle Relaxation

Tighten muscles in right arm by making a fist.
Hold the tension for a moment.
Open the hand and enjoy the feeling of the tension flowing away.
Repeat process with left arm.
In a similar way, tense and relax muscles in the leg, back, chest, shoulders, neck, and face.

Meditation (for older children)

Sit or lie comfortably.
Close your eyes and let your muscles relax.
Concentrate on your breathing.

Select a word (a mantra) and say it silently each time
you exhale. Think only of that word.
Open your eyes after ten or fifteen minutes.
Sit quietly for a few minutes more.

IMAGERY

Go to a park, forest, meadow, or another quiet place.
Observe the colors, sounds, and scents.
Later, close your eyes, breathe deeply, and spend a quiet
ten-minute break recalling those sights, sounds, and
scents.

EXERCISE

A game of tag, bicycling, skating, or other vigorous activity can be
an enjoyable and fun way to release tension. In addition to relaxing
the muscles, this activity causes the brain to release endorphins, a
tranquilizing neurochemical, throughout the body.

It is ineffective to advise the child to participate in a pointless,
unstructured activity, such as punching a pillow, in order to relieve
stress. This can actually increase the child's tension and anxiety.
Rather, advise him to complete an activity that has a measurable and
specific beginning and ending: "Go outside and shoot twenty baskets"
or "Take five laps around the yard."

HYPERFOCUS

It is a common belief that relaxation is enhanced if you "let
your mind go blank" and think about absolutely nothing. In fact,
the opposite is true. It is quite relaxing to focus intently on a simple
object or activity (e.g., screwing on and unscrewing a bottle cap repeatedly, stroking the dog's fur, drawing straight lines on a piece of
paper).

Find two surfaces of different textures (e.g., table top and fabric
on pant leg). Close your eyes and make circular motions on one surface with the fingertips of your right hand, and on the other surface
with the fingertips of your left hand. This strategy is particularly effective when used immediately prior to an anxiety-producing activity
(e.g., test, oral report, dentist appointment).

Coping with an Event or Task

Simple behaviors that you might consider routine can be sources of great anxiety for a child (e.g., boarding the school bus, talking to Grandma on the telephone, buying a treat from the ice cream truck). Prior to the activity, tell the child what you want her to do in very specific and observable terms: "When Grandma calls, I want you to tell her about the award you received at Girl Scouts last night. Don't forget to ask her if Grandpa is feeling better." *Not* "Be good when Grandma calls."

As always, the adult should praise and reinforce the child for "brave" behavior and should avoid overcompensating for the child's anxious behavior. For example, if the youngster is too anxious to approach the librarian's desk to check out a book, make this behavior a social goal. Divide the task into manageable steps and coach the child through the process: "This week I want you to accompany me when I check out a book for you. But next week, I will expect you to interact with Mrs. Colloton during the process. By the end of the month, you will be able to take out a book all by yourself!"

Coping with Sleep Problems

You might find that your anxious child also has difficulty sleeping or has unusual sleep habits. If so, discourage his napping during the day and encourage him to get regular exercise. Limit his caffeine intake and make bedtime a relaxed, soothing process. You may want to discourage him from using his bedroom for anything *but* sleeping. Have him do his homework, watch TV, and read in other areas of the home. Reinforce the idea that his bedroom is solely for sleeping. It can also be helpful to have the child go to bed and awaken at the same time each day.

Coping with Change

The anxious child does not react well to transitions or changes in his environment or routine. But, of course, it is impossible to structure a child's day so thoroughly that no changes occur. Change is an unavoidable aspect of modern life. There are numerous strategies that you can use to minimize the impact of change and to prepare the child for the inevitable transitions of everyday life.

First, design a phrase that you can use consistently whenever a change in the schedule or routine is imminent: "We have a little curve ball here," or "There's a little bump in the road now." This phrase prepares the child for the change, and the consistent use of the saying may be comforting to him.

Try to avoid introducing several changes simultaneously. For example, if you are going to visit family members for a long weekend, prepare the child gradually by discussing the trip over several days, packing gradually, and so forth. The child may not be able to deal with the typical "night before we leave" frenzy that often accompanies such an excursion. In these situations it is important to plan *with*, not *for*, the child. If he is involved in the planning process, he is less likely to become unduly anxious. This strategy may also provide you with valuable information regarding the source of his anxiety.

When the planning process is completed, assure him that he is well prepared and this preparation is likely to make all go smoothly. He will doubtless be buoyed by your confidence. When the transition or change is complete, congratulate him on his success and commend him for his efforts.

For younger children, *transitional objects* may help to reduce the stress of a doctor's visit, trip to Grandma's, or other surprise events. A transitional object is merely a familiar object that brings comfort to the child because it is familiar and reminds him of safety and security. It is no accident that children have, for generations, carried threadbare and tattered dolls and stuffed animals with them. The familiarity of these objects brings great comfort and peace of mind. In a variation on this theme, I once worked with a very anxious teenager who became quite troubled whenever I traveled away from the school. One day, he asked me if he could have one of my business cards to carry with him whenever I went away. He looked at it often in my absence and reported that it brought him great comfort.

Coping in School

There are several other strategies that parents and school personnel can use to assist the child who is experiencing significant anxiety. The adults in the child's life should receive information and training in the nature and needs of anxiety disorders. Too often care-givers minimize these disorders and the child is merely labeled as "nervous" or "high-strung." It is important that anxiety problems be viewed as significant mental health issues that can greatly complicate and compromise the child's day-to-day progress and performance. The avoidance behaviors (e.g., resistance, defiance) often manifested by anxious children should not be viewed as willful or disrespectful. Rather, they are understandable reactions to the child's uncomfort-able feelings of anxiety. Parents and school personnel should com-municate frequently to avoid the use of conflicting strategies and ensure consistency between home and school. The consistency and predictability will bring great comfort to the child.

The child is more likely to participate in (and enjoy) school activ-ities if he is assigned to a classmate or teammate during these ses-sions. Because of his tendency to be shy and withdrawn, he is unlikely to pair up with another student during academic or recre-ational activities. By assigning students to work in pairs or triads, the teacher is in effect doing the pairing for the child.

The teacher can also assist the child by making social interac-tions observable and measurable. That is, instead of merely encour-aging the child to "interact more frequently" with classmates, provide him with specific "social assignments": "At recess today, I want you to ask two kids what they think they will be getting for Christmas." Or "This week, I want you to volunteer three times when I ask a question or ask for assistance in class."

Most students with social difficulties benefit from having an in-school case manager or ombudsman who is assigned to coordinate the child's program and facilitate effective communication between and among the youngster's teachers. This supportive structure is par-ticularly important for children with anxiety difficulties. This child thrives on a predictable environment with limited transitions and sur-prises. Ongoing communication among his teachers will go far in en-suring this consistency. The school personnel must be understanding and tolerant of the child's anxiety and his pronounced need for struc-ture and predictability.

The anxious child's teachers must be aware of his self-defeating tendency toward perfectionism. He may become easily upset about minor mistakes or miscues and overreact. He needs constant reassurance that mistakes are a normal and necessary aspect of the learning process. His focused attention on "details" prevents him from seeing the "big picture." As a result, he becomes so upset about his incorrect answer on a specific test item that he fails to recognize that he achieved a 95 on the exam and improved significantly over his previous test. The teacher should assist him in gaining a more realistic and positive perception of his performance. Encourage him to understand that perfection is generally unattainable and that mistakes are inevitable and valuable. I once had an anxious student who became distraught whenever he made an error on his math worksheets or during oral drills. I explained to him that his mistakes were signals to me that allowed me to learn where and when I should begin to teach him. Until he made a mistake, I did not know what skills he needed to learn. Without mistakes, there can be no learning or teaching.

Afterword

Children with anxiety disorders often have severe and catastrophic reactions to problems or incidents that are quite trivial in nature. This is a chief characteristic of these disorders. If these children overreact to minor problems, one can imagine their significant reactions when a major crisis or disaster occurs. In the weeks following the September 11 attacks, anxiety clinics and therapists reported severe anxiety reactions in their patients. Many practitioners reported that patients who had not required treatment for several years experienced significant relapses as a result of the terrorist attacks.

For this reason, teachers and parents should be acutely aware of the needs of the anxious child if a crisis, disaster, or tragedy occurs. The child will doubtless react more strongly to the incident than will his siblings or classmates and may do so for an extended period of time. In a crisis (such as severe weather, accident, serious illness), the adult must remain mindful of *his own* needs and reactions. You will be of limited use to the child if you are having a catastrophic reaction yourself. Seek guidance, counseling, or assistance from those in your personal support system. Take care of yourself. This is not a sign of selfishness or self-centeredness on your part. It is merely recognition of the fact that it is difficult to heal someone if you are wounded yourself. There is a reason that airlines advise that you "put on your own oxygen mask before attempting to assist others."

In a crisis, an anxious child feels an intense loss of control. His inability to control events, coupled with the realization that the adults in his life *also* cannot control or eliminate them, can trigger overwhelming anxiety. This anxiety is enhanced by the concurrent disruption of schedules and plans. These abrupt changes in the "order of things" can produce great anxiety for the child.

The child's initial reaction to a crisis is generally self-centered. He will need assurance that he is safe. Be patient with and understanding of this response to a crisis. Suppose Jerry's cousin is injured in an accident and Jerry begins asking endless questions about whether *he* will ever be in an accident. Jerry's reaction may seem selfish, but it is a typical anxious response to a crisis. During the atom bomb scare of the 1950s, many children reported that they were extraordinarily fearful that their parents would die in a nuclear holocaust. Upon further investigation, however, the main root of the fear did not lie in the children's concern for their parents' welfare. Rather, the children feared that their parents' death would cause them to be left alone and uncared for.

It is important that the adult be honest and candid with the child during the crisis period. Avoid the temptation to give the child temporary comfort by minimizing the problem or lying. Merely assuring the child that "everything will be okay" will do little to comfort him, particularly if the child later discovers that all is *not* okay and that the results of the crisis are permanent and lasting (e.g., death, serious illness, major destructive fire).

After a crisis, the anxious child may react with anger, denial, and depression. Again, the child will need patience, understanding, acceptance, and unconditional love as he maneuvers through these stages. He may need significant amounts of attention and affection during this period. Help him to express his emotions through guided and supportive conversations.

Be aware that the child may have a delayed or continuing reaction to the crisis. The death of a friend's grandfather may trigger the anxiety and sadness that the child experienced at the passing of his own grandfather; a television news story about a near-drowning may cause the child to relive his own swimming accident some years earlier. Be supportive during these periods and encourage the child to voice his concerns and anxieties.

Below are some warning signs that a child may be experiencing an anxiety reaction to incidents in his life and environment.

- complaints of unusual physical symptoms with sudden onset (dizziness, difficulty breathing, tightness in chest, rapid heartbeat)*
- change in eating habits
- cruelty toward pets or younger children
- nightmares
- compulsive behavior
- cold hands, feet*
- irritability
- poor concentration
- nervous laughter
- explosive crying
- shyness
- free-floating anxiety (worry with no discernible cause)
- defiance
- avoidance behaviors

Any one of these symptoms in isolation is not indicative of a child with an anxiety problem or a stress reaction. When attempting to discern if your child has an anxiety problem, analyze her behavior using the above list and carefully consider the three Cs:

1. *Change:* Does the behavior represent a significant *change* in his behavior (e.g., a formerly sound sleeper now has difficulty sleeping)?

2. *Chronic:* Is the behavior (symptom) occurring often?

---

* Be aware that the physical ailments and complaints voiced by anxious children are very real. Anxiety can greatly increase heart rate and blood pressure, which can cause the physical symptoms.

3. *Clusters:* Are several of the symptoms occurring simultaneously?

RECOMMENDED RESOURCES

Children and Trauma, Cynthia Monahan, PsyD (New York: Lexington Books, 2002).

Emotion: The On/Off Switch for Learning, Priscilla Vail (Rosemont, N.J.: Modern Language Press, 2002).

The Grieving Child, Helen Fitzgerald (New York: Fireside Press, 2001).

Helping Your Anxious Child, Ronald M. Rappe, PhD (Oakland, Calif.: New Harbinger Press, 2002).

Nurturing Resilience in Our Children, Robert Brooks, PhD, and Sam Goldstein, PhD (Chicago: Contemporary Books, 2003).

Seven Steps to Help Your Child Worry Less, Robert Brooks, PhD, and Sam Goldstein, PhD (Plantation, Fla.: Specialty Press, 2002).

CHAPTER THREE

Language Difficulties

Getting and Giving the Message

Language is a tool. We use this tool to inspire, inform, ignite, illuminate, illustrate, initiate, immortalize, imply, impose, impress, improve, and impugn.

Teachers and educators often refer to "the language arts" when discussing a child's progress and performance. The language arts consist of four distinct but interrelated skill sets. There are two *media* of language—*written* and *oral*. If you wish to inform a colleague that you will be out of your office for awhile, you can communicate that information to her by writing her a note (written) or by telling her (oral). There are also two *elements* of language—*expressive* and *receptive*. If you write a note or tell your colleague you will be absent, you are expressing language. When she reads the note or listens to your announcement, she is receiving language.

The language arts consist of a combination of these four media and elements.

MEDIA	ELEMENTS
Written	Expressive: writing
Written	Receptive: reading
Oral	Expressive: speaking
Oral	Receptive: listening

43

Difficulties or deficiencies in a child's ability to *speak* or *listen* will compromise his social adjustment or acceptance. In order to establish and maintain social relationships, the child must be an enjoyable, effective, and efficient conversational partner. If he has a language disability, this deficiency will have a marked and observable impact upon his ability to function and interact socially.

There are two basic kinds of verbal communication disorders. *Articulation* involves the ability to speak in a clear and comprehensible manner. Children with articulation deficits may have difficulty pronouncing words properly. They may stutter or stammer, making their speech difficult to understand. Even minor and occasional articulation problems can cause the child great embarrassment and insecurity. When the child is young, her "baby talk" may be viewed by the family members as cute and may even be encouraged by well-intentioned caregivers. However, when the child enters school, classmates may tease her and adults may demonstrate frustration with her speech. As a result, the child may become withdrawn, shy, or incommunicative.

Articulation problems can often be remediated and improved through speech therapy. Speech sounds are produced by passing air through the voice box (larynx). Movements of the tongue and lips then adjust the sound. If these movements are performed improperly, misarticulation can result. A speech therapist can assist the child by teaching the proper movement and placement of the tongue and lips.

The second and perhaps more significant kind of verbal communication problems are known as *language disorders*. These difficulties can have a measurable impact upon the child's ability to communicate verbally. These disorders may be receptive (e.g., auditory processing) or expressive (e.g., dysnomia, the inability to recall words and name objects). Children with measurable and observable language disorders may experience significant difficulties mastering and applying social skills. A child's ability to function socially is largely dependent upon his ability to communicate his needs, feelings, and opinions to others.

For most children, language develops quite naturally and in a predictable, sequential manner. Mastery of basic oral language skills is impacted by several factors, including:

- chronological age
- intelligence
- learning environment
- language role models
- quality and quantity of social interactions
- basic language capabilities
- sensory stimulation

Even when the above listed factors are satisfactory and appropriate, some children have difficulty developing effective language skills. The academic and social progress of these children can be greatly compromised as they struggle daily to understand the language of others and to have their own language understood. As with the child with articulation deficits, the frustration involved in attempting to communicate effectively may cause the child with language disorders to avoid social interactions and become withdrawn and reclusive. These children require significant support, encouragement, and specialized training to overcome their language deficits.

Children with significant language disorders may manifest several of the following symptoms:
- difficulty discriminating or locating the source of sounds
- difficulty sequencing ideas
- circumlocutions (imprecise, roundabout communications)
- inappropriate use of tenses
- grammatical errors
- difficulty following oral directions
- difficulty differentiating fact from opinion
- limited vocabulary
- word-finding difficulties
- mispronunciation of common words
- delayed reading skills
- difficulty summarizing

Children with attention problems may have particular difficulty with conversations because of their distractibility, impulsivity, forgetfulness, and processing difficulties.

The Art of Conversation

One area of language development that has a significant and lasting impact upon social competencies is *pragmatics*. This crucial skill is defined as the "social side of language." Pragmatics involves skills such as taking turns in conversations, maintaining eye contact, adjusting speech patterns to the audience, and asking relevant questions. Children with pragmatic difficulties are unable to use language as a social tool.

A child who has disorders in the areas of expressive and receptive language will have significant difficulty participating in day-to-day conversations and discussions. Such language-based exchanges are fundamental to a child's acceptance and participation in social settings at home, in school, and in the community. A child who is unable to converse is at a great disadvantage in these settings.

Conversational skills appear to be quite uncomplicated. They are so basic to our daily functioning that they seem quite natural and simple. However, for children with language disorders, a conversation is a complex, challenging activity that requires myriad skills and competencies. A good conversation can be compared to a volleyball game wherein each "player" is required to volley, pass, set up his partner, and ultimately score.

To effectively participate in a conversation, one must use a wide variety of language skills. First, you must screen out all of the irrelevant stimuli competing with the message (e.g., background noise, other conversations). You must focus your attention on the content and mood of the conversation in which you are participating. In order to determine the mood and intent of your conversation partner, you must be able to "read" his body language, tone of voice, and facial expressions. These tasks require complex perceptual and memory skills.

Social conversations also include a set of complicated conventions and rules that must be adhered to and followed. These rules may vary from culture to culture and must be closely obeyed lest your conversation partner view you as boorish or boring. These rules may involve appropriate eye contact, turn taking, body language, tone of voice, volume, vocabulary, and basic manners. If any of these "ingredients" strike the listener as inappropriate, the conversation will not go well. Again, conversational speech is so natural for most adults that parents and teachers often fail to realize how truly complex this skill is. An effective and enjoyable conversation requires a degree of flexibility and responsiveness that many children with learning problems lack.

When a person is involved in a conversation, he must master and apply the following skills:

- Comprehend the message being sent by the conversation partner: What are the *words* saying?
- Observe, analyze, and respond to the partner's body language: What message is the body language communicating?
- Consider the partner's perspective.
- Consider the partner's social status: Peer? Authority figure? Family member?
- Consider the setting of the conversation: School? Church? Playing field?
- Organize an appropriate response.
- Determine a partner's prior knowledge: What do I know about my partner that should be considered during this conversation? What is the extent of my partner's knowledge of the topic under discussion?

Failure to accurately and appropriately tailor your conversation using these skills will result in a difficult, inappropriate, and ineffective conversation. For children with language problems, group conversations (e.g., dinner table conversation, classroom discussion) are particularly difficult because these settings require them to evaluate and respond to several conversation partners simultaneously. Teachers and parents should be mindful of this in group settings. A child who may be quite conversant in a one-to-one discussion may have significant difficulty when involved in a group conversation.

Interrupting

Children with social skill deficits tend to inappropriately interrupt conversations. Although this behavior is troubling and off-putting, the reasons for the behavior are quite understandable when one considers the variety of challenges and difficulties that these children face in the areas of language, memory, and emotional needs. The child may interrupt an ongoing conversation, for example, because he feels that he has an important message to deliver and he knows through past experience that he is likely to forget the message if he does not deliver it immediately. Many children with social deficiencies also have great difficulty delaying gratification because of their impulsivity related to Attention Deficit Hyperactivity Disorder (ADHD), and this may result in a tendency to interrupt conversations. Other reasons for this behavior may include the child's tendency to feel threatened and left out when a parent or teacher is attentive to another person. This reflects a degree of self-centeredness that is a common—albeit troubling—trait.

Whatever the reason for these interruptions, the parent or teacher should devise a strategy to deal with them. One is to forewarn the child that you will be involved in an activity or conversation that is not to be interrupted: "Jack, I am going to be making a very important phone call to Mr. Middleton, and I do not want you to interrupt me during the call. If you need help with your homework, I will help you as soon as I get off the phone." If the child does not interrupt the call, be certain to reinforce that behavior by thanking and praising him. As always, remember that behavior that is reinforced is more likely to be replicated. You may want to give him something to do to prevent the interruption. "Ms. Vita is going to come over to our house in ten minutes to talk with me about the garden. We can't be interrupted. Here are some glue and paper. Why don't you make a birthday card for Grandma?"

Agree on a gesture to signal that a conversation should not be interrupted (e.g., open hand with palm facing out, crossed fingers). If you are engaged in a conversation and the child interrupts, give him the prearranged signal and continue your conversation. If the child waits patiently, respond to him when a lull occurs in your discussion. If the child's interrupting behavior is caused by faulty memory and his anxiety that he will forget his message, modify this technique by allowing and encouraging him to provide you with a keyword that you can use later to trigger his memory of his message. For example, if he remembers that he needs to have you sign his permission slip for tomorrow's field trip, he would approach you during your conversations with another and merely say "field trip" and depart. At the end of your conversation, you can give him the keyword and he will deliver his message.

If the child is a chronic interrupter, the most effective strategy to reduce this behavior is to reinforce and recognize the child when he does *not* interrupt: "Mikey, thank you for not interrupting my conversation with the plumber. I know that you had a question to ask me and really appreciate your waiting and your patience. Now, how can I help you?"

Failure to Follow Conversations

Memory deficits can have a significantly negative impact upon a child's ability to participate in routine conversations. The child may lose her place in the discussion, forget the topic at hand, be unable to find the right word, or forget that she has already made a comment and repeat herself several times during the conversation. The child also may fear that she will forget a comment that she wishes to make and so she interjects the comment inappropriately. Encourage the child to jot down key words related to the comments she wishes to add to the discussion. This can be easily and unobtrusively done during informal conversations. Also encourage the child to carefully concentrate during conversations. This vigilance will increase her ability to use her memory skills.

Monopolizing the Conversation

For the child who has a tendency to monopolize conversations, teach her to ask questions often during informal discussions. By asking questions—and listening attentively to the responses—she will become a more attractive conversation partner. The child will realize that she need not monopolize the conversation in order to participate actively in it. Asking questions, listening, and observing are appropriate ways to participate in a conversation. Again, reinforce the child when she does not interrupt or monopolize.

The Art of Small Talk

In order to participate comfortably and appropriately in most social settings, it is necessary to master the art of small talk. This practice should not be viewed as trivial or unimportant; rather, it is a strategy used to pass time between and among people. Think for a moment about the two or three most social and amiable people you know. The chances are that they are quite skilled at small talk, and they use this skill to engage, include, and charm others. Small talk is a valuable social skill.

We have all experienced the dreaded silence in conversation. A conversation that suddenly falls silent creates an uncomfortable social situation. Each participant struggles to think of a comment that will break the silence and restart the conversation. Instruct the child to observe the setting in which the silence is occurring and to comment on something or someone in the immediate environment to get the conversation moving forward. "Look at how high this ceiling is! I wonder how they change the lightbulbs," or "See that man over there? Doesn't he look like Abraham Lincoln?"

Provide an appropriate role model by engaging in informal conversations with others when your child is present. Waiting in line at the grocery, in an elevator, or on the train platform, turn to a stranger and initiate an informal conversation. Discuss this strategy with the child after the exchange. Ask the child to recount how you initiated the conversation and ask how the stranger responded. Encourage the child to use small talk with strangers and with people with whom the child is familiar. Naturally, you will want to caution him that topics used with strangers should be general and global. The child should never ask intimate questions of a stranger ("How much did that watch cost?" or "I'm here at the doctor's office to get a flu shot. What's wrong with you?"), nor should she divulge any personal information to someone she does not know.

It is a generally accepted fact that people enjoy talking about *themselves*. Therefore, small talk is more likely to be effective if it is about the person with whom you are conversing. Encourage the child to comment favorably on a person's clothing ("That's a great hat") or the person's behavior ("You did a great job at basketball practice today"). Topics for small talk should be upbeat and light; avoid introducing depressing or distressing subjects. If the child is in a group, the small talk should include everyone in the immediate area.

There are times, of course, when small talk is inappropriate and unwelcome. Tell the child that if someone appears to be concentrating on a task, it is not a good idea to attempt to initiate a conversation. I recall an interminable Boston-to-Dallas flight when I was desperately trying to complete some long-overdue correspondence while my seatmate made innumerable attempts to engage me in conversations ranging from the recent presidential election to Major League Baseball to the latest antics of his new nephew. He was unable to effectively read my body language or the sense of urgency and annoyance that it was conveying. By the conclusion of the flight, I am sure that the man viewed me as unsociable or unsocialized. Actually, it was *he* who made the social error by not responding to my signals that I was not eager to participate in three hours of informal communication. I had other, more pressing matters that needed attention.

In order to initiate a conversation, one must first select an appropriate and effective topic. This can be very challenging for a child with poor social skills. Many children who struggle socially have a tendency to perseverate on a single topic (i.e., baseball or horror movies) and they are unable to "read" that this topic may be of little interest or importance to others. It is quite common that such children have interests and hobbies that are somewhat narrow and unique, like 1930s jazz, World War II tanks, or NFL logos. The child may find these topics fascinating, but his conversation partner may not. When the child's conversation focuses solely on his favorite topic, social isolation and rejection are the natural results.

As I travel around the country, I sometimes cross paths with students with whom I worked in the '70s and '80s. Invariably, they will initiate our conversation with topics or events that are significant and important to *them* but of little interest or importance to *me*: "My uncle bought a new car last week" or "My boss at work shaved off his beard yesterday." It is difficult to respond to such inappropriate conversational initiatives. It is encouraging to meet alumni from the '90s, who had been exposed to intense social skill instruction during their high school years. Their conversational entrees are far more appropriate and effective: "How are Mrs. Lavoie, Christian, Danny, and Meggi?" "How long will you be in the area?" "How are things on Cape Cod?"

Assist the child in selecting appropriate conversation topics by encouraging him to choose a subject that is topical and based on the news of the day, provides happy news about mutual acquaintances, invites comments on a current entertaining film or television show, or poses a question related to his conversation partner's job, home life, or family. Again, most people respond favorably and participate actively when the conversation focuses on them and their interests. If the child realizes that the bulk of the conversation has focused on himself, he can redirect the discussion by saying, "But enough about me. What have *you* been up to?"

Children with social problems may have difficulty staying on a single topic during a conversation and may have a tendency to jump from subject to subject. Of course, it is not uncommon for several topics to be explored within one conversation, but care must be taken not to switch topics too suddenly or to introduce information that is only loosely related to the subject under discussion. "Look how high that bridge is! My uncle lives right near a bridge. He has a dog named Taffy and she bit me once and I had to go to the hospital and the doctor was about 6'7" and played basketball once for the Celtics . . ." Encourage the child to stay on topic by gently pointing out that his discourse has gone off track a bit and reminding him of the initial topic under discussion: "That's interesting, Zak, but remember that we were talking about the bridge."

First Impressions

Studies show that most people form a lasting impression of someone within minutes of their first meeting. These initial interactions cause each person to evaluate whether their new acquaintance is interesting, fun, and sincere. This research also shows that it takes several subsequent *positive* interactions in order to offset an initial *negative* impression.

Encourage your child to be entertaining, attentive, and interested when she meets someone for the first time. Urge her to use the person's name during the conversation and to disclose something memorable and somewhat personal during the initial meeting: "I met Elton John at an airport once," or "We live in the oldest house in town." This disclosure can help to move the relationship along and also serve to make the first exchange a noteworthy one: "Oh, I remember *you*! You met Elton John once, right?"

The goal of any initial meeting is twofold: (1) to make the new acquaintance feel good about himself, and (2) to demonstrate that you are an interesting person.

Many children (and adults!) become unduly concerned if a first impression goes poorly. Remind the child that if an initial meeting does not go well and the child feels that he presented himself appropriately, he can chalk it up to simple incompatibility.

Adjusting Your Own Language

Parents of children with social skill problems often report that they have difficulty conversing with their child. Be mindful of the fact that oral language is difficult for the youngster, and his lack of language fluency can hinder his comprehension and production of the spoken word. Adults should adjust their own language to accommodate the child's language deficits.

If you ask a typical adult a broad, global question, you generally receive a broad, general response. For example, the question "What did you think of last week's election?" results in a lengthy response. "Well, I feel that the Democrats . . . and the Republicans . . . and the young voters thought . . . and the results demonstrated . . ." Conversely, if you ask a specific, focused question—"Who did you vote for in last week's election?"—you will receive a brief, specific response ("Jim Smith").

Interestingly, this dynamic works in just the opposite way when conversing with children with limited language skills. A general, broad question renders a specific response—"How was school today?" might receive the response, "It was good"—while a specific question—"How was your third-period science class today?"—results in a detailed and lengthy response: "Oh, it was neat! We hooked up a magnet to an electric motor and it made all the iron filings go into a straight line, and the teacher said that magnets have two poles . . ." By asking more specific questions, you are enabling the child to focus his language skills on a narrow topic, which enables him to generate a more detailed and factual response.

Generally children will send discernible nonverbal signals when they are ready to end a conversation with an adult. They often begin to stare off into space or become silly. It is time to end the exchange. Gracefully take the lead and end it.

Teaching the Basics of Conversation

In summary, an effective conversationalist generally does the following during an informal discussion. He

- constructs a positive beginning and ending to the conversation
- makes appropriate eye contact with his conversation partner
- takes turns and does not monopolize the conversation
- asks questions in order to keep the conversation going
- effectively reads and responds to the body language of his partner, and in return sends appropriate body language that reflects interest, agreement, and camaraderie (e.g., nodding, smiling)
- adjusts his vocabulary, language, and tone to reflect his partner's age, social status, knowledge, and the setting
- adheres appropriately to the topic at hand
- ensures that all conversation partners feel listened to and appreciated
- comprehends the message being sent and recognizes figurative language
- thinks and reflects before speaking
- enters and exits a conversation appropriately

Appropriate and appealing conversational skills are significant factors in a child's ability to make and maintain friendships. Here are several tips and techniques that you can provide to the child in order to enhance his conversational skills and abilities.

Be interested, *not just* interesting. Whenever we are involved in a conversation, we make an understandable effort to be an interesting conversation partner. But it is more important to be an *interested* partner, by asking questions and providing the other person with body language signals that demonstrate that you find his input to be compelling and important.

This interest is reflected in a *softening* of your behavior. Suggest that the child soften her voice, her posture, her touch, and her body language. This communicates a signal of genuine interest in her partner and her message.

Understand silences. Many people—particularly those with poor social skills—mistakenly interpret a partner's silence during a conversation as representing agreement. There are many reasons why a conversation partner may fall silent in response to something that you have said. Possible explanations for his silence are many and varied, including reflection, anger, shock, revulsion, confusion, and stalling. Teach the child how to read body language to determine the meaning behind a sudden silence.

Use effective body language. Encourage the child to avoid fidgeting, yawning, or breaking eye contact when involved in a conversation. He should use his eyes, facial expressions, and posture to demonstrate his interest in the other person's ideas and comments. Suggest he lean in toward the speaker, maintain an open posture by keeping his arms by his side or gesturing appropriately, maintain an appropriate distance, avoid crossing his arms (it communicates defiance), and make and maintain eye contact.

Remember that whenever two people are in each other's company, they are communicating, even if neither is speaking. Their body language is sending a message. It is, quite simply, impossible *not* to communicate.

Listen carefully and effectively to your conversation partner. Attentive listening can actually improve the quality of your partner's speaking. In a classic experiment, a young professor was noted for his dry, monotonous lecturing style. His department head enlisted the professor's students in an experiment that had intriguing results. The students were asked to be inattentive and distracted during the professor's lecture. Their body language clearly reflected boredom and

tedium. At a prearranged signal, all of the students changed their demeanor and acted interested and engaged in the lecture's content.
With this, the professor became more expansive and expressive, using
gestures and engaging in stimulating exchanges with his students. At
a second predetermined signal, the students returned to the previous
disengaged demeanor. The professor became less animated and re-
verted to his dry lecture style.

Teach the child to communicate the fact that she is listening by
nodding, smiling, and making brief comments ("No kidding," "wow,"
"great") while the other person is talking. She should respond to the
other person's thoughts and feelings. A good conversation consists of
effective turn taking with no single party dominating or monopolizing
the discussion.

A good conversation has a defined beginning and ending. Explain
to the child the best way to begin a conversation is to ask a question.
Earlier in this chapter, a conversation was compared to a volleyball
game, wherein one player may set up a teammate with a short pass
that allows the teammate to score. A well-placed question—"What
did you do last weekend?" or "What did you think of today's assembly?"—provides the child's conversation partner with a similar setup
that allows him to share information and opinions.

It is equally important to conclude a conversation in an appropriate way. Children with social deficits often have difficulty ending a
social interaction. Throughout my career, I have had countless informal conversations with such children and have been struck by how
often a child will simply walk away during a conversation once he has
delivered his intended message. Instead, the child should conclude
every conversation by bidding his partner good-bye and bringing
some sort of closure to the conversation: "Well, it's been nice talking
to you," or "I have to run because I'm late for my dentist appointment."

A good conversation may cover several different topics. A *discussion* is generally focused on one specific topic and it is inappropriate
to divert it from that subject. However, a *conversation* is far less for-

mal, and a wide variety of topics may be considered during the conversation.

"I like that CD player."

"Thanks. My aunt gave it to me. It belongs to my cousin, but he moved to California."

"No kidding? I just returned from California. Where did he move?"

"He is in San Diego. He goes to school there. He wants to be a veterinarian. He wants to work with horses."

"You have a horse, don't you?"

"Yeah. Her name is Taffy."

Help your child become aware of the appropriate timing and techniques of changing conversation topics. It is appropriate to switch topics if the subject area being discussed is making someone feel badly, if a single topic is discussed for a long time, or if the child knows little about the topic. She can change topics directly ("Well, enough about that. Let's talk about something else") or indirectly, by asking questions about another topic or ceasing her participation and allowing the topic to exhaust itself.

Listening

Effective conversationalists are also responsive listeners. The skill of listening is often overlooked, and direct instruction in this important area is seldom provided to children. This is unfortunate, because the ability to listen attentively is fundamental to social success.

Once again, listening is a challenging skill for children with language-based learning disorders. The best way to foster effective listening (oral receptive language) is to *model* effective and appropriate listening skills. Unfortunately, discussions between adults and children often do not provide very positive models for responsive listening. A recent survey asked adolescents about their pet peeves regarding their parents. The most common response cited the fact that parents simply do not listen to their children. If you wish your child to become a better listener, it is important that *you* listen more attentively to *him*.

How to Model Listening

Below are some suggestions that will enable you to become a more attentive listener when conversing with your child.

- Drop what you are doing: put down the dish towel or the newspaper, establish eye contact with the child, and really listen.

- Initially, accept what he is saying *without* passing judgment on the content.

    CHILD: "I'm not going to put a project in the science fair."

    BAD RESPONSE: "No way! You *are* going to finish that project and have it ready for Tuesday and—"

    GOOD RESPONSE: "You don't want to finish the project?"

- Listen to both the words *and* the feelings that the child is expressing.

    CHILD: "But all the other kids are going to go to Jake's swimming pool for a party on Sunday."

    BAD RESPONSE: "I don't care what the other kids are doing, you are going to stay in on Sunday and finish that science project."

    GOOD RESPONSE: "It sounds like you really want to be with your friends."

- Reflect back what you hear the child saying *and* feeling.

    CHILD: "But all the kids will be mad at me if I miss Jake's party."

    BAD RESPONSE: "That's ridiculous! Why would they be mad at you? Let them get mad! What do *you* care?"

    GOOD RESPONSE: "You *really* think they will be upset with you if you miss the party?"

- Avoid introducing topics and events that do not relate directly to the situation under discussion.

    CHILD: "I don't want to submit anything to the science fair this year."

BAD RESPONSE: "No way! This is just like this summer when you wanted to quit tennis lessons, or last fall when you didn't want to write a poem for the poetry festival."

GOOD RESPONSE: "You don't want to submit a display this year? I thought you were excited about the electricity experiment you were working on. Has something happened to change your mind?"

- Avoid attempting to read the child's mind.

CHILD: "I don't want to submit a project to the science fair this year."

BAD RESPONSE: "I know why! It's because you think that Tim will make fun of you! When are you going to learn to stand on your own two feet and stop worrying so much about what other people think?"

GOOD RESPONSE: Listen attentively to the child and provide him with body language responses that indicate that you are interested in what he is saying.

- Avoid cutting off the child or interrupting him in midsentence.

CHILD: "I'm not going to submit a project to the science fair this year. Instead, I've decided to—"

BAD RESPONSE: "I don't care what *you decided*. This is not your decision to make! Why didn't you tell me before I bought the materials? Your partner is counting on you. You need the extra credit."

GOOD RESPONSE: Listen patiently and wait until the child finishes speaking before offering your input or advice.

"My Child Doesn't Listen, but His Hearing Test Is Fine"

Margie Gollick of Montreal's McGill University tells a charming story about a child who had difficulty with auditory discrimination. This is a problem that causes children to hear speech differently and ineffectively, even though their hearing acuity is normal on standard hearing tests.

Margie was conducting an informal hearing/language assessment on an eight-year-old boy at her Montreal clinic. She was saying stimulus words to him and he was instructed to define each word or use it in a sentence. The exchange went as follows:

MARGIE: "John, the first word is *carousel.*"

JOHN: "Oh, I know *that.* We learned it in math lab. Carousel lines are two lines that run right next to each other but never meet."

MARGIE: "Okay, John. How about the word *inspiration?*"

JOHN: "I know that, too. Inspiration is stuff that Dad puts up in the attic to keep the house warm in the winter. It's made from fiberglass and comes in big pink rolls."

MARGIE: "All right. And what about *poultry?*"

JOHN: "Poultry is what your Mom puts on the couch if you get a rip in it. She gets new poultry."

John's pattern of responses clearly indicated that he was not hearing words properly, so Margie decided to continue the assessment with a lengthier listening assignment. "I'm going to read you a story now, John, and I want you to listen carefully because I will be asking you questions about it later. But the story is not true . . . it's *make-believe.* Do you know what *make-believe* is?"

"Sure," John responded confidently. "It's a hockey team from Toronto."

There are two areas of language functioning that commonly present challenges for children with social problems. These weaknesses make it exceedingly difficult for the child to receive and process oral language effectively, and create significant social difficulty.

The first language problem is *central auditory processing*. It is important to understand that the child with a CAP deficiency does not have a hearing loss or a difficulty with auditory acuity. However, he is inattentive during conversations and discussions, and he has marked difficulty following oral directions or comprehending verbal input. His behavior is often mistakenly labeled as distracted, unmotivated, or inattentive.

To understand and assist the child who has central auditory processing difficulties you must be mindful of the difference between "hearing" and "listening." Children with CAP difficulties are able to *hear* satisfactorily and often go undiagnosed because they are generally able to pass routine hearing (acuity) evaluations. *Listening* requires the child to process and comprehend the message that he is receiving. This presents a particular challenge for the child who cannot adequately discriminate between similar speech sounds, particularly in settings with significant competing background noise (e.g., classroom, fast-food restaurants, sports practice).

Children with CAP problems are generally diagnosed in second or third grade, a time when attentive listening in school becomes increasingly important. Children report that the speech sounds of others seem distorted and unclear. They may continually ask others to repeat what they have said and often misinterpret the verbal input of others. These children are easily distracted and have particular difficulty comprehending speech in noisy and stimulating environments. They become easily fatigued when required to listen for extended periods of time. As a CAP child once told me, "It's a lot of work to listen!"

Children with CAP deficiencies have difficulty hearing the subtle differences in the sounds of words. *Here* sounds identical to *hair; four* and *door* sound the same; they cannot discriminate between *bureau* and *squirrel.* The verbal messages are confusing and garbled. Even when they focus their concentrated attention on the incoming message, they have difficulty understanding it. Again, the problem is not caused by a hearing *loss* of any kind. Rather, it is caused by the child's inability to *perceive* the incoming sounds. An analogous situation would be the frustration and confusion that you might feel when speaking to someone with a strong foreign accent. The person's frequent mispronunciation of the English words will cause you to miss many words and force you to use closure to fill in the words that you are unable to clearly understand. For the CAP child, conversations are equally frustrating and anxiety producing. He may respond to this chronic frustration by tuning out of conversations and discussions. Children with CAP problems must work hard to understand and follow conversations, which can be very tiring. They often complain about being exhausted at the end of a school day. Again, imagine how frustrated and fatigued *you* would be if every one of your daily conversations was nearly indecipherable, and you had to focus and concentrate on even routine conversations in order to understand and respond to them.

This child's daily challenges are compounded by his inability to localize sounds. He has marked difficulty finding the source or direction from which a sound is coming. He may also have difficulty identifying voices, even those of members of his family or his teachers. This seemingly minor deficiency becomes quite significant when one is conversing on the telephone or listening to the public address announcements at school.

Children with CAP problems are commonly misdiagnosed as having attention deficits. The CAP child, however, has little difficulty staying on task, and she is not as distractible or impulsive as the child with attentional problems. In fact, her behavior and responses may be quite satisfactory when in a quiet, one-to-one setting.

If you suspect that a child has a CAP disorder, you should consult an audiologist for a diagnosis. Among the symptoms that the child may manifest are:

- frequent mispronunciations in verbal speech
- poor spelling skills
- history of ear infections
- difficulty focusing during conversations
- frequently asking for directions or instructions to be repeated
- reading comprehension problems
- poor memory for information received orally
- difficulty learning phonics

Because the school environment is far more auditorily challenging than the home (due to classroom discussions, assemblies, athletic practice, and other distractions), teachers may notice a CAP disorder first. School is full of background noise, unfamiliar voices, and competing auditory stimuli that CAP children find confusing and frustrating. A ten-year-old with whom I worked was constantly criticized by his teachers for "cheating and copying" from his classmates during academic activities. The *actual* cause for his behavior was rooted in the fact that he was unable to fully comprehend the teacher's oral directions, so he would look at other students' papers in order to determine if he was doing the assignment correctly.

It is easy to see how a CAP difficulty would have a significant impact upon a child's social competence, his relationships with others, and his reputation at school and in the community. When working with such a child, be certain that you have his full attention before giving him an instruction and avoid conversing with him when he is involved in another activity. Do not attempt to carry on a discussion with him when he is in another room and unable to see you. Hold important conversations in quiet, distraction-free settings. Speak slowly and distinctly, and take occasional pauses so the child can comprehend and process your message. Repeat, emphasize, and/or rephrase the most important portions of your message. "Jackie, I want you to be home by nine . . . that's nine o'clock . . . and wash the kitchen floor. Remember: nine, and get the floor good and clean."

Inability to Follow Directions

The second auditory difficulty that can have a significant impact on a child's social competence is *auditory memory*. This differs from CAP disorder in that the child is able to perceive, comprehend, and understand auditory input, but she quickly forgets the message. This behavior is puzzling and frustrating for the adults who deal with the child because her memory for names, dates, and places is often quite effective and functional. This disparity results in the child being labeled unmotivated or defiant because of her failure to carry out simple instructions.

An effective, informal way to evaluate a child's auditory memory is to say several sentences of increasing complexity and detail (e.g., "The boy had a dog. The tall boy had an old dog. The tall boy with a red hat had an old dog with a hurt paw.") and ask her to respond to questions related to the detail within the sentences. The child with auditory memory problems will have difficulty recalling the details of the sentences when quizzed immediately after hearing them. These children often complain that everyone is talking too fast and can become easily frustrated and disruptive when required to listen for a prolonged amount of time.

This child may well remember a *portion* of the auditory information that she receives, but she is unable to commit the entire message to memory. For example, she might be instructed to "go into the cellar and turn off the dryer and get your red sweater." She might remember to go to the cellar and retrieve her sweater, but may not recall where the sweater can be found. So she goes into the basement, searches for the sweater, and returns, exasperated, to her equally exasperated mom to announce that she "can't find it." Again, this problem is more pronounced in school than it is at home because of school's increased language demands and expectations. Most instructions on the home front are briefer and less complex: "Pass the salt" or "Turn off the TV" versus "Get out your science book, open to page 135, read the chapter on photosynthesis, and answer the odd-numbered thought questions at the end of the chapter." Current research indicates that auditory memory difficulties often cause children to have negative relationships with parents and receive far more scolding and criticism than their siblings.

The child with auditory memory problems benefits from instructions that are given slowly and repetitively. Always be certain that the child is listening closely when you are giving directions. Discourage her from doodling or fingering objects when listening, and encourage her to focus and concentrate her energies when being given instructions or listening to lectures. Again, this child may be easily fatigued and frustrated by settings that require a great deal of attention and listening.

Strategies for Improving Social Language

When these deficiencies are considered, it is easy to understand why some children have poor conversational skills and, further, why they find little enjoyment in participating in discussions. It is often a frustrating and difficult experience for them. However, their unwillingness and inability to converse with others has a very negative impact upon their relationships at home, at school, and in the community.

Below are some tips and strategies to assist a child in developing appropriate social language and giving him more confidence and willingness to engage socially with others.

- If a child makes a statement that is replete with grammatical and syntactical errors ("I holded my cousin's hamster on yesterday!"), do not scold or even correct the child at that time. Research on language development indicates that if you constantly correct a child's language or reprimand him for poor grammar, he will generally respond by avoiding conversations and refusing to participate in discussions. His logical reasoning is: "The less I talk, the fewer mistakes I am likely to make." Rather, respond by letting him know that he *did* communicate a message and then reframe his message using correct grammar: "It must be fun to hold an animal that is so soft."
- Provide the child with opportunities to have language experiences with a wide variety of people in numerous social situations. ("Billy, go ask the waiter if they have a Sunday brunch here," "Sally, go ask Grandpa what time his dentist appointment is.")
- Many children have difficulty telling a story or recounting an experience in the correct chronological order. Assist by providing "prompts" in the form of words and phrases designed to remind him of the next phase of the story. Avoid completely taking over the storytelling when he has difficulty sequencing the events. ("Billy, you've got it all wrong. Let *me* tell Grandpa what happened.")
- Older siblings, relatives, or friends can be of great assistance in developing a child's conversational skills. They usually discuss topics of interest to the child (e.g., sports, popular music, video games) and he will be greatly motivated to participate actively and appropriately in these high-interest discussions.
- Successful conversations are rooted in common ground. En-

courage the child to find some trait or interest that he shares with his prospective conversation partner in order to make the interaction more meaningful.

- Encourage children to ask questions during conversations and reinforce them when they do. But remind them that the questions they ask should be related to their conversation topic and should be designed to enhance the discussion. I recall regaling an applying student with tales of our school's athletic program. I then asked if he had any questions. He said, "Yes, do you have sports here?" His question gave the distinct impression that he had not been listening to our conversation.

- Instruct the child to avoid beginning a conversation by saying, "What's up?" or "What's new?" This gives his conversation partner the impression that it is his duty to entertain the questioner and that the child does not intend to participate actively or equally in the interaction. Rather, remind the child of the volleyball analogy. It is his job to set up his partner by asking a question that will yield a solid, informative response. The question should be more specific: "What did you think of that thunderstorm last night?" or "How was your trip to Boston?"

- Teach the child how to give *and receive* compliments. Children often feel uncomfortable when they are given a compliment and may respond inappropriately by denying or refuting the praise. ("Ben, I really love that sweater." "Oh, it's an old one and it has a tear in the back. I should have worn the blue one that I got for my birthday.")

- When giving instructions, directions, or commands to a child with a learning problem, avoid abstractions and generalizations. ("When we go to Uncle Jim's I want you to *be good*" or "We can leave for the game *when you are ready*.") Instead, give more precise instructions. ("When we go to Uncle Jim's house, don't tease the dog or go into the woodshop" or "We can leave for the game when your bed is made and you have put your soccer uniform in the hamper.")

- If your child has difficulty meeting new people and initiating conversations, help him to prepare a brief "script" about himself to use when he meets someone. "My name is Paul and I am in the fifth grade. My dad is a veterinarian, and we have a clinic and kennel. I help him feed the animals and keep them clean."

- Each evening, tell the child about your day and require him to listen and respond. Then inquire about and discuss *his* day. This daily process, conducted in a spirit of warmth, interest, and acceptance, can greatly enhance a child's conversational skills.
- Provide the child with opportunities to practice a wide variety of conversational skills, including:

     asking/answering questions
     giving/receiving instructions
     giving/receiving compliments
     giving/receiving apologies
     giving/asking permission
     negotiating
     giving/receiving complaints
     making/responding to an accusation
     giving/gathering information
     beginning/interrupting/ending a conversation

  At some time, the child will be required to participate in each of the preceding types of conversations. You can do much to ensure her successful participation by practicing and role-playing the discussion in a positive, nonjudgmental, and supportive setting.
- Parents are often troubled by a child's tendency to use "back talk" and this behavior is often interpreted as rude and disrespectful. However, perhaps this back talk is merely an immature and inappropriate attempt to *negotiate*. The child is *saying*, "I hate this show and you'd better change the channel *now*!" when his intended message is, "I really want to watch my favorite cartoon for a while." Therefore, it is crucial that you attempt to separate the *message* from the *language*. Assist the child in developing negotiating skills. They will be useful in innumerable future social settings.
- The old adage "Fight fire with fire" is ineffective when dealing

with back talk. Avoid responding to the child's rudeness with *your* rudeness. If you instantly lash back at the child, he will be hesitant and fearful to express his needs or opinions. Rather, teach him how to express himself appropriately. Don't interrupt his tirade. Wait until he is done and then calmly explain that his behavior was intolerable and unproductive. Provide him with language strategies that would be more successful in meeting his needs. Then discuss his requests only when he has rephrased and reframed them.

- Emphasize the fact that the child can use one of four methods to communicate his needs: direct, indirect, polite, and impolite.

  Situation: The child's brother used her bicycle without her permission.

  Direct   = "Don't ever take my bike again."
  Indirect = "I really needed my bike this afternoon."
  Polite   = "Please ask me the next time you need my bike. If I'm not using it you can borrow it."
  Impolite = "Never, *ever* borrow my stuff again."

  Advise her that polite/indirect is generally more effective and appropriate than impolite/direct!

- Remind the child that if someone asks him a question it is both appropriate and expected that the child will ask a similar question of his conversation partner.

  "Good morning, Don. How was your weekend?"
  "It was terrific. My dad took me to the boat show and then we met my uncle at a real neat Chinese restaurant. *How was your weekend?*"

Afterword

Dealing with Vulgar Language

The use of vulgar language is a particular concern for children with learning and language problems. This is not because these children have a tendency to swear more often than other children, but because they may be unable to determine when and where cursing may be appropriate. Children with social difficulties are often unable to make transitions or "shift gears." They may not understand that curse-filled language that might be socially acceptable in the boys' locker room when talking to friends would *not* be appropriate at the dinner table when Grandma is visiting. Once the child begins to swear habitually, it is a difficult pattern to break.

This difficulty is rooted in the child's pragmatic language skills. An important pragmatic skill is the ability to adjust your language and vocabulary to meet the needs and profile of your audience. For example, you would not explain a solar eclipse to an adult in the same manner that you would describe it to a four-year-old. The child who develops vulgar language in his day-to-day vocabulary is likely to use it in *all* conversations to *all* audiences.

Parents are often advised to *ignore* a child's swearing in the hope that the behavior will eventually go away. This strategy is based on the belief that the child is "doing it for attention" and that refusal to grant that attention will eliminate the behavior. In truth, adults generally find that ignoring is unsuccessful and that children view it as tacit approval. If the foul language bothers you, deal with it.

Another timeworn—but largely ineffective—technique is known as *satiation*. This strategy requires the child to say or write the offending word hundreds of times in order to eliminate it. This strategy only builds resentment in the child and does little or nothing to change the behavior.

When attempting to eliminate swearing, it is important to remember the adage "Positive feedback *changes* behavior; negative feedback merely *stops* behavior." Your immediate goal here is to *stop* the offending behavior, so you will want to design and implement effective consequences for the use of vulgar language. These consequences should be swift and definitive. This technique will probably *stop* the behavior and the child will no longer swear in your presence. However, if you want to truly *change* the behavior and eliminate swearing in all settings, you need to praise and reinforce the child when he uses appropriate language. ("Way to go, Tim! You didn't lose your temper or swear when Adam took the ball from you. Good decision!") This reinforcement will make it more likely that the target behavior (no swearing) will generalize to other settings.

When dealing with children, adults must remain mindful of the difference between *disrespect* and *back talk*. The former is unacceptable and the latter is less so.

Consider these responses to a parent saying, *"Molly, please pick up the popcorn that fell on the floor."*

- "But I didn't put it there." (back talk)
- "Oh, I hate vacuuming." (back talk)
- "But why do I have to do it?" (back talk)
- "Do it yourself if it is so important to you." (disrespect)
- "@##% you!" (disrespect)

Back talk is sometimes tolerable and reflects the child's growing need for independence. You may choose to respond to back talk with cajoling, humor, or gentle reminders. "Gee, I thought that you *loved* vacuuming. I thought *everyone* loved that!"

However, disrespect should not be tolerated and should be confronted. Children must learn that authority figures are entitled to be treated with respect. Swearing is disrespectful and rude and is, therefore, intolerable.

Be aware, however, of the difference between swearing and venting. The latter occurs when a child utters a curse impulsively as a result of fear, anger, or frustration (e.g., a missed basketball shot or dropped cafeteria tray). This type of cursing does not reflect disrespect and should be responded to in a nonpunitive way. ("I know that you are frustrated, Sasha, but that type of language is unacceptable.") Tell her that an occasional "slip" is understandable, but she should make a genuine attempt to curb her swearing in these situations.

RECOMMENDED RESOURCES

Childhood Speech, Language and Listening Problems, Patricia McAleer Hamaguchi (New York: John Wiley and Sons, 2001).

Learning Disabilities: The Interaction of Learner, Task and Setting, Corinne Smith, PhD (New York: Little, Brown Publishing, 1983).

Roadblocks to Learning, Lawrence J. Greene (New York: Warner Books, 2002).

Teaching Students with Learning Problems, Cecil Mercer, PhD (Columbus, Ohio: Charles E. Merrill Publishing, 1992).

CHAPTER FOUR

Paralinguistics

Words Carry the Message, Body Language Carries the Emotion

Mrs. Nelson teaches a fourth-grade class that includes some children with learning disorders. The teacher is at the classroom door having a quiet, brief conversation with the school principal regarding plans for that evening's parent open house. Her students have been told that they can have short "conversation time" while their teacher confers with her colleague.

Let's take a bird's-eye view of some of the interactions occurring in the classroom.

- Elizabeth is bored with Brian's interminable recounting of his dog's operation. She makes a face indicating disinterest, but Brian fails to interpret her attitude and continues to prattle on.
- Erick talks excitedly about his recent trip to Disney World, but his blank, emotionless facial expression contradicts his mood and puzzles his conversation partners.
- Corbett sees a picture in a book that his friend Josh *must* see. Corbett beckons excitedly to Josh to come to his desk. Josh is unable to interpret Corbett's body language and remains at his desk.

- Melinda is discussing the upcoming math quiz with Patti, but stands inappropriately close to Patti during the conversation. This bothers and troubles Patti. She backs away and Melinda responds by moving ever forward.
- Pauline discusses recess plans with Linda but fails to make eye contact during the conversation.
- Jeff becomes offended and angry when his friend Roger makes a sarcastic remark about Jeff's new haircut. He takes offense even though Roger was obviously joking and meant no harm.
- Doug asks James if he can go to his house some afternoon to use the new pool table. James smirks and says, sarcastically, "Sure, any time!" Doug smiles with delight about the open invitation and fails to recognize the sarcasm and rejection attached to the message.
- Joey wears a plaid shirt with polka-dot sweater vest and striped pants.
- Tracey wears a party dress with an oversize bow in her hair.
- Jackson tells a bawdy joke to the teaching assistant.
- Susan blurts out to Annie, "Your sweater really smells funny."
- Jo Ellen tells the new student about her parents' pending divorce and nightly arguments.
- Diana and Tara are involved in a private conversation about next week's church outing. Mary walks over uninvited and crashes the discussion.
- Ronald tells Dennis and Scott that his dog is very sick—for the twentieth time that day. The two boys roll their eyes.
- Cheryl approaches the new girl in class and asks her if her facial birthmark hurts.
- John tells a group of boys that he got a new video game called *Stomper*. Frank disagrees and insists that John's new game is called *Treacherous*. John argues that he is in a better position to know the name of the game that *he* purchased, but Frank will not relent.
- Luis describes, in great detail, the rotting cat carcass that he found under his porch that morning, much to the horror and revulsion of his audience.

- Chip's explanation of last night's episode of *The Simpsons* is peppered with obscene language.

What is going on here? All of these behaviors are caused by the children's inability to understand and utilize *paralinguistics,* or *nonverbal language*.

Paralinguistics is another significant contributor to social isolation and rejection. Drs. Stephen Nowicki and Marshall Duke of Emory University have conducted much of the pioneering work in this critical area. They have coined the term *dyssemia* to describe the nonverbal social skills deficits that are so common among children with relationship problems. The term, derived from *dys* (inability to) and *semia* (signals), is defined thusly: "A difficulty in understanding and using nonverbal social signs and signals."

As human beings, we constantly send nonverbal messages to one another. Interestingly, these signals can have a variety of meanings, depending upon the social interaction, the setting, and the emotional states of the participants. For example, consider the wide variety of interpretations that can be applied to these simple gestures or behaviors.

- A person nods his head up and down: agreement? threatening? anxiety?
- A person turns her head rapidly in a certain direction: fear? anger? surprise?
- A person breaks eye contact and looks downward during conversations: shame? embarrassment? fear? anxiety?
- A person's voice becomes high-pitched: anger? fear? frustration?
- A person's eyes suddenly open widely: surprise? delight? anger?
- A person shrugs his shoulders: "I don't know," "I don't care," "I give up."
- A person inhales quickly: surprise? delight? anxiety? shock?
- A person squirms in his seat: anxiety? excited? fear?

During social interactions, we constantly observe these behaviors in others and must interpret (and respond to) the signal that is being sent. The child who is unable to do so is at a significant social disadvantage.

The concept of nonverbal social communication extends well beyond "body language." Rather, it is a complex and extensive language system that parallels and supplements verbal language. The importance of nonverbal language is clear when one examines the statistics related to this skill. When two people are involved in a face-to-face interaction, approximately 55 percent of the messages they are sending and receiving are expressed *nonverbally* (via gestures, posture, facial expressions); 40 percent of the messages are communicated through the tone of voice. Only 5 percent of the intended messages are communicated by the words.

For example, suppose a man escorts a woman to her apartment following a dinner date. At her door, she puts her hand gently on his shoulder, makes eye contact, smiles, and coos, "I had a *great* time with you tonight." She is sending a clear signal that she enjoyed his company and hopes that he will call her for another date in the future.

However, suppose she puts her hands on her hips, scowls, and says sarcastically, "I had a great time with *you* tonight." Even though her *words* are identical, her message is significantly different: "Don't call me . . . and I won't be calling you." Her message has been greatly altered by use of body language and tone of voice. Basically, words carry the message of a discussion; paralinguistics carries the emotion.

Unfortunately, many children with learning or social problems fail to understand or recognize these subtleties. Their inability to read these signals can cause social isolation, rejection, and humiliation.

Several years ago, I was working with a young girl who had significant difficulty understanding the nonverbal signals of her teachers, siblings, parents, and peers. I was using a common strategy that is quite effective in diagnosing and remediating dyssemia. I had videotaped several scenes from television soap operas that depicted social interactions between people in a variety of settings. Because many of the actors are young and somewhat inexperienced, they tend to overact and are quite animated in their body language. These scenes provide a treasure chest of examples of body language and gestures.

My student, Lyndsey, was twelve years old. I showed her a scene in which a petite, well-dressed woman was seated behind a desk. Suddenly, an unshaven, unkempt young man barged into the office and stood across from her. He pounded on her desk and waved his index finger in her face as his arms flailed about. The woman reacted by raising her hands in a defensive posture and leaning back in her chair. A look of fear and apprehension was obvious on her face. Within a few moments, a secretary carrying a stenographer's pad entered hurriedly through the open door. She positioned herself between the man and the desk and maneuvered him toward the exit. As the man backed out of the room, he continued to make threatening gestures toward the seated woman by thrusting his index finger in the air. Although the volume was turned off, the facial expressions on the man's face clearly showed that he was yelling angrily. The secretary finally pushed the man out the door, which she then closed and locked. She walked quickly over to the woman, who was now crying. The secretary hugged the woman and comforted her by gently patting her back.

After Lyndsey watched the silent video, I asked her if she could characterize the relationship between the man and the woman. I was surprised by her response. "They must be good friends or relatives," she said.

I asked her why she felt this way. "Well," she began, "my mom works in a big office. Whenever anyone comes to visit her, the secretary always enters the office first to announce the visitor. The guest then enters when instructed by the secretary. However, if the visitor is a family member or close friend, he can enter without being announced. Because the man went into the office alone, he must be a friend or relative of the woman."

Lyndsey failed to observe or comprehend the several body language signals that were obvious on the videotape. Her inability to interpret and respond to these paralinguistic clues greatly compromised her ability to interact with peers and adults.

The ability to read and interpret body language is known as *kinesics*. A child's difficulty reading body language will manifest itself in several ways. She may be unable to read facial expressions (e.g., smiling, grimacing, puzzlement) and will, therefore, respond inappropriately in conversations or social interactions. She will also have difficulty "reading" the moods of other people. She will be unable to determine when Dad is angry, when her teacher is frustrated, or when Grandma is pleased and happy.

Children with kinesic difficulties often have facial expressions that belie their actual feelings and attitudes. For example, a child may have a sullen expression when expressing good news or—conversely— may smile when being scolded or reprimanded. This incongruent behavior is confusing for her social partners.

These children seldom use gestures, and their conversations are noticeably lacking nods, winks, shrugs, and other kinesic signals. This can make discussion tedious and uninteresting for the conversation partner.

These gestures and body language signals are extraordinarily significant in human interactions. As an example, it is widely accepted that President George Herbert Walker Bush lost the presidential debate against Bill Clinton and Ross Perot in 1992 because of a simple but significant body language signal: on several occasions during the debate, he glanced at his watch. This gesture indicated that he was bored with the event and felt that the debate was not a worthy investment of his time. Many viewers were greatly offended. Their collective reactions were, "If it's worth *my* time to watch this debate, it certainly ought to be worth the president's time to participate." The gesture was viewed by many as somewhat arrogant and dismissive. President Bush's poll numbers dropped 20 percent in the days after the debate. Although he *said* nothing offensive, his body language had an extraordinarily negative impact upon the voters' perception of him.

Nonverbal errors are actually more damaging to social interactions than are *verbal* errors. When a person makes a verbal error by using inappropriate grammar or vocabulary choices, his social partners will doubt his *intelligence*. However, if a person makes significant *nonverbal* errors, his partners will make the assumption that the speaker is somewhat emotionally unstable.

Suppose you are seated in a plane and a man approaches you and takes an adjoining seat. He looks at you and says, "I ain't never seen nothin' like *this* before! Ain't this big plane somethin' else?" You would make the assumption that your seatmate is not very bright. His grammatical errors and the inappropriate informality of his language would cause you to doubt his intellectual ability.

However, suppose the person were to sit next to you, put his arm around you, pull you close to him, and say loudly, "This is one of the largest planes that I have ever seen." Although the man's *words* were appropriate, his message was greatly intensified and altered by his inappropriate body language. In this situation, you would not necessarily doubt the man's intelligence; you would doubt his *emotional stability*. You would be made to feel uncomfortable by your seatmate's strange behavior and would wish to move to another seat immediately. Clearly, nonverbal language skills can have a greater impact upon a person's social acceptance than can his language or verbal skills.

It is important to recognize that a child's difficulties in nonverbal language will manifest themselves in receptive *and* expressive situations. That is, the child who is unable to interpret and understand the nonverbal behavior of others will also have marked difficulty understanding the effects of his own body language and paralinguistic skills. The student who is unable to understand or correctly interpret a teacher's humorous or sarcastic remarks (e.g., "Bill, when you are finished talking to Rob, I will begin the lesson. I don't want to interrupt you, because your social life is of the utmost importance to me!") will doubtless also have difficulty monitoring his *own* verbal and nonverbal language. For example, a teacher might say during a scolding: "I want you to listen to me—"

The child might respond, in a sarcastic tone, "I'm *listening* to you!"

The teacher responds to this rudeness by sending the child to the principal's office. When the principal asks the child why he was sent to the office, the puzzled boy responds, "I don't know! I told the teacher that I was listening to her and she threw me out of class!" Because the child does not understand how his tone of voice and body language altered his message, he does not understand the teacher's reactions. He is simply unaware of the message that he has sent to her.

When Conversation Is Stiff and Wooden:
Gestures and Posture

The innumerable gestures that we use in everyday social interactions form an important aspect of nonverbal language. These gestures supplement, complement, and—in some cases—*replace* verbal language. If a person waves while he says "hello," his gesture is *supplementing* his verbal message. If a person gives a teammate a thumbs-up after a good play, his gesture is *replacing* his verbal message.

Consider for a moment some of the gestures that we use in informal communication.

- Rolling your eyes communicates disbelief or dissatisfaction.
- A throat-slashing gesture using your index finger communicates that something should be stopped or discontinued.
- Shaking or waving a finger in a person's face indicates scolding or threatening.
- "Crossing your heart" indicates sincerity or reassurance.
- Rubbing your index finger with your thumb refers to money.
- Scratching your head indicates confusion.
- Extending your hand flat and waving it from side to side indicates "so-so" or a lukewarm response.
- At a restaurant, achieving eye contact with the waiter and pantomiming writing communicates "Check, please!"
- Extending your thumb and little finger and placing your hand to your ear indicates "Call me!"
- Crooking your index finger communicates "Come here."
- Forming a circle with your thumb and index finger and splaying the other fingers upwards means "okay" and indicates support.
- Crossing your fingers wishes your partner good luck.
- Placing one open hand upright and putting the other hand perpendicular to it communicates "Time out" or "Hold on."
- Tapping your foot reflects impatience.

There are countless gestures and postures that we use daily to communicate our thoughts, opinions, or needs. If a child is unable to interpret and/or utilize these gestures appropriately, he is at a great social disadvantage. Again, these gestures are used to amplify or replace verbal language. For example, a teacher might say "Stop that!" to a child who is behaving badly. However, if the teacher accompanies the statement with gestures (e.g., hands on hips, extending her open hand, or pounding the table), the message is greatly magnified. This nonverbal language communicates the seriousness of the misbehavior and the degree to which the teacher is troubled by it.

When observing many children with special needs, it becomes obvious that they seldom understand or use gestures. They often assume a stiff, wooden posture when involved in conversations and seldom use animated gestures to reinforce or supplement their conversations. It is important to help them use and interpret gestures if they are to have successful social interactions. Interestingly, the meaning of gestures may vary from culture to culture. For example, in our society, extending the middle finger to a person is a significant insult. However, the same gesture in Middle Eastern cultures is an expression of affection and good luck. American children are expected to make and maintain eye contact when addressing a teacher, coach, or parent. Conversely, children in Asian societies are taught that eye contact with authority figures is rude, inappropriate, and disrespectful. It is important to consider these cultural differences when working with international students.

I once consulted with a school that was concerned about a child who had recently enrolled in the program. The ten-year-old had transferred from Seoul, Korea, where he had been born and raised. His teachers were puzzled by his poor adjustment to the school. He told his parents that the teachers did not like him and were rude to him. I observed the teachers' interactions with the child. One of the adults beckoned to the child with her hand during recess. She encouraged him to join his classmates in a game. The child became upset and the teacher attempted to comfort him by holding his head between her open hands and speaking gently to him. The teacher was unaware that she had unintentionally sent very troubling and upsetting nonverbal messages to the boy. In the Korean culture, it is considered a great insult to beckon someone with your hand. That is a gesture that is reserved for animals. Because Koreans believe that a person's soul is contained in his head, it is inappropriate and insulting to touch another's head. The child was puzzled and hurt by the teacher's unintentionally rejecting behavior. Again, nonverbal gestures communicate important and valuable messages.

One effective method to improve a child's use of gesture is the aforementioned activity wherein you require the child to view and interpret videos of human interactions with the sound turned off. This requires the child to rely exclusively on body language in order to interpret the interaction.

"People watching" is also effective. In the mall, the grocery store, or the airport, point out a couple who is out of earshot. Ask the child to interpret the relationship between the couple by observing the body language. "Do you see the little boy and his mother over there by the window? Do you think she is happy with him right now, or is she angry?" Or "Look at that group of people over there. Which one do you think is the boss? How can you tell by the interactions among the group?"

Make your child aware of the tremendous number of gestures that we use daily. Use charades and pantomime activities to enhance his awareness of gestures and body language. Cut out photographs from newspapers and magazines that show various gestures. Remove the captions from the photos and assist the child in generating captions that appropriately match the body language depicted in the photo. Emphasize that several body parts can be used in gestural language, including arms, shoulders, fingers, and hands.

Give your child a card that has the name of an emotional state written on it (e.g., *anger, fear, disgust, love, admiration*). Ask him to pantomime the emotion using only gestures or facial expressions and have his classmates attempt to determine which emotion he was miming. Below are some emotions and feeling states that you may want to include in the activity:

angry	hurt	hesitant
proud	sick	nervous
suspicious	arrogant	amazed
stressed out	curious	eager
sad	exhausted	bored
panicky	shy	frightened
aggressive	puzzled	

These activities will require the child to use facial expressions and gestures to communicate effectively.

Norwicki and Duke remind us that body *postures* are also very important in nonverbal communication. For example, a student who sits in his history class slouching and stretched out is clearly—but perhaps unintentionally—communicating boredom and disinterest. Conversely, a pupil who sits up straight, visually tracks the teacher's movements around the classroom, and maintains eye contact with him is clearly communicating her interest and motivation. Even if the student does not participate in classroom discussions, the teacher will be impressed with her. Again, use mirrors and photographs to demonstrate various postures and the social message that each posture communicates. Ask the child to walk like a soldier, an elderly person, an injured person, a monster, a drum major, or a puppet. These activities make him more aware of his posture and the posture of others.

Often, children with social difficulties assume unusual or odd postures when merely standing or during periods of inactivity. These idiosyncratic postures (e.g., hands on hips, slouched shoulders, head down) send an unintentional message to others in their environment. For example, when a comedian relates an anecdote or joke about a "nerd" or an undesirable social partner, he assumes this posture and the audience immediately recognizes the character and laughter begins even before the comedian delivers the joke.

A person's posture often communicates mood, intent, or attitude. During a meeting, your boss may lean back in his chair with his hands interlocked behind his head and his legs outstretched. However, as the meeting proceeds, he may suddenly lean forward, fold his hands on the desk in front of him, and move his face closer to yours. These postural changes clearly demonstrate that the tone and the content of the meeting have changed significantly. If you fail to respond to these changes, the meeting will go badly. Again, it is important to note that socially deficient children have difficulty understanding the postural signals that they *see* (receptive) as well as the signals that they *send* (expressive). As with gestures, mirrors and videotapes can be used extensively to provide remediation in these skills.

A child with kinesic difficulties may
- rarely use gestures to supplement verbal language
- use gestures inappropriately
- have difficulty understanding how other people feel about him
- constantly interrupt others due to his inability to determine when others are busy or preoccupied
- not respond appropriately to the facial expressions of others
- not match his facial expression to what he is saying or feeling (e.g., has a sad face when sharing good news)
- seem aloof or disinterested by staring aimlessly
- be unable to tell when a conversation or interaction is going poorly due to his inability to accurately read the body language of others
- continue to talk even when others are obviously not listening

Vocalics:
How Tone of Voice Communicates
("It's Not What He Said, It's the Way That He Said It")

Another subset of paralinguistics or nonverbal language is *vocalics*. This refers to the role that tone of voice plays in interpersonal communication. The loudness, pitch, or tempo of a person's verbal message conveys the emotion in the same manner that gestures and body language do. By adjusting the tone of voice, a message can be significantly altered.

Suppose that I were to conclude a speaking engagement by looking at the audience, putting one hand in my pocket, shifting all my weight to one foot, smirking, and saying sarcastically, "Boy, I had a great time with *you* people today!" Even though the words conveyed a positive message, my body language and tone of voice served to negate and, in fact, contradict that message.

In social situations, we constantly use pitch, pause, and tempo to communicate or amplify the verbal messages that we send. By speeding up our speech, we communicate a sense of urgency. By slowing it down, we convey importance. We raise our voices to communicate anger, excitement, or emphasis. We whisper to denote privacy or intimacy.

For example, consider the innumerable ways that the following simple sentences can be spoken by modifying the volume and tone in which you say them. These sentences can be spoken in such a way that they communicate anger, fear, frustration, joy, criticism, support, trepidation, or assurance.

"The bus is coming in ten minutes."
"It's time for you to go."
"I've never seen a house like this."
"That was some trip."
"Close the door and come in."
"How many times have I told you?"
"Get off the couch and come here."

You can actually say "I love you" in a manner that conveys hate. You can also say "I hate you" in a manner that expresses love and affection. Try it! (Note: You can also say "Try it" in a manner that encourages someone to attempt something or in a manner that forbids him to attempt it!)

The child who has difficulty with vocalics will be unable to correctly interpret the intent or the meaning of his conversation partner's message. He will not understand when a comment is a subtle insult or he will be inappropriately offended by a jocular comment. He fails to see the humor in jokes and puns and cannot identify transparent lies.

Beyond being unable to interpret the vocalic language of others, the child may also send out vocalic signals that can be misinterpreted. He may speak too loudly, too softly, or too fast. He may speak in a monotone, with little expression or emotion in his voice. Giggling or laughing at inappropriate times can also cause social problems.

If a child is unable to understand the way that vocalics modify a message, she will constantly misinterpret the verbal statements of others and will, therefore, respond inappropriately to that input. For example, suppose the child boards the school bus wearing a mismatched, outdated outfit. One of her classmates sees her, smirks, and says sarcastically, "Nice dress! Where'd you get *that*?" Unable to sense the sarcastic tone of the message, the child tells her mother that everyone "really liked" her new clothes. I recall entering a classroom as a child was departing. As he passed his teacher, she said sarcastically (and inappropriately!), "Boy, *you* had a great day today." The child passed by me, smiling, and said, "Did you hear that, Mr. Lavoie? Miss Handled said I had a good day today." The intent of the teacher's message was lost.

Tone of voice can alter the meaning of a sentence as well as the emotional intent. Asian languages fascinate English-speaking people because the loudness with which a speaker says a word can actually alter the definition of the word. However, the English language can be equally complex. For example, consider this simple sentence that John might say to his neighbor Kevin: "*My* son didn't break the window."

That sentence conveys one simple meaning. John is communicating his belief that his son is not responsible for a broken pane of glass. When the sentence is spoken in a neutral, unemphasized cadence, John's message is clear. He is not accusing anyone of breaking the window. Neither is he implying who the guilty party might be. He is suggesting that his son is not involved in any wrongdoing.

Now let's have John repeat the sentence several times, but he will now emphasize a different word each time by merely saying that word a bit louder than the other words in the sentence. The meaning of the sentence is changed significantly as a result.

- "**My** son didn't break the window." Implication: *Your* son did.
- "My **son** didn't break the window." Implication: My daughter did (who, interestingly, is not even in the sentence).
- "My son **did not** break the window." Implication: I emphatically deny my son's involvement and I am offended by the accusation.
- "My son didn't **break** the window." Implication: John's son was—somehow—involved in the incident and may have even *cracked* the window, but he wasn't the one who *broke* it.
- "My son didn't break the **window**." Implication: My son may have broken the door, the drain spout, or the mailbox, but he *didn't* break the window!

Many children with language difficulties are unable to understand these language subtleties. They also need to learn to modify the vol-

ume of their voices to reflect the social environment. Children generally grasp the concept of "indoor voice/outside voice" at a very
young (preschool) age. However, many children with learning or social problems have great difficulty adhering to these social rules.
When they fail to use appropriate volume in social situations, they
can become isolated or rejected by others. The child who speaks too
loudly can be a source of embarrassment to his peers and may also
cause unwelcome adult attention ("The four of you in back: *keep it
down!*"). Even adults are embarrassed by a dining partner who speaks
or laughs loudly in a restaurant.

Discuss with the child the importance of modifying his voice to
meet expectations in a variety of settings (e.g., mall, theater, classroom, hallway, library, church, museum, plane, car). You can also try
another remedial strategy, in which you say sentences to the child
and have him listen and respond with his eyes closed. Modify your
volume and tone as you speak the sentences to communicate a variety of moods and emotions. Ask him to identify the message you are
delivering (e.g., "Do I sound angry? Do you think I'm happy?").

We also communicate a great deal by the pace of speech that we
use. By speaking in a hurried manner, a person communicates urgency, anxiety, or confidence. By speaking slowly, the person conveys
uncertainty or comfort. In an emergency, one will speak rapidly;
when giving instructions, the pace of speech is slowed considerably.
Children with learning problems often tend to use one pace of
speech in all situations. People who speak slowly with little inflection
in their speech are often viewed as boring or unintelligent.
Conversely, people who talk excessively fast can be seen as manipu-
lative or untrustworthy. Consider how professorial types or used-car
salesmen are portrayed on television.

Politicians and statesmen quickly learn how to master effective
tone and pace in order to communicate. In the extraordinary book
Helping the Child Who Doesn't Fit In, Drs. Nowicki and Duke use
President Ronald Reagan as an example of someone who understood
how to use tone and pace. Dubbed the Great Communicator, Reagan
applied his acting training to use his voice effectively. When he addressed the nation on the evening of the *Challenger* shuttle tragedy,
he spoke in slow, comforting, reassuring tones. His message commu-

nicated our collective grief and sympathy for the crew's families while, simultaneously, providing subtle hope for the future of space travel. Contrast that with his forceful "Mr. Gorbachev, *tear down this wall!*" speech in Berlin. The kindly, comforting grandfather became a contentious, demanding leader merely by modifying the delivery of his message.

Conversely, consider the fate of Vermont governor Howard Dean at the conclusion of the 2004 Iowa Democratic caucuses. Before the caucuses, Dean was the leading contender for the Democratic nomination for president. After a disappointing showing in the caucuses, Governor Dean took the stage and said: "We are going from California and Texas and New York. And we're going to South Dakota and Oregon and Washington and Michigan. And then we're going to Washington, D.C., to take back the White House. Yeah!"

Those thirty-five seemingly benign words cost Dean the nomination. Although the *words* were appropriate, he delivered them in a loud, raving manner accompanied by broad and expansive gestures. The impromptu presentation became widely known as the "I Have a Scream" speech. His well-intentioned attempt to motivate his disappointed supporters backfired, and he was widely viewed as unstable and unbalanced. The manner in which he delivered his message—not the message itself—became his undoing.

Try reading notable speeches (e.g., Martin Luther King, Jr.'s "I Have a Dream," John F. Kennedy's inaugural address) to the child or have her read them aloud. These notable speeches are also available on videotape or DVD, which allows the child to view the speaker's body language and facial expressions. Discuss how tone of voice, pitch, and speech rate can deliver a message effectively. Demonstrate how inappropriate use of volume and rate can miscommunicate.

Assist the child in gaining an understanding of these concepts by conducting exercises wherein he is expected to compare various speaking rates and volumes. For example, "Bill, say this sentence loud and slow; now say it soft and fast; now say it soft and slow." Continually emphasize that *how* you say something is just as important as *what* you say.

A child with vocalics difficulties commonly:

- overreacts to playful "insults" due to his inability to sense sarcasm in tone of voice
- talks in a monotone with little emotional inflection
- is overly loud (or soft) or fast (or slow) when speaking
- fails to understand jokes or puns
- cannot understand the impact of emotional inflection in conversations
- laughs inappropriately (e.g., too loudly) or at inappropriate times
- yawns inappropriately (e.g., too loudly) or at inappropriate times
- uses baby talk
- fails to adjust the content and tone of his language in light of the age and status of his conversation partners (e.g., tells an off-color joke to Grandma)
- talks about inappropriate or confidential topics in public
- fails to remain on topic during conversations

Eye Contact:
Look at Me When I'm Talking to You

Another critical area of paralinguistics is a person's use of eye contact. In our society, people are expected to look into the eyes of a conversation partner in most situations. Eye contact demonstrates understanding, caring, sincerity, intelligence, honesty, truthfulness, integrity, confidence, and respect. Conversely, when a person fails to make and maintain eye contact during a conversation, he is generally viewed as dishonest, insincere, disrespectful, and intellectually limited. Eye contact—or the lack of it—sends a clear and significant social message. Eye contact also allows a person to observe the facial expressions of the conversation partner. Correct interpretation of the other person's expressions will be of immeasurable value in understanding the intent, attitude, and emotions that underlie the conversation.

Many children seem adverse to establishing and maintaining eye contact, particularly with authority figures. This is a natural response to anxiety or confusion. When an adult is confronted with an adversary who is overpowering, he, too, will break eye contact. Children with social deficits have learned, through bitter experience, that social interactions with peers or adults often are disastrous. As a result, these children are threatened by social situations and fail to make eye contact. This, of course, only serves to make them less desirable social partners.

You can help a child to improve eye contact skills by having staring contests with her to see who can maintain eye contact the longest. This simple activity will enable the child to recognize that eye contact is painless. If a child feels very uncomfortable establishing eye contact with another person, encourage her to gaze at the person's *forehead* during conversations. This will reduce the child's discomfort and the partner will feel that appropriate eye contact is being established and maintained.

Another technique to increase eye contact is to hold a conversation with the child about a topic that is of particular interest to him. Instruct him to make eye contact with you while you talk, and tell him that you will stop talking whenever he breaks eye contact and continue the discussion when he reestablishes it.

Tell the child that at sometime during dinner, you will wink at him. If he sees you wink (which means that he was making eye contact), you will go out for ice cream after supper.

Another game involves four children. Each child has a partner. One partner closes his eyes and the second child keeps his eyes open and makes eye contact with his partner. On occasion his partner will open his eyes. If the first child sees his partner open his eyes, the team gets a point. Of course, the child must make and maintain eye contact in order to see if his partner opened his eyes.

Hygiene:
The Importance of Good Habits

Hygiene is another form of nonverbal communication. You communicate a great deal to others via your daily cleaning and grooming.

Ineffective or inconsistent hygiene makes a telling statement about a person's self-esteem, self-respect, confidence, and intelligence.

Younger children tend to be fairly tolerant of a lack of proper hygiene. But as children enter puberty and adolescence, poor hygiene can result in social rejection and humiliation. The pubescent body is undergoing significant changes and the child with social skill difficulties often fails to recognize that these changes require significant adjustments in daily cleaning rituals.

The pubescent child begins to sweat a great deal and the oil glands in his skin become increasingly active, particularly on his neck and face. These two factors can combine to create offensive body odors and breakouts of acne and other skin problems. Encourage the child to wash his face several times each day, avoid greasy food, and get sufficient sleep and exercise. Allow and encourage him to change his pillowcase frequently, as it can become a repository for skin oils that can cause breakouts.

The pubescent girl will require frank and honest guidance regarding menstruation. This bodily function can be frightening and puzzling if she is unprepared for its onset. Discuss her options related to sanitary products and warn her of the social and medical repercussions of ineffective hygiene during her menstrual period.

The natural increase in body fat in the adolescent can result in significant weight gain. Counsel the child to eat healthy foods and exercise regularly. This will also enable his lungs, heart, and bones to develop appropriately. Discourage dieting, however. Instead, encourage the child to eat balanced meals and develop the habit of drinking several glasses of water daily. Assist the child in developing regular hygiene habits. Provide him with the reminders and reinforcers he needs to develop these rituals.

Artifactual Systems:
Appearances Are Everything

Another important method of nonverbal communication involves *artifactual systems*. This refers to our use of artifacts to communicate with others. These artifacts may include clothing, hairstyles, jewelry, hats, handbags, or makeup. People generally use these forms of non-verbal language in a purposeful and intentional way in order to express their values, attitudes, feelings, and status. Clothing is also used to communicate age, gender, role, socioeconomic status, personality, and group membership.

People often form instant impressions of others upon viewing their outward appearance. A good friend of mine is a Catholic nun, and it is interesting (and entertaining) to watch the reactions that she receives from others when wearing her religious habit. People automatically smile and soften their voices and their attitudes when interacting with her. Although the clerks, waiters, or pedestrians do not *know* her, they make automatic positive assumptions about her based upon her clothing. Conversely, a high school friend of mine had a penchant for wearing the garb of a motorcycle gang member, although he was actually a sweet and scholarly person. He never understood why his efforts to hitchhike to school (an acceptable practice in the 1960s) were unsuccessful. His chosen mode of dress identified him as dangerous and threatening.

Clothing communicates a culturally shared message. Adolescents are generally obsessed with their clothing. Their mode of dress identifies them as being with one group, clique, or gang. In effect, their choice of clothing is nothing short of a *uniform*. Nearly 50 percent of shoplifters are adolescents, and the most commonly stolen items are articles of clothing. Many communities are plagued with incidents of youth-on-youth assaults and robberies wherein the stolen objects are jackets, sneakers, or hats. This reflects the adolescent's desperate need to have artifacts that identify and classify him. Even the slovenly, unkempt teenager may be purposely communicating his rejection of the values of his parents or his peer group. Clothing choices can reflect conformity with a peer subgroup or rejection of a subgroup.

For many preadolescents and adolescents, clothing comes to reflect their identity and self-esteem. Convinced that *everyone* will notice what they are wearing that day, they invest significant time and energy selecting and preparing their outfits. Some teenagers may appear to have selected their clothing blindfolded, but these mismatched, wrinkled clothes might actually be quite studied and purposeful. They are, again, sending a distinct social message: "I'm not going to go to school all ironed and orderly like the jocks do! I'll just throw on any old thing to show my disdain for those 'pretty boys.'" Clothing can reflect and/or actually *satisfy* a child's need for self-esteem and self-worth ("I have more sweaters than anyone else in my group!"). The clothing-obsessed child takes great pride, joy, and satisfaction in dressing for school each day.

Again, youths use clothing to reflect membership in a group and express their attitudes and beliefs. Because these artifacts clearly separate the various groups in a school, conflict often results between and among these subgroups. In response to this, many public and independent schools have begun to require and enforce dress codes. This controversial approach has enjoyed limited success. Schools that have introduced dress codes have noted a decrease in gang-related activity, a reduction in social comparisons related to brand-name clothing and economic ability, and a slight improvement in the school's overall educational performance. Opponents of dress codes argue for the children's rights of self-expression and cite the temporary nature of the aforementioned improvements.

Interestingly, even in schools where dress codes are enforced, the children will attempt to express their identity and membership in a particular subgroup. I consult with a private girls' school that features a fairly rigid dress code. One group of girls demonstrated their camaraderie by wearing mismatched socks, while another group took to wearing distinctive neon necklaces.

It is important to understand that the child's obsession with clothing and other artifacts may also be linked to his or her distorted body image. Many children are quite dissatisfied with their height, weight, build, or facial features. While they may feel that they have no control over these variables, they *can* control the clothes and artifacts they wear. Comedian Eddie Izzard makes a telling observation:

Isn't it odd that nature has played such a cruel trick on adolescents? At the precise time when we develop an interest in the opposite sex and we wish to appear attractive and desirable ... we become doughy, squeaky, pimple-faced, gawky beings who are instantly unappealing to all.

In adolescence, clothing is not regarded as an object separate from the person; rather, it is a portrait or mirror that reflects his self-image, personality, values, beliefs, attitudes, and group membership. The teen or preteen generally selects and coordinates clothing in order to send a clear and instantaneous social message to peers and adults in his environment. When a child feels that he is dressed appropriately for a social environment, he conducts himself with confidence and self-assurance. Conversely, when dressed inappropriately, he feels insecure and inordinately uncomfortable.

Many children with social skill difficulties simply do not understand this significant social concept. They are totally unaware of the signals that others send via their outward appearance. More important, they do not understand the signals that *they send* via their clothing choices and attire. They often wear mismatched clothes or fail to take proper care of their clothing. As a result, they provide their peers with additional evidence that they are "square pegs" and unattractive, unappealing social partners.

A child's inability to conform to peer norms related to clothing is often due to his poor observational skills. He may fail to observe or analyze social situations and, as a result, fail to recognize which clothing styles are currently "in" or "out." So when his schoolmates are all wearing Hawaiian shirts or reversed ball caps, he fails to comply. He is instantly viewed as odd or out of step with the others. Often, the child will have a delayed response to the clothing trends— donning a Hawaiian shirt long after the fashion has come and gone, for example.

The essence of adolescence and preadolescence is conformity, and a child's social acceptance is closely linked to this compliance. Assist your child in selecting clothing that mirrors the latest local trend. Observe the other children at the mall or at the bus stop. Older brothers and sisters are also valuable resources for information about the latest fashions. If everyone is wearing short denim jackets with sheepskin collars, buy one for your child. This conformity will not necessarily increase his popularity markedly, but it may serve to de-crease the rejection and isolation that he is experiencing.

You will find that each community has its own unique clothing styles and rituals. Not only is it important to own a certain type of ball cap or backpack, it is also important that it be worn or carried in a certain way. An uncreased peak on a ball cap or the use of *both* shoulders to carry a backpack can brand a child as "a loser" to his peers. That is the nature of adolescence. And it has always been so.

It is worth noting that children are very aware of (and responsive to) the manner of dress used by the adults in their lives. ("Dad, you're not going to wear *that* coat to take me to the swim meet, are you?") When our daughter was in middle school, my wife asked her who her favorite female teacher was. Her response consisted of a detailed critique of the clothing, earrings, perfume, and shoes of each teacher. Not once did she mention the teacher's knowledge, skills, or abilities. In a research study, two pictures were shown to a group of children. One showed a clean-shaven, well-groomed man in slacks, a sport coat, and a tie. The second showed a slightly disheveled man in jeans and a sport shirt. The children were asked which person was the most trustworthy and which they would go to if they were in trouble and needed help. The overwhelming majority of the children selected the first man. When these data are considered, one questions the wisdom of the lack of *staff* dress codes in our schools.

Again, children with social skill problems are often quite unaware of the fact that clothing sends an instant social message to others. The adage "You never get a second chance to make a first impression" is true. If one makes a poor first impression, one often loses the opportunity to make a second impression. Clothing is a critical aspect of this all-important first impression.

When critiquing a child's outfit, be gentle and supportive. Remain mindful of the "communication sandwich" wherein you cushion the "bad news" in a conversation by beginning and ending the discussion in a positive way. "Robbie, that ball cap is terrific. I love the Red Sox, too. But you probably want to change that sweater because it's all stained and needs to be cleaned. Where'd you get the boots? They sure look warm!" Always praise the child when he makes appropriate clothing choices.

Assist the child in making appropriate clothing choices by pointing out that there are four things that must be considered whenever one gets dressed in the morning. For most adults, these factors are nearly automatic and require minimal thought or concentration. However, children with social problems often require training and reminders in order to consider these factors when dressing.

Weather: Are you dressed appropriately for the weather conditions? Do you need a coat, umbrella, or boots? As the child prepares for bed, have him listen to the weather on the television or radio. Create a bedtime ritual wherein he reads the weather forecast from the daily paper and lays out the appropriate clothing.

Activity: When I deliver a seminar on weekends, I often point out that I am the only male in the room who is wearing a suit and tie. Even though I am dressed very differently from the other male audience members, we are all dressed *appropriately.* I dressed for *my* activity and they dressed for *theirs.* It would be odd for me to deliver a keynote in jeans and a sweater, just as it would be odd for a teacher to wear a suit to attend a Saturday seminar.

Encourage the child to consider the activity that he will be participating in and to select clothing appropriate to that activity. It is unfortunate for children with social skill deficits that the concept of "school clothes/church clothes/play clothes" has vanished in recent years. This tradition clearly highlighted that different modes of dress were appropriate for various settings.

The child should be made aware that the outfit that he wears to a school dance may be inappropriate for a church dance; his clothing for a birthday party should differ from what he wears to mow the lawn. This child also may be unable to care for his clothing properly and may ruin articles of clothing by wearing them at inappropriate times. Gently remind him: "Hang your new jacket on the fence before you begin to play football" or "Take your shoes off and roll up your pant legs if you are going to walk along the beach!"

Comfort: When you dress in the morning, you consider your comfort during the day's activities. If you will be attending an all-day lecture in an air-conditioned auditorium, you might select loose-fitting clothing and dress in layers that will enable you to add or discard clothing according to the room's temperature. If you will be shopping for an extended period, you will want comfortable shoes.

Many children with learning and social problems may also have difficulties in the area of *sensory integration.* As a result, they may be highly sensitized to any sort of sensory stimulation. This may manifest itself in significant discomfort regarding clothing. Many of these children report that they constantly feel the sensation of their clothing touching their skin. Of course, this sensation exists for *all* of us, but we are able to "screen it out." These children cannot. They constantly tug at their clothing and squirm endlessly in response to this discomfort. A freshly starched shirt, a tight collar, or the label inside an undershirt can cause significant discomfort or distraction. For this reason, many children prefer well-worn, loose-fitting, comfortable clothing and will resist new or unfamiliar outfits. On long car rides, allow the child to wear pajamas or drawstring dorm pants. Remind him to wear sneakers or hiking shoes to walk home from soccer practice. (He may be unaware that it will be uncomfortable for him to make the mile-long walk in his soccer shoes.) Avoid buying restrictive clothing such as turtlenecks and tight-fitting sweaters.

A parent once suggested to me that as part of a teacher's training, every prospective teacher should be required to take an ADHD child on a shoe-shopping excursion. Many children find shoes and socks to be very restricting and uncomfortable and would generally prefer to go barefoot. This confirms my long-held belief that Huckleberry Finn was America's first documented case of Attention Deficit Disorder! Parents should consider this when advising children to match their footwear with the activity in which they will be participating.

Teach the child to consider his personal comfort when dressing. Encourage him to don his Scout uniform or his suit jacket *immediately prior to* his pack meeting or school chorus performance.

Style: When a person dresses, he considers the current fashion and contemporary style. The clothes that you wore to work today, you will not be wearing five years from now and probably would not have worn five years ago. Fashions change and failure to embrace and reflect that change can create social isolation and rejection. Children must also learn to consider what is age appropriate. The sixth grader who brings a Cookie Monster umbrella or a Mister Rogers backpack to school is doomed to isolation and social failure.

A child with difficulties in the area of artifactual systems may
- wear mismatched clothing
- look unkempt
- have poor hygiene
- dress inappropriately for his age (e.g., wears a Sesame Street raincoat in fifth grade)
- seem unaware of current fads and trends in clothing
- fail to match clothing to the activity (e.g., wears jeans and T-shirt to church; wears dress pants and new sweater to play football)
- fail to dress appropriately for weather conditions

Proxemics:
Close Talking and Other Special Issues

The use of space and distance in social interactions is another form of nonverbal communication. This skill set, referred to as *proxemics,* provides another clear example of a Zero Order Skill. We are generally unaware of the importance of space in social settings until someone violates the "rules" by standing too close or too far away or by intruding on our personal or physical territory. These territorial boundaries have a significant impact upon daily encounters and can impede or promote communication.

If a child is skilled in proxemics, she understands the concept of *physical territory.* For example, when students are working at the art table on a project, an informal territoriality is adopted. Each student is expected to utilize the space in his immediate area, and his tablemates anticipate that he will keep his materials in his section. On an airplane, the passengers develop and respect territoriality by using their armrests to define "their" space. Human beings become quite protective of their space and become offended and anxious when this territoriality is breached.

People are often fascinated by wild animals and their extreme territoriality. These beasts mark their territory by forming borders using
urine or saliva, which they then jealously guard against any and all in-
truders. However, human beings are equally territorial. We mark our
territory using signs (PRIVATE PROPERTY), walls, fences, geographic
borders, or furniture. Your office is *your* space. Imagine how troubled
you would be to enter your office one morning and find a coworker
sitting in *your* chair behind *your* desk. As I write this, I am sitting on
a plane. I have lowered my tray table to serve as a writing surface.
This is *my* tray table, at least for the duration of this flight. Imagine
my angst if the gentleman sitting next to me finished his orange juice
and placed the empty cup on *my* tray! Appalling!

This human tendency toward territoriality came in clear focus for
me recently. My wife and I had enjoyed a great breakfast at a San
Francisco art deco diner. While we ate our meal, the fourth booth on
the right was *ours*. It was *our* territory and everyone in that diner understood and accepted that. Several minutes after leaving the restaurant, Janet realized that she had lost a unique pewter button off her
new coat. I ran the several blocks back to the restaurant to see if it
was under "our" table. When I arrived, a young girl was sitting at the
fourth booth on the right. It was now *her* booth. I had no right of possession or ownership. I now had to intrude on *her* territory. I went
through a complex and embarrassing social ritual of explaining the
situation to this total stranger, who—somewhat unwillingly and sus-
piciously—allowed me to search under *her* space. A half hour later,
some other person sat in that booth and it was temporarily *his*. The
ownership of "our" booth changed hands a dozen times that day, with
each customer strongly believing that the booth was *his* or *hers*.

I am always fascinated to observe an audience when I present a
multiday seminar. On the second day of the presentation, attendees
invariably sit in the exact seats that they sat in during the first
session. Human beings assume territoriality quickly.

We establish territoriality by forming physical boundaries. The
velvet rope in a bank that blocks the entrance to the offices could be
easily breached by anyone. But we respect it as a signal from the bank
that admission to that area is restricted. We carefully walk between
the lines in a crosswalk and make certain that our tires are not touch-

ing the painted lines in the parking lot lest we intrude on the space of another driver. The executive's placement of his mammoth desk facing out toward the door sends a clear signal that a visitor is not welcome to go behind his desk. That is the *executive's* space.

Children with proxemics difficulties are often unable to under-stand—or respond to—these physical signals or boundaries. This is particularly difficult when the boundaries are imaginary ones that are assumed by others (e.g., standing in a straight line at the fast-food counter). As a result, they may intrude upon the physical territory of others and, unwittingly, send a signal of insensitivity or self-centeredness. These intrusions can also be viewed as threatening and intimidating.

When in public with the child, point out the different "fixed fea-tures" in various environments and discuss the social signals that each sends. Grandma's placement of a vase on the piano sends the message that she prefers that the child not play the piano during his visit; the presence of a hostess podium at the restaurant entrance in-dicates that you should not seat yourself upon entering; the ribbons taped on the church pews show that those rows are reserved.

If a child is to master proxemics, he must recognize and respect *personal territory.* This involves the social distance that people use in order to communicate. This distance can be used to modify or en-hance a spoken message. For example, suppose you are standing at a jewelry counter and speaking to the clerk about a diamond necklace that you are interested in purchasing. Suddenly, the clerk lowers her voice and leans closer to you. "Next week they are having a fifty-percent-off sale on diamonds. You may want to wait," she whispers. By softening the tone of her voice and leaning closer to you, she is communicating that she intends to share a secret. Her proxemics modifies the customer-clerk relationship and converts it to a far more intimate and personal exchange.

Suppose you are having dinner with your husband in a fine restaurant. You are enjoying each other's company greatly and you are holding hands on the table. You lean close together and whisper softly to each other. Suddenly, you inform him that you have agreed to take on an extra project at work and this will preclude your long-planned golf vacation. He sits bolt upright, removes his hand from yours, and leans away. In this case, his proxemics communicates his dissatisfaction with your announcement . . . and you.

The human being is the only animal who actually carries his territoriality around with him. It is comparable to being surrounded by a large bubble or hula hoop that defines and marks our personal space. The social message is clear: *Do not enter my space unless you have some business to transact with me. Otherwise, stay out!*

Consider for a moment the discomfort that one often feels when standing in a crowded elevator. Strangers surround you. They are solidly in your personal space, even though you have no business to transact with them. You and your elevator mates stare at the flashing numbers indicating the elevator's movement, eager to reach your floor and depart this uncomfortable social situation.

Several research studies have observed and analyzed elevator behavior. People cope with this common but uncomfortable situation in fairly predictable ways. When two strangers are in an elevator, they tend to lean against opposite walls; four strangers will occupy the corners of the elevator; five or six elevator riders will face the door and look up to avoid eye contact.

There are basically four types of personal space that we use to communicate with others. These are best explained by this example.

Suppose I am walking down the main street of a small town. It is 9:00 in the evening and the area is all but deserted. As I walk down the sidewalk, a young woman walks toward me from the opposite direction. As we pass one another, it is appropriate that I maintain *public space* between us—a distance of three to five feet. It would be inappropriate and possibly even threatening to move any closer to her. It would also be appropriate to make quick eye contact and even offer a small smile. This sends the clear message (via kinesics) that she is safe and assures her that I mean her no harm. If—as we pass one another—I moved closer to her, she would doubtless recoil and sidestep in order to maintain the appropriate public space.

Now imagine that I am lost in the town and am searching for the local post office. I want to ask her for directions. It is now appropriate to assume *social space*. This is a distance of approximately two feet. I stop, stand still, establish the two-foot distance, make eye contact, and ask her if she knows the location of the post office. It would be inappropriate to make this inquiry from five feet away and it is entirely appropriate to decrease the distance between us. However, it would be quite inappropriate to stand *too* close to her or to have physical contact of any type with her. If I were to touch her arm, for example, while asking for directions, she would feel quite uncomfortable and threatened.

In the third scenario, suppose that I have delivered a seminar in that town earlier in the day. As I walk down the street that evening, I notice that the woman coming my way was in the audience. We recognize one another, smile, stop, and move closer. We shake hands and begin a conversation. This situation requires *personal space,* a distance of about one foot. We share a brief handshake and then unclasp our hands. To hold hands during the conversation would be sending a very different social message. Unlike when sharing social space, it *is* appropriate to make physical contact of some kind in this scenario. However, exchanging a hug or other more intimate gesture would be inappropriate. Our relationship simply does not warrant such contact.

In the final scenario, suppose that the woman who approaches me is a former colleague whom I have not seen in several years. We are surprised and delighted to see each other. We approach and hug. This is referred to as *intimate space*. However, the duration and tightness of the hug *also* communicate a message. It would be inappropriate to exchange a kiss in this instance. It would be inappropriate to hold the embrace for an extended period. Again, within each zone there are levels and gradations.

These social rules are quite complex and are subject to nuance. I recall Janet and myself hurriedly leaving my office at the end of the day one Friday. We were heading for the airport to catch an evening flight to a Saturday speaking engagement. As I passed my secretary's desk, I exchanged a quick "Good-bye, Barbara"/"Good-bye, Rick" with her and wished her a good weekend. Two hours later, we were walking down the concourse at Boston's Logan Airport and—much to our surprise—saw Barbara standing at the gate waiting to board a flight. We laughed and hugged one another.

Now, it would have been quite inappropriate to hug her as I was leaving work. However, the setting (an airport) and the situation (our mutual surprise at seeing one another) made it quite appropriate to exchange a more intimate greeting. Many children fail to understand or enact these nuances.

Lest we think that this complex concept of "appropriate spaces" is reserved for the adult world, let's follow Alexander, a ten-year-old, as he walks across his grade school cafeteria to dispose of his empty juice box. As he ambles across the room he passes the vice principal. Since he has no business to conduct with the administrator at that time, he assumes *public space* and allows three or four feet between them as they pass. He may make brief eye contact with the vice principal and even manage a quick smile.

As Alexander proceeds across the cafeteria, a newly arrived student stops him and asks where the boys' room is located. This exchange requires *personal space* because they will be participating in a conversation. Alexander stands a few feet from the boy and gives him directions. However, Alexander does not touch him or have any physical contact with him.

A few feet later, Alexander sees his best buddy, Chester, who is talking to another boy and facing away from Alexander. Putting his hands on Chester's shoulders, he playfully spins Chester around and they have a brief joyful conversation about that afternoon's long-anticipated soccer tournament. Standing only a foot apart—*social space*—they exchange high fives, and Alexander heads for the trash barrel. He looks into the school lobby and is surprised—and delighted—to see his grandmother entering the building. She has driven a long distance from her home to see Alexander's afternoon soccer game. He runs to greet her and they exchange a warm hug— *intimate space.*

In this scenario, Alexander used all four spaces (public, personal, social, intimate) very appropriately. However, "your" Alexander might have hugged the vice principal, high-fived Grandma, and distanced himself from the new student! The use of these four zones is quite

natural for the socially competent. However, this concept of proxemics can be quite confusing for children with social skill difficulties.
They may use inappropriate spaces at inappropriate times. They
might hug your boss when they are introduced, or ask you an intimate private question from ten feet away ("Mom, doesn't that fat lady
look like Aunt Helen?"). Again these inappropriate behaviors often
cause the child to be viewed as insensitive or boorish.

In many American schools, administrators have responded to the
recent spate of molestation incidents by initiating "no touch" policies, wherein school personnel are prohibited from having any physical contact with students for any reason. Although the objectives for
these policies are understandable, I believe that the regulations are
somewhat misguided. Rather than prohibiting contact between children and adults, it is preferable to provide children with guidance regarding the appropriate use of touching and contact. For example, a
"sideways hug" might be an appropriate greeting with a child's former
teacher at their first chance meeting at the beginning of the year,
but it would be *inappropriate* to continue this ritual throughout the
semester.

The child who fails to understand and utilize appropriate space is
likely to be ostracized by peers. Although the child's classmates and
teammates may be unable to recognize or identify his specific social
difficulty, they view him as "weird" or "strange." The atypical social
interactions of the child will cause others to reject his overtures of
friendship. Adults will also be troubled by the child's proxemics problem. They may misinterpret these behaviors and attach unintended
motives to the child's actions: "He's always touching me! He must
have a sexual attachment to me!" or "He stands so far away from me
when we talk. He must be frightened."

It is important to consider the serious consequences of a child's
inability to understand and effectively use these proxemics concepts.
If the child does not understand the various zones and their uses, she
may become vulnerable to molestation or inappropriate sexual contact by adults or peers. If the child does not have a natural sense of
her personal space, she will not think it strange or inappropriate
when her bus driver or babysitter rubs her thigh when they are sitting together. Such behavior *is* inappropriate, but these children have

poorly developed "radar" to detect when another person is touching them inappropriately.

Although it is troubling to consider this, recent research also indicates that children with proxemics problems are also more likely to molest others, particularly children who are much younger than they. An adolescent who does not understand the various zones is more likely to violate them. When a boy is nine years old and his female cousin is three, it is entirely appropriate for the boy to tickle and wrestle with the younger child. Even a playful pat on the girl's backside is acceptable. However, as the years pass and the boy is sixteen, such contact with his ten-year-old cousin is now inappropriate and, perhaps, illegal. This underscores the importance of providing the child with instruction and guidance in this critical area of social development.

An important subset of proxemics is *touch*. Many children with social skill deficits are unaware of the appropriate social use of touch. They may touch others when it is inappropriate to do so. When it is appropriate to touch someone, they may unintentionally hurt the other person. Ironically, some of these children are very resistant to physical contact and may be quite reluctant to touch or be touched. Their tendency to recoil from the touch of others can be offensive and hurtful. They handle crowded social settings like the proverbial bull in a china shop and will constantly bump into others and intrude on their "social space."

Many anthropologists feel that American society holds significant misinterpretations and misunderstandings related to touch. As a society, we have far less physical contact with one another than do most cultures. As a result, many Americans traveling in other countries are viewed as "cold" by their hosts. The American mind-set often equates "touch" with "sexual." Therefore, our children are exposed to a consistent mantra from the adults in their lives: "Don't touch anyone; don't let anyone touch you; don't touch yourself!" This viewpoint is greatly out of step with the traditions and practices in other countries. Studies have shown an inverse correlation between the amount of human touching children receive and the amount of violence in a given society. An oft-cited example is the Aparesh tribe in New Guinea. As infants, members of this tribe are constantly carried by their parents in a manner that features a great deal of skin-to-skin contact. The Aparesh are one of the most peaceful and productive peoples on earth. Conversely, their southern neighbors, the Mundugamor, are raised in stiff reed baskets with minimal human touch. The Mundugamor are warlike, and their traditions feature fierce competition between and among their members.

Unfortunately, America is widely viewed as one of the world's most violent societies. Our culture also provides our children with considerably less physical contact than many other societies do. Infants in the United States are often and consistently shuttled to playpens, high chairs, and car seats in lieu of being carried and held. Anthropologist Desmond Morris once cited Americans' "massive inhibition of our natural tendency to touch."

The sense of touch has been referred to as the "mother of all senses." The largest organ of the human body is the skin. Therefore, skin-to-skin contact between and among members of a society is extremely important. A lack of this basic human contact has been linked to depression, anxiety, violence, and aggression. Touch can be of great benefit. Some asthma attacks can be aborted or alleviated by merely hugging the person who is afflicted. A mother's stroking of her newborn can actually arrest postpartum hemorrhaging, contract the uterus, and speed up the expulsion of the placenta. Even an inch-long fetus responds to stroking. Human touch is a valuable communication tool. Touch has been proven to improve rapport and reduce tension.

Again, our society mistakenly equates touch with sexuality. This is a *cultural* and not at all *natural* equation. Our ape cousins groom and stroke one another for hours with no lust or sexual gratification. Other cultures are far more accepting of touch than we are. In the East Indies, a dying patient is held and comforted in the caretaker's lap like a child. The Kaingang tribe of Brazil customarily encourages children to lie at the feet of their elders while being stroked and petted for hours. These societies have minimal conflict among their members, and betrayal, infidelity, and sibling rivalry are virtually nonexistent.

All that said, our society has developed—and strictly enforces—a firm set of rules and conventions regarding inappropriate touching. I was recently standing in a line at a ticketing counter at an airport. A young woman was standing in front of me wearing headphones and listening to music on her portable CD player. The agent called for her to approach the counter, but she failed to see his signal. I wished to get her attention, but her headphones prevented me from using oral language ("Excuse me . . .") to accomplish this. I would have to make physical contact with her. I reached out and touched her gently on the area between her neck and her right shoulder. She turned to me, smiled, removed her headphones, and leaned toward me a bit to receive my message.

Imagine how this woman would have reacted if I had touched the top of her head, her knee, or her hand. What if I had jostled her roughly by pushing my open hand into the small of her back? Or if I reached over and yanked the headphones off her head? Or kicked her leg with my foot? Our societal conventions dictate that, in this situation, my contact with her should be gentle, quick, and in a very specific location on her body. Had I violated this convention, I would have sent a troubling and worrisome social message to her.

Reinforce the "silhouette concept" with your child. Show him the silhouette of a person's body and tell him that he should only touch another person on the outer outline of the silhouette (e.g., shoulders, outside surface of arms). It is generally inappropriate to touch a person anywhere else (rib cage, nose) and would transmit a troubling social message. Discuss the appropriate and inappropriate situations, locales, and methods of touching another person. Because many children with social skill deficits also have expressive language problems, they are often overly physical with others and may poke, push, shove, or grab in order to communicate their feelings, opinions, or needs.

Touching can be more effective if accompanied by appropriate verbal statements. For example, suppose you are telling your doctor that you are experiencing severe pain in your knee, and he reaches across and pats your back. This gesture might well be interpreted as patronizing and placating. However, if the doctor accompanies these actions with eye contact and the statement, "Well, let's see if we can get you some medication to take care of that pain," he would be viewed as responsive and empathetic.

Children, too, must learn to accompany physical contact with an appropriate verbal message. For example, when Johnny hugs Grandma when she arrives for a visit, it is appropriate that he accompany the hug with a greeting of some kind ("Happy Thanksgiving, Grandma"). When he gives a teammate a high five, he should simultaneously say, "Nice play, Mickey." In these instances, the physical touch and the verbal message complement one another and *either* action on its own may be inappropriate.

We should be mindful that there are significant cultural differences regarding proxemics. For example, Asian children are often taught to avoid eye contact with authority figures; people from Hispanic cultures tend to touch one another often during conversations. As I travel throughout the country, I note significant differences in proxemics in various geographical regions. Children should be advised to observe and adhere to the accepted behaviors in each setting that they enter. When in Rome, do as the Romans do.

The final subset of proxemics involves an overall respect for the *privacy* of others and an understanding of the informal "boundaries of information" that exist in social relationships. Children with social difficulties may have great difficulty understanding the concept of "public versus private" and may create tremendous embarrassment by divulging confidential family information or asking questions of others that are inappropriately personal and probing: "Does that wart hurt?" "Is that diamond real?" "How much did your new car cost?" A twelve-year-old student of mine once told me that he would enjoy having a younger brother. I responded by telling him that I hoped that his wish would come true someday. He responded, "No, it'll never happen. My parents don't even sleep together anymore. My dad mostly sleeps in the den." *Too much information!*

Counsel the child to be reflective before he divulges information or asks questions of others. Topics related to money ("How much money do you make, Grandpa?"), health ("How come you cough so much?"), or physical conditions ("How much do you weigh, anyway?") present the most common problems. Urge the child to avoid these subjects when conversing with others. Provide him with examples of subjects, topics, and information that are off-limits. Teach him the importance of confidentiality, privacy, and keeping secrets.

Demonstrate and model these concepts by respecting *his* privacy and keeping secrets that he shares with you.

A child with proxemics difficulties may
- stand too far away from others during social interactions or conversations
- stand too close to others during interactions and continue to move in even when the conversation partner moves back
- begin conversation or interaction before he has appropriately gotten the attention of others (e.g., begin a conversation with his teacher even though the teacher has her back to him)
- fail to read the social signals of furniture arrangement in a social setting (e.g., seats arranged in a circle indicate a free, interactive discussion; seats arranged in rows indicate a lecture)
- stare inappropriately or avoid eye contact
- stand close behind people, and often get bumped into
- touch others when not appropriate (e.g., put hand on someone's shoulder when asking directions)

Again, much of nonverbal language is culturally based. A firm handshake in America is a sign of integrity and strength. In Japan an appropriate handshake is gentle. People in Central and South America tend to touch one another often during conversations, while North Americans have far less physical contact. The American "okay" sign means "zero" in France, "money" in Japan, and is a sexual insult in Germany. *But the two universally positive paralinguistic signals are eye contact and a smile.*

Afterword

As difficult as it is for children with social difficulties to *establish* friendships, it is even more challenging for them to *maintain* or *sustain* these relationships. Many of their friendships will be temporary and short-lived and generally end with a bang, not with a whimper. A common lament of these youngsters is, "Dougie used to be my best friend, but now we hate each other."

Throughout my career, I have analyzed and "autopsied" countless friendship breakups involving special-needs children. Invariably, the cause of the relationship's demise is rooted in the child's paralinguistic weaknesses. His inability to read the subtleties of language, coupled with his tendency to misinterpret the verbal and nonverbal language of others, causes the relationship to have an unnecessary—and often explosive—conclusion. Of course, these weaknesses are further complicated by the child's inability to resolve conflicts and effectively repair damaged or dented relationships.

Janet Giler, a California therapist and author, cites children's inability to understand the "language of friendship." They misinterpret playful joking and teasing and overreact to statements or gestures that were not intended to be hurtful or negative. They are unable to see the gray areas of language and tend to view the social statements of others as being black or white. These rigid perceptions are partly due to paralinguistic difficulties, but may also be caused by the child's need to oversimplify a confusing and complex social world. He views everyone in his environment as either friend or foe, beauty or beast, buddy or bully. Of course, the social world is far more complex and subtle than that. The child perceives his social life as consisting of relationships that are either extremely positive or painfully negative. Therefore, when a friendship ends, the former friend is immediately and permanently relegated to the category of lifelong enemy.

This phenomenon provides a compelling reason to focus on the child's ability to understand and respond appropriately to nonverbal language. Failure to do so will continue the cycle of misinterpreted joking, misunderstood gestures, and mismatched reactions to unintended insults or offenses. Countless daily social messages are sent via nonverbal language. The ability to understand and interpret this communication is fundamental to social success and fulfillment.

RECOMMENDED RESOURCES

Helping the Child Who Doesn't Fit In, Stephen Nowicki, PhD, and Marshall Duke, PhD (Atlanta, Ga.: Peachtree Publishers, 2000).
How to Start a Conversation and Make Friends, Don Gabor (New York: Fireside Press, 1990).

Painful Passages, Elizabeth Dane (Washington, D.C.: NASW Press, 1999).

Promoting Social Competence, G. Gordon Williamson, PhD (San Antonio, Tex.: Therapy Skill Builders, 2001).

Teaching the Language of Social Success, Stephen Nowicki, PhD, and Marshall Duke, PhD (Atlanta, Ga.: Peachtree Publishers, 2001).

CHAPTER FIVE

Attention Deficit Disorder

The Social Lives of the Unhappy Wanderers

The field of special education has long recognized the significant impact that attention deficits can have upon a child's academic performance and progress. There is no valid research evidence that indicates that Attention Deficit Disorder (ADD) is caused by diet, environmental toxins, or poor parental management. Rather, it is caused by a chemical or neurotransmitter imbalance in areas of the brain that control attention, inhibition, impulse control, and motor functioning. The symptoms of ADD (e.g., impulsivity, distractibility, inability to plan) inhibit the skills and behavior required for academic success (e.g., remaining seated in class, paying attention to directions and instructions, completing long-term assignments). It is also important to realize that ADD has a significant impact on a child's social development, peer interactions, and personal relationships. Attention deficits affect a child's ability to observe, understand, and respond to his social environment.

The three basic commandments of childhood social success are (1) share, (2) wait your turn, and (3) follow the rules. A child with attentional deficits will find these three tasks nearly impossible. It is easy to see why the majority of children with ADD are isolated and rejected by their peers. The social behaviors of ADD children are often described as "insensitive" and "immature." These terms may seem rather harsh, but they give an accurate assessment of the child's day-to-day social performance. Because he is impulsive, he gives little thought to the consequences of his actions and seems insensitive to the feelings and needs of others. His hyperactive, distractible, and impulsive behavior resembles that of a younger child, so he is often viewed as immature.

This chapter examines the most common ADD symptoms and their impact upon a child's social competence, and provides some suggestions to deal with these behaviors. It is important to note that ADD is an *explanation* for poor social skills, not a justification for asocial or antisocial behavior.

Hyperactivity

The symptoms of hyperactivity include:
- chronic restlessness
- tendency to be overly verbal
- inappropriate roaming, running, climbing
- fidgeting
- unnecessary movement (e.g., tapping, stretching)
- limitless energy

A teacher once told me, "If Adam would just stay in his seat, be quiet, and pay attention, I could *deal* with his Attention Deficit Disorder." Unfortunately and ironically, those behaviors *are* his Attention Deficit Disorder!

Although peers and siblings are often tolerant of *some* ADD symptoms, they are often unforgiving and judgmental about the child's hyperactive behavior because of the impact that behavior has upon social settings. Unfortunately, caregivers, classmates, and team-mates often view these behaviors as *purposeful* and, therefore, assume that the child is deliberately disruptive. Admonitions to "sit still" or "behave yourself" are ineffective. Peers will label the hyperactive child a troublemaker because his erratic and disruptive behavior often angers adults and results in restrictions upon the entire group. ("We don't go to visit Grandma anymore because Todd always messes up her new furniture," or "Mrs. Bennett doesn't let us go to the media center on Fridays because Jesse is in our class that day and he broke a projector once.") Children have difficulty understanding that their classmate's behavior is largely beyond his control. When examining relationships between children, it is important to be aware of the basic principle of sociologist John Thibault's Social Exchange Theory: people tend to maintain relationships that are beneficial to themselves in some way. We constantly weigh the "cost/benefit" of relationships and decide whether the cost of the affiliation outweighs the benefit. Unfortunately, the child with ADD often is the loser when this equation is applied by peers.

Teachers, coaches, and parents also have difficulty dealing with hyperactive behaviors. The child seems to be unwilling to listen to directions, often fails to complete assignments, is constantly distracted, and jumps (quite literally) from one activity to another. His constant and unpredictable movement causes difficulty and disruption in all social settings, and he requires far more supervision and care than his peers or siblings.

Teachers and parents should be tolerant of overactivity (e.g., excessive movement, squirming, fidgeting) if the child is "on task" and the behavior is not disruptive to others. Demands that the child constantly sit still cause needless anxiety, frustration, and embarrassment for him. When it comes to excessive movement, remain mindful of the sage advice, "If it doesn't make a difference, what difference does it make?" If the child is squirming in his seat *but* is doing his math assignment appropriately, the teacher would be well advised to ignore or tolerate the excessive movement. This behavior is largely beyond the child's control. It is important that the adults in the child's life be flexible and accommodating.

Teachers can make several modifications and adjustments that will allow the hyperactive child to function more effectively in the classroom. These techniques take a "fight fire with fire" approach: rather than constantly battling with the child's need for activity and movement, provide the child with ample opportunities to be active during classroom activities. In effect, you are legitimizing the child's need to move by making movement part of your lesson plan!

For example, provide the hyperactive child with a standing desk and allow him to complete written work while standing. This simple adjustment may satisfy the child's need to be active during a sedentary activity. Give the child a clipboard to use during writing activities and allow him to work on the floor or in a beanbag chair. One teacher reported remarkable results after allowing her hyperactive students to sit in rocking chairs during silent reading activities. Another teacher assigned a child two seats in the classroom and allowed him to change seats whenever he needed to move about. Ask the hyperactive child to do classroom chores (e.g., water the plants, erase the white board, deliver messages). You can also legitimize the child's movement by doing quick (thirty-second) calisthenics between class activities. Again, these modifications recognize that the excessive movement is beyond the child's control.

Parents can replicate this approach by allowing the child to stand at the rear of the church during religious services, or encouraging him to walk around using a cell phone during Grandma's Sunday phone call.

Children with ADD generally do not respond well to traditional behavior-management interventions. They view the world quite differently than their peers do, and their perceptions, background information, and memory functions are—by definition—idiosyncratic. There is, therefore, no reason to believe that traditional interventions like "time out" would be effective in curbing or improving hyperactive behavior. However, hyperactive children often respond quite well when they are given an opportunity and location to take a break when feeling anxious, frustrated, agitated, or restless. Establish a location where the child can cool off at these times. Emphasize that placement in the "cool-off corner" can be initiated by the child or by the adult, and that the corner is *not punitive*. It is merely a comfortable, solitary location where the child can go to get himself together. The caregiver should watch for warning signs or behaviors that indicate that the child is beginning to lose control. Advise him to go to the cool-off corner *before* he begins to act out or act up. A calming break may prevent a behavioral outburst.

Janice Dickens, a former colleague, once observed, "It takes a lot of work for a hyperactive kid to do nothing." How true. When a child sits quietly for a period of time, recognize and reinforce that behavior. ("Thanks, Donna. I really appreciated your not interrupting me while I was on the phone with Grandpa. He told me to say hello to you.") Also, alternate stimulating activities with more sedentary tasks. This may provide the child with the break he needs to better control his hyperactive behavior. This rotation of activities (sedentary, active, sedentary, active) should be an integral part of a teacher's lesson plan or a family's day at home. Hopefully, the child will begin to integrate this cycle into his own life as he plans free-time activities: "I will work on my math homework for forty minutes, then feed the dog and brush her, then get to work on my English essay."

The hyperactive child often has difficulty with organization skills and executive processing. Therefore, she will respond positively to a school and home environment that is predictable, structured, and features well-defined expectations and rules.

Although hyperactivity is not *caused* by the setting in which the child is placed, elements of the home or school environment can improve his behavior or contribute to its decline. Observe the child carefully in a variety of settings, environments, and situations. Make note of the times and places when his hyperactivity is severe (e.g., spelling bees, when his cousin visits, in church) and take steps to minimize his hyperactivity by adjusting the activity in some way. For example, provide him with ample notice prior to a spelling bee, limit cousin visits to one hour, and attend church services early in the morning, when his hyperactivity is controlled by his first medication dosage.

When dealing with hyperactive behavior, the adult should do everything in her power to remain calm and controlled. Yelling and shouting will be ineffective and may, in fact, feed the child's hyperactive behavior. Your goal is to provide a positive model of controlled, responsive, mature behavior for the child to emulate.

For the hyperactive child, the need for activity is very real. His dervishlike behavior is not purposeful or willful. He *needs* to be active. Therefore, provide him with ample opportunities to be active. Common punitive strategies such as taking away recess are counterindicated and counterproductive. A ten-minute recess is the *solution* to the child's hyperactive behavior! Barring him from 10:30

recess because of a 10:20 meltdown is simply inappropriate. Several years ago, when consulting with a school system that simply didn't "get" hyperactivity, I added the following phrase to a hyperactive student's Individualized Education Plan (IEP):

"Under no circumstances is Sammy to be prevented from participating in recess for punitive reasons or as a reaction to his classroom behavior and performance. In Sammy's case, recess is a *right* . . . not a *privilege*."

By restricting Sammy's access to recess, the teachers were actually increasing his hyperactive behavior. Although Sammy desperately needed recess in order to channel his hyperactivity, he was unable to make an effective transition from the rough-and-tumble of recess to the structured environment of the language arts class that immediately followed. His teacher found it effective to restrict Sammy to a specific area of the playground and assign him a daily "recess buddy" to assist him in keeping him relatively calm during play period. (The buddy might be another child who is isolated by others during recess.) She also divided his twenty-minute recess period into four sections: ten minutes of free play; two minutes of "cool down"; five more minutes of free play; and two more minutes of cool down before reentering the building. This format was very useful in controlling his behavior, and he understood that these modifications were not punitive but designed to assist him in making a successful recess-to-classroom transition.

Impulsivity

The impulsive child usually experiences significant difficulty in the social arena. His poor impulse control often causes him to take action without considering the consequences of his behavior or its impact upon others in his environment. These children lack *consequential thought* and the ability to reflect upon the consequences of their behavior prior to acting on their impulses. As a result, impulsive children often manifest behaviors that are off-putting and offensive to their peers, siblings, teachers, and parents. They constantly interrupt conversation, intrude on the personal space of others, fail to wait their turn, and have significant difficulty delaying gratification.

They appear to be insatiable. A colleague once referred to impulsive children as "MNM" kids: **Me, Now, and More!**

Impulsive children also may pose major safety challenges for caregivers. Because they do not consider the consequences of their actions, they may take risks and chances that endanger themselves or others. Lacking reflective/consequential thought, these children usually do not look both ways before crossing or make sure the strange dog is friendly before petting it. Consequently, they often have preventable mishaps and accidents. This child requires closer supervision and guidance than his peers. A graduate student of mine wished to do some research with impulsive children. He asked me where he could find some children with poor impulse control. I advised him, tongue in cheek, to go to hospital emergency rooms . . . *they will come!*

Impulsive children have significant academic problems because they rush through their schoolwork without understanding and following directions. They often give impulsive, irrelevant, and "off the wall" responses to oral questions posed in the classroom because they fail to reflect on the appropriateness of the answers before they give them. Their impulsivity affects their ability to take written tests, as this activity requires reflection and consideration before recording an answer.

As one can imagine, impulsivity also has significant social consequences and can make a child an unattractive social partner. His impulsivity can result in chronic stealing ("I see it; I want it; I take it!"), lying (blurting out an impulsive lie to cover for a mistake or misdeed), and disrespect (impulsively challenging an adult decision or reprimand).

Caregivers for impulsive children are well advised to prepare the child in advance prior to any challenging social situation. For example:

"Here we are at Grandma's. Remember, you can pet her white cat, but the black one doesn't like being touched."

"Before we go into basketball practice, remember that the coach doesn't like you to yell when he is conducting drills."

"Before we get to the auditorium, remember: Don't applaud unless everyone else is applauding."

•   •   •

In seminars, I often describe the lifestyle of the impulsive child as "Ready—Fire—Aim." This means that the child fails to give his actions appropriate reflection and forethought. Assist him in developing reflective thought by rehearsing upcoming social situations: "What are some things that you might say to Grandma today when she visits?" "Let's talk about how you will ask Mrs. McNamara about her new baby."

One of the greatest gifts that an adult can give an impulsive child is the gift of *time*. Provide him with ample time to reflect upon his response *prior* to responding. ("I want everyone to think of three words to describe Mount Rushmore while I erase the board.") Encourage him to inhibit his behavior and reflect before he answers or responds.

These children often impulsively begin a task before they truly understand the instructions. They fail to ask questions or request clarification because they are so eager to begin the task. Basically, they are missing the "set" in "ready, set, go!"

An enjoyable and effective activity that helps a child develop reflection is called "Go Get It." Have the child take a seat and tell him that you are going to ask him to retrieve articles around the room. However, some of your commands will be impossible to follow because the requested item is too heavy to carry. Instruct the child that he should retrieve the item if it is light enough to carry, but if you name an item that is too heavy to lift, he should remain still in his chair. Create an air of excitement by giving the instructions in a dramatic fashion:

"Ready? Set? Go get me the *piano*!"
"Ready? Set? Go get me the *stapler*!"
"Ready? Set? Go get me the *desk*!"

Another useful strategy is to require the child to fully repeat the *question* before giving his answer. This will require him to listen to and comprehend the question prior to responding and will reduce incorrect, impulsive answers.

One of the more unappealing social traits of impulsive children is their tendency to tell lies. When they are challenged about a mistake, misbehavior, or situation, they often tell impulsive and transparent lies ("Rodney, did you eat all the ice cream?" "Mom, I don't even like ice cream!"). Again this unattractive behavior is rooted in the child's neurological deficit, but his lying causes embarrassment, peer rejection, and distress.

Parents and teachers often overreact when a child tells a lie because adults view lying as a *behavior* and a *character trait*. We fear, unrealistically, that the child's lying will become chronic and that he will become a dishonest and untrustworthy person. Again, it is important to note that many ADD children will tell lies impulsively, without malice aforethought. Therefore, it may be inappropriate to punish the ADD child for lying. That would be akin to punishing him for being hyperactive or for having a reading problem. Remember: Punishment is designed to eliminate learned behavior. In this case, the lying is rooted in the child's biology.

Consider this exchange: "John, did you leave the door open? The cat got out!" "No, the cat must have opened the door by herself!" If you feel that a child's lie is a result of his impulsivity, do not punish him for lying, although you may wish to punish him for the behavior that he lied about. You may also want to give him an opportunity to retract the lie *without a consequence*.

Suppose that Joey uses his father's hammer to break rocks and the handle of the tool gets cracked. When Dad finds the broken tool, he confronts Joey.

DAD: "Joey, my good hammer is cracked! Did you do it?"

JOEY: "*No!* I don't know anything about it!"

DAD: "Wait a minute, Joey. I saw you using the hammer yesterday in the backyard. I think that you are not telling me the truth. Now, why don't you take a breath and tell me what happened. I don't think that you meant to lie to me."

JOEY: "Okay, Dad. I'm sorry. I didn't mean to do it. I tried to bust that big rock near the garage and the hammer broke."

DAD: "Well, I'm glad that you decided to tell me the truth, and I appreciate it. It's real important that we be honest with each other. I am not going to punish you for lying, but I don't want you to use the tool shed for the rest of the weekend. If you ever break something again, Joey, it's best that you tell me about it, okay?"

Dad may also try giving Joey a few moments to reflect *before* answering an incriminating question, thereby compensating for his son's impulsivity: "Joey, my best hammer is broken. I think that you were the last person to use it. Take a minute to think, and then meet me in the kitchen to tell me what happened."

Impulsive (or compulsive) lying is seldom eliminated by punishment. Sincere and calm discussions about this behavior are generally more effective. Tell the child that lying is socially unacceptable and that this behavior has a negative impact upon *trust* in a relationship. Because of the emotional impact of the label *liar,* be sure to label the *behavior,* not the *child* (i.e., "What you said is a lie" versus "You are a liar!"). Always praise and reinforce a child when he tells the truth.

Impulsive children also tend to be poor and inefficient listeners and often tune out others during conversations.

Impulsive behavior is particularly troubling as the child enters adolescence. These young people may make impulsive—and inappropriate—decisions regarding sexual activity, driving, and drug or alcohol use. Impulsive adolescents often practice risky, dangerous, and thrill-seeking behaviors. (For more on substance abuse and the ADD child, see page 132.)

Inattention

The ADD child's inability to pay attention to a task can create significant social problems. For example, classmates and teammates of the inattentive child may be quite unforgiving and judgmental about this behavior. A Little League coach once told me, "Jack's teammates are pretty tolerant about his hyperactivity and impulsivity, but they get really upset with him when he misses a fly ball because he's not paying attention in the outfield. They feel that he is *not trying . . .* and letting the team down."

The inattentive child is often disorganized and forgetful. Teachers bemoan his lack of follow-through on assignments, his poor listening skills, and his inattention to detail. Peers and parents complain about his tendency to lose his (and others') possessions, and his "spaciness." Again, he is viewed as an unattractive social partner and is often ignored or isolated by his peers.

An inattentive child will have difficulty focusing or concentrating for long periods. He may become easily confused or bored. He seldom finishes assignments or chores and may lose interest in a board game and quit at its midpoint. (Interestingly, inattention is more common among girls with ADD than boys.) By increasing the child's ability to pay attention, his social competence and acceptance will generally increase as well.

Teachers and parents can help a child focus his attention by giving instructions clearly and concisely. Be certain that the child is looking directly at you when giving a direction and speak in a clear, direct manner. Keep your directions simple. Use motivating and stimulating hints to help the child to focus his attention. Say something like, "The next thing that we are going to talk about is *very* important . . ." or "John, you are going to want to *really* pay attention to the next part . . ."

Many inattentive children respond well to visual cues that supplement auditory (hearing) input. When giving verbal directions, simultaneously write the directions on the blackboard; when explaining how to fold the construction paper, provide a visual demonstration of the proper way to make the fold.

Routine, daily conversations can pose a significant challenge for the inattentive child. He may easily lose track of the discussion and stare blankly at his conversation partner. He may have a tendency to free-associate during conversations and disconnect from the discussion. Encourage the child to make eye contact during conversations and to concentrate intensely upon the purpose, content, and direction of the discussion.

The inattentive child is often highly disorganized, due to his inability to attend to detail. Provide him with techniques and strategies to assist him in keeping track of his belongings. Encourage him to place his keys, books, glasses, and other items in the same place every day.

Sleep Problems

Many children and adults with Attention Deficit Disorder have significant difficulty sleeping. They report that they are often unable to fall asleep, to remain asleep, or to awaken in a typical way. Enuresis (bedwetting) and nightmares are also common complaints for ADD children. Because ADD is a neurologically based problem, it should not be surprising that the idiosyncratic neurological functioning also affects a person as he sleeps.

There is a good deal of conjecture regarding the connection between ADD and sleep disorders. One theory holds that the child is unable to "turn off" his highly active brain and nervous system. Another theory is that anxiety and worry about past and future events do not permit the child to rest peacefully. A third explanation cites the severe distractibility of the child and his inability to focus his energies on the sleep process.

Recent research indicates that many ADD children are unable to reach the deep, restful, regenerative rapid eye movement (REM) sleep that most people reach. Although the child "sleeps" all night, he never has the REM sleep that provides him with the energy that he needs to function successfully at school. The teacher complains that Jonathan is listless, tired, and yawning in class. She requests that Mom ensures that Jon go to bed early, and Mom complies, but the lethargic behavior continues.

The behavioral/social impact of sleep deprivation is obvious. Consider for a moment how *you* feel when you have had an inadequate amount of sleep. You tend to be irritable, grouchy, overly sensitive, and emotional. You may also have difficulty focusing on tasks and be easily distracted. These are all feelings and behaviors that are common for the child with Attention Deficit Disorder. Interestingly, *partial* sleep deprivation (similar to the aforementioned sleep experience of many ADD children) is more debilitating than *total* sleep deprivation (staying totally awake for extended periods of time).

Doctors on long hospital shifts used to be encouraged to take quick catnaps when opportunities arose, but current research indicates that it is preferable to remain awake during these extended shifts, because "total deprivation" has less physiological impact than "partial deprivation" does.

Parents often become upset because of the adolescent tendency to sleep for twelve or fourteen hours each day. As adults, we consider this to be unproductive and "lazy." The fact is that adolescence features more physical growth and development than nearly any other phase of human growth. The only developmental period that features *greater* growth is infancy. What do babies do with most of their days? They *eat* and *sleep*. How do teenagers spend most of *their* days? They *eat* and *sleep*. Nourishment and rest are necessary to accommodate these growth spurts. Parents are well advised to be tolerant and understanding of these biological needs of the adolescent. Let 'em sleep and forgive the daily raids on the refrigerator.

Some sleep experts feel that snoring is a significant sign that a child may have a sleep disorder. If your child snores loudly or manifests excessive movement during sleep, she may have a sleep problem that is affecting her ability to function socially or academically. This sleep problem may be the cause—or consequence—of her attentional problems. As with any other medical issue, you will want to consult with your pediatrician.

If you find that your ADD child is having difficulty sleeping, here are some suggestions that you may want to implement.

- Bedtime should be a quiet, peaceful, and calming time. The activities that immediately precede bedtime should be passive and restful. Read him a story. Give him a restful bath. Sit and talk. Gradually soften and decrease the lighting in the house as the evening proceeds. Put on a classical music CD. All of these activities indicate that sleep time is imminent.
- Avoid roughhousing, active play, or stimulating, exciting television programs before bedtime. These children have marked difficulty handling dramatic transitions. Early in her career, my wife, Janet, was a dormitory counselor at a residential school for special-needs children. Each night at bedtime, her supervisor would enter the dorm with great fanfare, play roughly with the

kids, and then carry them into their rooms and heave them onto their beds. Great fun! But these wired, highly stimulated kids would lie awake for hours after the supervisor's nightly visits.

- As much as possible, establish and maintain a consistent schedule for bedtime and waking up that allows the child to get as much sleep as he needs. This will help the child to develop regular sleep patterns. Avoid the understandable temptation to permit the child to sleep in on weekends, or to extend bedtime during vacations. Discourage naps during the day. Again, a consistent schedule will allow the child to establish sleep styles that are adequate, predictable, and constant.

- Many children sleep better if they are allowed to sleep with an object that is soft, comfortable, and comforting. Allow and encourage the child to do so, even though this activity may not seem age appropriate.

- Many families develop unfortunate rituals that indefinitely extend the child's bedtime. The ADD child will implore the parent for "one more story," "just a glass of water," or a final bathroom trip. Try to avoid falling into these traps. When the child calls you from his bedroom, do not respond immediately. Wait a moment or so. He may fall asleep on his own or lose interest in the "crucial need" that he had. When you *do* enter his room in response to his call, remain in the doorway. Don't approach the bed. Assure him that you are in the house and that he is safe, but avoid stimulating him in any way. Do not allow him to sleep with his parents.

- For children with severe sleep disturbances, you may want to contact your pediatrician and explore medication. Some parents report that "white noise" machines, which are available at many retail office supply stores, have been effective in helping a child fall asleep more easily.

Impaired Sense of Time

Many, perhaps most, children and adults with attentional problems have difficulty dealing with *temporal* (time-related) concepts. This weakness can have a significant negative impact upon the child's social life. Failure to adhere to curfews, deadlines, schedules, and commitments can cause others to view the ADD person as irresponsible, unmotivated, and discourteous.

A child with *temporal concept deficiencies* has great difficulty determining how long a given activity will take to complete. As a result, he may begin to shovel the driveway only ten minutes before Dad's scheduled arrival home from work. Dad, of course, views this behavior as dawdling, laziness, or even confrontational. Actually, the boy simply has no idea that this mammoth task requires many hours to complete. He is simply unable to estimate and plan for such things. This weakness is also a primary cause of test anxiety.

Imagine the significant impact that such a difficulty would have upon a child's day-to-day social functioning. He is chronically late (or early) for meetings, meals, appointments, and events. He allows too little (or way too much) time to get to the school bus every day. He begins his long-term science project the evening before it is due. His friends are greatly frustrated by his casual relationship with punctuality.

Learning disabled children often have great difficulty learning to tell time. As a result, they may avoid social interactions that are time related. Interestingly, they seldom make references to specific times in casual conversation. They might say, *"Once* I went to the amusement park," versus *"Last Thursday* I went to the amusement park." Or, "I have to go home when *The Simpsons* is over," versus "I have to go home at nine o'clock."

For these children, time is a confusing and frustrating concept. They are extraordinarily impatient and despise waiting. Time appears to creep for them, and they react strongly when they are required to wait their turn in a game or wait for the family to finish dinner. Moments truly seem like hours. It is important to understand that this behavior is not rooted in selfishness or self-centeredness. Rather, the five-minute wait for Mom to cash out her grocery order seems like interminable hours for the child.

Additional Symptoms

There are several additional, but less common, symptoms manifested by children with ADD that have a severe impact upon their social-emotional behavior. For example, many attention-disordered children are unable to learn from past experiences. As a result, traditional behavioral strategies of punishments, rewards, and warnings simply do not work. These children repeat negative behaviors over and over despite reprimands, interventions, and reminders. Adults often rhetorically ask the child, "How many times have I told you not to—" Unfortunately, the frequency or severity of these interventions is irrelevant. The child simply does not learn from experience. Traditional behavioral interventions are frustrating for the child and the adult. These children require immediate reinforcement of good behavior and immediate feedback about misbehavior or social miscues.

ADD children also have marked difficulty dealing with frustration. They tend to react in an emotionally charged way to seemingly insignificant problems, inconveniences, or setbacks. This child may have a hair-trigger temper or give up easily when confronted with an academic or social challenge. He may panic or withdraw when facing a task that is demanding or complex. This child benefits greatly from *chunking,* a technique wherein the parent, teacher, or coach divides the overwhelming task into small, manageable steps.

Many children with ADD have extreme emotional reactions. Their emotions are poorly modulated and are subject to rapid fluctuation. This makes them quite susceptible to bullying because other children recognize how easy it is to "set them off."

Memory deficits are also common among children with attentional problems. They may forget directions, requests, appointments, or curfews. They will have difficulty retrieving facts, names, or rules and may forget the social demands and expectations in daily interactions.

Difficulty with executive functioning will also have an impact upon the social skills of the ADD child. His inability to plan and problem-solve makes social situations difficult and challenging for him. He tends to do things the hard way, complicating even routine daily interactions and activities. Children with executive functioning problems also have difficulty determining *saliency.* This means that they are unable to recognize or respond to the important details within a social setting or situation. For example, a child may tell an off-color joke to a group of his friends without noticing that his teacher is within earshot.

• • •

Attention deficits can have a profound impact on social skills. Unfortunately, these social deficits continue into adulthood because the child and adolescent with attention problems is unable to learn appropriate social behaviors. As human beings, we master social skills in an incidental way. That is, we *observe* the behavior of others, *replicate* that behavior, *practice* that behavior, and *respond* to positive or negative feedback related to the behavior. Children with severe attentional problems are simply unable to follow this process. Because they do not learn social skills *incidentally,* we must teach them these skills *directly.*

Adolescents and adults with ADD often fall into a "downward spiral" in the social arena. In contrast, most typical children become involved in an "upward spiral" in which

- the child learns social skills
- the child applies social skills and utilizes these skills
- positive social skills serve to broaden his social contacts
- additional social contacts increase the child's social opportunities
- social opportunities improve and enhance his social skills

Unfortunately, the child with attentional problems finds herself in a continual "downward spiral" as a consequence of her ADD-related behaviors. As a result:

- the child fails to learn social skills
- the child fails to apply or utilize appropriate social skills
- negative social skills serve to limit her social contacts
- lack of social role models and experiences have negative impact upon her development of social skills

In addition to the strategies and techniques discussed above, there are other ways parents, teachers, coaches, and caregivers can slow or stop the downward spiral and improve a child's academic and social performance.

1. *Be aware that the behavior of most ADD youngsters is often dependent upon the setting.*

For example, Grandma's house may have a calming effect on the child, and so his behavior is relatively appropriate. However, the stimulating and unpredictable environment of soccer practice or the grocery store may cause the child to act out or be disruptive.

A useful analogy compares ADD to allergies. In certain environments (e.g., hospitals, city streets), an allergy sufferer has little difficulty breathing or functioning. However, in other settings (garden, park, ballpark), he will suffer from watery eyes, congestion, and sneezing. Remember: a person's *response* to his environment is not his fault and, further, is beyond his control.

2. *Unfortunately, many ADD children develop troubling behaviors— bullying, clowning, cruelty, manipulating, or bossiness—as a reaction to their perceived powerlessness in social situations.*

The child fears embarrassment or humiliation in a social setting, so he attempts to circumvent this by taking control of the situation. All of the above-listed behaviors are related to *control*.

3. *Many parents find it useful to redefine the traditional function of babysitter when dealing with a child with a severe attentional problem.*

If you are fortunate enough to find a responsible, responsive, and effective sitter for the child, use her as a companion for the youngster. Have the sitter accompany the family when dining out or attending important social functions (e.g., family wedding, company picnic). The sitter can be of great assistance in monitoring and controlling the child's behavior, leaving Mom and Dad free to fulfill their social obligations at the event. If the child becomes totally overwhelmed by the activity, the sitter/companion can leave with him or conduct a calming activity in private for the child.

4. *Many ADD adolescents develop emotional or psychological problems in reaction to their attentional weakness.*

In high school, the adolescent is expected to utilize the skill areas (e.g., organizational skills, productivity, cognitive speed, memory) that have been compromised by ADD. If you see your child becoming depressed or withdrawn, you should seek counseling for her. Among the most significant symptoms of depression are:

- shyness, withdrawal from social situations
- significant changes in eating habits

- feeling of incompetence or inadequacy
- rigid, inflexible attitudes and behaviors
- chronic fatigue
- excessively critical attitude about self or others
- refusal to accept advice, help, or constructive criticism
- memory loss
- constant complaining

Among the intervention techniques that are generally effective with ADD students are:

- providing physical outlets
- providing immediate feedback
- providing consistent, predictable, structured environment
- providing reasons and rationales for regulations
- encouraging and fostering independence
- involving the child in decision making, planning, and problem solving
- remaining success-oriented through reinforcement, praise, encouragement
- providing noncompatible diversions during periods of inappropriate behavior (e.g., if a child is staring aimlessly out the window, call his attention to a picture in his book; if he is distracting others by tapping his pencil, give him a ball to squeeze. Basically, the undesirable behavior is incompatible with the desired behavior. They cannot occur simultaneously).
- anticipating and preventing problems
- defusing escalation
- remaining flexible and willing and able to accommodate
- providing clear, consistent limits
- establishing effective communication between home and school
- providing motivating, stimulating, activity-oriented, concrete experiential instruction
- providing positive, supportive, preventive behavior management strategies
- focusing on strengths to remediate weaknesses

- providing unconditional love and acceptance
- cueing, prompting, reminding
- assisting in dealing with failure and frustration
- providing occasional options and choices

Among the intervention techniques that are generally *ineffective* with ADD students are:
- punishing, removing privileges
- confronting
- yelling, shouting
- lecturing, moralizing, threatening
- nitpicking
- fostering dependence
- engaging in home-versus-school "turf battles"
- branding the child "lazy" or "unmotivated"

Some Thoughts on Substance Abuse

Of course, the use and abuse of illegal drugs is among any parent's greatest fears. Some research has indicated that children with attentional problems are especially at risk for becoming involved in experimentation with alcohol and illegal drugs. If you suspect that your child is involved in drug use, closely monitor her and be mindful of the various physical, social, emotional, and attitudinal behaviors that often indicate a child's involvement with illegal drugs.

Physical changes: fatigue, sleepiness, difficulty waking, red or watery eyes, frequent colds, pale complexion, coordination difficulties, change in appetite, unusual food cravings, weight loss.

Emotional and attitudinal changes: irritability, depression, paranoia, slurred speech, lack of emotion, absentmindedness, losing train of thought frequently, authority conflicts, mood swings, outburst of anger or crying.

Social changes: withdrawal from usual social contacts and activities, new circle of less desirable friends, obsession with music with drug-related lyrics or themes, secretive and brief phone calls or visits from strangers, strange odor on breath or clothing, lying, stealing (particularly money).

Parental fears about drug usage by adolescents with learning and social problems are, unfortunately, well founded. The youngster who is experiencing repeated failures in his academic *and* social lives is vulnerable. It is a widely accepted fact that a person's feelings and emotions are often directly linked to his tendency toward substance abuse. The child who feels sad, lonely, and isolated is able to find temporary relief by using substances that alter his feelings, emotions, and perceptions. This is particularly true if the child feels that he has no outlet or format to discuss these painful and troubling feelings.

This is one more reason that parents and caregivers must establish and maintain open channels of communication with the child. The youngster must feel that he can discuss his social problems openly with a caring adult and, further, that such conversations will be devoid of criticism, lectures, and harsh judgment. If the child feels that he cannot *express* his feelings, he will, naturally, *repress* these feelings. These repressed emotions can easily lead to the "self-medication" of drug abuse. Teach the child how to identify and communicate his emotional states. Reinforce the idea that there are several "shades" of emotions within the common feeling states of *sad, mad,* and *glad.* These shades may include:

Glad: accepted, welcomed, confident, secure, proud, loved, relaxed, relieved, happy, determined, excited, grateful, important.

Sad: afraid, nervous, confused, disappointed, embarrassed, discouraged, rejected, unloved, unappreciated, ashamed, lonely.

Mad: furious, angry, annoyed, disgusted, irritated, grumpy, fed up, bored, weary, frustrated, uncertain, guilty, indifferent.

Also: jealous, surprised, sympathetic, puzzled, insecure, cheated.

Encourage the child from a young age to share her emotions with you. Be comforting, supportive, and nonjudgmental during these discussions. Put an arm around her and express your empathy through your body language and your focused attention. Although the child's emotional upset may seem trivial to you—a lost toy or a squabble with a playground friend—the problem may be quite significant to her. Teach her that she will not be ridiculed or dismissed when she shares her feelings with you. If this open dialogue becomes a part of your relationship, she is more likely to confide in you when her peers begin to pressure her to try drugs or alcohol. A recent survey by *Weekly Reader* magazine indicated that one third of America's children have tried alcohol by age eight and that marijuana use has doubled in middle schools since 1995.

When discussing drug or alcohol abuse with the child, do not hesitate to talk about incidents in your own life that required you to make similar decisions. Discuss the significance of peer pressure, and do not attempt to minimize it by telling the child to "stand up for himself" and to "be his own man." Such platitudes are easy to say but extraordinarily difficult to apply. Use this opportunity to discuss some problems and disappointments that *you* experienced in the past. Parents sometimes make the mistake of portraying themselves as "perfect" in the belief that the child will be inspired by this flawless role model. This approach often backfires. I once encouraged a twelve-year-old girl to discuss her social problems with her mother. "Oh, she'd never understand," the girl replied. "She's always had a million friends. She's always talking about how popular she was in high school. I love her, and we talk about a lot of things, but she would not be able to help me with *this* problem. What does *she* know about being left out and picked on by other kids?" The daughter might be surprised (and encouraged!) to know that *everyone* feels isolated and rejected at times.

Experts in drug abuse prevention encourage parents to initiate open discussions about this topic rather than wait until the child brings up the subject. Unfortunately, drugs and alcohol are significant factors in every child's social landscape. Avoiding the issue will not make it disappear. Ask the child directly about the drug scene in her school and neighborhood. Ask if she has ever been offered drugs and advise her on what to say in the event that this occurs. Remind her that drug and alcohol use by minors is against the law and discuss the social and legal consequences of these activities. Acknowledge the fact that a sad or lonely person may understandably seek temporary solace in drugs, and provide her with safe, effective alternatives to use when feeling depressed (e.g., vigorous physical activity, conferring with a close adult or peer, relaxing or pleasurable activity).

Although peer pressure is a significant causal factor in adolescent and preadolescent drug use, it is not the sole cause. A recent California survey of children involved in drugs indicated five main reasons for their drug use:

1. to get away from problems
2. to experiment
3. to replicate the behavior of friends
4. to make themselves feel good
5. because they had nothing else to do

When these factors are analyzed, it becomes clear that parents and caregivers should utilize strategies that address these needs.

1. Provide the child with strategies to discuss and handle these problems.
2. Warn them of the dangers of drug experimentation. For example, there are several documented cases of fatalities as a result of a single dose of the designer drug Ecstasy.
3. Discourage friendships with peers who use drugs.
4. Provide the child with alternative activities that decrease stress and build self-esteem.
5. Assist the child in developing a full, complete, and productive lifestyle.

Parents are often blamed when a youngster becomes involved in drug or alcohol abuse. Although it is unfair to place all of the responsibility on Mom and Dad, it is important to remember that children who view their family and their home as a safe and accepting "haven" are less likely to become involved in drug-related activities. The parent should work diligently to create a home environment that provides guidance, structure, support, and—most important—unconditional love for the child with a learning problem, who is unlikely to view school as a safe and supportive refuge.

Afterword

Girls with Attention Deficit Disorders

At a recent speaking engagement, a teacher approached me with a litany of complaints and concerns about a child in her class. I suggested that she might want to explore the possibility that the child had an attentional problem. "No, it couldn't be ADD," the teacher responded. "She's a girl."

Her response reflects the common misconception among parents and caregivers that ADD is very rare among girls. Although most of the early research in attentional problems was focused upon boys, the field now recognizes that girls can also struggle with attentional issues.

As discussed in this chapter, ADD has long been associated with hyperactivity. In fact, for a long time, hyperactivity was one of the diagnostic criteria for ADD. Without hyperactivity as a symptom, a child could not be classified as ADD. We now realize that many children have all of the symptoms and struggles of ADD but no observable hyperactivity. This type of attention problem is quite common among girls. Young girls, because of biological differences and sociocultural expectations, are generally less disruptive and more compliant than boys. Therefore, they use a significant amount of energy to maintain nondisruptive behaviors. Their hyperactivity may be channeled into being hypertalkative, hypersensitive, hypercurious, or hyperreactive. Their physical restlessness is channeled into fine-motor fidgeting (e.g., hair twirling, foot tapping). They are mistakenly viewed by adults and peers as "ditzy," "empty-headed," and "spacey." They are seldom taken seriously, and the adults in their lives often have inappropriately low expectations of them. As a result, many girls with ADD do not reach their full potential.

Girls with attentional problems often have significant social difficulties. They are rejected by peers or isolated because of their odd behaviors. They are unable to follow the rapid-fire conversations that are common among young girls, and they may make comments that are out of step with the discussion at hand. They misinterpret social cues and are often unaware of (and therefore unresponsive to) the feelings and needs of others. They often act silly and immature in social situations.

Girls with attentional problems:
- are easily bored
- are careless
- have poor listening skills
- are disorganized
- have difficulty with temporal (time) concepts
- are overly sensitive; easily hurt or offended
- are highly distractible
- have poor sleeping patterns; stay up late
- are forgetful; procrastinate often

Girls with ADD are at risk for developing a wide range of behaviors, including eating disorders, immaturity, substance abuse, and promiscuity. The world is a confusing and rejecting place for them. They find themselves in constant conflict with authority figures and often experience a rocky relationship with their mothers because of their inability to adhere to accepted feminine norms. As the girl with ADD progresses in school, her inability to organize herself and her environment begins to take a significant toll on her academic performance. She is unable to perceive, prioritize, or understand the tremendous amount of academic material that she is expected to process and memorize. She begins to fall further behind and may become extremely anxious or depressed. It is unfortunate that girls with ADD are often not diagnosed or treated, simply because their symptomology is less obvious than their male counterparts'. Because adults view the child's behavior as immature, an ADD girl is often held back in school in the mistaken belief that "she just needs another year to mature."

RECOMMENDED RESOURCES

The ADD/ADHD Behavior Change Resource Kit, Grad L. Flick (West Nyack, N.Y.: Center for Applied Research in Education, 1999).

ADHD and Teens, Colleen Alexander-Roberts (Dallas, Tex.: Taylor Publishing Company, 2001).

"Attention-Deficit/Hyperactivity Disorder Briefing Paper," Mary Fowler (Washington, D.C.: NICHCY, 2002). Available online at www.nichcy .org.

Driven to Distraction, Edward Hallowell, MD, and John Ratey, MD (New York: Touchstone Press, 1995).

Maybe You Know My Kid, third edition, Mary Fowler (New York: Kensington Press, 1999).

Maybe You Know My Teen, Mary Fowler (New York: Broadway Books, 2001).

Teenagers with ADD, Chris Zeigler Dendy (Bethesda, Md.: Woodbine House, 2000).

PART TWO

Social Skills on the Homefront

Dealing with Parents, Siblings, and Other Strangers

> "The dark, uneasy world of family life—where the greatest can fail and the humblest succeed."
>
> —RANDALL JARRELL

CHAPTER SIX

Enhancing Organizational Skills

Bringing Order and Structure to the Disorganized Child

One of the primary causes for social isolation and rejection is an inability to organize and structure oneself. At first blush, this may seem a bit puzzling. Why would a lack of organizational skills cause a person to have conflict with peers, teachers, and family members?

If a person has significant organizational difficulties, she becomes an unpredictable and undependable friend, often complicating social plans because of her chronic tardiness and inability to adhere to social schedules. As a student, she often ignites her teacher's wrath by failing to complete homework, study effectively for tests, or make productive use of class time. Her family members find that her chronic disorganization creates havoc at home, and the family's activities are often compromised and complicated by her confused and confusing lifestyle.

It is important to assist the child in increasing and improving his organizational skills. This is a tall order for children with learning and attentional difficulties. Unfortunately, the organizational techniques contained in most books on the topic are generally unsuccessful for

141

children (or adults) with learning disorders. Due to my own ADHD-related organizational difficulties, I have spent significant time, energy, and resources attempting to integrate these "anti-clutter" strategies into my lifestyle—with minimal success. The techniques that are so effective for most people (e.g., datebooks, electronic calendars) simply do not work with many people with attentional deficits. We lose the datebooks and forget to buy batteries for the electronic devices!

These techniques also fail because ADD people view the world in a unique way. We tend to be very visual and need to *see* something in order to remember and organize it. Therefore, elaborate filing, categorizing, and storing systems are doomed to fail. If it is out of sight, it is literally out of mind. That is why people with ADD tend to be "pilers"; we place all of our important and necessary documents and materials in piles that can be easily and readily accessed. For years, my office at school featured a conference table with innumerable piles of papers, periodicals, memos, and documents. My colleagues found this disconcerting, I am sure, but I was always able to find the scrap of paper for which I was searching. The system was not pretty, but it was productive. Any organizational system should be judged on its effectiveness, not its appearance. The *function* of the system is more important than the form. "Messy" doesn't *necessarily* mean "disorganized."

Although the behavior patterns of disorganized children may seem similar, there are at least four distinct etiologies (causes) for this problem and four distinct profiles of disorganization that we see. Below is a brief outline of these subtypes and some suggestions to deal effectively with each.

Material-Spatial Disorganization

Children with material-spatial disorganization have significant difficulty managing the tools (e.g., pens, rulers, clothes) that they need in everyday life. They tend to lose things frequently and often fail to follow directions efficiently. They seldom know the proper places to put things: "Mom, where should I hang Aunt Jane's coat?" "Where do the eggs go?" "Have you seen my backpack?" Their rooms and desks are overrun with clutter and they have great difficulty using organizational tools (e.g., notebooks, assignment pads).

Children with this type of organizational deficit are constantly searching for pencils, pens, hats, and gloves. Our typical admonition of "Well, where did you put it?" is ineffective, because they don't remember! These youngsters often also have difficulty distinguishing left from right, have a poor sense of direction, and have difficulty interpreting visual symbols (e.g., reading, face recognition, visual memory).

- Assignment pads are somewhat useful but *must* be monitored by the teachers and parents. Merely requiring the child to maintain an assignment pad will not work.
- Teachers may wish to assign the disorganized child to a study buddy, who helps him record and understand assignments.
- Write all assignments on the board; it is insufficient to merely give oral directions.
- In elementary schools, have regularly scheduled desk cleanup days. A good technique for disorganized "hoarders" is this: "Kids, take everything out of your desks and put it on your chair. Now, as I name the item, put it in your desk: history text, science notebook, math workbook, dictionary, thesaurus, ruler, two pens, three pencils, and an eraser. Everything left on your seat is unnecessary. Throw it away or take it home."
- If your child continually leaves his books at school or at home, ask if he can be issued an extra set of texts. Keep one at home and one at school.
- The three-ring binders should have specific sections for homework, class notes, handouts, and so forth.

Temporal-Spatial Disorganization

Youngsters with temporal-spatial disorganization have difficulty dealing with time and sequence. Dr. Mel Levine describes these kids as being in a permanent "time warp." They have difficulty understanding any and all temporal (time) concepts. Therefore, they cannot allocate or predict how long an activity will take. ("I'm going to the mall to get a CD, Mom. I'll be back in ten minutes.") They cannot sequence activities well, and they complete sequenced activities out of order; have a tendency toward tardiness and procrastination; and constantly lose track of time. They do not use time well or efficiently. In effect, time is their enemy, and that enemy often wins. Their lack of time management skills is a complicating and disruptive aspect of their lives.

Children with this (dis)organizational pattern also have great difficulty understanding and utilizing sequential skills. They cannot remember events, directions, or instructions in correct order. Consequently, they experience significant difficulty completing multistep tasks (e.g., long math problems, complex instructions, relating stories).

Adults become frustrated with how little these children accomplish in the allocated time. The child views timed, multistep activities as frustrating and overwhelming. Because of their inability to break down large projects into manageable, sequential steps, these youngsters are easily overwhelmed.

- Emphasize effective time management skills by maintaining calendars and meeting with the child weekly (Sunday night is best) to discuss the activities and plans for the upcoming week. This prevents the child's catastrophic reaction to surprises.

- Use checklists to assist in the organization of multistep routines (e.g., getting ready for bed, preparing for soccer practice).

- Require the child to estimate the amount of time a task might take and then evaluate the accuracy of his answer. "John, we have to go to Billy's house to drop off his coat, then go to the car wash and wash the car, and then go to Blockbuster to return last night's videos. How long do you think that will take?" You may be surprised at how inaccurate the responses will be!

- Divide long-term major projects into smaller segments. Clearly communicate due dates and expectations for each section of the project.

- In order for your child to function effectively at home, you *must* provide a structured and predictable family schedule. Mealtimes, bedtimes, arising times, chore times, and so forth must be as consistent as possible.

- As a child completes his list of duties, chores, or steps in a long process, allow him to cross the tasks off the list. This builds motivation and self-esteem by providing visual evidence of his progress.

- Keep directions brief, clear, and to the point.
- Children with organizational problems have difficulty with goal setting and prioritizing. They often decide to put covers on their books the evening before exams when their time would be better spent studying! Help them with these important skills.
- Consistent communication between home and school is critical for long-term assignments.

Transitional Disorganization

Many students experience their greatest organizational confusion and frustration at transitional times. They have significant difficulty "shifting gears" and are often unprepared for the next step. Even seemingly minor transitions (e.g., "Amalia, please put away your homework and go into the living room") can cause difficulty and confusion. Many children begin to dislike, fear, and avoid transitions. Most incidents of classroom misbehavior or noncompliance occur during transitional activities.

Because of the difficulty transitions create for these children, they tend to procrastinate during transitions (dawdling), *or* they attempt to speed through the transition in order to "get it over with." Both approaches are ineffective and disruptive. These children also have significant difficulty adjusting to new settings or situations, and are often described as being inflexible, obstinate, or "set in their ways." They tend to move frenetically from one task to another and are often criticized for failing to bring appropriate materials to class. They may also have difficulty settling down at the beginning of class, particularly after stimulating or exciting activities (e.g., recess, lunch, physical education). They may be unable to understand and comply with daily routines, and their performance on recurrent tasks (e.g., cleaning room, making bed, filing) is often described as "slow and dawdling."

Transitional disorganization can manifest itself as frenetic, unpredictable movement from task to task *or* as hyperfocused reluctance to move on to another activity.

- Talk directly and frankly about this weakness to the child with transitional difficulties. Guide him through transitions and provide him with ample forewarning and support before and during transitions.
- Disorganized children often enjoy deadlines! Play Beat the Clock. Help the child estimate how long it will take her to clean her closet. Set an oven timer for the predicted time. Tell the child to see if she can complete the task before the timer goes off.
- Transitions should be as predictable and uneventful as possible. In the classroom, teachers should *plan* the transition as an integral part of their lessons.

Prospective Retrieval Disorganization

This subtype of disorganization is greatly affected by memory deficits. The child is simply unable to remember instructions and directions over a period of time. When given a task or assignment that is to be completed in the future—"When you get home, call Dad at the office"—the child forgets completely and is viewed as a "spaceshot" or a "flake." Often, adults accuse the child of willful or intentional failure to complete the task.

This lack of dependability can be very frustrating for adults. As soon as the child is reminded of the task ("Weren't you supposed to call Dad when you got home?"), the child instantly remembers. This often causes the adult to misinterpret the behavior as being purposeful.

- These children need assistance and guidance in budgeting and planning their time. However, this instruction must be aimed at the student's eventual *independent* ability to plan his time. Doing it *for* him is simply not enough.
- Use enjoyable, motivating activities to teach and reinforce effective organizational skills (e.g., putting on a play, building a clubhouse, installing a computer).
- Teach and require consistent formats for all assignments (e.g., name and date in upper left corner, required margins).
- Use Post-it notes to remind, cajole, and nag!

- It might surprise you to know that some disorganized, distractible children are actually *better able* to function with music in the background. It serves to eliminate some of the other distractions.
- Disorganized children often benefit from effective modeling. Don't just *tell* him what you want him to do—*show* him by demonstrating it.
- Establish and maintain structure and routines. As the structure *in*creases, the child's anxiety *de*creases.
- Homework should be collected and corrected consistently. The child should receive feedback on a homework assignment within twenty-four hours after it is submitted. Otherwise, he has little motivation to organize and structure himself.
- Tape the child's class schedule *everywhere!* Inside books, lockers, notebooks. Maps of the school, too!
- A locksmith can reset the child's combination lock to any combination you wish. Choose a familiar set of numbers.

Executive Processing Difficulties

Many children with learning disabilities have a deficiency in executive processing skills. They have minimal internal structure. The executive functions include the following critical skills:

Self-talk: The ability (via internal language) to "talk oneself through" a situation. This self-talk is used to solve problems, predict consequences, and control behavior.

Emotional control: The ability to tolerate and deal with frustration and anxiety. A person with appropriate emotional control is able to monitor his stress level and utilize effective strategies to deal with anxiety, anger, or fear in stressful situations.

Activation, Arousal, and Effort: The ability to get started on a task, maintain alertness, and complete the task. These three skills are fundamental to success in all social, academic, and vocational settings.

Impulsivity control: The ability to inhibit inappropriate speech and actions. The highly impulsive child can greatly complicate and compromise social settings at school, at home, or in the community. Inappropriate, uncontrolled impulsivity can also present a safety hazard for the child and others.

Memory and recall: The ability to process and remember information and past experiences. Children with executive functioning deficiencies have particular difficulty with active working memory that requires the child to hold facts in mind while manipulating other information (e.g., "Name the past four U.S. presidents in alphabetical order").

Complex problem solving: The ability to analyze a situation and reconstruct it in order to solve a social problem.

Children with difficulties in the various areas of executive functioning may
- be forgetful
- have weak short-term memory
- be unable to learn from mistakes and past experiences
- perceive time as passing very slowly; be impatient with waiting or rote tasks
- have minimal self-awareness
- demonstrate minimal "future orientation," poor planning skills
- have difficulty beginning tasks and maintaining motivation
- have low energy and poor sleep habits
- be distractible and irritable
- rarely engage in reflective or consequential thought (ready, *fire*, aim)
- be emotionally reactive
- seem immature and self-centered
- be excessively sensitive to criticism or slights
- be unable to delay gratification
- have difficulty analyzing problems and devising solutions

The symptoms of an executive processing deficit can affect a child's ability to organize in the following ways:

Inability to plan. The child is unable to "think ahead" or to determine the equipment that he will need to accomplish the task at hand. Even the simplest daily rituals (e.g., brushing teeth, making a sandwich, going for a swim) require planning, sequencing, and organization.

Difficulty recognizing priorities. Each day, we are required to initiate and complete many activities. These tasks range from unimportant to crucial, and we need to constantly prioritize our actions to ensure that the important tasks are completed. Children with executive processing difficulties are often unable to distinguish between important and unimportant activities, and so they become involved in mundane tasks, leaving the crucial tasks undone.

Difficulty allotting time effectively. Children with executive functioning deficits often have difficulty mastering temporal (time-related) concepts. They have significant difficulty understanding how much time a specific activity will take to complete. As a result, they budget their time ineffectively.

Difficulty understanding space. Just as these children are confused by concepts related to time, they have difficulty with spatial concepts as well. This affects their ability to order their environment. For example, they may try to cram three square feet of folded T-shirts into a one-foot-square dresser drawer.

Difficulty developing effective study skills. In order to complete homework and class assignments, the child must organize his materials and order his study environment. This is an exceedingly difficult task for children who are highly distractible, disorganized, and impulsive.

How to Help Your Child Organize Himself

To assist the child who has minimal *internal structure*, parents and teachers need to provide him with a good deal of *external structure*. Regrettably, the concept of "structure" is often misinterpreted and misunderstood; it is mistakenly viewed as harsh, unyielding, and militaristic. Actually, a structured environment is merely a *predictable* and *external* structure that compensates for the lack of internal structure.

When assisting the disorganized child, continually remind him of the benefits of bringing order to his environment. Emphasize the fact that *his* life is easier and more effective when he organizes himself, plans, and prioritizes. It is difficult for a child to overcome his disorganization, and he often fails to recognize that you are offering this instruction for *his* benefit, not for yours. Reinforce the fact that there are observable payoffs for him if he becomes better organized (e.g., saving time, losing things less often, more efficient use of study time).

Structuring a Task

The disorganized child becomes easily overwhelmed when approaching an unfamiliar or complex task. She tends to see the task as huge and formidable because she cannot perceive that the large task (cleaning up after supper) is actually a series of small tasks (clear the table, put away the milk and butter, wash the table, push in the chairs, rinse the dishes, and so forth). Assist the child in breaking large activities into smaller, manageable ones. By converting the task into "bite-size pieces," the child learns to restructure larger tasks at school and in the community as well. This greatly enhances the child's independence and self-sufficiency.

When a child approaches a task (e.g., cleaning the garage), he should ask himself three questions as he attempts to complete it:

1. *"What's the job that I need to complete?"* He peruses the garage and observes that the bicycles need to be lined up, the tools must be reshelved, the sports equipment must go into the bins, and so forth.

2. *"What will I need to use to complete this job?"* He will need to go to the basement to retrieve the push broom, and he may want to get work gloves from Dad's tool chest in the hallway.

3. After the task is completed, he should ask the final question: *"How did I do?"* This self-evaluation process is often difficult and overlooked by children with social skill difficulties. This important step enables the disorganized child to judge his own performance (and possibly make corrections or improvements) rather than depending on adults to evaluate him.

These children also become easily frustrated during a lengthy or complex task because they are continually evaluating their progress as they work. They should be encouraged to delay their evaluation until the task or part of the task is completed. Continual, ongoing assessment only causes frustration and may result in the child's quitting prior to completing the process. Reinforce and praise the child when the task is completed. Also, encourage him to reward *himself* as he works on a multistep assignment: "I have ten questions to answer. When I get five of them done, I will go to the freezer and get an ice cream bar."

This three-step strategy also teaches the child when and how to ask for help. He should request assistance during the second stage of the process. Often these children request help during the first stage, before they have analyzed the task and determined what their real need will be.

A primary reason for the child's disorganization is his lack of impulse control. Activities or objects that are unrelated to the task at hand easily distract him. For example, the child is asked to go to Dad's bedroom to retrieve the television's remote control. As the boy climbs the stairs, he sees his brother playing with their new kitten. He impulsively turns to his brother's room and—five minutes later—Dad angrily enters and inquires as to why the boy has not completed the simple task. It is often helpful to require the child to repeat the instruction prior to completing a task: "Sean, please go into the kitchen and bring me the phone book. Now, what are you going to bring me?" Often, the child will impulsively run off to complete the task without fully understanding what he is supposed to do. He arrives in the kitchen and stares blankly around the room, unaware of the next step in the process.

Before your child begins, ask him how much time he thinks he will need in order to complete the job. You may be surprised at the inaccuracy of his estimation! Discuss the demands of the task with him and mutually arrive at a realistic estimate. Use that time frame as the deadline. ("Okay, then. You should have your room cleaned and the dog walked by noon.") Children enjoy working against the clock and this tends to reduce their dawdling or distractibility.

When monitoring the child's progress on a task, the intervention should be positive ("How are you doing on the project, Danny?") rather than negative ("When I come back, this room better be cleaned up!"). Be affirming if he is proceeding well; be supportive if he is experiencing difficulty. Reinforcements or rewards are very appropriate when the task is satisfactorily completed. ("The garage looks great, Scottie. Wanna shoot a few hoops together?") Always thank a child for a job well done. This common courtesy is often neglected in the parent-child relationship. I once counseled a dad to thank his son when the boy completed a task appropriately. The father resisted. "But if I thank him when he merely carries out his responsibilities, he'll expect me to be saying 'thank you' all the time!" I was—and still am—unsure as to why that would be a *bad* thing. Living in a home where people thank one another regularly sounds pretty good to me!

Children with learning disorders also have difficulty understanding that larger tasks can (and should) be completed in "chunks." Their strategy for having a clean room is to allow the room to deteriorate to the point at which it is nearly unrecognizable and then spend a weekend completing major urban renewal. They are unable to understand that it is far more efficient and effective to *maintain* room cleanliness by eliminating clutter on an ongoing basis.

Organizing the Morning

The most challenging time of the disorganized child's day is usually the morning. Conflicts with parents and siblings are common at wake-up time! Much of this conflict can be eliminated by establishing bedtime routines that include preparations for the morning. Clothing (especially shoes!) should be selected and laid out, books and assignments should be put in the backpack, and lunch money should be placed in the pants pocket. This will prevent confusion and conflict the next morning.

Post lists or picture cards that remind the child of the various chores, responsibilities, and routines that he must complete before departing for school. Mom and Dad should take turns being responsible for assisting the child with the morning rituals. This prevents the child from being nagged by both parents. ("Dad already *told* me to make my bed! Get off my back!")

When I ran a residential school, I always recommended that live-in residential staff be fully dressed and groomed *before waking* the children. Kids seem to respond better when awakened by an adult who models structure, enthusiasm, and preparedness, and who appears to be ready to start the day.

The wake-up ritual is an often overlooked and underutilized opportunity for relationship building. Mornings need not be tense and difficult. Try to remain calm and upbeat. Your child may be anxious and upset about the upcoming school day, and he may be disagreeable and short-tempered. Remember the old adage, "Kids need love most when they deserve it least." Try to remain calm. Your obvious tension and angst will serve to frighten the child. The frightened child will often manifest attention-seeking behaviors. The more harried you are, the more likely the child is to misbehave.

We know that many children with learning problems have idiosyncratic sleep habits and patterns. Even though they may have been "asleep" for eight hours, their sleep may have been fitful and not restful. The transition from sleep to wakefulness may be a difficult one for them. They should be awakened gently and they should not be expected to arise on the "first call." They will need a second or even third reminder in order to become fully wakeful. Let the "second call" become a part of your wake-up ritual, not a scolding. Avoid threatening or belittling your child during this process. That's just a lousy way to start the day, for both of you. Some children respond positively to physical contact during this process, but avoid shaking them. A gentle back rub or stroking is preferable.

Nutritionists and psychologists agree on the importance of a calm, nutritious breakfast. This ensures that the child will have sufficient energy throughout the day. Again, the breakfast table provides a great opportunity for parents and children to converse, share, and discuss the upcoming day.

You should remain mindful that the child's "home leaving" is only a *portion* of his morning ritual. The manner in which he travels to school will also have a significant impact upon his attitude and performance when he arrives at class. If his carpool, school bus, or walk to school is difficult, your calm and organized wake-up rituals will be for naught. Evaluate the quality of his daily "commute" and try to ensure that it is as stress-free as possible.

If mornings are an ongoing problem and source of conflict, try discussing the issue in a calm way *in the evening*. Solicit the child's feelings and opinions about the morning routine, and generate ideas and processes that could make mornings less hectic and frenetic. Seriously consider her input and use this discussion as a method to improve her problem-solving skills.

Calendars, Schedules, Clocks

An oversized calendar in a child's room can be useful in developing a child's organizational skills and of invaluable assistance to his day-to-day functioning. Appointments, assignments, and activities can be written on Post-it notes and placed on the calendar. This allows him to change and adjust the schedule as the need arises. The stickies can be color coded to indicate the nature or importance of the activity.

The child may also benefit from carrying a copy of the weekly/monthly calendar to assist him in planning and remembering upcoming activities. When posting school assignments on his calendar, it is a good idea to record the day the assignment was given ("Dec. 1—Holiday customs report assigned"), the date it is due ("Dec. 15—Customs report due"), and the dates the child plans to work on the assignment ("Dec. 5—library research on customs"; "Dec. 7—Internet search on customs"; "Dec. 9—Interview Papa re: Christmas during World War II"; "Dec. 11—Write first draft, etc.").

Schedules and calendars should be placed prominently in the child's room or at another easily accessible location in the house. The schedule should be continually updated and should contain lists of "Things to Buy," "People to Call," and so on, in addition to upcoming activities, responsibilities, and deadlines. Foster the child's sense of accomplishment by encouraging him to cross out the activities as he completes them.

The child's alarm clock can be a valuable tool in the development of his organizational skills. This device can be used for many functions beyond the traditional wake-up. If dinner is at 6:30, have the child set his alarm for 6:15. When it rings, he knows it is time to initiate the predinner rituals of washing his hands, putting away his toys, and so on. The clock can also be used to remind him of bedtime or "homework time." You may wish to have an alarm clock in every room of the house. Kitchen timers are also useful for this purpose. ("Okay, John, we agreed that you should be able to take a bath and get dressed in thirty minutes. Let's set the timer, and when it rings, you should be all done.") Eventually, the child should be encouraged to set the timer himself.

A side benefit to the use of these devices is that it makes an inanimate object (the clock or timer) the reminder or "nag." Instead of Mom constantly reminding the child of the passing of time, the device plays this role. This can take considerable pressure off the parent-child relationship.

Dr. Robert Brooks, a noted psychologist who specializes in family issues, once told me of a mother and son who were involved in an ongoing conflict regarding her constant reminders to the child to take his daily medication. When Dr. Brooks interviewed the eleven-year-old, his primary complaint centered on Mom's constantly asking him, "Did you take your medicine?" A workable compromise was reached when Dr. Brooks and the boy taped an index card with the word "Medicine?" on it to a pencil. Mom agreed to simply hold up the sign whenever she wanted to know if the child had taken his daily dosage. No more nagging. No more conflict.

Cleaning and Maintaining the Bedroom

A source of parent-child conflict is the cleanliness and orderliness of the child's bedroom. It is exceedingly difficult for many youngsters with learning disorders to maintain the bedroom in a manner that meets adult standards. Although room cleanliness *is* important, the wise parent also knows that the child is entitled to a degree of privacy and must be allowed some choices regarding the bedroom. After all, that room is likely the only piece of "real estate" that truly belongs to her, and it is natural that she feels possessive of her bedroom and its contents. Children have minimal choices in their lives. They cannot select their homes, their schools, their relatives, or even their names! They often view their bedrooms as their sanctuaries.

Ask your child about her needs and desires related to the bedroom. Discuss various options for the storage of her belongings and her preference for open shelving or containers. Allow her to hang posters and pictures on the wall or provide her with bulletin boards. Again, it is *her* bedroom, and it is appropriate that it reflects her hobbies and interests.

The child may become easily overwhelmed when asked to clean a particularly messy room. Assist him by structuring the task and dividing the job into manageable chunks: "Pick up and put away all the clothes [or books or "blue things" or "sports stuff"] and let me know when you are finished."

Many children cannot clean their rooms effectively because they have difficulty with the skill of *revisualization*. This skill enables a person to recall a picture in his mind's eye. For example, if I were to say "Walter Cronkite," you could automatically retrieve a picture of Cronkite's face, even though you may not have seen him for several years. His visage is stored in your memory, from which you can access it on demand; you can *revisualize* it. You also use the skill of revisualization whenever you clean a room. When cleaning your cluttered, messy kitchen after a meal, you basically create a mental picture of the clean kitchen in your mind. Then you proceed to perform various tasks (clear off the counters, put dirty dishes in dishwasher, sponge off the table) until the kitchen matches the picture in your mind.

Many children with learning problems are deficient in the skill of revisualization. This accounts for their weakness in the area of spelling; they are unable to visualize the correct spelling of a word, so they cannot determine when a word has been misspelled. These children will also be unable to clean a room effectively.

On a Saturday morning, Dad sends the youngster to his bedroom with instructions to remain there until the room is clean. The child enters the room, is unable to picture what it looks like clean, and proceeds to be distracted by his baseball card collection or his skateboarding magazines. Because he is unable to picture the room clean, he has no idea how to begin the cleaning process. Dad enters the room an hour later and reprimands the boy for his lack of progress. He is unaware that he has assigned his child a true Mission Impossible.

Asking the child who is unable to revisualize to clean his room independently is identical to asking an adult to assemble a 400-piece jigsaw puzzle without having seen the picture on the puzzle box cover. Because the adult is unaware of what the finished product should look like, he is unable to develop a strategy to assemble the puzzle. Because the child is unable to picture his clean, orderly room, he is unable to construct a process that will organize it.

The solution to this problem is relatively simple. Assist the child in cleaning the room and putting all of his belongings in their proper places. Then take photographs of the room from several angles and post them on the child's bulletin board. Now he doesn't need to revisualize in order to clean the room. He need only refer to the photos and arrange things in the manner that matches the picture.

Children with learning problems are often "pack rats" who tend to save useless objects ("Grandma, are you gonna throw away that broken radio? Can I have it?") and are reluctant to discard *anything*. Discuss this with the child and occasionally assist him in purging his belongings and throwing away the more useless articles in his collection. Although it is not a particularly attractive option, some parents have found it useful to place a large, industrial-size trash barrel in the child's room. He is then far more likely to discard the 3'-by-3' sheets of Styrofoam that the school's janitor foolishly discarded . . . and he carried home on the bus because he *had* to have them!

Many parents have found it useful to use color coding and labeling. Label each dresser drawer to indicate that drawer's contents (e.g., pants, underwear). Color code the poles in his closet to indicate where he should hang his shirts, pants, or jackets.

Organization experts point out that kindergarten classrooms are among the most orderly and user-friendly spaces on earth. There is a place for everything and everything is in its place. But the real reason that kindergartens are so orderly is because the room is divided into "centers," each with a single, specific function. There is an arts and crafts center, a story center, and a building block center. Everyone knows where to go for each activity, and further, they recognize that it is not appropriate to use a center for a nondesignated purpose.

If possible, set up the child's bedroom in a similar fashion. Provide him with a desk for homework and a table for models. Discourage him from using his table or his bed to read or study. Each area should contain the tools needed for the designated activity. The study area, for example, should have pens, pencils, tape, a stapler, scissors, and any other material the child might need. His model table should have all the tools and materials that he needs to construct his toy planes. This type of structure enables the child to know where to put and store his materials. Use bookcases or folding screens as room dividers to denote the various sections.

Children are often reluctant to discard souvenirs or mementos from activities that they have enjoyed. Ticket stubs, programs, or postcards become treasured possessions. Install a "memory bulletin board" in the bedroom where she can tack her mementos. Avoid being overly judgmental about the objects that the child considers precious.

Remember that one man's treasure is another man's junk. I have carried a ticket from a Eugene McCarthy for President rally at Fenway Park since 1968 and have *never* thrown away a Red Sox ticket stub! You probably also have cherished mementos that would be meaningless to others. Your child is entitled to have some as well.

Below are some additional suggestions for helping your child maintain a relatively clean and orderly room:

- Install hooks in the closet so he can hang appropriate items.
- Lower the closet poles and shelves to the child's height.
- Keep a "cleanup kit" in the child's room containing a sponge, whisk broom, etc., and encourage the child to clean up messes as they occur.
- Reserve and label a shelf in the bathroom for the child's toiletries and supplies.

- Allow the child to have a table in his room for unfinished puzzles and ongoing building projects.

The Book Bag

For many children, the book bag is a black hole that contains countless worksheets, handouts, clipped newspaper articles, baseball cards, toys, and innumerable inanimate and even living objects. Again, this may be due to the child's inability to prioritize and organize. Unable to discriminate between objects that are important and those that are useless, he saves *everything*.

Telling the child, "Clean out your book bag," is an exercise in frustration for you and for him. He requires significant and sensitive assistance for this seemingly simple task.

Begin by having the child remove *everything* from his bag. Then assist him in deciding what material he *needs* to function effectively in school (e.g., history book, science notebook, ruler, five pens, five pencils, eraser). One by one, place these objects in the bag. Once the "needs list" is completed, allow him to select two or three items that he *wants* (as opposed to *needs*) to take to school (yo-yo, picture of Fido, baseball cards) and allow him to place those objects in his bag. Any material that remains in the pile is thrown away or placed somewhere else. By completing this ritual on a regular basis, you prevent the "black hole" phenomenon, and he will find that the objects that he *needs* for school will be more readily available.

Some parents find it helps to provide the child with two book bags: one for morning classes and one for afternoon courses. Or perhaps the child may have one book bag that she keeps in school and a second that she brings home each evening. Many children respond well to this format and learn to transfer materials from one bag to another.

Homework

There is no task that is more challenging for the disorganized child than homework. The completion of nightly homework often creates a whirlwind of chaos, confusion, and conflict in the home. Some parents have asked that a "no-homework" clause be added to the child's Individualized Educational Plan. I believe that this is counterproductive and inappropriate. Children who have difficulty learning benefit greatly from a nightly review or reinforcement of the skills that they are covering in school. Homework is more than a "necessary evil." It is a fundamental part of a child's academic development.

Homework that is appropriate serves several valuable functions. It provides an unparalleled opportunity to review material that has been mastered and to reinforce material that is nearly mastered. It also fosters responsibility and can add immeasurably to the child's fund of general knowledge and cultural literacy. Homework should be a priority in every family's daily schedule.

Sometimes, however, the homework assignments are not appropriate. Such assignments can be the source of parent-child conflict and frustration. That's because many teachers assign homework that is ineffective and inappropriate. A good homework assignment is designed mindful of the Rs.

Homework should be:

- *Relevant*: The assignment should be directly related to the area of study that is being currently covered in class.
- A *Review*: New, unexplored subject matter should *not* be assigned for homework. Rather, the assignment should be a review or reinforcement of material *already covered* in class.
- *Realistic*: While in school, the child is in an "academic mindset" and in a relatively distraction-free environment. There he may be quite productive. In contrast, at home he is fatigued and besieged by innumerable distractions and diversions. He will be far less productive. Therefore, I recommend that a teacher keep in mind the "3:1 formula": the child will require three times as long to complete an assignment at home as at school. A worksheet that he can complete in ten minutes in the classroom will require thirty minutes at home.

If your child's homework assignments do not meet the 3R criteria, talk to the teacher.

Parents can assist the child in completing homework by increasing the structure of the home environment. One of the most useful devices is the assignment sheet. The traditional assignment sheet used by most schools is generally ineffective for the child who has significant difficulty with organization. These sheets were designed to assist children who learn and remember in a traditional way, and they do not meet the unique needs of the child with learning problems. In fact, these interventions may actually *increase* the child's sense of disorganization and frustration. This child requires an assignment sheet that addresses her memory, attention, and organizational deficits.

The assignment sheet should provide ample room for the child (or teacher) to record the assignment in detail. The child with ADD will often require specific instructions to accompany the assignment in order to complete it effectively and efficiently: for instance, "Be sure to use pencil only on this assignment," or "The information for this assignment is in your science book. You will need your science notebook to complete this assignment."

Assignment sheets should be individualized for each student. It is always a good idea to place a checklist of the child's books at the bottom of the assignment sheet. Instruct the child to place a checkmark next to each book that he will need to bring home *as soon as the teacher posts or announces the assignment*. This way, he can scan the book list at the end of the day and retrieve the books that he needs. A parent of one of my students once lamented that he was on a first-name basis with the school's janitorial night crew due to his innumerable after-hours trips to the school to retrieve the books that his LD daughter "just *had* to have"!

The Learning Project at Park Tudor School in Indianapolis made a very effective addition to its assignment sheet by adding a section wherein the student could write in his evening and weekend plans, appointments, and activities. This enables the child to better organize and prioritize his time. For example, if he writes in "Cub Scout meeting at 7 P.M. on Tuesday," he is aware that his homework must be completed *before* dinner on that evening. He is prepared to address his nonschool activities and his academic responsibilities.

The child might also benefit from an assignment sheet that requires him to write in an estimate of how long it will take him to complete a given assignment. When the teacher assigns twenty math problems, the child can estimate that he will need thirty minutes to compute these examples and he writes "30" in the designated section of his assignment sheet. At the end of the school day, he can total up the amount of time that he will need to complete that evening's assignments.

If the child is not assigned homework in a class or subject, he should be encouraged to write "no homework" on his assignment sheet rather than merely leaving the block blank. That way, he will definitely know that no assignment was given, rather than wonder later if he forgot to record it. Require him to maintain three folders in his book bag: one for "Homework to Do," one for "Completed Homework," and one for "Notices and Permission Slips."

Many children with learning problems have bursts of energy and creativity and may work on an assignment with great zeal for ten or fifteen minutes and then wish to put it aside and tackle a different task. As a result, they often arrive at school with several half-completed assignments. This is a source of frustration for them and for their teachers. Parents should discourage this work pattern and encourage the child to work on one assignment to completion. In fact, some parents will collect all the assignments before the child begins his homework and then give the child one project at a time once the previous task is completed.

If this intervention is not successful or possible, encourage the child to maintain a pile of half-finished assignments that must be completed before the homework is considered "done." If the child puts the uncompleted homework away in his book, it is highly unlikely that he will remember to retrieve it or complete it. Once again—out of sight, out of mind.

Academic Accommodations

Under federal laws and guidelines, schools are required to make modifications and accommodations for children with measurable special needs. Many adjustments have been devised to assist children with organizational and executive functioning difficulties. Unfortunately, many of these well-intentioned accommodations are misguided and actually *add to* the burden of the child who is unable to plan, prioritize, and organize his environment.

One of the most ineffective accommodations is *extended time* on tests, quizzes, and assignments. This strategy is often viewed as a "cure-all" for struggling students, but it is generally ineffective. As University of Utah professor Sam Goldstein reminds us, "Learning disability is not a disorder of ability, but rather a disorder of consistency." The child's inability to perform and produce on a consistent basis is a source of great frustration for him. Merely giving him extra time to complete a task will do little to solve or ameliorate the problem. In fact, this strategy may actually *reinforce* the child's tendency to dawdle and procrastinate, because it decreases the external structure and negatively impacts his ability to focus on the task.

A more effective strategy would be to divide the large task into several smaller, more manageable tasks. For example, on Monday, the class is assigned twenty state capitals to memorize by Friday. For the struggling child, the teacher should require him to learn five capitals by Tuesday, ten capitals by Wednesday, fifteen capitals by Thursday, and the remaining five by Friday. This *restructuring* of the assignment is far more effective than merely shortening the requirements (only memorizing ten capitals) or changing the due date (five extra days to learn the twenty capitals).

A second overused accommodation is *untimed testing*. Although this strategy may alleviate a child's test anxiety a bit, it generally does little to improve his test performance. This technique is appropriate and effective for children with significant processing difficulties, but it often has a deleterious effect on other struggling students. It merely gives them more time to stare blankly at the assignment. Again, a more effective strategy is to divide the test or task into manageable chunks and give the sections to the child one at a time.

Here are some strategies and techniques to help a child organize his environment.

- Provide the child with a heavyweight cardboard or plastic envelope marked "Completed Homework" and instruct him to put completed assignments in the envelope as he finishes them. They will be readily available for him to submit the next day, and thus you prevent the "I know that I did it, but can't find it" phenomenon.
- If your child has a series of tasks or assignments to complete,

encourage her to do the most difficult and challenging ones *first*. Her natural tendency might be to save such tasks for *last*. Explain to her that it makes more sense to tackle the toughest task while she is fresh rather than when she is fatigued and frustrated.

- Many well-intentioned parents provide *too much* help with homework. Mom invests hours of blood, sweat, and tears guiding, coaching, assisting, and copiloting the child through a difficult worksheet. The end result is a letter-perfect assignment submitted to the teacher. In response to this, the teacher (unaware that the assignment required hours of work and caused the child to go to bed in tears) merely continues to assign work that is of similar difficulty and complexity to the child. If an assignment is inappropriately difficult for a child, write a note to the teacher explaining this. If you fail to do this, the child will continue to receive work at that level, because all the evidence that the teacher is receiving (completed, well-done assignments) indicates that the work is well within the child's capabilities.

- Maintain a shoebox or old briefcase filled with homework supplies (pens, rulers, paper, eraser, dictionary) that the child has readily available to him during homework time.

- An additional *R* in the aforementioned three Rs of homework should be *R*esponse. The teacher should collect and correct homework assignments, and the child should be recognized and reinforced for performing well on homework assignments. If your child reports that he never sees his homework after it is submitted, talk to the teacher.

- Provide your child with a dry-erase board and/or bulletin board to keep in his room. Use it to post reminders and display souvenirs.

- Evaluate the child's ability to tell time. Many children with learning disabilities become quite adept at "faking it." By mimicking the behavior of others, they can *appear* to tell time but actually cannot. Encourage the child to wear a watch.

- A disorganized child will have marked difficulty dividing large tasks into smaller, more manageable ones. This skill requires a significant amount of organizing, monitoring, and prioritizing. When the child receives a major long-term assignment, assist her by dividing the task into substeps and designing a schedule for the completion of these steps.

- Encourage the child to create, use, and maintain to-do lists in which she outlines tasks and assignments and crosses each one out when complete. This strategy improves organization skills while also celebrating and reinforcing the completion of each task.

- Provide the child with a positive model of structure and organization by adhering closely to the family's schedule. If Thursday is Take-Out Food Night, try to vary from this ritual as little as possible. Children with special needs prosper in a more predictable environment.

- Praise and reinforce any and all efforts that your child makes toward improving his organizational skills at home and at school. Remember to praise the *effort,* not the *result.*

- Children should be encouraged to complete homework at the same time and in the same place each evening.

A wise man once counseled, "You need not attend every battle to which you are invited." In other words, "Pick your fights!" This is valuable counsel for a parent of a disorganized child. His room may *never* meet your ideal criteria regarding cleanliness and orderliness, and may well not meet the standard of the other children's rooms in the home. Remember that this may be beyond the child's control. If this issue is a constant source of friction and conflict between you and your child, you may want to adjust your standards a bit. That's why bedrooms have doors . . . just close it!

Afterword

Here are more organization strategies that may be helpful:

- Set aside a specific and consistent time period each night for study time. Discourage any interruptions (e.g., no visitors or phone calls during this time). This time can be used for homework, reading, writing letters, and so on.

- Dr. Mel Levine reminds us that "the longer a child is disorganized, the more difficult it is for him to become an organized person." Begin organizational training with the child in the early grades.

- Remember that just as you are frustrated by a child's lack of organizational skills, it is also a source of anxiety and embarrassment *for the child.* Never publicly embarrass or humiliate the child for his organizational difficulties.

- Children with severe organizational deficits require intensive, consistent, and supportive communication between home and school.

- In order to motivate students to invest themselves in improving their organizational skills, try this: if a student fails to bring in appropriate materials (e.g., sharpened pencils, composition paper), do not reinforce this by providing him with the materials he failed to bring. Instead, give him less desirable materials to use (short, chewed-up pencils, scrap paper). This is not a punishment but a natural consequence.

- Reward, recognize, and reinforce improvements and progress in organizational skills.

- Color code, color code, color code! It works!

- These children can become quite skilled at indicating that they understand instructions or directions although they actually do not. Check for understanding by asking the child to repeat or rephrase your directions before she begins the task.

- Help your child improve her organization skills with respect and consideration for her individual goals, temperament, and affinities. You may view her collection of teen magazines as useless junk, but you need to appreciate and recognize her attachment to them. You may be a morning person and prefer to shower before breakfast; however, your child's temperament may be more receptive to an evening bath and a less hectic morning.

- Unfortunately, many children with learning problems have great difficulty keeping track of their belongings. As a result, they often lose or misplace things. Consider this when making purchases for them. It may be best to buy the low-end portable

CD player and the less expensive pocket calculator. These items may very well end up "among the missing," and you will be less distressed when you need to replace them.

- Allow your disorganized child to make decisions, but provide him with only a few options. Don't ask, "What would you like to wear to school tomorrow?" Rather, ask, "Would you prefer to wear your blue sweater or your brown one?"

- Parents are often reluctant to assign chores that are to be completed in the early morning. Interestingly, morning chores are often beneficial for the disorganized child, because they contribute to the structure of the morning. Don't hesitate to assign the child a task such as feeding the dog, helping with breakfast, or watching the baby while you make your bed.

- Although it will be a difficult skill for the disorganized child to master, reinforce the concept of "a place for everything and everything in its place." Assist him by providing special hooks for him to hang his keys on, a soap dish on his dresser for his wallet and watch, and a designated place for his book bag. This will help to decrease time spent searching for things and may also enable him to develop a useful, lifelong organizational habit.

- A child with organizational problems may have great difficulty understanding and complying with a general instruction such as "Clean the garage" or "Pick up the yard." Provide her with a list that *describes* what constitutes "cleaning the garage" (e.g., sweep floor, put tools in proper drawers, discard empty boxes, stack paint cans).

- It is important to understand that most children with learning disorders do not necessarily learn from experience as other children do. Keep this in mind when the child makes the same mistake repeatedly.

- Your child may benefit from "hurdle help" when attempting an organizational task. This technique consists of assisting the child with the initial stages of a task in order to get him started: "Spencer, you need to put your clothes in your closet. I will help you with the first few, and then you can finish while I walk the dog." The child is often able to complete the task once he is given a good start.

CHAPTER SEVEN

Siblings and Other Strangers

Two Stories

Andrew stormed into my office ten minutes after our meeting was scheduled to begin. He heaved his overloaded book bag onto the couch and glared at me. "I *know* that he's my brother and I *know* that he has trouble in school . . . but Paul is making me nuts! *He's* the older brother. *I'm* the one that is supposed to get the extra attention, but it's always about Paul! My family plans their whole lives around him. Mom tells me that Paul has an attention deficit, but—if you ask me—I'm the one that has a deficit in attention. Nobody pays attention to me. It's just not fair."

After several minutes, Andrew calmed down and was able to rationally explain his very legitimate concerns. "Last summer we had to sell our cabin by the lake so we could pay Paul's tuition at his special school. Every afternoon Mom takes Paul to some kind of appointment or another. I can't remember the last time she was home when I got off the bus. Mom, Dad, and even Grandma are always arguing about Paul, and we don't go to Uncle Frankie's house anymore because Paul plays so rough with their new puppies. The kids on the school bus are always asking me why Paul acts so strange, and last

169

week Paul's teacher had to get me out of class to help Paul because he refused to take off his boots.

"I can usually handle all of this, but sometimes he makes me so mad. He argues about everything, and he's always asking me for help doing things, but he never thanks me. He borrows my stuff without asking, and last week he forgot that he had my headphones on and he jumped into the pool. Wrecked 'em."

I tried to explain to Andrew that sibling rivalry and conflict were both normal and natural, but he wasn't buying it. "I know that brothers fight," the eleven-year-old responded. "I fight with my other brother Eric all the time. But it's different with Paul. I try to get along with him. I really do. But we fight a lot, and Mom always takes his side. 'Give him what he wants,' she says, 'or he'll cry.'

"But I feel badly about something I did last night," Andrew continued. "Paul had been working on his Scout workbook last night. I was watching TV and he came in and took the remote control. Mom told him to get back to work and he got mad and threw the remote. Mom said no more TV—for anyone—for the rest of the night.

"I was so mad that I snuck into his room and hid his workbook under his dresser. He went to bed upset and crying. But I don't care. He had it coming! He embarrasses me and never helps around the house."

"But he's your brother," I replied.

"You know what, Mr. Lavoie," Andrew responded slowly. "I didn't ask for a brother like Paul. Sometimes I wish he wasn't my brother. My life would be *much* easier."

Conversely . . .

Several years ago, I was facilitating a meeting of families at a Cape Cod hotel. All of the participants were facing the challenge of helping their learning disabled child make the transition from adolescence to adulthood—no easy task. We discussed a wide range of topics, from academics to employment to housing issues.

At the end of the day, we conducted a free-flowing discussion in an informal round-table format. All attendees were encouraged to contribute their ideas, feelings, and opinions.

As invariably happens at such a gathering, the discussion soon turned to sibling relationships. Several parents decried the heightened sibling rivalry that they battled daily in their households; others debated "fairness issues"; still others shared anecdotes about the unique pleasures and pressures of raising a family that includes a child with special needs.

Midway through the meeting, Brooke took the floor. A twenty-one-year-old college student, she has a sister, Hayley, with profound learning and language problems. She began, "I love my sister very much. I am probably her best friend. I know that my parents are getting older and they worry about what will happen to Hayley after they're gone. I recognize the fact that I will be responsible for Hayley some day. But that's fine with me. Like my mom often says, 'Brooke, we don't expect you to become Hayley's mom and dad—just be the best sister you can be!'"

Brooke continued, "But I know and welcome one simple fact: any man who says 'I do' to me had better realize that he's saying 'I do' to my Hayley, too."

The audience broke into spontaneous, heartfelt applause . . . and a tear or two.

Sibling relationships are a necessary and invaluable ingredient in the development of social competencies. These relationships form a child's first social network and will have a lifelong impact upon his ability to function successfully with people outside the family. Over the years, siblings may play many varied roles in one another's lives, including friend, companion, guide, nemesis, teacher, protector, leader, follower, enemy, confidant, competitor, and role model.

These relationships are particularly valuable—and decidedly more complex—when one of the siblings has a learning or social disorder. As a longtime administrator of residential schools, I have seen hundreds of these relationships in action. These sibling relationships can be a source of inspiration, guidance, and support for the child who struggles daily in school. However, the complexity of these relationships and the unique challenges created by the learning disability can also create great tension and frustration among family members.

Reflect for a moment upon your own sibling relationships as a child. Recall the myriad social/interpersonal skills that you learned from your brothers and sisters. Among these crucial skills were:

- sharing
- turn taking
- empathy
- regulation of aggressiveness
- cooperation
- trust
- ability to deal with change
- compromise
- loyalty
- ability to deal with conflict
- teamwork
- sportsmanship
- accepting/giving criticism
- accepting/giving compliments
- following rules

Clearly, a child who does not have the benefit of positive sibling relationships is at a marked disadvantage. The sibling relationship is the only truly lifelong relationship that we have. Our relationships with our parents will last forty to fifty years, but our link to our siblings is likely to last sixty to eighty years. This relationship takes on even greater significance in the opening of the twenty-first century because of some recent cultural and sociological changes. As family size decreases and human life span increases, our sibling relationships become even more significant and meaningful in our lives. Today's children are being raised in families that are mobile and stressed; further, both parents are often employed full time. Those factors increase the child's dependency upon his or her siblings for support, care, and friendship.

The relationship between siblings develops and changes throughout the life span. As young children, we are greatly dependent upon our siblings for companionship. Throughout the elementary school years, this dependency decreases as we make contacts with classmates and teammates in our communities. At adolescence, the sibling relationship can assume a degree of ambivalence or even hostility. As we become adults, the relationship becomes more solid and mature as we recognize that our common heritage and shared experiences are far more significant than the petty differences and disagreements that had previously been the flashpoints for conflict. At old age, as children move away and spouses die, siblings often become significant sources of support and comfort to one another.

Rivalry, jealousy, and conflict among siblings is normal and natural. Parents should be cautious not to overreact to the typical rough-and-tumble relationships between brothers and sisters. The bond between most siblings is strong enough to overcome the ritualistic teasing and hassling that often characterize these relationships in the preteen and adolescent years. Again, reflect upon your own sibling relationships and you will realize that most of the rivalries, slights, and skirmishes that you shared with brothers and sisters during childhood are now long forgotten and forgiven.

The reasons for sibling rivalry and skirmishes are quite understandable. A child's relationship with his parents is characterized by the fact that both the child and the parent are fully aware that the latter has more experience, knowledge, and control than the former. However, in a sibling pairing, there exists an ongoing battle for superiority, power, and control. Contributing to this conflict is each child's persistent belief that his sibling is receiving a disproportionate amount of parental time, energy, resources, attention, and love. This makes fighting between siblings far more common than conflict between classmates or teammates. It has been said that you can select your friends, but you can't choose your family. This fact, coupled with the intense exposure that siblings have to one another, creates a hotbed for hostility and conflict.

The complexity of these relationships is greatly enhanced when one of the siblings has significant learning and language problems. The pleasures, pressures, and intensity of the sibling relationship are magnified. Research in this area indicates that the quality of the sibling relationship within a "special-needs family" is influenced by a wide variety of factors, including family size, ages and genders of children, and parental attitudes.

LD or CLK?

Several years ago, I developed a workshop entitled F.A.T. City. The acronym stands for "Frustration, Anxiety, and Tension," and the workshop was designed to give parents and teachers a brief firsthand experience with having a learning disability. Every year, I would also do the seminar with siblings of the children at the school where I was employed. The workshop was generally held on Saturday morning, and, as you can imagine, I usually had a less than enthusiastic audience.

The classroom would be filled with adolescents who did not know one another. They generally had only two things in common:

1. They had a brother or sister with a significant learning disorder.
2. They would prefer to be home in bed!

I started the session in a unique way. "Tell me," I began, "all the things that you *cannot stand* about your LD brother or sister! What does he or she do that really drives you nuts?"

The participants generally cast their eyes downward. They were understandably reluctant to share this personal information in such a public setting. They shuffled their feet and avoided eye contact. After a few moments of uncomfortable silence, one of them would raise his hand. "It bothers me when he keeps asking me how to spell words when he is doing homework."

A second sibling added, "Yeah, and how he always borrows my stuff and embarrasses me whenever my girlfriend comes to the house."

A third chimed in, "My brother embarrasses me a lot, too. But what really makes me crazy is when it takes him so long to get ready in the morning. He's always making me late for school."

Once we had thirty or so behaviors listed on the board, we stopped to examine and discuss each one. I introduced a key to categorize each of the behaviors. We wrote "LD" next to each behavior that is a direct result of the sibling's learning disability. We wrote "CLK" next to each behavior that occurs, quite simply, because the sibling is a "crummy little kid."

This simple activity is used to teach a profoundly important concept: Siblings disagree. Siblings fight. Siblings tease, argue, embarrass, and frustrate. The relationships between brothers and sisters are inherently conflictual. Problems among siblings are normal, natural, and nearly unavoidable. Therefore, the child who has a learning disabled sibling cannot blame every skirmish on the LD! Even if the sibling did *not* have a learning disorder, interpersonal problems would still occur.

"My LD brother teases me!" That's CLK—*all* brothers tease.

"My LD sister uses the phone too much." That's CLK—most sisters monopolize the telephone.

"My sister is always late!" That could be a combination of CLK and LD. Lots of people are chronically late, but your sister's problem might be more complicated and severe because many kids with learning disabilities and Attention Deficit Disorder have trouble understanding concepts related to time.

"My mother is always going to meetings about my brother. She's gone a lot!" That's purely LD. It is your mom's responsibility to advocate for your brother so that he will receive an appropriate education.

"My brother uses my CD Walkman"—CLK.

"He uses it in the shower"—that would be LD!

It is critically important that *all* parties understand why you should not overreact to normal sibling rivalry, conflict, and friction. We need to remember that even if the brother did *not* have LD, siblings would *not* get along all the time. Further, each and every squabble is not related to the disability. Parents must be aware that when the LD child acts like a CLK, discipline and reprimands are both appropriate and necessary.

Early in my career, I worked with families who were raising children with severe physical disabilities. Many of these children used wheelchairs, hearing aids, or other orthopedic devices. They often had physical traits that made their exceptionality immediately obvious to all. I was consistently struck by the warm, supportive relationships that existed between the disabled children and their siblings. After thirty years of working with families of learning disabled children, I have found that these positive relationships occur far less often in the LD population. I attribute this to the fact that the LD child's problems are largely hidden or invisible. There is no outward appearance of a disability, so his idiosyncratic and age-inappropriate behavior is often misinterpreted as willful and purposeful by others in his environment—including his siblings. This "invisibility factor" makes it extremely difficult for a child to understand and accept his sibling's disability.

Development of
Normal Sibling Relationships

Before we discuss the unique relationships between disabled and nondisabled siblings, we should examine the "normal" development of the sibling relationship. Only when we understand what is normal can we begin to understand that which is abnormal.

The noted Gesell Institute has conducted extensive studies on the development of sibling relationships. It appears that in most families, these connections follow a relatively predictable and consistent trajectory. The process is a positive, albeit slow, one.

At eighteen months, a child's self-centered nature and brief attention span make sibling contacts fleeting and transitory. He generally receives caring and pleasurable contacts from his older siblings, who delight in his ability to imitate and entertain. Sibling conflict at this age is rare unless the children are very close in age.

From ages two through three, the child is generally "the baby" of the family, and older siblings accommodate his needs and wishes. They are cautioned never to hit the baby and are urged to keep him happy, lest he cry. This is the inalienable right of the youngest child.

If a new baby enters the family, the two- to three-year-old must abruptly surrender his appealing role as the baby and the rights and privileges that accompany it. Jealousy and confusion can occur. The child may even (intentionally or unintentionally) hurt the "new" baby. Many pediatricians feel that the fabled "terrible twos" are largely due to the child's inability to understand or accept the new baby's role in the family and the sudden, significant shift in his own role. Cooperative, sharing play is a developmental impossibility for the child at this age. His mantra of "Mine! Mine! Mine!" illustrates his possessiveness.

As the child enters his fourth year, he can become rather affectionate toward his younger sibling and—simultaneously—very desirous of the adventures and experiences of his older sibling. This stage is also characterized by increased inconsistency and unpredictability of behavior. This wide variation of behavior is often a source of conflict between the child and his older brothers and sisters. Parents are surprised by his well-mannered, cooperative behavior at nursery school when contrasted with his conflictual, erratic behavior at home.

In the fifth year, the child tends to become less bossy and demanding. He is often kind and mothering to his much younger siblings and is better able to share, take turns, and cooperate. He is eager for approval from parents and older siblings.

The six-year-old often experiences conflict with *all* siblings, both younger and older. At this age, the child tends to be domineering and demanding. He has significant difficulty conforming and compromising and becomes less tolerant of younger siblings. He also takes pleasure in seeing siblings cry and "get in trouble," and he will often instigate situations that create conflict. He may also become an inveterate tattler and involve himself inappropriately in affairs of others.

At this age, he may become extraordinarily competitive and be unable to tolerate losing. He will even cheat or quit the game if victory seems unattainable. He becomes intensely aware of the parents' distribution of attention and goods and will often complain that he is being treated unfairly. All of these behaviors may cause him to be viewed as a bully by his younger siblings and a pest by his older ones.

At age seven, the child tends to become less aggressive and less competitive. He may become a bit gloomy, and this new "mellowness" is welcomed by his brothers and sisters. He tends to get along better with his siblings but may focus his negativity and rejection on one particular brother or sister. Although he may tattle less, he continues to have a significant misconception of fairness and will complain vehemently and often about it. He may enjoy his role as teacher and protector of younger siblings. He will tend to have a contentious relationship with the siblings who are close to him in age, yet may "worship" his brothers or sisters who are significantly older than he.

At eight years old, the child may become more aggressive and outgoing. He tends to be dramatic and may be described as having "a chip on his shoulder." He enjoys arguing and is unlikely to overlook even the smallest mistake made by any household member. He may become extremely sensitive about younger brothers "tagging along" with him and desire the company of his older siblings (although he is often rejected by them). On the positive side, the eight-year-old tends to be less competitive and may become more gracious in victory or defeat.

The nine-year-old often begins to greatly improve his relationships with his siblings. He might become more protective of his younger brothers and more proud of his older ones (although conflict with those close to his own age may continue). In conflictual situations, he becomes fixated on "who started it." The nine-year-old is beginning to nurture friendships with nonfamily members, and his siblings may become a source of embarrassment and disgust for him.

The child's tenth year is often characterized by inconsistency. At times he will get along famously with his siblings, but conflict may erupt suddenly with little or no provocation. He may tire easily of younger siblings and complain often that they "get away with everything." However, there is also a good deal of good-natured horseplay and lively, animated conversation. He begins to recognize that his older siblings consider him a pest, so he may try to improve this relationship by acting more mature and worldly. Basically, the tenth year is characterized by an overall and substantial improvement in sibling relationships.

However, a significant downturn may occur during the eleventh year. At eleven, children often become temperamental and quarrelsome. Although physical skirmishes occur less frequently, arguments, name calling, and teasing are commonplace. Parents often cite the child's constant needling of siblings and his preoccupation with his possessions and his privacy. He also may tend to be bossy and intolerant of younger children, but become angry when older siblings attempt to boss *him*.

The twelfth year often heralds an improvement in sibling relations and a more mature understanding of the nature of fairness. Although conflicts continue between the child and his immediate younger siblings, he may be very helpful and affectionate toward the youngest children in the family. The child may develop strategies to avoid sibling conflicts, and he tends to find less enjoyment in squabbles with his brothers and sisters.

At thirteen, most conflicts center on the younger sibling's tendency to use, borrow, or damage the child's possessions. Physical conflicts are rare at this stage. Although the child may be moody and somewhat unpredictable, he is also gaining and reflecting greater insight into the needs and temperaments of the other family members. The greatest and most notable improvement occurs between the child and the siblings who are closest to him in birth order. True sibling friendships begin to emerge. The opinions and approval of older brothers and sisters become critically important to the thirteen-year-old.

The fourteenth year may feature another backslide in sibling relationships, as the child becomes critical and judgmental toward the overall personalities of younger siblings (e.g., "He's such a show-off," "I hate his voice") and may even find fault with the previously worshiped older siblings. The fourteen-year-old recognizes that he is not perfect and is willing to accept some blame for conflicts that may occur. Complaints about parental partiality decrease markedly. Positive relationships continue to grow between the fourteen-year-old and the sibling(s) closest to his age.

The fifteen-year-old may bask in the admiration of his younger siblings and often defend his brothers and sisters when the parents reprimand or punish them. ("Give Jimmy a break, Dad. He didn't mean to lose your fishing pole.") Although the child continues to be annoyed by the younger siblings' meddling, he may develop effective techniques to prevent difficulties from occurring. The relationships with siblings who are close in age are deepened and strengthened, as are those with much older brothers and sisters.

The sixteenth year finds a significant decrease in the amount of time that a child spends with his siblings. As his independence increases, he spends more time in the community and his most important relationships are with nonfamily members. Sibling conflicts decrease markedly, and children report that they do what they can to avoid these squabbles. The sixteen-year-old continues to enjoy the admiration of his younger siblings and the mature relationship that develops with his older brothers and sisters.

It may bring some comfort to realize that these relationships naturally change over the years and do tend to improve. However, it is important to remember that your child will not necessarily adhere to this typical pattern, and your experience may differ greatly from the "schedule" that was born of this research. As I reflect upon the relationship that developed between and among our own three children, I recognize that there were some departures and differences from the outline as their relationships were forming.

Sibling Relationships in the Learning Disabled Family

As we have seen, the connection between siblings is a complex and dynamic one. Many variables affect the development of the sibling relationship. This complexity is greatly magnified when one child has a special need. The balance of power and the defined roles in these relationships are significantly complicated and compromised when one child is disabled. I was told once by a frustrated twelve-year-old, "My parents are always telling me to help my brother with homework and chores. He's fourteen! *He's* supposed to be helping *me*!"

As parents, you will need to help the nondisabled sibling gain a better understanding of the nature and needs of her sibling with a learning or social disability. Without this guidance, a positive relationship between and among the family members is unlikely to develop.

Leo Tolstoy said, "Happy families are all alike; every unhappy family is unhappy in its own way." You must recognize that the special-needs child will present a significant challenge to the process of developing a "happy family." The child, through no fault or choice of her own, will serve to further complicate a highly complex process.

Primary among these complications is the family's need to alter normal family patterns to accommodate the needs of the learning disabled child. A disproportionate amount of the family's financial resources may be spent on tutoring, counseling, or special schooling.

Vacations and other "extras" may be scaled back. The younger children may be expected to assume some of the roles and responsibilities of the older special-needs child because he is simply unable to complete them. A frustrated sibling once told me, "It's as if Bobby is the sun and the rest of the family are the planets. All of the family's plans circle around Bobby. It's *always* about Bobby!" The child was right.

This family dynamic can greatly heighten the sense of competition among siblings. The children feel that they are thrust into an intense contest wherein they must battle for their fair share of parental time, energy, and resources. This can greatly complicate the relationships among *all* family members. The family dynamic may be further confounded by the nondisabled child's confusion about the nature of his sibling's problems. He may be unable to comprehend how his normal-appearing sister can act and behave in such an abnormal way. Feelings of confusion, anger, guilt, and jealousy can occur. As the sibling comes to better understand the struggles of the disabled child—and the parents—he may feel the need to be the "perfect child" to compensate for the problems of his sister.

Unfortunately, it appears that the presence of a learning disabled child in the family *does* have a negative or detrimental impact upon the development and dynamics of many families. Some studies have shown that nondisabled siblings suffer from increased anxiety, decreased sociability, and more conflicts with parents. They may be greatly confused by their own contradictory feelings of anger, embarrassment, guilt, and affection toward the child with a learning disability. This confusion may manifest itself in behavioral and/or emotional difficulties.

However, there also appear to be positive, long-term effects for the siblings of learning disabled children. These children tend to be more mature and less self-centered than their peers. They may have a unique insight into the human condition and be admirably intolerant of prejudice and stereotyping. As adolescents and adults, nondisabled children often develop a deep sense of pride and admiration for the struggles and accomplishments of their brothers and sisters. As Brooke, from my story of the meeting in Cape Cod, once told me, "Nothing comes easily for Hayley. Yet she keeps on trying. She is my hero."

Clearly, the presence of a special-needs child in the family can have positive *and* negative impacts. It is the parents' role to accentuate the former and minimize the latter. In order to do this, you must examine and understand the myriad factors at play. Some factors (e.g., birth order, ages) are beyond your control, yet many (e.g., attitudes, caregiving responsibilities) can be modified and adjusted. Let's examine some of the family characteristics that can affect sibling relationships in special-needs families.

Family Size: Although my personal experience finds glaring exceptions to this rule, the conventional wisdom holds that "the larger the family, the smoother the development." In smaller families (two or three children), the nondisabled child may feel great pressure to care and compensate for the LD child. In larger families, these responsibilities are spread over many children. It is important to note that the pressure felt by the nondisabled sibling is often self-imposed.

Gender: Girls tend to adjust to the special needs of the LD sibling more effectively than do boys. Girls are more often assigned the responsibility for caring for and guiding the disabled sibling. However, girls more often manifest behavioral problems in response to the LD sibling.

Severity of the disability: Siblings tend to adjust more smoothly to disabilities that are severe and visible.

Age and birth order: The generally accepted rule of thumb is that the children *closest in birth order* to the child with learning disabilities will be the most significantly affected. For example, a ten-year-old child may be constantly embarrassed, criticized, and isolated from *his* peers because of the behavior of his eleven-year-old LD brother. However, when a seventeen-year-old takes his "little LD brother" out for ice cream, he is viewed by the community as a generous and kind sibling.

Parental attitude: This factor is, undoubtedly, the most important contributor to the development of positive sibling relationships in the special-needs family. The parents, particularly the father, must consistently demonstrate to the family that they are not overwhelmed by the needs of the learning disabled child and, further, that they have confidence and faith in the child's potential and in the family's ability to face the challenges. Parents must work together to confront and solve family problems involving the special-needs child. Parents must discuss these issues openly and honestly. They need to support one another and demonstrate this support and respect for all family members. Allow yourselves to express your feelings without the discussion becoming negative or judgmental.

Parenting is a somewhat subjective practice, but both parents should come to a consensus regarding the critical issues of homework, discipline, and home-school communication. The children should recognize and appreciate that the two parents present a united front on important parenting issues.

Recognizing and Meeting the Needs of Special Siblings

All children have needs (e.g., safety, belonging, power), and our success as parents lies in our ability to meet these needs. Your children have unique needs because of the unusual circumstance of having a learning disabled sibling. You realize that, as a "special parent," you have some needs and challenges that other parents do not have. Doesn't it follow that your sons and daughters will also have unique needs as "special siblings"?

Primary among these needs is the need to be *understood*. Special siblings often have confusing and ambivalent feelings about their LD brother or sister. These feelings are often in flux and may range from anger to fear to embarrassment. They need to know that the adults in their lives view these feelings as valid and legitimate. They must feel comfortable expressing these feelings to understanding and empathetic adults.

A second need is *information*. The sibling may be quite confused about his sister's diagnosis and prognosis. He may develop unreasonable fears, fantasies, and assumptions regarding the disability that prevent him from establishing an effective, meaningful relationship with his sister. It is widely accepted that if a child is not provided with adequate information about an important topic (e.g., an illness in the family, a pending move to a new home), he will often fill the void with unrealistic and inaccurate "facts." Children have a natural need for such information, and if it is not provided to them, they will fabricate it. This can cause the child unnecessary worry, concern, and angst.

Discuss these issues in a clear and direct manner using language that he can understand: "On Tuesdays, I take Christine to an occupational therapist named Sarah. She helps Christine learn to hold her pencil and scissors correctly and does exercises with her that will make Christine's arms and hands stronger." Update this information occasionally; keep the sibling in the loop at his or her level of understanding. Create an environment where the sibling feels comfortable asking questions about his sister's disabilities.

This information will be comforting and will enable the special sibling to better understand (and tolerate) his sister's idiosyncratic behaviors. You might say, "One of Christine's problems is called 'temporal relations.' This means that she has difficulty understanding time, and so it is very hard for her to estimate how long an activity will take her to complete. That's why she started vacuuming while you were trying to watch wrestling on TV. She thought that it would just take a minute and that she could vacuum the whole living room during one commercial. She didn't mean to annoy you."

A parent's failure to provide this information can have serious consequences for the sibling of the struggling child. He may develop an unhealthy pattern of concealing his feelings and may even deny his fears and frustrations to himself. A discrepancy between his feelings and his actions can begin to affect other relationships in his life.

Some suggest that a lack of information about a sibling's disorder can actually diminish a nondisabled child's sense of independence. He may come to view himself as an "extension" of his brother and not understand that this sibling role is but one of the many roles that he plays at home, in school, and in the community. This makes it difficult for the child to view himself as a unique, valuable, and special person in his own right. Again, this can create patterns of belief and behavior that can plague the child into adulthood. As adults, we must recognize the legitimacy and importance of our *own* needs, lest we become a slave to the needs of others. It is no less so for children.

Special siblings have a heightened need for *respect*. Because so much of the family's resources and energies must be invested in the child with LD, it is easy for the siblings to feel forgotten and unappreciated. Special siblings may believe that their feelings and accomplishments go unrecognized. They need to be treated as individuals with unique personalities and affinities.

In order to demonstrate that respect, parents should avoid blanket restrictions that are often made to protect or provide structure for the child with special needs. A special sibling once lamented, "It's so unfair! My brother Luke needs a lot of sleep, so my parents make us all go to bed at nine P.M. I never get to see my favorite shows." The parents' failure to view the children as individuals—with individual needs—demonstrates a lack of respect.

Special siblings need to know that their efforts are recognized and appreciated. We sometimes ask the sibling to be his "brother's keeper" by assisting him at home and advocating for him at school (e.g., making sure he catches the bus, delivering his forgotten lunch). Simultaneously, the sibling may be hassled and teased by peers regarding his brother. All of these burdens are added to the typical angst of childhood. Let the sibling know how much you appreciate the role he plays in his brother's life.

Another important need of the special sibling is *attention*. If you do not provide the sibling with adequate attention, he may attempt to gain your attention in inappropriate ways (e.g., drug use, school problems, back talk). Remember, children need attention, and while positive attention is preferred, they will settle for negative attention if it's all that's available.

The special sibling needs to have a well-defined *role* in the family, lest he feel the self-imposed responsibility to be the perfect child or the "third parent." Neither of these roles is appropriate. Reinforce the fact that she is a unique individual with unique needs, affinities, and qualities.

It is normal, natural, and often necessary for the special sibling to assume the role of caregiver on occasion. This is a role that is relatively rare in typical sibling relationships, so it can cause confusion and concern for the child who is asked occasionally to play it.

When the special-needs child is the younger of the two, the older child is often asked to assist his brother in the completion of day-to-day tasks. This can create a sense of resentment or cause the younger child to become so overly dependent that it hinders his development, potential, and independence. It is important to carefully monitor the child's caregiver responsibilities to avoid these twin pitfalls.

Younger siblings are also occasionally asked to assume the caretaker role. This can also be problematic because it represents a marked reversal in traditional sibling roles. This may result in feelings of resentment, embarrassment, or even guilt. Be aware of the unusual dynamic that you may create when you ask your nine-year-old daughter to keep an eye on her twelve-year-old brother while you wash the car. A child may become understandably resentful when this request is made. When such a request is necessary and appropriate, express your empathy with this unusual situation and your gratitude.

Reaction of Siblings to the Child with Learning Disabilities

There is no truly "typical" way in which a child will react to his disabled sibling. The level of acceptance that each child demonstrates is greatly influenced by her personality and temperament. Little can be done to adjust those inborn factors.

However, parents should be aware that there are several predictable reactions or feelings. Rarely is the special sibling's reaction static and unchanging throughout the years that the two children live under the same roof. Rather, the child's response may change in response to each child's development, maturity, and circumstances. As you read about the feelings that special siblings often experience, view this information as a compass, not a road map. Your children may manifest unique patterns and behaviors.

At times, the sibling may experience *fear*. Younger children may be afraid that they may "catch" their sister's disability and that they, too, will experience school failure. Siblings who are susceptible to anxiety reactions may develop significant fears about the future of their sibling or that of the family. They may also have misgivings about the reactions of their friends to their LD sibling, or fears that their own children may be born with a disability.

The special sibling may also experience periods of *anger*. This fury may be aimed at the sibling, the parents, or even at God. This anger has its roots in the child's belief that the situation at home is inherently unfair.

Special siblings often report deep feelings of *embarrassment*. The sibling may be quite tolerant of his LD sister's idiosyncratic behavior inside the home, but may experience great embarrassment and resentment when the same behavior occurs in public. The sibling may be reluctant to invite friends home, fearing that the LD sibling will do or say something embarrassing. It is important to note that embarrassment is a primary fear of most adolescents and preteens.

Jealousy is another emotion often encountered by the special sibling. This, again, is rooted in the child's resentment over the disproportionate amount of time and energy that the family invests in the child with special needs.

Special siblings typically report that they have significant *confusion* related to their LD brother or sister. They may be unclear as to their role and responsibility in the family structure. This confusion is magnified when parents express sharply contrasting views and responses to the special-needs child.

Although their sibling's disability has occurred through no one's fault or choice, the non-LD siblings may experience periods of *guilt* and self-blame. They may feel guilty about their own hostile feelings about the special-needs child, particularly when they have been reprimanded for expressing these negative emotions. If the LD child is older than the nondisabled sibling, the latter may feel guilty about surpassing his older sister in academic and social tasks. A special sibling once told me that she rejected four invitations to her senior prom simply because her older LD brother had not attended *his* prom years earlier. She felt guilty celebrating a milestone that her brother could not attain.

Despite best parental efforts to avoid this, special siblings often feel great *pressure* in their lives due to the disabled sibling. They sometimes feel that they must achieve mightily in order to counter-balance or "make up for" their parents' disappointment in their LD sister's lack of progress and growth. They also may feel pressured to maintain a positive relationship with their sister, although the LD child does little to contribute to this connection.

Lastly, the special sibling may experience significant feelings of *loneliness* because he feels a lack of support, understanding, and empathy for his unique circumstances. He feels different, and resents the fact that there are very few people in his life to whom he can express his ambivalence and confusion. As one sibling told me, "Whenever I complain to my friends about Kevin, they just tell me that *all* kid brothers are a pain. They just don't get it!"

Again, these emotional states are not experienced by all special siblings, and the intensity of these feelings will vary widely. But it is important to know that these feelings do exist. As siblings of a special-needs child, your typical children are going through a challenging ordeal that you probably have never experienced. Listen to them and avoid being judgmental and reprimanding in your responses. Their feelings are normal, natural, and valid.

Fairness

One of a parent's greatest challenges is to handle their children in a fair and equitable fashion. The juggling of "fairness" and "equality" presents a never-ending conundrum for parents, and few of us realize that these concepts are not synonymous. In fact, they are often total opposites. The classic work in moral development conducted by Laurence Kohlberg at Harvard University indicates that children, in their initial stages of moral development, define "fairness" thusly: "Fairness means that everyone gets the same."

Unfortunately, in many households, children have convinced their parents that the above definition is a true and accurate one. For instance, how many fathers would return from a business trip bearing a gift for only one child? How often do you resist the temptation to purchase a special gift for one child because you would feel the wrath of the siblings who received nothing? At holiday time, do you carefully compute and monitor each child's gift list to ensure that all receive the identical number of gifts? If this sounds familiar, you should understand that your concept of fairness matches that of a seven- or eight-year-old child.

In truth, the definition of fairness has little to do with treating people in an identical manner. The true definition of fairness is: "Fairness means that everyone gets what he or she needs."

Consider the following analogy: The population of my town is five thousand families. Suppose a magnanimous philanthropist were to give us a grant of $5 million and ask that the funds be distributed *equally* to the townspeople. Each family would receive a check for $1,000. That's easy. However, if he were to request that the funds be divided *fairly* among the townspeople, that would require a far more complex and diverse distribution. We would be bound to consider the financial needs of each family. Suppose that a chronically ill child was not receiving treatment because his family could not afford it. Fairness would dictate that this family receive a disproportionate amount of the donated funds. *Fairness* and *equality* are not synonymous.

How do these concepts relate to parenting? Parents must realize that, in order to treat their children fairly, each must be treated *differently*. We must recognize their unique patterns of strengths and needs. In the life of a family, there will be times when the needs of one family member become paramount. In order to be fair, the parent must respond by investing a disproportionate amount of time, energy, and resources in that child. Parents should not become guilt ridden and should feel secure in the fact that the "offended" siblings will, at some time in the future, have unique needs that require some extra effort.

In a well-intentioned effort to balance the scales, parents will often attempt to compensate the siblings for the extra time and energy that they are investing in the special-needs child. The nondisabled child often recognizes the parents' situation and capitalizes on their guilt. This can create significant turmoil in the family.

After a recent seminar, a harried parent approached me and outlined her dilemma. "I spend three hours nightly with Jennifer and her homework and am constantly shuttling her from one tutoring session or therapy appointment to another. We had to sell our beloved boat to fund Jennifer's tuition at the special school. Her older sister, Francie, really resents this. How do I make it up to Francie?"

I responded, "You don't—and you can't. As long as you can look Francie in the eye and say, 'Honey, if it were *you* who had this problem—believe me—I would be working just as hard to help. It's *not* you . . . it's your sister who has the problem. And aren't you lucky that it's *not* you? But that doesn't diminish my responsibility to Jennifer.' "

In order for this "fairness doctrine" to work, the parent must also understand the difference between *need* and *want*. Stephen Glenn, noted author and parenting expert, helps us understand this distinction in the following dialogue between a mother and her fourteen-year-old daughter.

> DAUGHTER: "Mom, I need a pair of Guess? designer jeans. I need fifty dollars."
>
> MOM: "Nope. I have checked your closet, and I agree that you *need* a pair of jeans. However, you *want* a pair of designer jeans. I will gladly provide you with what you *need*. Please accept this check for thirty-five dollars, which will buy you the jeans that you *need*. If you *want* the designer jeans badly enough, I am sure that you will find some way to add fifteen dollars of your own to my thirty-five."

In summary, parents who go to great lengths to see that they give each of their children the identical amount of energy, time, and resources are probably being unfair to all of them. Let us celebrate the unique needs, goals, and personalities of each of our children.

The Good News

This chapter has focused on the complexities and difficulties experienced by the child whose sibling has a learning disability. The problems outlined are real and quite common. However, lest we forget, there are also positive aspects to this experience.

The special sibling often develops a maturity, insight, and generosity of spirit that is uncommon among his peers. It is not uncommon for these siblings to enter the helping professions as adults in a genuine effort to "give back" to society. When addressing audiences of special educators, I often ask the crowd to raise their hands if a member of their immediate family has some sort of learning disorder. Invariably, 20 percent to 30 percent of the audience responds in the affirmative.

In my career, I have dealt with thousands of special-needs families. Often, the unique challenges faced by these families cause significant dysfunction and discord. However, I have also met hundreds of siblings who provide their LD brother or sister with immeasurable love, patience, support, and encouragement.

Thomas H. Powell, author of *Brothers and Sisters: A Special Part of Exceptional Families,* once surveyed hundreds of special siblings and posed an interesting query to them. He asked, "If you could counsel your parents to do *one thing different* in terms of the way that they parent your brother/sister with learning disabilities, what would that be?"

The responses were interesting and insightful. They were:

- Be open and honest with us regarding our special-needs sibling.
- Limit and reduce our responsibilities as caregivers for our sibling.
- Make better use of the community services that are available; the family cannot do this alone.
- Learn to better accept my sibling's disability.
- Schedule some special time for *me.*
- Let us kids settle most of our differences by ourselves. Don't be so quick to jump in and referee and rescue!
- Welcome my friends and your friends into our home. Sometimes I feel like we have isolated ourselves.
- Praise us, *all* of us, a lot!
- Recognize the power that you have to get through this, and to get all of us through it, too!
- Listen to us.

- Involve us in important decisions. We have input and insights that might help!
- Recognize each of us as individuals with unique personalities and qualities.
- Give my LD brother/sister more freedom and independence. He can handle it. You're smothering him!
- Recognize that there are times in the year (e.g., final exams, tennis season) that are particularly stressful for me. Modify my responsibilities to accommodate.
- Teach my LD sibling how to interact more positively and give me some strategies to deal with him when he is having a rough time.
- Help our family to be a normal family that participates in normal activities as much as possible.

How many of these suggestions would *your* children make to *you*?

Advice to Kids with Learning or Social Problems About Siblings

Parents should explain that you know it is difficult to get along with brothers and sisters. There is, naturally, a degree of rivalry and competition between kids who are living under the same roof. Help the child with learning disabilities focus on the goal of building positive relationships with siblings and to have as few battles as possible. Here are some suggestions for the child:

1. *Try to avoid taking your problems out on your siblings.*
    School can be very frustrating, but it is not fair to bring all of your frustration home with you. Because you cannot yell at your grouchy math teacher, you sometimes come home and yell at your kid sister. This isn't fair! Calm down!

2. *Don't hide out.*
    You may think that the best way to avoid fighting with siblings is to stay in your room all day. That's not a good idea. You'll have better relationships and fewer fights if you try getting positively involved with your family.

3. *Choose your battles carefully.*

If you fight or argue with your brother about every single minor issue that comes up, you will be fighting all day—and night. You need to decide which issues are worth fighting about and which issues you can live with and ignore. Maybe you can learn to live with the fact that he calls you names, but you cannot tolerate him going into your room and taking your CDs.

4. *Talk about it!*

Wait until things are peaceful with your brother. Tell him—firmly—that you can no longer tolerate a certain behavior and clearly state that it must stop. Don't ask. Tell.

5. *Be honest with yourself.*

If you fight often with a brother, you may begin to believe that the problem is 100 percent his fault. That is probably untrue. Try to determine *your* role in these battles. Look at the situation from your brother's point of view. What behavior can *you* change?

6. *Beware of "hot buttons."*

Siblings are very skilled at discovering the specific behaviors that make you lose control. Try not to let them bait you into making a mistake. If you pretend it doesn't bother you when they push your hot button, they may lose interest and move on.

7. *Try not to compare yourself with your siblings.*

Sometimes it seems that your brothers and sisters are perfect. They have little difficulty getting good grades, have plenty of friends, and excel at sports or the arts. This can be tough to deal with. Remember, your siblings' accomplishments have nothing to do with your own potential. Be yourself and try to improve your own behavior and performance. Try not to compete constantly with your siblings.

By the way, try to view things from your brother's or sister's perspective once in a while. Nobody's life is *really* perfect. The sibling who is a sports star or who gets great grades *also* makes tremendous sacrifices in order to accomplish these things. He also has his share of frustrations and failures.

Tips for Helping Special Siblings

- There are no steadfast rules regarding the relationships between special-needs children and their siblings. The nature of this relationship is influenced by numerous factors, including family resources, lifestyle, severity of disability, size of family, birth order, age spans, intrafamily relationships, and community involvement.

- Learning to adapt to the needs and idiosyncrasies of a sibling with LD is a challenging and difficult process. The sibling's feelings, actions, and responses may vary over time. The intensity and variation of these feelings will be unique to each individual child. There, unfortunately, is no road map or cookbook for this complex process.

- Older siblings may develop concerns that their brother's disability is genetic and will be transferred to their own children.

- Some siblings will feel an inappropriate obligation to compensate for their disabled sibling by becoming the "perfect child." They may also try to act as "the third parent" and develop a domineering attitude and relationship with their LD sibling. These reactions are understandable but inappropriate.

- Nondisabled siblings have a tendency to overreact to normal sibling rivalry, conflict, and friction. They need to be reminded that even if their brother did *not* have LD, they would *not* get along all the time. Further, each and every squabble that they have is *not* related to the LD. In short, "You don't have an LD brother; rather, you have a brother who has LD."

- The special sibling's need for current, factual information about his brother's or sister's special condition is very significant. Because the sibling has limited life experience, he has difficulty putting the disability in perspective. Parents should share the information about the child's problems (e.g., diagnosis, prognosis) openly. Absent this information, the sibling will develop assumptions and beliefs that are inaccurate and, generally, overblown.

- The older nondisabled sibling should be informed of the

whereabouts and format of his brother's educational, vocational, and medical records.

- The sibling of the child with LD must come to understand that family life will be uncertain and unpredictable. However, the sibling *can* control his responses to the LD sibling's behavior. Parents should discuss—and even role-play—the child's reactions to the LD sibling's behavior (e.g., tantrums, public misbehavior).

- Explain to the non-LD sibling that moodiness and inconsistency are primary symptoms of children with learning and attentional problems. Caution the child to take his sibling's behavior seriously but not personally. You might say, "Sally, Dick didn't mean to embarrass you in front of Mrs. Clinton. He should not have said that you got a D on your science project, and I will talk to him about it. Sometimes Dick says things without thinking, and Dr. Rogers is working with him on that. I don't blame you for getting mad at what Dick said. But try not to get mad at Dick, okay?"

- Encourage the non-LD child to discuss his concerns, problems, anxieties, and opinions openly. When these feelings are expressed, avoid being judgmental or reprimanding.

- Encourage the special sibling to talk to you about what it is like to have a sibling with special needs. Remember: you probably have never experienced what she is experiencing.

- Recognize that it is okay for the sibling to have mixed feelings about his special sibling.

What Can Parents Do?

At times, it seems that children live in an isolated world beyond the influence of parents and adults. A frustrated mom once lamented, "It's not fair. When I was a kid, I was afraid of my parents. Now I'm a parent and I'm afraid of my kids."

However, there actually is a great deal that a parent can do to improve and enhance the sibling relationships in the household. Below is a list of do's and don'ts that you may find helpful.

Do surprise kids with your love and affection! A loving note hidden in a school lunchbox or an unexpected treat can do much to express and confirm your love for your child. I developed the habit of leaving cryptic Post-it notes on my first-born's mirror before leaving for work each morning. I was surprised (and delighted!) to learn that he has saved these notes for nearly twenty years!

Do understand that children view parental love as a finite commodity. They live in constant fear that Dad's love for one child will leave him without adequate love for another. Promote the concept that although parental *time* is finite, parental *love* is infinite.

Don't become a full-time referee of sibling squabbles. Avoid involving yourself in normal, petty bickering. Keep your powder dry for the *major* battles that truly need your intervention. Remember, you need not participate in every battle to which you are invited!

Don't overinvestigate sibling conflicts in an attempt to determine which of the children is to blame for the incident. Most battles between brothers and sisters have mutual starting points and become quite convoluted as they progress. Law enforcement officers often refer to bar fights as "mutual combat" situations wherein there is no clear-cut instigator or victim. This is analogous to most skirmishes between siblings. Be brief and decisive in your interventions.

Do "pull rank" when necessary. If *every* Monopoly game between your LD child and his sister ends in a battle royal, forbid them from playing Monopoly together.

Don't let 'em see you sweat! You may be at your wits' end, but avoid revealing your frustration and exasperation with the situation. Communicate that you are in control.

Don't compare your children to one another. Appreciate and celebrate their uniqueness. When a parent constantly compares one child to another (e.g., "Why can't you be more like Sean?"), *nobody* wins.

Do attempt to create a home environment that is calm and controlled. This provides the children with a sense of comfort and optimism. Confusion begets confusion.

Do allow the nondisabled child to maintain a lock on his bedroom door or keep a lockable trunk if the LD child is constantly borrowing and/or breaking his possessions. This may seem like a drastic and harsh measure, but it demonstrates your understanding of the situation and your respect for the nondisabled child and his privacy.

Don't allow the children to manipulate the parents by playing one against the other. Discuss and share decisions that will have a direct impact on the children.

Do have realistic expectations and demands for your children. Surrender the fantasy that your family will be perfect and conflict-free. A family consists of individuals with disparate goals, needs, desires, and personalities. Occasional conflicts are normal, natural, and necessary.

Do establish and enforce family rules (e.g., no TV during dinner; no phone calls after 9:00 P.M.). This provides the children with structure and predictability on the home front and minimizes squabbles and disagreements.

Do discourage tattling by minimizing your response to it. Respond to "Mom, Bobby went into Mr. Marshall's yard today and he's not supposed to!" with "Oh, is that so? What time is your soccer practice next week?"

Do serve as a positive, consistent role model. As the saying goes, "Children learn what they live," and if the parents lead a jealous, competitive, or judgmental lifestyle, the children are likely to replicate it.

Do use logical and natural consequences. If the children are fighting over the TV, turn off the television. Don't respond by putting the pool off limits or decreasing their allowances. The punishment should fit the crime.

Do praise—often and loudly. Your LD child's social and interactional skills will grow *only* in an environment of support and encouragement.

Do make an attempt to spend one-on-one time with each child. In the 1960s, a popular avant-garde psychological movement urged parents to practice "togetherness," wherein the entire family did things as a group. This is a laudable idea, but it is also important that each parent take the opportunity to spend some solitary time with each child on occasion. This is particularly important when there is a special-needs child in the family. Our hectic schedules may make this one-on-one time difficult to arrange, but look for opportunities to do it: "Hey, Jack, I have to go to the hardware store. Want to come along?" or "Sally, how about if you and I give the dog a bath?"

Do reinforce the fact that the special sibling cannot control his LD brother's behavior, but he *can* control his response to it.

Do try to be *pro*active rather than *re*active. If you know that Jonathan and Jim always argue when they go to the video store, deal with the issue *before* they go! This may prevent your having to react to their argument in the store.

Don't misinterpret a sibling's silence or lack of questions to mean that she fully understands the nature and needs of the child with learning disabilities. It is common for children to be silent about issues that are very important to them. It may be exceedingly difficult for the sibling to discuss the feelings of guilt, shame, and embarrassment that she may have.

Do allow and encourage the children to make decisions. This will enable them to develop faith in their own judgment. Also, solicit their opinions about major decisions that will affect them.

Don't allow a child's disability to become the focal point of the family's relationship, interactions, activities, or decisions. The disability is only one factor in the family's development.

Do understand that each child has eight basic needs: limits, attention, acceptance, power, success, belonging, safety, and love. "Acting out" occurs whenever one or more of these needs are not being met. You can prevent a good deal of misbehavior by making a concerted attempt to meet these needs for each child.

Don't encourage competition among the siblings. This rarely motivates children and can become quite destructive. Encourage the siblings to work together on cooperative projects.

Don't threaten children! Instead, *promise* them. Compare the threat "If you don't get your room cleaned by noon, you can't go to the movies" to the promise "If you get your room cleaned by noon, you can go to the movies." Promises make the child's behavior *his* responsibility and provide a realistic sense of control.

Don't use collective punishments such as, "Because Jeremy misbehaved at the mall today, we are not going to go to the movies tonight." This creates resentment among family members and will do little to improve Jeremy's behavior. Rather, use collective *rewards*. "I was so pleased with Jeremy's behavior at Grandma's that I decided that we will all stop for ice cream on the way home." Everybody wins! The siblings get ice cream and Jeremy is a hero!

Do emphasize the concept that the family is a team. Each player should assist in the others' success while providing support and encouragement when problems arise. The group is stronger than any individual. Each member of the team has defined responsibilities, rights, and roles.

Do occasionally discuss and evaluate the "State of the Household." Sit down and assess the levels of impact and stress that the family is experiencing. Be honest. If the levels are unusually high, what can be done to reduce them? Don't wait for a crisis. These sessions should be positive, structured, solution oriented, and preventive.

Do recognize that the child with special needs has an impact on your marriage. It is important to support one another as you face the challenge of raising a child with a learning disability. This experience can be fraught with conflict and tension, particularly if your family communication system is ineffective.

Afterword

Voices Through the Bedroom Wall
by Noreen Boyle

Again tonight I hear my brother's voice carrying out a conversation—sometimes playing the part of two people, at times just one.

When we were younger, in the same setting—he in his bedroom and me in mine—I would hear him through my bedroom wall and would yell out, "Who's in there with you?" and he would stop his talking and yell back, "Nobody."

"Then stop talking to yourself." For a few minutes there would be quiet. But gradually and inexorably, I'd hear his voice again, at first muffled by his pillow, but as his conversation would grow more intense, the volume would slowly increase.

Eventually, I began to realize that this was his way of getting through his days and gathering up the courage to face tomorrow. He was rewriting a script in which he didn't like the way his character was portrayed. This way his character could fight back against the bully, charm the heroine, or score the winning run.

And every night I'd listen to him rewriting and then rehearsing the revised script. But on the following day, never did he win the battle, the girl, or the game. Too many in the cast of his day-

time play were ignorant and insensitive actors. But for a few minutes in his darkened bedroom, he held the spotlight and had his chance to shine.

Again tonight I hear this voice through the walls. But tonight I don't interrupt—I let him change the ending of his daily nightmare, if only for a few minutes, so that he can face the sun the following morning.

Noreen Boyle is a registered nurse. This piece was written when she was leaving high school and her brother was just entering.

RECOMMENDED RESOURCES

Mothers Talk About Learning Disabilities, Elizabeth Weiss (New York: Prentice Hall, 1993).

Sibshops: Workshops for Siblings of Special Needs Children, Donald J. Meyer (Baltimore, Md.: Paul H. Brooks Publishing, 1995).

Special Children, Challenged Parents, Robert A. Naseef, PhD (Secaucus, N.J.: Carol Publishing Company, 1995).

Strategies for Helping Parents of Exceptional Children, Milton Seligman (New York: The Free Press, 1996).

CHAPTER EIGHT

Playdates

The Social Coin of the Realm

Two brothers, Brad and Tom, are sitting on their front lawn. It is ten o'clock on a Saturday morning and the boys are anxiously awaiting the arrival of their cousin Skip. Tom is twelve and attends special class. Brad, two years younger, is an accomplished student and gifted athlete. Both boys have been eagerly awaiting Skip's monthly visit.

Tom, who is slashing at the shrubbery with an old broom handle, says, "When Skip gets here, we're gonna play street hockey. I get the good stick."

"Maybe we should wait and see what Skip wants to do," Brad counsels. "He's the guest."

"Yeah, but it's my house and I'm the oldest," Tom responds loudly. "We're playin' street hockey!"

Brad rolls his eyes and secretly hopes that this playdate would not conclude badly, as most previous playdates had.

When Skip arrives, Tom insists that the street hockey game begin. Brad and Skip reluctantly join in. Tom demands that he be the goalie. When Skip scores a goal, Tom throws his stick and loudly protests that Skip must have cheated because no one had ever—EVER—scored against him before . . . and he plays every day . . . with high school kids. The game ends abruptly when Tom angrily throws the puck and it rolls into a nearby drainpipe.

Tom's mom and dad come out of the house in a near panic. They have forgot that Tom and Brad each have appointments at the orthodontist that morning. Because the hourlong appointments are at 11:00 and 1:00, Mom will take Tom to the first appointment and then return home to retrieve Brad for his session. Tom reacts very negatively to the sudden change in plans and wails loudly as she escorts him to the car. As they back down the driveway, Tom hollers last-minute instructions to his brother and cousin: "Stay out of my room and don't play Monopoly without me! Don't touch my bike. I just painted it and it's wet. If you wreck the paint job, I'll wreck something of yours—"

Brad and Skip, feeling both relieved and a little guilty, retire to Brad's bedroom. Brad asks his guest if he wants to play a board game and they agree on checkers. Brad sets up the game board while Skip admires Brad's CD collection. Skip asks if he can borrow the sound effects CD and Brad explains that his mom doesn't allow him to lend his CDs, but he would gladly burn a copy of the specific sound effect that Skip wants.

The boys then decide to call some mutual friends and spend twenty minutes on a rollicking three-way phone conversation. One of the friends invites Brad to come to his house to play pool, but Brad tells him that he has a guest and that he will be unable to come over. Maybe next time.

For ninety minutes, Brad and Skip enjoy each other's company. They laugh, joke, wrestle, giggle, snicker, crow, cackle, and guffaw. At 12:30, Brad's mom arrives to retrieve him and drop off Tom.

Tom immediately insists that Skip go to the playroom with him. Tom dons headphones and listens to his latest CD, leaving Skip to read yesterday's sports page.

After a half hour or so, Tom announces that the two cousins are going to play cards. Tom tries—unsuccessfully—to teach Skip the rules for Hearts; Tom calls his guest "stupid" when he is unable to master the game after only one try. They become em-

broiled in a dispute over the rules, and Tom loudly reminds Skip that they are his cards so he can make the rules. In an attempt to reduce the tension, Skip asks if Tom knows how to play 52 Pickup. He heaves the cards into the air, saying, "Okay, pick 'em up!"

Tom is unable to recognize that Skip intends this as a joke and stomps out of the room. "I'm not picking those up!" he bellows. "You threw 'em—you pick 'em up!" Tom sits on the swing set and refuses to talk to Skip. Eventually, Skip picks up the cards in an effort to assuage Tom and to rescue the playdate from disaster.

Tom then tells Skip that he wants to watch a video. Tom says that he will be the only one to use the remote control. At a particularly exciting scene in the movie, Skip asks Tom to rewind the video so that he can view the scene again. Tom attempts to comply, but becomes confused and sets the remote to fast forward by mistake. Trying to correct his error, he inadvertently ejects the cassette from the VCR. With that, Tom flings the remote control against the wall and storms into his bedroom.

Brad and his mother return from the dentist and—just as they pull into the driveway—Skip's mom arrives to retrieve him. All say their good-byes, and, as Skip departs, Tom reminds him that his street hockey goal "didn't count."

On the drive home, Skip's mother asks him if he enjoyed his visit.

"Yeah," Skip responds. "It was okay. I want to go back next Sunday."

"That's good," Mom says, "except Sunday is the day that Tom has marching band practice. He won't be home. It will be just you and Brad."

"I know that, Mom. I know."

In many communities, playdates have become the social coin of the realm. Parents find themselves transporting their children out of their neighborhoods to spend afternoons with classmates in other communities. These activities can be a minefield for children with social skill deficits. This chapter will provide advice to parents and children on the successful planning of playdates and overnight visits, and the roles, rights, and responsibilities of both the guest and the host.

It is difficult and often painful for a parent to watch a child struggle socially. Earlier conventional wisdom held that there is little that a parent can do to ignite a friendship for a child. However, in the past decade, a significant amount of research has explored the nature and development of friendships among school-age children. Landmark research was conducted at the University of California in recent years. The findings of these studies and observations provide parents and professionals with valuable information and strategies. Now that we better understand how these friendships are formed, we can take a more active and constructive role in promoting them.

One troubling finding in the research indicates that children who report having "no friends" are at greater risk for drug abuse, school problems, and mental health issues. They also have significant difficulty dealing with social situations and conflict resolution as they grow into adolescence. This is, of course, understandable, as the child never experiences the "social laboratory" that allows him to learn, practice, and reinforce these critical skills.

Among the recommendations made by the researchers is the importance and effectiveness of one-on-one playdates. Parents often attempt to improve a child's social skills by enrolling him in group activities or team sports. These attempts often result in very public failure and frustration. However, the one-on-one playdate provides an opportunity for the child to learn and practice the critical social skills of sharing, negotiating, problem solving, intimacy, and turn taking in a less threatening environment.

Of course, this activity has several pitfalls and drawbacks, particularly if both children involved in the playdate have social difficulties. But it remains the most effective approach in promoting friendships skills for children with special needs.

Finding Friends

When attempting to find a playdate partner for your child, ask her for information and feedback about her selection and preference. Ask her if there is a girl whom she plays with at recess or on the bus. Be aware that she may overreach a bit by stating her desire to become friends with the most popular and desirable girl in her class. This girl's popularity is doubtless based on her superior social skills. It may be exceedingly difficult for your daughter to "keep up" with this girl, and she may be rejected and hurt. Solid friendships are based upon similar interests and compatible social competence.

Consider the friendships that you hold dear in your own life. One of the most significant aspects of those friendships is the fact that you and your friend hold similar interests (e.g., golf, sailing, shopping, politics). It is rare that two people with totally diverse interests can develop a lasting and deep friendship. Therefore, it is important that you assist your child in developing and cultivating interests that will be appealing and attractive to other children. These interest areas must be interactive. They must provide the child with an opportunity to cooperate with others. Unfortunately, children with social skill deficits tend to develop solitary interests such as drawing, reading, or collecting.

If your child is unable to identify a potential playmate, drop by school or her church group and observe. Perhaps you will see the spark of a potential friendship as you watch her interact with the other children. Be sure to consult with your child before extending an invitation. When playdates are arranged exclusively by the parents, both children feel trapped and are seldom willing to invest themselves in making the date successful.

Once you have identified a child, contact her parents and arrange a playdate. Again, this may seem contrived and artificial. After all, most parents do not make these arrangements for their children. But your child may be incapable of successfully completing the preliminary activities involved in establishing a relationship, so you must assist her. Your goal is to provide the child with an opportunity to develop a special relationship with another child. Be aware that this is only the initial step in the process. She will continue to need your guidance, support, encouragement, and intervention in order to maintain the relationship.

Planning the Successful Playdate

Like Tom, many children have significant difficulty dealing with play-dates. Below are some suggestions that can help to ensure that your child's next playdate goes more smoothly.

- Establish "house rules" for playdates (e.g., no visitors are allowed in Grandpa's workshop). In that way, the child can avoid conflict with a guest by citing the rule: "Yeah, I know that the shed looks like it would be neat for a fort, but my mom doesn't allow us in there when we have visitors. All of my grandfather's tools are in there."
- Playdates should generally only involve two children. To invite two guests is to court disaster! A grouping of three children invariably deteriorates into a two-on-one situation, and the child with the least social competence is usually the odd man out.
- Another common cause of playdate failure is the involvement of the host child's siblings. The presence and participation of a sibling can have a negative impact on the dynamic of the play-date. The visiting child may find the sibling more appealing and reject the host. This will cause hostility and understandable resentment. To avoid this, include guidelines for siblings in the house rules for playdates. These may include making the child's room off-limits to his siblings whenever he has a visitor.
- You may want to "hover" in the background so you can intervene if a conflict arises. If trouble *does* occur, enter the room and whisper a cue in the child's ear (e.g., "Remember, Bobby, the guest is always right").
- The host child should greet the guest at the door, show him around the house, and introduce the guest to the family.
- You will also want to be conscious of the length of the proposed playdate. The initial sessions should be relatively brief (one to two hours). The all-day playdate outlined in the introductory scenario was obviously too much for Tom to handle. The allotted time can be lengthened as the relationship and the child's social skills develop.
- Prior to the arrival of the visitor, assist your child in straightening his room or the play area to make it as attractive and ap-

pealing as possible. He is anticipating the arrival of a guest and it is socially appropriate and desirable to make such preparations. These preparations should be a pleasurable experience. Don't threaten to cancel the playdate if the child does not cooperate. A child should not have to *earn* the right to play with a friend.

- If the child has a particular toy or possession that is unusually valuable or breakable, you may want him to put it in a closet to prevent conflict if his guest wishes to play with it. Explain to your child that toys in the common area must be shared.
- Make your home an inviting and enjoyable place to visit! Have great toys, games, and snacks. Be welcoming to visitors. Does this mean that you are *buying* friendships for your child? Possibly. But it works! I refer to this as "the American foreign policy approach to friendship"!
- Children tend to vividly remember the final fifteen minutes of any experience. Be sure to end each playdate in a positive, upbeat way. This will enhance the chances that the guest will wish to return another day.

It may seem strange and unnecessary to invest so much planning in a routine social activity. But this preparation is necessary to ensure success. Be mindful of the adage, "People don't plan to fail, they just fail to plan."

Helping Your Child Be a Good Host

- A successful playdate must be supervised. This does not mean the parent must (or should!) be an active participant in the activities, but you must be available to provide counsel, assistance, and refereeing when necessary. Remember, your *child* is the host. You should greet the guest warmly, make small talk, then move to the background and allow your child to play the host role.
- Especially with a new friend, it may be helpful to begin with a moderately structured activity and then allow the children to interact independently. For example, display a collection of

Popsicle sticks, pipe cleaners, or modeling clay on the kitchen table. Help the visitor and the host construct a few simple structures, then quietly walk away.

- Some children are extraordinarily territorial and overly possessive and anxious about their toys and belongings. If this is the case with your child, you can prevent conflicts by conducting the playdate at a "neutral site" (e.g., playground, park).

- Your child's playmate is a guest and should be treated as such. It is part of your child's "social contract" to make his guest feel welcome and comfortable. Be sure to review and reinforce the "host rules" immediately prior to each playdate. If a conflict occurs during the visit, cite the specific rule when you intervene ("I know that you are tired of playing checkers, but Chip wants to finish the game. He's the guest, so he's always right, remember?").

- Basically, in a guest-host relationship, the guest is always right and the guest always goes first. Again, this concept will run contrary to the child's belief that "this is my house and we'll do things my way." By establishing and communicating this rule, you will solve most conflicts before they occur. When a disagreement arises, it is easily defused by citing these two rules! If a guest takes unfair advantage of these gracious guidelines, you may want to reconsider a future invitation.

- Discourage noninteractive activities during the playdate. Watching TV and using the computer are not desirable or effective playdate activities. Again, boredom will set in easily and quickly with these passive activities. In addition, these activities provide little opportunity for social interaction or conversation.

- Teach your child some appropriate strategies for changing an activity that he may find boring or unexciting. These skills can be used whether your child is the guest or the host. He should be told that it is impolite to criticize the activity (e.g., "This is boring," "This game stinks"). Rather, he should politely suggest a modification in the activity ("Can I use the steam shovel for a while?"). Better yet, he can suggest an alternative activity

("Hey, do you want to see the pictures of Fenway Park that my dad took last week?").

- It is always a good idea to include snacks in a playdate. Ask your child to participate in selecting—or even preparing— these snacks. Again, his playmate is a guest and should be treated as such. It is part of your child's "social contract" to make his guest feel welcome and comfortable.

- It is highly unlikely that you would criticize an invited guest in your home. Similarly, the child should be told that it is inappropriate and unmannerly to criticize his visitor during a playdate.

- You should emphasize the importance of *loyalty* in a playdate situation. If the host abandons his visitor by retiring to his bedroom or joining a more attractive group of children during the playdate, it is highly unlikely that the guest will return. It is part of the host's social contract to remain with his visitor for the duration of the visit.

- For younger children, it may be helpful to provide duplicate toys (e.g., two dump trucks, two dollhouses) so that each child has a toy to play with. This prevents conflicts and encourages parallel play.

- Occasionally, arrange a playdate with a youngster who is older or younger than your child. This will give her an opportunity to learn from an older child or teach a younger one.

Playdate Postmortem

- When the playdate is finished, discuss the visit with the child. What parts went well? What parts went poorly? Why? These conversations will enable you to remediate the problems, reinforce his positive behaviors, and demonstrate your interest in him and his social life. This will also assist you in planning future playdates.

- The child should have several successful "at home" playdates before you allow her to go to another child's home for a date. When you retrieve her from her first "away" date, ask the host's parents for specific input regarding her behavior during the visit. Don't expect the parent to volunteer the information if you don't solicit it, particularly if the visit has not gone well. Most parents will prefer to "suffer in silence" and simply not invite your child for another visit. Tell the host parent that you would appreciate honest and candid input. Otherwise, you will never learn the specific problems that she experienced and you will be unable to assist her in improving her behavior.

- You should attempt to establish a relationship with the guest's parent(s). By doing so, you present yourself as a responsible, involved adult who will provide a safe and secure environment for the child to visit. It is always advisable to compliment and commend the visitor when speaking to his parents. ("Bill was a perfect gentleman while he was here. He even helped Tom's grandfather bring in the groceries.") Nothing is more appreciated by a parent than to hear her own child praised!

One of the longest afternoons of my life was when my wife and I foolishly invited our son's entire second-grade class to our home for an end-of-the-year celebration. We cavalierly rejected the offers from other parents to assist us. We were confident in our professional abilities to control, corral, and entertain twenty-five kids for a mere four hours. I still shudder at the thought of that long, eventful afternoon.

If you are hosting a party or outing for a group of children, be mindful of the following:

- Reward and reinforce the entire group for positive social interaction. ("You kids are being so terrific! Let's bowl another string!")
- Be flexible. Use your party plan as a compass, not a road map.
- If the children seem bored, change activities.
- Use I-messages to correct behavior. ("Tom, I can't hear Jennifer when you are blowing your horn" versus "Tom, stop that noise!")
- State rules positively. ("Please stay in the front yard" versus "Don't go in the backyard.") Let them know what you *want* them to do, not what you *don't* want them to do.

- De-emphasize winning. Emphasize having fun!
- If behavior begins to deteriorate, have kids pair off. ("Okay, let's pair off. Each pair should finish the scavenger hunt together.")
- If a child appears to be left out, give him a leadership role.
- Plan games and activities that require problem solving and luck (scavenger hunts, guessing games), not skill.

Overnight Guests

Your child may have the occasion to be an overnight guest at the home of a friend or relative. This can be a particularly challenging social situation for the child, and she may need a significant amount of coaching prior to the event.

First, it is important that she bring any and all of the things that she will need or want during her visit (e.g., grooming aids, clothes, toys, medication). Careful, thoughtful packing will save you from being called to deliver the sweater that she "absolutely *has* to have." If your child has organizational or memory problems, she will need significant assistance with packing. Help her make appropriate decisions by providing her with a suitcase or duffel bag and informing her that all of her "stuff" must fit in the bag. This will require her to make some priority decisions and will prevent the inevitable overpacking.

Remind her to be sure to bring all of her possessions back home when she returns. It is a good idea to make a checklist of the items that she brought and put the list in her suitcase. Then she can use the list to ensure that she retrieves all of her possessions upon her departure.

When the child is a visitor, it is important that she carefully *observe* the host family. Each family has its own unique culture and an unwritten set of rules. For example, some families may say grace before meals or may remove their shoes upon entering the house; other families may not follow these rituals. Remind the child of the wise adage, "When in Rome, do as the Romans do." She should do her best to carefully observe the behavior of the hosts and replicate it. Some behaviors that are acceptable in your home (e.g., feeding the dog scraps from the table, singing loudly along with the radio) may be unacceptable to the host family.

The child should be reminded that—as the guest—it is important to be nice to *everyone* in the host family. If the hosting child is rude to her parents or bullying to her younger brother, that does *not* give your child permission to do the same. Reinforce the importance of manners, politeness, and kindness. This may be a difficult concept for the child to grasp. ("Well, Sarah called her brother a jerk! Why can't I?")

You or the child should notify the host family of any problems or complications that they might need to know about. ("Bill is really frightened of dogs," "Sarah is allergic to milk," "Jody needs to call her grandmother at seven o'clock on Saturday.") It's best to communicate these issues prior to the visit.

It is a good idea to pack a book or a deck of cards so the child can entertain herself during downtime.

It is common for a host to tell a guest to "make yourself at home," but the child must not take this welcoming statement *too* literally. Remind her to ask permission before using the telephone, television, computer, and so forth. The child must also avoid sharing the friend's secrets with the family. ("Mrs. Rockwood, did Sally tell you about the trouble she got into in Ms. Cavanaugh's class last week?") She should avoid getting involved in family squabbles and should never, ever complain about the food or accommodations. It is also a good idea to ask the host's parents if they need help or assistance in any way (e.g., cleaning the kitchen after a meal, walking the dog, taking out the garbage).

A common mistake made by children during sleepover visits is *snooping*. Although it is tempting to explore the host family's closets, cupboards, desks, and dressers, it is extremely inappropriate to do so. Care should be taken *not* to read letters, bills, mail, and notes, even if they are left lying around.

It is the child's social responsibility to say good-bye and thank the hosts for their hospitality at the end of the visit. It is not sufficient for her parents to thank them.

Part of the fun and enjoyment of a sleepover or playdate lies in the opportunity to experience another family's rituals, customs, and habits. But the visitor must remain mindful of her social duty to adhere to the conventions of the host family.

Receiving the Guests of Others

What role should the child play in receiving and welcoming *your* guests? For example, you probably invite guests to your home for dinner, and these visitors may be significant and influential people in your life—perhaps your boss, colleague, or friend. As a result, you wish to impress and please your guest. You become anxious about the menu, the cleanliness of the house, and—particularly—the behavior of the children.

As always, any transition or change in routine can create anxiety for the child with social difficulties. So, at a time when you want him to be at his best, he may not be. Try to prepare the child for the guest's arrival. Avoid threatening him or increasing his anxiety. ("The Marshalls are coming for dinner, and if you don't behave, you will be one very sorry boy!") Rather, assure him that very little will change at home, despite the presence of a visitor. Remind him of your basic rule: When Mom or Dad asks you to do something, do it!

If the child acts inappropriately with the guest (e.g., asking her to read him a story), try talking to the child *through* your guest. ("Sometimes Jody gets so excited about company, she forgets our rules about courtesy.") In this way, you can communicate your dissatisfaction to your child while avoiding a confrontation.

Instruct the child to return to his room in a firm and supportive manner. ("Jody, we spoke earlier about the fact that Mr. Middleton and I have an important meeting tonight. Please go to your room and read by yourself. If you can't do that, I will help you.") This approach protects you, the guest, and the child from embarrassment and communicates to *all* parties that you are in control of the situation.

If a second interruption occurs, take the child out of earshot of the guest and reinforce the rules that you outlined prior to the guest's arrival. Provide him with another opportunity to follow the rules appropriately. Inform him of the consequences for failing to adhere to the rules. "Jody, I *know* that you are excited about Mr. Middleton being here, but we told you this afternoon that we cannot be interrupted during our meeting. Remember? Now, if you interrupt again, you will have to go to your room for the rest of the evening."

If Jody interrupts again, excuse yourself from your guests by saying, "I'm sorry, but it is important that Jody understand the rules of our house when we have company. Please excuse me. I feel that it is important to deal with this now." This strategy, again, minimizes the embarrassment factor and demonstrates to the child the importance of the rules. This demonstration of follow-through can have lasting impact on Jody and her behavior.

If visitors consistently create havoc in your household, you may want to examine *your* role in the problem. It is inappropriate—and anxiety producing—to ask your child to perform (e.g., read, recite poetry, play piano, sing) for guests. The child may be unable to handle this temporary spotlight and it could cause embarrassment or a reluctance to surrender center stage. Remember that your agenda and expectations for the evening may be quite different from Jody's.

Visits from Relatives

The child with social skill problems may also have difficulty when relatives visit the home. Even though the relatives' intentions may be laudable, their visits can present a challenging social transition for the child with social competency problems. The complicated dynamics can create significant discord and havoc.

For example, Grandma stops by. She wants to spend some time with her beloved grandchild. Mom is trying to keep the child's behavior consistent and appropriate. The child views Grandma's visit as an opportunity to dispose of all rules and regulations. Conflict and confusion reign.

Don Fleming, PhD, offers a unique solution to this challenging situation. He recommends that you advise the child that you *will* relax rules a bit when Grandma comes to visit (e.g., *three* cookies rather than the customary two, extended bedtime) *under the condition* that the rules return to "normal" when Grandma departs. If the child attempts to take advantage of the situation, rules will be consistently enforced whether Grandma visits or not. This communicates a true sense of fairness to the child and also signifies your recognition that visits from Grandma are special and significant.

Visits and Playdates: Rules for Kids

When you are the guest . . .

If you say you are going to go, *go!!* It is inappropriate to accept an invitation and then not show up.

Be on time! Arrive at the preappointed time. It is not right to be too early or too late.

Enjoy the food, but watch your manners and don't pig out.

Don't snoop. Respect the host's privacy.

Bring everything that you will need. It is rude and inconvenient to call your mom to bring stuff that you forgot.

Observe! Observe! Observe! Carefully watch the host family and do things the way that they do.

Be nice to *everyone!* If your friend ignores his parents or teases his sister, that does *not* give you permission to do the same.

Clean up after yourself and ask the adults if you can help in any way.

Don't "make yourself at home." Ask permission to use the phone, turn on the TV, get some food, or let the dog out.

Don't share your friend's secrets or squeal on them to their parents.

When you are the host . . .

Always ask your parents for permission to invite a guest.

Introduce your friend to your family. That is part of your job as a host!

Explain the various house rules to your guest: "We don't let the dog out of his pen," or "We have to be quiet in the front yard because my little sister is taking a nap."

Help out! When a guest is in the house, it means extra work
for Mom and Dad.

Remember: the guest is always right, and the guest always
goes first.

Be loyal to your guest. Never abandon her in midvisit if
something (or someone) better comes along!

PART THREE

Social Skills at School

Reading, 'Riting, 'Rithmetic, and Relationships

> "You can't dry tears with notebook paper."
> —Charles Schulz

CHAPTER NINE

Bullies, Victims, and Spectators

Strategies to Prevent Teasing, Intimidation, and Harassment in School

June 12, 2001

Responsibility of a Good Citizen

Teasing, if you ask me, should not be legal. It is the worst thing to happen to any school, and anyone. Teasing is just a way of angry people to gang up on someone who is maybe a little different, or maybe just unfortunate. I also think that there are not only children, but also teachers who, maybe not on purpose, make fun of people, but they have no punishment. I saw an example this year. One of my teachers was going around signing homework books when one kid, a sort of troubled kid, came up to him and started to get frantic, waving his arms and saying, "Mr. Potter, Mr. Potter, what's my homework!" By then he had the whole class's attention, and my teacher, being very mean at the moment, turned to him and started waving his arms and chanting, "Do you like it, do you like it?" I don't know what was so funny, but the whole class cracked up, and the kid stood in the middle of them, hanging his head, red-faced, and on the verge of tears.

I think the victims have the worst fix. Imagine if you were one of those people, and every day, every single day, at least one person comes up and makes fun of you for your clothes, race, accent, smartness, family, and anything else that you can think of. I think teasing should be stopped for them.

Bystanders, huh, they're the worst. They sit around, afraid to go against the teasing, and sometimes join in. There are the teasers, who are bad, in the school, but they aren't nearly as bad as a bystander. They should be the ones to stop teasing. They don't have to support the teasers, but they do. For one of two reasons, they might want to do what's cool, pick on the un-cool, or they are just very, very bad people.

So these are my reasons to stop teasing. If you can't stop it, then I hope you at least try. Remember, if you go along with it, try to imagine what pain you are causing to another human being. They may be less fortunate, and have the worst clothes, a bad house, or might not be the brightest, but just imagine you are in their position, and tell me if you are proud of who you are.

This insightful and poignant essay was written by my nephew, Daniel Marshall, when he was eleven years old. Unlike many education professionals, Daniel recognized that there are three "roles" in a bullying scenario: the Bully, the Victim, and the Spectator. Children with social skills deficits often find themselves assuming one of these roles voluntarily or involuntarily. It is important that parents and teachers understand the tremendous impact that bullying can have upon a child's social development and self-concept.

Unfortunately, many adults view bullying as a harmless rite of passage that every child must experience and tolerate. We must adjust our thinking regarding this attitude and realize that all three players (bully, victim, and spectator) in these daily dramas are negatively impacted by bullying. As we learned from the unspeakable violence at Columbine High School, children who are chronically bullied may take violent and terrible revenge on their perceived tormentors.

The parental reaction to bullying is often quite ineffectual. I well recall an incident when our son came to me and told me that several of his fellow fourth graders were teasing and intimidating him on the school bus. I asked if he was doing anything to cause this reaction from others. He responded that he was not. I asked if he was pushed or struck at any time during the incidents. He responded that he was not; his classmates teased him, called him names, and spread hurtful rumors about him.

I advised him to "toughen up" and assured him that the situation was temporary. I told him to inform me if they ever actually *struck* him, but, until then, to remember the adage about "sticks and stones."

What an ineffectual, dismissive, and insensitive response! When bullying becomes so severe that the child seeks counsel and assistance from an adult, we need to provide him with advice and strategies—not slogans and proverbs.

The proliferation of cell phones, personal computers, camera phones, instant-messaging, and the Internet has provided bullies with a new and limitless platform to intimidate or harass their victims. Children now become involved in vicious, ongoing instant-message exchanges that escalate in their cruelty as the electronic conversations proceed. The exchange is then printed out and distributed to others in order to humiliate and embarrass a child. In a recent incident at a midwestern high school, a girl secretly photographed other girls in the locker room with her camera phone and distributed the embarrassing pictures to dozens of classmates as e-mail attachments.

The dictionary definition of the term "bullying" is "intentional, repeated hurtful actions (including name calling, intimidation, and shunning) committed by one or more children against another. These acts are neither provoked nor welcomed by the victim and reflect a significant imbalance of power between the victim and the bully." Note that the definition pointedly includes nonviolent actions (name calling) against a child. Bullying can be physical, verbal, emotional, or sexual in nature. It includes such behaviors as humiliation, ostracizing, and defaming.

This broader definition of bullying and our enhanced understanding of this issue have resulted in startling data regarding the prevalence of bullying in our schools. In a recent survey, 88 percent of school-age children report that they have observed significant incidents of bullying and intimidation, and 76 percent report that they have been victims. Fourteen percent state that bullying plays a major, negative role in their lives. Tens of thousands of American schoolchildren are truant every day due to fear of intimidation and tormenting at the hands of schoolyard bullies.

Most incidents of bullying occur away from adult supervision. The average incidence of bullying lasts about thirty seconds. The supervising adult is often unaware that the bullying incident even occurred. This creates a climate of fear and anxiety among the victims, and they may avoid all school or community settings, even at activities where adults are present. Of course, this has a great impact on the intensity and frequency of the child's peer interactions.

As previously stated, all children are affected by bullying in school, not just the victim. When most adults think of a bully, we picture a large, hulking, glowering loner who torments others as a result of his own insecurities. However, the majority of bullies do not fit that profile. Bullies come in an assortment of sizes, shapes, and packages. There is no accurate stereotype for a bully. Many of the aggressors in schools are bright and confident children who feel that intimidation is an effective and appropriate method to solve problems and achieve social goals. They often have an extensive group of friends who admire them and—explicitly or implicitly—encourage their behavior. Bullies tend to share some common characteristics, including impulsivity, dominant personality, difficult-to-control temper, and little tolerance for frustration. Bullying is increasingly common among girls, who tend to use threats, rumors, and ostracism to intimidate their victims. Girls who bully tend to be highly verbal, capable, and fashionable in their language and manner of dress.

The bully himself does not escape the negative impact of bullying. Children who chronically bully others are also at greater risk for dropping out of school and developing tendencies toward violence and criminality in adolescence and adulthood. The bully's distorted sense of power and control becomes habitual, and such behavior is generally unacceptable in adult life. One federal study found that 60 percent of school bullies had criminal convictions by age twenty-four.

Children who observe bullying are also negatively affected. They are distracted from their learning and may be afraid of associating with the victim out of fear of becoming victims themselves. Insecurity and intimidation may become deeply rooted in these students. Bystanders may also experience feelings of guilt and helplessness because of their reluctance to assist or intervene.

Spectators should be urged to publicly support the victim of bullying. Failing this, the students should offer support and empathy in private. They should be counseled not to join in the rumors, gossip, laughter, or teasing inevitably associated with bullying. One school greatly reduced the incidence of fighting and physical intimidation by announcing that if a teacher came across a fight between two students, *all* of the students present (including bystanders!) would be suspended. The bullies suddenly lost their audience, and the bullying stopped! Bullying is about humiliation, and a willing audience is necessary in order for humiliation to occur.

The impact of bullying upon its victims is more obvious. They often suffer more than physical harm. The constant intimidation and resultant anxiety can result in decreased school performance, truancy, dropping out, increased absenteeism, withdrawal, depression, social anxiety, and an aversion to risk taking. Some victims may take drastic and ill-advised measures to protect themselves (e.g., carrying weapons) or avoid the intimidation (running away).

In the elementary and middle school years, the bully can gain status and even a degree of popularity among peers. His classmates may be somewhat entertained by his intimidation of less popular children. In high schools (and increasingly in middle schools), bullying may also occur under the guise of hazing and initiation rituals. However, during the high school years, students recognize the inherent inequity and cruelty of bullying and will begin to ostracize the tormentor. It is very difficult for the bully to establish relationships with his former victims and bystanders, and he often becomes isolated and lonely. One effective antibully program involves former bullies of high school age conferring with middle school bullies. The older students delivered a timely message: "Kids think that bullying is cool *now*, but you won't have any friends once high school begins. So stop it!" The voice of experience.

Parents are becoming increasingly aware of the dangers of Internet chat rooms, but there are other cyber dangers as well. Youngsters who are exploring their own burgeoning sexuality may visit X-rated sites and receive a very troubled and troubling perspective of the role and function of sex in our lives. Many students compete with one another in order to locate the most bizarre website and may spend hours surfing from site to site. Although cyberspace is the home of tremendous information and inspiration, it also contains its share of depravity and degradation. Other students may compete to see who can establish the longest "buddy list." As a result, they often add individuals who are practically strangers, and then share confidential and private information with them.

It is altogether appropriate for you to inquire about the child's computer activities, and you should clearly explain that you will be asking to see the websites that she is visiting. If she turns off the computer as soon as you enter the room or attempts to block the screen, you have the right and responsibility to ask for an explanation. If you are looking over her shoulder while she is writing or instant-messaging and she types "PAW," she has warned her cyber-companion that "parents are watching."

School Programs to Prevent and Eliminate Bullying

Many schools have instituted schoolwide bully-prevention programs. These well-intentioned projects have met with inconsistent success. However, a schoolwide approach is the only approach that holds promise as we attempt to identify, quantify, and eliminate bullying. Anything less than a full commitment from all members of the school community (parents, faculty, administration, and students) will not be effective. It truly *does* "take a village."

Some programs have used mediation sessions to deal with bully-victim disputes. I feel that this approach is misguided. The relationship between a bully and a victim is based upon a significant difference in power (real or perceived) between these two students. Therefore, compromise and negotiation is neither advisable nor appropriate. The victim has done nothing wrong and should not be required to compromise or modify his behavior. This approach would be akin to requiring a battered wife to enter negotiations with the husband who beats her.

One approach which has been quite effective in identifying and eliminating bullying behavior is a confidential reporting strategy wherein *any* member of the school community can anonymously inform the administration of patterns or incidents of bullying. In this way, the bully does not know who the reporter was and the spectator has a vehicle through which he can reduce his feelings of guilt and fear by reporting these incidents without reprisal. If a person wishes to make a report about bullying that is occurring on or off the school grounds, he can leave an anonymous message in a designated box. The best way to prevent bullying is to make it safe for students to report these incidents.

A common complaint from students is that school personnel do not deal with incidents of bullying that *are* reported and, further, that many teachers are unaware of the scope and severity of the bullying that occurs at their school. One Midwest school principal asked teachers and students if bullying was a problem in his building and if incidents of bullying were dealt with appropriately. The overwhelming majority of teachers reported that they felt that bullying was *not* a major problem and that these incidents were dealt with decisively and appropriately. In contrast, the overwhelming majority of the students surveyed felt that bullying was a *significant* problem at the school and, further, felt that the staff was *ineffectual* in dealing with the issue. Denying the existence of a problem only serves to exacerbate it. It is our fundamental obligation to ensure the physical and psychological safety of the children in our charge. If a child feels that school personnel will not protect him, he may take matters into his own hands. Several incidents of major school violence in the United States were instigated by bullied students who felt ignored by the authority figures and chose to seek relief and vengeance against their tormentors.

What Can a Parent Do
If a Child Is Being Bullied?

Children tend to exhibit a specific set of symptoms if they are being bullied in school. Parents may notice a significant change in eating habits, irritability, ability to focus, sleep patterns, or self-imposed isolation from family and community. Be on the watch for torn clothing or missing possessions. The bully may be extorting from him.

Your first step is to determine what exactly is occurring. It may be difficult to secure this information because your child may be ashamed or embarrassed to admit to you that she has allowed another child to exercise such control over her. She may even offer excuses or lie about her bruises or missing possessions. She may also fear that your involvement will make the situation worse.

Select an appropriate time and place to discuss the matter with her. The purpose of this discussion is threefold: (1) to gather detailed information, (2) to design strategies to improve the situation, and (3) to offer support, empathy, understanding, and—if appropriate—sympathy. The child must feel that you care and that you are on her side. The situation has already caused her to feel terribly alone. Any sign of rejection or disappointment from you will serve to confirm and intensify these feelings.

Wait until a time when she appears relaxed, and choose a place where you are unlikely to be interrupted. This conversation should not be rushed. Listen carefully and empathetically to her concerns. Some of her input may seem trivial to you, but it is significant and important to *her*. Acknowledge her feelings of fear, anger, and embarrassment.

You will also want to avoid overreacting to her predicament. Of course, it is upsetting to hear that your child has been intimidated or attacked, but it is important that you remain calm. Communicate to her that the situation makes you angry and that the bully's behavior is wrong. Assure her that the two of you—together—may be able to figure out how to stop these incidents. Promise her that you will not make matters worse, but also avoid promising her that you can "make it all better."

The child may feel that she is a "wimp" or a "baby" for allowing the bullying to upset and control her so. Assure her that her feelings are quite normal, understandable, and appropriate. Try sharing a similar experience from your own childhood. It may be comforting for her to know that others have experienced—and survived— bullying behavior.

You will want to probe a bit in order to determine exactly how severe the situation is. Sometimes children with learning problems may "overgeneralize," and you may find that despite her report that "Steph always steals my lunch," there was actually only one incident of theft. This does not mean that the child was intentionally lying. Her concern and embarrassment merely caused her to enhance the tale a bit. It is important that you determine the accurate details—the who, what, when, where, how, and why of the situation. You may even want to take notes. If you are putting the details in writing, she may take more care to be accurate and factual.

Unless the bullying is severe or dangerous, you should view yourself as her coach in this matter. As in sports, the good coach never goes on the field or makes the difficult pass or shot for his player. Rather, the coach remains on the sidelines, offering counsel, advice, support, and encouragement while the player actually plays the game.

Brainstorming can be an effective and efficient problem-solving strategy in this situation. Together you can generate ideas designed to change or improve the situation. Avoid evaluating any of the suggestions until you have come up with a dozen or so ideas. Some of the suggestions may be silly or unworkable, but the goal of the activity is to "think outside the box" a bit. Brainstorming will help the child begin to view the bullying as a problem to be solved, rather than an inevitable part of her daily life. This will greatly enhance her sense of power and control. Brainstorming will also provide her with a feeling of ownership regarding the solution. This is preferable to Mom merely *telling* her what to do.

Once you have generated a list of possible solutions, evaluate each one by predicting the consequences and effectiveness of each. Determine the "best solution" (which may combine features of several solutions) and design a plan. If the child has a significant language problem, this step may include writing scripts or listing step-by-step instructions. Review the plan with her prior to her departure for school and ask her for a "report" as soon as she arrives home. Reinforce and celebrate if the plan works. Comfort and restructure if it does not.

Strategies for Dealing with Bullies

There are several strategies or tactics that may be successful for the child who is being bullied. He should first be encouraged to try to handle the incident calmly. If he cries, whines, or shows fear when bullied, the incidents are likely to continue. The bully wants a reaction from the victim, and, if he fails to get a reaction, he may cease the intimidation. Remember that bullying is an attempt to have power and control over another person. No reaction equals no power! A strong reaction tends to escalate the frequency and intensity of the bullying.

Victims tend to be shy and sensitive children, and, as a result, it may be difficult for them to ignore bullying. Counsel the child to count to ten or take several deep breaths. Encourage him to talk silently to himself and remind himself to remain calm. Again, you are not urging the child to ignore the bullying. You are merely coaching him to minimize his public reaction to the teasing. He may even want to smile at his tormentor and walk away. Initially, this reaction will tend to escalate the teasing, but the frequency of the incidents will eventually decline. Again, you are not dismissing or minimizing the child's predicament by using this strategy. Rather, you are providing him with a specific and effective technique. His lack of response to the teasing will eventually have an impact. Your child will need much encouragement during this process. Ask him to inform you daily of the progress of this approach and praise him for his perseverance.

Bullying often follows a pattern and has a specific, petty cause. For example, if the child reports that the bully always picks on him when he wears his Yankees ball cap on the bus, advise the child to leave the cap at home for a while. This is not cowardice. It is merely an effective technique to break the established pattern and, hopefully, end the teasing.

Children who are verbal and glib can be taught to verbally diffuse a bullying situation by using a comeback of some sort. This strategy is effective because the bully doesn't expect it. In effect, the embarrassed victim neutralizes the bully by embarrassing *him*. This strategy will require a good deal of practice at home; it would not be adequate merely to instruct the child in the technique and then send him off to use it at school or on the playground. It is also important to realize that verbal techniques are effective for teasing and taunting; they would be less effective against physical intimidation or extortion.

One of these verbal strategies involves actually *agreeing* with the bully's taunts. Again, this technique arms the victim with the element of surprise. Suppose the victim is continually teased because he is overweight. He can respond to the teasing by saying—in a very calm, detached manner—"You know, you're right. I am overweight. Maybe I ought to do something about that." This strategy immediately reverses the balance of power. The key is to keep the retort unemotional and to repeat the agreeing statement verbatim whenever teasing occurs. Eventually, the teaser will tire of this and the bullying will decrease.

Teasing can also be halted by embarrassing the teaser by criticizing something about *him*. This strategy works only for mild teasing and must be done with an audience present to be effective. For example, if a teaser constantly taunts the child about his performance in math class, the victim can wait until he is being teased on the bus or in the hall, turn to the teaser, smile, and say, "Yeah, I have trouble in math, but *you* got a lousy mark on the geography quiz last week." This technique tends to extinguish the bullying and may prevent future incidents as well.

One particularly ingenious "table-turning" strategy is to counterattack *before* the attack. When the teaser and his group approach the victim for the daily litany of taunts, the victim turns to the teaser and says, "Well, good morning. What are you going to tease me about today? My hat? My coat? My glasses? What's it going to be? I'm eager to find out." Only the most verbal teaser will be able to mount an effective retort to such an onslaught. Most teasers will simply leave with their tails firmly between their legs!

The victim might also be assertive and direct with the teaser. Assertiveness—unlike aggression—is not intended to hurt another person. Rather, it merely tells the tormentor that the victim is worthy of respect and has certain rights that cannot be infringed upon. This response is far more effective than whining or complaining when teasing occurs. The assertiveness strategy is also effective when the intimidation or harassment has indirect sexual overtones.

Once again, the LD child may require intensive practice and rehearsal to master the scripts involved in this approach. This technique requires simultaneous use of verbal language *and* body language, which may be difficult for many children with learning problems.

When making an assertive statement to a teaser, the child must stand up straight, make direct eye contact, and speak in a firm, authoritative tone. The child must move toward the teaser as he speaks. Failure to utilize the proper body language will render his "assertive script" ineffective.

Unlike the previous strategies, assertiveness is more effective when the teaser and the victim are alone, without an audience present. This setting enables the teaser to respond to the message rather than perform for the audience.

The assertive script consists of a direct, brief confrontive statement that does not threaten. Rather, the statement serves to firmly condemn the teasing and insist that the child be treated with respect in the future. Below are some examples of effective assertiveness scripts:

> "John, I hate it when people call me 'Shorty.' I am tired of
>   being pushed around every day. Now stop it!"
> "Bill, I have had it with you and your teasing. From now on,
>   I want you to leave me alone on the bus ride."
> "Joey, I never make fun of you, and I get sick of you making
>   fun of me. Leave me alone."

Notice that these statements focus on the *victim's* feelings and are not accusatory or threatening. The child should be taught to break eye contact immediately after making the statement.

Another effective technique to prevent and eliminate teasing is the use of peers and friends. Bullies tend to focus their unwanted attention on loners. If your child is accompanied by a small group of friends at school, on the playground, and on the bus, he is far less likely to be bullied or teased.

When to "Tell"

When the above strategies fail to halt the teasing, your child will need assistance from an adult. Do not assume that your child will know how and when to solicit adult intervention. The anti-tattling credo of childhood is strong, and children are often reluctant to seek adult help.

I often counsel children about the difference between *tattling* and *telling*. Tattling is done in order to get someone in trouble. ("Mrs. Munro, on the way to school today, Billy threw a snowball and almost hit a window.") In contrast, telling is done to get someone *out* of trouble. ("Mrs. McCue, Jim hits Lenny on the bus every day and takes his lunch. Lenny is afraid to tell you.")

Children with learning problems often have difficulty determining the roles and functions of people within an organization. As a result, they may not know *whom* to go to when they are being bullied. I remember a confused maintenance man entering my office and saying, "Rick, Scotty just told me that Jeffrey beats him up at the bus stop every morning. I don't know why he told *me* and I don't know what to do about it." Assist your child in making a list of adults who would be effective confidants if the child is bullied or intimidated.

Also, counsel the child to attract an adult's attention if he is being bullied. If the victim loudly protests the bullying or yells out "Ouch! Stop that!" when he is physically hurt, he will attract adult attention and assistance without directly requesting it. Bullying incidents are often very brief and sneaky. By loudly bringing attention to the behavior, the bully's sinister, covert strategy is rendered ineffective.

Creating Support Systems

Children who are chronically bullied or isolated report that they have no established "support system." They feel, often correctly, that they have no defined group or individual to turn to when they are bullied or harassed. The ability to establish a support system is an integral step in achieving social acceptance and a sense of belonging.

Many children believe—incorrectly—that being independent means that you don't depend on *anyone else* for *anything*. This is simply untrue. Even the most successful and accomplished adults have a well-developed support system. This system consists of individuals who can provide assistance or guidance for a variety of situations. You know that Rolodex on your desk with hundreds of names and phone numbers? That's your support system.

It is important that the child develop his own system and learn to use it appropriately. His success in school, at home, and at work will be enhanced by an effective support system. These supportive relationships require a lot of work to develop and maintain.

One of the main functions of a support system is to provide encouragement and assistance. The system is particularly valuable during times of stress or risk taking. Some people refer to the support system as a "safety net." The child will be more likely to try new things and take some chances if he knows that there is a group of people to catch him if he falls or fails.

There are four important factors involved in the development of an effective support system.

1. You must communicate honestly with members of the system. Say what you mean and mean what you say. Honest communication is the key. Be willing to say what you are thinking and feeling. These relationships are based upon trust.

2. You cannot merely "make withdrawals" from the system; you must "make deposits" as well. The child must be willing to assist the other person when help or counsel is needed.

3. Access your support system when you are anxious, fearful, or vulnerable. Approach a member and tell her honestly about the issue or concern you are facing. Ask for objective (honest) input. Be prepared! The member may not agree with you. Being a member of a support system does *not* require 100 percent approval of everything you do!

4. Support systems take time to develop and need to be nurtured. Because these relationships are based upon trust, they do not develop overnight. In order for a support system to be effective, the child must nurture and cultivate the relationship by random and unsolicited acts of kindness and generosity toward those in his system. He cannot access the system only when he is in trouble.

When *Your* Child Is the Bully

This chapter has dealt extensively with techniques that can assist the socially incompetent child when he is teased or bullied. But in some instances the LD child is the *aggressor*. How should you handle the situation if *your* child is the bully? Children who bully tend to have several common traits, including a need to control social situations, a notable lack of empathy, difficulty with anger control, cockiness, and arrogance.

None of us is happy to learn that our child intimidates and torments other children. When we receive such a report—or when we witness our child's cruelty toward others—our natural tendency is to deny the behavior or develop myriad excuses for the bullying. Try to resist both of these responses and deal with the problem directly and openly.

Although you should not tolerate the behavior or invent excuses, it is important to realize that bullying behavior occurs for a reason. Very few children are simply mean and bad. Bullying may occur for reasons beyond the child's control. The behavior is inappropriate and should not be tolerated, but the causal factors should be considered.

For example, the child may develop a pattern of bullying behavior because he has poorly developed problem-solving and conflict-resolution skills. He simply does not know how to use language in order to meet his needs and wishes. So he uses physical intimidation—rather than discussion and compromise—to get others to do what he wishes.

We must remember that the classroom is a very frustrating place for children with chronic learning problems. His bullying may be reflective of this frustration and failure. Again, this does not make the behavior appropriate or tolerable, but it may shed light on its cause.

As previously stated, bullying generally occurs when there are no adults around or available. Many children with LD are very rule governed and dependent upon adults to guide their behavior. When adults and rules are not readily apparent or available, the LD child's behavior is likely to regress.

There may be a developmental reason the LD child bullies. At ages six and seven, for example, it is common for children to be so self-involved that they are unaware of how hurtful their bullying behavior is to others. By age eight, children begin to learn about friendship and kindness, and these hurtful comments and behaviors decrease markedly. However, the nine-year-old child with a learning problem may have a developmental delay in this area and so continue to treat peers in an insensitive and hurtful manner.

It is an established psychological fact that all human beings have a need for power and control in their lives. Because of their academic difficulties, children with LD often feel powerless and may feel that they have minimal control over their lives or futures. Therefore, they may seek to achieve power in inappropriate ways (bullying). Again, this is not an *excuse* for the behavior, but a possible *reason* for it.

An LD child who often bullied others made a very insightful comment to me during a counseling session. "The other kids don't like me," he said, "so I make them *afraid* of me. At least it's *something*." For some children with social skill differences, their lack of popularity deteriorates into intimidation of others.

Seriously consider these causal factors and try to ameliorate or neutralize them by providing the child with success, offering counsel, or instructing him in friendship skills. Also recognize that your child's victims must be defended and protected. There may be reasons for your child's bullying behavior, but these do not make the behavior appropriate or acceptable.

You must deal with incidents of bullying immediately after they occur. Firmly tell the child that the behavior is unacceptable and explain to him the impact that his intimidation has upon the victim. Provide him with alternative behaviors: "If you don't like Gabe, just stay away from him," or "Joanne felt very badly when she dropped her tray in front of everybody. By making fun of her and calling her a name, you made her feel even worse!"

If you witness your child bullying another, comfort the victim first. *Then* discuss the behavior and its impact with your child.

When an adult approaches a tormentor to reprimand him for his behavior, the child will often defend his behavior by saying that he was "only joking" with the victim. Do not accept this as a response. Joking occurs between friends or equals and brings mutual enjoyment. Bullying does not fit this definition. I reprimanded a bully once by saying, "John, don't tell me that you were joking. Joking is between friends and is fun. Billy is *not* your friend; you don't like him, and your goal was not to have fun. Your intent was to humiliate and embarrass Billy. You were not joking!"

Confer with the other adults in your child's life and try to find the pattern of your child's bullying. How frequent and intense is the bullying? Is he focusing on one child or a group of children? When and where do these incidents occur? This information will better enable you to develop a strategy to reduce harassment.

Because many kids with social problems are eager to be accepted and liked by peers, they become extremely susceptible to peer pressure. Perhaps your child's bullying behavior is an inappropriate attempt to impress and please others. Explain to him that bullying is unacceptable and, further, that it is an inappropriate and ineffective strategy to establish friendships. In fact, this behavior is likely to increase his isolation and rejection.

Reinforce the importance of kindness. The philosopher William Blake was once asked what the three most important ingredients in a successful, happy life were. The wise man responded, "Three things in human life are important: the first is to be kind; the second is to be kind; and the third is to be kind." Do all in your power to teach—and model—kindness to your child. Show him the benefits and joys inherent in being kind to other human beings.

The first step in this kindness instruction is to teach the child to be increasingly aware of the feelings and emotions of others. Utilize television shows, movies, or community excursions to point out people's emotions and feelings. ("How do you think the boy felt when his father didn't come to the awards dinner?" "Look at that woman

over there near the door. She looks very happy and seems to be waiting for someone's arrival. How can you tell that she is happy?") It will
be easier for your child to be kind to others if she becomes more
adept at reading the emotions of people in her environment. A significant subskill of empathy is the ability to "walk in the shoes of another" and respond to the emotions of classmates, family members,
and other people that you may encounter.

Empathy is the ability to view a situation from another person's
point of view. I cannot overemphasize the importance of this skill in
building social competence. A child with poorly developed empathy
will be viewed as self-centered and insensitive and will have frequent
conflicts and misunderstandings with peers and authority figures. He
may be unaware that he has offended someone or hurt another's feelings. He will have significant difficulty solving social problems.

One effective strategy to enhance a child's empathy is to consistently outline your emotional reaction to her behavior or comments.
You might say, "That really hurt my feelings when you criticized my
dress in front of Becky," or "I was very proud of you when you cleared
the table at Grandma's house without being asked." This strategy will
help the child become more aware of the impact of her behavior on
others.

Children will not develop empathy simply because their parents
wish them to. Empathy is a skill that must be continually taught and
fostered. Be sure to reinforce and praise the child when he is kind,
thoughtful, or responsive to the needs of others. As always, remember: behavior that is reinforced is replicated.

As the child develops empathy, he will benefit from reminders
and prompts. For example, "Your sister is pretty disappointed that her
softball game was rained out. Maybe you could go into her room and
try to cheer her up," or "Grandpa is really happy about his picture
being on the front page of the newspaper. Why don't you call him and
tell him about your teacher hanging it up on the bulletin board?"

Modeling continues to be the most valuable and effective strategy
to improve your child's empathy and responsiveness. When you
demonstrate kindness in your own daily behavior, this value is reinforced and celebrated. Let the child know how rewarding and fulfilling it is to assist others. "I had a great day at work today. Sally was

really swamped with a big project and had a lot of photocopying to do. I took a quick lunch and spent most of my lunch hour helping her collate. She was so grateful and it made me feel great to be able to help her out."

Peer Pressure

To understand and deal effectively with bullying, you must consider the dynamics of peer pressure. The interrelationship between bullying and peer pressure is significant, particularly during adolescence.

"Peer pressure" is a concept often misinterpreted and misunderstood by parents and caregivers. The term inevitably elicits a negative response and is often viewed as synonymous with "mob rule." It brings to mind a child doing or saying inappropriate things in an attempt to please and ingratiate himself to his peers. As in a mob mentality, the child would *not* have behaved in this manner if not for the negative influence of his peers. However, there are also positive aspects to peer pressure. The opinions and perspectives of peers have a significant impact upon the behavior of children *and* adults. The human desire to conform to group norms is one of the most civilizing and significant forces in human history. We all alter our behavior, our thoughts, our language, and even our clothing to gain acceptance and approval. This is altogether natural and necessary.

Peer influence can be a positive and motivating force in a child's life. His eagerness to gain peer acceptance may result in his joining a team or a club. It may inspire him to work harder in school, maintain his hygiene, and be more mindful of his physical health. It is our collective hope that our children select peer groups with appropriate and positive goals and that the groups' influence becomes a source of motivation and inspiration for them. Our great collective fear is that a child "falls in with a bad crowd."

Peer pressure affects all of us throughout our lives, but it has very significant impact on adolescence. This complex developmental stage finds the child with one foot in adulthood and the other foot in childhood. As the child's physical appearance becomes more adult-like, his parents, teachers, and coaches naturally begin to expect more mature behavior from him. Unfortunately, the child does not have the experience or background to make adult decisions and his actions are often based on his childhood experiences. He finds himself torn between his desire for independence—"Leave me alone! Stay out of my life!"—and his continued need for security—"Can I have twenty dollars for a movie?" This duality is complex and confusing for the adolescent *and* his parents. Adolescence can be characterized as a period of great joy and great sadness, of camaraderie and isolation, of significant growth and measurable regression, of high hopes and depressive pessimism. Throughout these difficulties we often remind the child, "These are the best years of your life." The confused adult-child often receives this optimistic message with great skepticism.

Parents often interpret adolescence as a period of rebellion in which the child loses respect and affection for the family. We view the peer group as conspirators in this rejection and revolution. This is an unproductive way to view this life stage.

A more productive perspective involves the recognition that the child is equidistant between the dependence of childhood and the independence of adulthood. He feels that he has little in common with his prepubescent siblings and even *less* in common with his aging parents. These two sources of support and confirmation have little influence on the adolescent. But the child still needs acceptance and approval, so he turns to his peers. He is not looking for a *conspiracy,* just a little confirmation. Parental attempts to guide or assist are viewed as interference and disrespect by the adolescent, while you may view your adolescent's desire for independence as a rejection of you and your values. Both of these perspectives are inaccurate and damaging to the parent-child relationship.

The adolescent has significant fears and feelings that he may not be "normal." His physiological changes can be a source of great concern and confusion. It is this fear of "abnormality" that drives the child to think, dress, talk, and walk in a manner identical to his peers. If he can see that he looks and acts "like everyone else," these fears of "weirdness" are greatly reduced. This also accounts for the cruel rejection often suffered by teenagers who do not fit into the norms that the peer group had created. Any departure in dress, speech, behavior, or interests is viewed with great suspicion by peers.

The Dreaded Spotlight

When I conduct parent seminars, I often ask the audience to brain-storm a list of adjectives to describe adolescents. Invariably, the word *mean* is among the very first responses given. Indeed, teenagers can be rejecting and hostile toward their peers. Who among us does not have memories of our own adolescence wherein we were cruel or re-jecting of a peer? Teenagers are not inherently mean. But their treat-ment of their peers can be brutal.

An example may be useful. Suppose four girls—Paula, Nancy, Janet, and Joanne—are daily commuters on the same school bus. Each morning, each girl enters the bus with the same wrenching, *secret* fear: that she will say, do, or wear something that makes her stand out and appear dumb or different. In her mind, one misstep could destroy the relationship she shares with the others. One mis-take could result in the permanent and indelible brand of *loser*.

The four girls carefully navigate the minefield of adolescent con-versation, careful not to say anything controversial or dumb. As the carefully choreographed conversation proceeds, Janet expresses her admiration for a singing group that is decidedly "out" and "uncool." Joanne grabs this opportunity to keep the spotlight off *herself* by mer-cilessly taunting Janet for her out-of-step opinion. The other two girls—also wary of the spotlight—gladly join in. Basically, as long as the spotlight focuses on Janet, the others are safe from the glare. Upon arrival at school, Janet staggers from the bus, humiliated and embarrassed. Are her fellow passengers pathologically mean and cruel? Not really. They're merely trying to survive! By focusing the group's hostilities on another child, the adolescent ensures her own well-being. This also allows her a modicum of control over her life and her environment.

Teenagers with learning disabilities are often the objects of peer ridicule and cruelty. Again, in the world of adolescence, "different" is automatically "bad." Because of his learning, language, and social problems, the LD adolescent is different. This becomes a source of humiliation, isolation, and rejection.

It is important to remember that adolescents, particularly adoles-cents with learning disorders, are "managed by the moment." That is, whatever event is occurring at that time in the adolescent's life (e.g., Halloween dance, class play, band tryouts) is—to her perception—the most important event in the history of humankind. She perceives no *future* and no *past*. She lives intensely and exclusively in the present. Therefore, relatively minor problems or difficulties (e.g., a snub from a friend, a dropped tray in the cafeteria, an incorrect oral answer to a teacher's question) are viewed as catastrophic and life altering. Her present-oriented mind-set does not allow her to put the incident in an appropriate perspective: "Sally didn't invite me to her pool party. My life is over. . . ."

Communication with the LD adolescent is difficult, especially when discussing peer issues. The teen may be extraordinarily critical of others and yet hypersensitive to criticism himself. Adolescents want their opinions and ideas to be taken seriously, and yet may be very dismissive of any ideas that you may offer. The adolescent wants (and needs) to make many independent decisions and becomes very defensive when others question these decisions. Adolescents want *their* opinions to be accepted on blind faith even as they continually criticize the beliefs of others. Obviously, this dynamic makes parent-teen communication quite difficult.

If a child *does* ask for your advice about a peer problem, recognize that he is not seeking a lecture, a scolding, or even a *solution*. He may merely want you to listen and to take the situation seriously. In such an instance, it is often useful to tell him of a similar incident that you faced when you were a teen and discuss your response. At times, such a story will assist the child in knowing what to do; in other cases, your anecdote may outline unsuccessful responses that the child will want to avoid. This approach demonstrates that you are taking the child's concerns seriously, and it also places you in the role of an ally and source of information.

Because peer pressure is such an important aspect of the teen's daily existence, she may attempt to modify *your* behavior by exerting pressure from *your* peers. ("But Cathy's mom lets *her* go to R-rated movies. Why can't you be cool like her?") This approach can make a parent feel rejected and hurt. It is important to realize that this is merely an attempt to manipulate you by making you feel uncool! Your child is testing your resolve. In most cases, it is important that you pass this test.

Because adult-adolescent communication can be challenging and difficult, parents often avoid interactions with their teens. I have seen many families in which parents are virtually uninvolved with their adolescents and each family member functions in his or her own solitary orbit. While this approach may bring temporary peace to the household, it has damaging and dangerous long-term effects. If the parent is unwilling to offer advice, comfort, and counsel, the child's peer group becomes his only source of guidance by default. Your teen ends up receiving advice from people with limited life experience and maturity. Adolescents *need* adults in their lives to serve as guides and role models. This is a primary responsibility—and right—of parents.

The Role of Self-esteem in Bullying

Interestingly, the trait shared by both the bully and the victim is low self-esteem. This lack of strong self-concept causes the victim to accept the bullying and causes the bully to inflict the intimidation. There is much that parents and teachers can do to foster self-esteem in their children and so disrupt the cycle of harassment.

Below are suggestions for effecting a positive change in a child's self-concept.

- Value the uniqueness of your child. Recognize that each of us has different preferences, skills, weaknesses, and needs.
- Focus on these strengths. Find areas of skills that bring success to your child. List them; emphasize them; celebrate them.
- When reprimanding the child, be cautious to reject the *behavior*, not the child himself. Use affectionate terms when scolding (e.g., "Come on, honey, get in there and finish that homework").
- Show a sincere interest in what the child is doing. This is often more effective than praise.
- Establish and maintain reasonable, realistic expectations for your child. Research indicates that children often behave in a

manner that is reflective of the adult's expectations. If you expect them to succeed they will. If you expect them to fail . . . they will.

- Avoid sarcasm when dealing with the child. Their language deficiencies often prevent them from understanding the humor or the intent of sarcastic statements.

- Provide the child with constructive feedback. Feedback should be specific and nonjudgmental. Address the immediate issue; do not bring up issues from the past.

- Help your child develop effective decision-making skills; provide him with regular opportunities for making choices. Provide effective modeling by outlining your reasons for decisions that you make. Encourage the child to do the same.

- Increase the child's sense of responsibility and self-reliance; allow him to do those things that he can do for himself, even if they don't get done as well as if you had done them. Before you leap in to offer assistance, determine whether the child should complete that task independently.

- Strike a balance between competition and cooperation; focus on enjoyment, satisfaction, contribution, and participation in competitive games and activities. Emphasize individual skills, improvement, and strategy development. Avoid comparing one child's performance to another's.

- View a child's errors as an opportunity to teach, not an excuse to belittle. We all make mistakes, and no one makes errors on purpose. When a child states that Abraham Lincoln was our first president, you have learned two things from your child: (1) he does not know a great deal about Lincoln, and (2) he probably knows less about George Washington! Use his mistake as an opportunity to diagnose and remediate his weakness.

- Avoid treating the child like a guest in his home. Expect the child to complete assigned (albeit modified) chores. Insist that he complete tasks that are expected of his siblings (e.g., writing thank-you notes, corresponding with relatives, wearing appropriate clothing for social occasions). He may require some assistance with these tasks, but it will decrease the resentment his siblings may feel regarding his "special" treatment.

- Divide large tasks into several small ones. This enables the child to enjoy success and is effective toward the mastery and retention of the skill.

- Encourage him to use spoken language to communicate his needs and interests. Encourage him to address "safe" groups (e.g., family gatherings) in preparation for the dreaded "oral talks" in school. This will help him to overcome his embarrassment and fear.

- Maintain a file of his academic work. Discuss this material with him on occasion in order to demonstrate his progress, achievement, and development.

- Give the child a weekly allowance. The child should be taught how to *spend* before he learns how to *save*. His allowance should not be tied to his chores, his behavior, or his academic performance. Rather, he is given an allowance as a "learning tool," so that he may better learn the skills related to money and consumerism.

- Encourage the child's participation in one-on-one and individual sports (e.g., tennis, swimming, skiing). These activities often provide the child with opportunities for success, exercise, and positive peer interaction. Encourage the child to learn bike riding. This activity provides her with much-needed independence and allows you to celebrate her personal best.

- Encourage the child to maintain "collections" (e.g., baseball cards, stamps, coins, rocks). This enables the child to become the resident expert on one topic.

- Avoid comparing your child to his siblings. Such comparisons are hurtful, unproductive, and unfair. When a parent says, "Danny, why can't you keep your room neat like your sister Meghan does?," it hurts both children. Danny is hurt by the unfavorable comparison, and Meghan begins to feel that her mother's love for her is based exclusively upon her room-cleaning skills.

- Communicate your confidence in your child.

- Encourage and compliment her daily.
- Permit/encourage the child to be involved in a variety of activities and, thus, play a variety of roles.
- Allow or encourage the child to follow the normal fads of his peers (e.g., in clothing, music).
- Emphasize the positive aspects of a child's behavior, even if the task was not entirely successful. *Reward direction . . . not perfection!*
- Anticipate that the child will have plateaus, failures, setbacks, and regressions. Encourage and assist him during these times.
- Listen to your children, celebrate their victories, and comfort them in defeat.

Remember: "There are only two lasting bequests that we can give our children—one is *roots,* and the other is *wings.*"

Afterword

This chapter began with an essay by my nephew, Daniel. He was occasionally a victim in the bully-victim-spectator triangle but was, more often, a spectator. His poignant essay reflects the spectator's feelings of guilt and powerlessness.

And what price does *the bully* play? That is shown in an essay by Daniel's cousin, our son, Danny. He is an exceedingly sweet and generous young man who now works as a journalist in Chicago. He constantly humbles and amazes us with his blazing insights and his greathearted worldview. He is as fine a man as I know.

He was the new kid at his middle school and was desperately seeking his role in that community. He was quick-witted and extraordinarily funny, and he found acceptance and approval by becoming a verbal bully. He used his verbal skills to belittle, embarrass, and isolate other kids.

Dan and I share his 1996 college application essay with you in order to make a point.

RUE
by Daniel Lavoie

I am deeply ashamed.

Perhaps the above sentence gets tossed around a little too loosely these days. But to this Connecticut-born son of special educators, the sanctity of those words has remained true. As a matter of fact, I do not believe that I have ever said or written that sentence in my sixteen and one half years on this planet. But tonight, on October 9, 1995, I feel that I must "come clean," as they say, for the feelings bouncing around in my head have been stewing for too long.

To set the stage—for years, I had always been the pleasant, agreeable (albeit bland) nerd, for lack of a better word. In sixth grade, though, I discovered the power contained within a humorously caustic remark; the superficial respect that a scathing, slashing retort commands. Just as I realized this key to preadolescent success, my life sustained a major blow as my family up and moved to an entirely new state. Starting over was difficult, but my newfound "comic sense" (as it seemed at the time) came to my rescue. Soon, I was relied upon as the self-declared "Pundit of Putdowns." I took that role to heart. And so my tale begins . . .

As is sadly destined to happen in any class full of faux adults, one classmate is chosen to be the "loser," the "outcast." In my particular class, this boy was Toby (his name has been changed due to his absolute innocence). Not only was Toby extraordinarily medically hyperactive, he was also a Jehovah's Witness. These two differences made him easy prey for even a halfway "witty" young student. During the Pledge of Allegiance (which his religious convictions prohibited him from taking part in), a group of sad, desperate classmates, myself included, would ridicule his belief system beyond the point of his ability. Furthermore, whenever Toby's Ritalin would lose its potency, we were the first to provoke him to the point that he had little choice but to retaliate with his only weapon: violence. But this just made the "game" that much more fun. Slowly, though, the attacks on Toby became

more severe, and, with them, so did the retaliations. The "game"
had escalated to a level none of us could anticipate. But to six
cocksure, seventh-grade bastards, the fun was just beginning.
One day, after a particularly rough day for Toby, my compatriots
and I crossed the line. After school, we sneaked into Toby's locker,
his private space, his one safe bastion away from our ridicule. We
removed and threw away all of Toby's school books, replacing
them with a chillingly simple note reading only: "Go to Hell,
Toby . . . Oh, sorry, you don't believe in it."

We thought nothing would be funnier than the expression
on Toby's face when he found the note the next day. We all waited
around the corner the next morning in giddy anticipation. As
Toby began to slowly pull open his locker door, my hordette could
do nothing aside from giggle incessantly. The sheer horror on
Toby's face did not disappoint my partners, or myself. We had fi-
nally put the proverbial nail in Toby's coffin. Thus, it was little
surprise to my "friends" when, the next day, we were told that
Toby was transferring schools, effective immediately. At that one
moment of epiphany, I realized the impact that the actions of one
immature, malevolent, vicious, Connecticut-born son of special
educators can have.

I'd like to say that this episode changed me instantly. I'd like
to say that, from that day forth, I went on to live an exemplary
life. But I can't. What I can say, though, is that this incident
helped to shape my ideals. Since that day, I have had a height-
ened sensitivity to even the smallest miscarriage of justice. I've
been told that, if I try, I would be able to forget this one unfortu-
nate altercation that occurred so many years ago. I choose not to.

Bullies are often *not* cruel, malevolent, sadistic, ruthless people bent
on the destruction and humiliation of others. Often, they are merely
insecure kids from good families whose need for acceptance temporarily overcomes their moral code and societal obligations. Dan
wanted friends. He met that goal at the expense of another. But his
behavior was a negative blip in a life filled with generosity, selfless-
ness, courage, and caring. Keep Danny's essay in mind the next time
you reprimand a bully. If the offender is lucky—and receives appro-

priate guidance—the incident might lead him to better understand the human condition. For Danny, it did.

RECOMMENDED RESOURCES

And Words Can Hurt Forever, James Garbarino (New York: Free Press, 2001).

Bullies and Victims, Suellen Fried and Paula Fried (New York: M. Evans and Company, 2002).

Sticks and Stones, Scott Cooper (New York: Random House, 1999).

CHAPTER TEN

Mastering the Hidden Curriculum of School

The Unwritten, Unspoken Rules

Jack was chronically late for class at his suburban high school. The sophomore often arrived at class without his books and materials, and he frequently failed to complete his homework. He was obviously unmotivated. A slacker. A ne'er-do-well. His own worst enemy.

A university consultant was contracted to investigate educational options for Jack. After the professor interviewed the student, he was puzzled by the inconsistencies between Jack's obvious eagerness to please his teachers and the spottiness of his day-to-day performance in school. The consultant surmised that Jack's problem might be caused by his inability to understand and adhere to the Hidden Curriculum of his school—the unspoken, unwritten "rules" that create the school's culture.

The consultant arranged to have Jack followed or "shadowed" by a graduate student who looked young enough to be mistaken for a high school senior. With no one's knowledge—including Jack's—the grad student followed Jack to and from his

251

classes and attended most class sessions. She was attempting to discern if Jack's tardiness and lack of preparation were caused, in some way, by his inability to understand or adhere to the Hidden Curriculum of his school. The consultant's suspicions were on target!

What was causing Jack's chronic tardiness and failure to arrive at class prepared? Was it lack of motivation? Disrespect for teachers? Lack of concern for his academic progress? No. He simply was unaware of the procedures involved in the effective and efficient use of his locker!

On the first day that Jack was observed, he was unable to correctly input the combination to his locker despite struggling with it for ten minutes. He was several minutes late for class and arrived without his books.

On the second day, he went to his locker prior to first period and retrieved all of his books for all six of his classes. He staggered to his first-period class under the heavy load. Immediately after his first-period math class, he returned to his locker, opened it, and placed his math book inside. Of course, if he had been planning to return to his locker after first period, there was no reason to lug all of his books to his first class. He could have retrieved them when he dropped off his math book!

On the third day, he went to his locker but retrieved the wrong books and experienced each teacher's wrath for being unprepared.

On the fourth day, he forgot to go to his locker at all. On the fifth day, Jack arrived at school with a soaking wet raincoat after walking to school in a torrential storm. Instead of hanging his jacket on the hooks in his locker, he elected to carry his coat through the corridors, soaking other students as he passed, confirming—once again—his reputation as a "loser."

Jack's story is a clear example of a child who has not mastered the Hidden Curriculum of school. The standard curriculum of a school consists of the published course of study—the rules, regulations, and standards. The standard curriculum is clearly understood by all; it is generally presented in student handbooks and other publications.

The Hidden Curriculum, however, consists of the *unwritten, unspoken* rules of school. It is the Hidden Curriculum that defines each school's unique culture. This culture makes each school an individual institution with specific expectations for each member of the community. The school's Hidden Curriculum is its *culture* and includes shared norms, values, beliefs, traditions, rituals, and customs. Your child is tested on his academic skills every few days, but his social interactions are "tested" and evaluated hundreds of times each day.

Compare Jack's story with an experience I had with our own son, Dan. On his second day of kindergarten, the bus failed to arrive at its scheduled time. I decided to drive him to school. On the drive the following conversation took place:

DAD: "What are you going to do when you arrive at school, Dan?"

DAN: "Well, the first thing I'll do is put this toy car in my cubby. I brought a toy to school yesterday and one of the big kids took it away from me. But we each have cubbies with our names on them and—if you push your stuff way back in the cubby—no one can see it, so it will be safe. Then I'm going to say, 'Good morning' to the teacher."

DAD: "And why will you do *that*?"

DAN: "Well, Dad, remember when you took me to the school gym during the summer and they gave me some tests?"

DAD: "Yes. It was kindergarten screening."

DAN: "The lady who tested me that day ended up being my teacher. Yesterday when I saw her I said, 'Hi, I remember *you*! You tested me last summer. I had fun that day.' The teacher smiled at me and called me 'Danny Boy' and she let me pass out the napkins at snack time, so I'm gonna do that again. Then I'm going to go sit at the far end of the long, white table."

DAD: "You've lost me, Dan. Why are you going to sit at the far end of the long, white table?"

DAN: "Well, at the beginning of class, we all sit at that table while the teacher reads us a story. After that, we have free play with the toys . . . and if I sit at the very end of the long, white table I will be closer to the toy box and I will be able to get the yellow dump truck that I missed out on yesterday."

In a single day, kindergartner Dan had discovered and mastered the Hidden Curriculum in his classroom. Conversely, teenaged Jack had been at the high school for two years and was still puzzled and confused about the Hidden Curriculum of his school.

Schools are not the only organizations that feature Hidden Curricula. In fact, nearly all institutions, agencies, and offices have a Hidden Curriculum. Consider your own office. It doubtless has a policy manual that clearly outlines the office's standard curriculum. But there also exists an informal—albeit important—set of unwritten rules that demands compliance. Failure to adhere to these rules will cause the offender to be viewed as rude, insensitive, or worse.

Suppose a custom has developed wherein employees bring regional snack foods to the office lounge when they return from a business trip to another part of the country. There is no written requirement to do so, but it has evolved as a customary practice over the years. Suppose a new employee returns from a trip to El Paso *without* salsa and tortilla chips. He is immediately viewed as less than a team player and his status tumbles. There is no *contractual* requirement that he brings food for all, but the *culture* of the office demands it. Your workplace doubtless has a Hidden Curriculum that dictates everything from the length of coffee breaks to the usage of office supplies. Failure to adhere to these unwritten rules will result in social isolation, rejection, and embarrassment.

An analogy to a Hidden Curriculum problem in the business world might be helpful to better understand this concept:

The Japanese culture is gentle and amiable. An integral part of this culture is the custom of "saving face." Being embarrassed—or embarrassing another person—is a source of great shame and angst for a Japanese man or woman. People take great care to avoid insulting others.

This charming virtue has permeated the Japanese business world. Suppose you were a Japanese merchant who planned to place a large order with a supplier. The two of you have conducted several meetings to finalize the deal, although no contract has yet been signed.

Suddenly, you discover that you can get a far better price from your supplier's competitor. Now you want to cease negotiations with the original supplier. It will be embarrassing for you to have this conversation—and embarrassing for the original supplier to hear it.

A business custom—part of the Japanese business world's Hidden Curriculum—has evolved that allows you to halt this negotiation without undue embarrassment to either party. At the next scheduled meeting, you merely bring a gift and hand it to the supplier at the beginning of the session. This gesture informs him that the deal is canceled, without making either of you uncomfortable. Interestingly, after the gift is given and accepted, the meeting is held as if the negotiating process is continuing.

Now, suppose you are an American executive doing business in Japan. You are involved in a complex negotiation with a contemporary in Tokyo. Midway through the process, you arrive in Japan for a crucial meeting. Remembering that your colleague is a golfer, you arrive at the meeting with a gift of a dozen top-grade American golf balls. You hand him the gift at the outset of your meeting, participate actively in the conclave, and depart. You arrive at your Tokyo office and are greeted by your irate supervisor who has just received an e-mail informing him that you canceled a huge and lucrative deal.

So it is with schools. Your child's school has an established culture, and his social success will be largely dependent on his ability to understand and navigate this culture. In fact, success in the standard curriculum is often secondary to his success in the Hidden Curriculum.

A 1986 University of Wisconsin study of school cultures discovered this about the Hidden Curriculum.

- The Hidden Curriculum has a significant impact upon the performance, productivity, progress, and attitudes of students.
- The Hidden Curriculum is created, maintained, and manipulated by the students and the staff of the school.
- The Hidden Curriculum is unique for every school.
- The Hidden Curriculum is both destructive and constructive in nature.
- Changes in the Hidden Curriculum are slow and laborious; innovations are often viewed skeptically. The skepticism can border on paranoia.

Unfortunately, this book cannot teach you the Hidden Curriculum of your school. Each school's Hidden Curriculum is unique. Like snowflakes, no two are alike. I attended a high school in a small city in central Massachusetts. The standard curriculum at that school stated that students could enter the building via any entrance after 7:30 A.M. However, the *Hidden* Curriculum dictated that underclassmen *never* used the east entrance until 8:00 A.M. You see, the seniors hung out there daily from 7:30 to 8:00, and they enjoyed nothing more than hassling the occasional underclassman who wandered unknowingly onto their turf. This custom had existed for years, although it was never printed in the student handbook and no signs outlining this regulation were posted about the building. Yet everyone knew about it—*almost* everyone!

Students with learning problems often lack the observational and conceptual skills to comprehend the Hidden Curriculum of their school. They may have few friends who can coach and counsel them about the school's culture. As a result, they unknowingly violate the Hidden Curriculum, and that results in rejection, isolation, embarrassment, and humiliation. It is critically important that we *teach* the Hidden Curriculum to socially incompetent children with the same commitment and planning that we present the standard curriculum. Failure to understand and adhere to the Hidden Curriculum is a primary cause for children's failure in the mainstream.

Find the Hidden Curriculum
in Your School

Before we can teach the Hidden Curriculum to children, we must come to understand the school's culture ourselves. There are several techniques you can use to quantify and analyze a school's culture. Surveys, brainstorming sessions, and questionnaires can be used successfully in this process. Teachers can conduct staff meetings wherein they explore the concept of the Hidden Curriculum and then solicit input from their colleagues regarding the nature and details of the school's culture. Unfortunately, many special education teachers are unaware of the Hidden Curriculum in their schools. The majority of their time and energy is spent in lesson preparation, teaching, and attending meetings. However, if the specialist is not knowledgeable about the specifics of the school's culture, she is ill equipped to teach this culture to her students. It is always a good idea for the special education teacher to be involved in a variety of school-related activities and functions. In this way, she gains a better understanding of the school's Hidden Curriculum and can be extraordinarily helpful in assisting her students to understand it. It is advisable for the teacher to be an advisor or coach for committees or teams that are unrelated to special education. This enhances the teacher's status in the school and gives her a greater understanding of the unwritten rules that dictate the school's culture.

The faculty is not the only—or the best—source of this information. The *students* are an excellent resource because it is they who actually *design* much of the school's culture. *They* dictate the behaviors, modes of dress, and styles of music that are accepted and acceptable. The staff of a school develops the standard curriculum; the students at the school develop the Hidden Curriculum. This accounts for the fact that some aspects of the Hidden Curriculum change from year to year.

Another valuable source for data about the Hidden Curriculum is the support staff. Secretaries, lunch monitors, and the janitorial staff observe a school's culture every day and often have significant insight and knowledge about the unwritten regulations that pervade a school.

You may also want to examine your school's publications to better understand its culture. Yearbooks, newsletters, and other publications written by students can often render valuable insights. For example, the standard curriculum of a school may claim that *all* varsity sports are of equal importance and status. However, a review of the senior yearbook—which features twenty pages of football photos and a solitary picture of the tennis team—clearly illustrates that the Hidden Curriculum bestows disproportionate status and importance on the gridiron.

Identifying and analyzing a school's culture requires an exploration similar to an anthropologist's examination of an ancient civilization. Several cultural phenomena must be considered.

Physical Plant

Does the child understand the physical plant of the school? Does she know the shortcuts? Can she navigate the hallways? Can she effectively and efficiently utilize the cafeteria, infirmary, library, and lockers? You might be surprised at the difficulty that the child has with these tasks and the impact this difficulty has upon her academic and social success.

I once consulted with a large public high school in central New York. A sophomore with significant learning problems was being harshly criticized for his chronic tardiness. He would enter each class several minutes late, panting from his run to the classroom. His teachers resented his lateness and viewed it as reflective of disrespect and a lack of motivation. The student was—quite obviously—spending his time between classes with his friends and then running to his classroom after the bell.

Upon examining the situation, we realized that his chronic tardiness was not caused by lack of motivation or interest. Rather, it was caused by his inability to master the school's physical plant. The student had a significant spatial deficiency and was consistently confused by the layout of the school. For example, his homeroom was on the school's first floor, his second class was on the fourth floor, and his third class was on the third floor. After interviewing the student, we realized that he was returning to his first-floor homeroom between each class because that was the only way that he could locate the other classrooms. He was unnecessarily scaling dozens of flights of stairs daily, and *that* was the cause of his tardiness. When he was informed that he could go directly from class to class without returning to his homeroom each time, he laughed and said, "That explains it! I'm a jock in good shape and there are lots of little girls in my classes. At the end of each class, I would run, full speed, to my next class. When I would arrive, those girls were already seated and working. I couldn't understand it! I figured that I was the only kid in school without an elevator pass!"

Again, the boy's behavior was misinterpreted as a lack of motivation and respect when it was actually caused by his inability to understand the physical layout of the school. A school presents a very confusing maze for students with spatial difficulties.

Analyze the various Hidden Curriculum demands related to the physical plant of the school. The child may be unaware of the procedures required to access the various services offered at the school (infirmary, restrooms, cafeteria, student store, and so on). Jamie, a sophomore, was constantly in trouble with his mother for devouring everything in the refrigerator upon his return from school each day. It was not uncommon for him to eat an entire casserole that was intended to feed the whole family for dinner. In a counseling session, he confided to me the reason for this behavior. He had missed September's orientation sessions wherein the procedures for purchasing a cafeteria lunch were outlined. He did not understand how to enter the appropriate lunch line and was too embarrassed to ask for assistance from students or staff. As a result, he did not eat lunch for the entire year and arrived at home famished each day. He preferred to face the daily ire of his mother rather than admit his incompetence at school. Most children would prefer to be viewed as bad rather than dumb.

Consider the following aspects of your school's physical plant when defining its Hidden Curriculum:
- location of restrooms
- shortcuts within the building
- use of media center
- use of cafeteria (e.g., clearing tables)
- infirmary, health suites
- school store

- auditorium do's and don'ts
- location of classrooms
- exits, entrances
- passing in hallways
- off-limits areas
- use of lockers
- main office
- playground
- parking lot
- gymnasium
- locker rooms
- preventing theft
- informal location names (e.g., cafeteria = "caf")

The Schedule

Many schools have devised schedule formats that are extraordinarily confusing for children. These schedules are often adjusted on a daily basis in order to accommodate assemblies, testing, or special events. This presents a significant challenge to students with spatial or memory problems. Many children with social skill deficits have difficulty handling transitions, particularly unexpected ones. As a result, the ever-changing school schedule can become a significant source of anxiety and angst. Several years ago, I worked with a middle school child who, inexplicably, began skipping school regularly. An average of one day each week, he would arrive at school on time but would leave the building prior to his first period. These absences were so frequent that he was in danger of expulsion.

After analyzing the situation, his teachers came to realize that each of the absences occurred on a Wednesday. It seems that each Wednesday the school would rotate the class schedule according to some indiscernible pattern. The boy was unable to understand this rotation and, being too embarrassed to request help, he elected to leave the building and hide in the nearby woods all day. Once we determined the root cause of the behavior, we arranged for the boy to go to the guidance office every Wednesday to receive a handwritten schedule. He never missed another day of class.

Consider the following aspects of your school's schedule when defining its Hidden Curriculum:
- passing bell/late bell
- block scheduling
- function of homework
- absence/tardiness policies
- dismissal policies
- schedule changes
- fire drills

The Social Scene

The child with poor social skills may be confused and challenged by the social scene at school. Does she understand the cliques, rivalries, and current trends? Does she comprehend the dating customs? Does she know what's in and what's out?

My children attended a large, fine public high school on Cape Cod. When you enter the cavernous school lobby in early September, you see huge banners covering the walls and bulletin boards. The banners promote the annual Welcome Back Dance sponsored by the incoming freshman class. The sign reads:

Come One, Come All!

Freshmen, Sophomores, Juniors, and Seniors

are invited to the Welcome Back Dance

Sponsored by the Freshman Class

See you there!

The banners represent the *standard* curriculum of the event, but the Hidden Curriculum of that dance is very, very different.

The Hidden Curriculum assigns specific roles to the students based upon the class in which they are enrolled. If you are a freshman, you attend the dance. If you are a sophomore, you hang out in the school parking lot and enter the dance after nine o'clock. If you are a junior, you would *never* attend the dance but attend a house party hosted by a classmate. If you are a senior, you go to the party for a while and then meet at a local ice cream parlor. *That* is the Hidden Curriculum of that event. Any student who violates these unwritten regulations risks social isolation and rejection.

Clothing, slang, and music are also components of a school's Hidden Curriculum. Students with poor social skills often fail to observe and follow the customs of their school. These customs demand great uniformity, and youngsters who dress or speak differently are often rejected. If your child has a social skill deficit, he may not have noticed that all of the other boys are wearing short leather jackets with upturned collars. As a result, he buys a long corduroy coat with enormous buttons and becomes an object of ridicule. Parents should observe the other students' mode of dress and should assist the child in selecting clothing that is stylish and appropriate.

Dating customs may be confusing for the child with social deficiencies. He may be unaware of what constitutes "going out" or the steps in his school's dating rituals. As a result, he may make inappropriate or ineffective advances toward girls he is interested in. Consult with his siblings to gain insight into the dating rituals at his school.

Consider the following aspects of your school's social scene and extracurricular activities when defining the Hidden Curriculum:

Social Scene
- cliques
- "in" and "out" clothing
- "in" and "out" slang
- "in" and "out" music
- bully prevention
- gossip and rumors
- dating mores
- school events (e.g., dances, rallies)
- friendships
- rivalries
- "in" and "out" jewelry, accessories, backpacks
- "in" and "out" clubs and activities
- lunchtime culture
- peer pressure

- current hairstyles
- locker decorations
- nicknames
- parties
- school arrival rituals
- school spirit rituals
- holiday, birthday customs
- cultural/racial tenor
- types/brands of school supplies

Extracurricular Activities
- sign-up procedures
- extracurricular schedules
- intramural sports
- competitive sports
- clubs
- uniform usage
- performing arts
- band, chorus, drama
- function of student council
- election customs
- school newspaper
- volunteer opportunities

The Administrative Team and Teachers

In order to successfully negotiate the school's Hidden Curriculum, your child must understand the unique nature of the administrative team. What is the power hierarchy? Who works for whom? Who should the child approach regarding a problem that he may be experiencing? How should he approach an administrator with a request? Are appointments required? The child must understand the political infrastructure of the school in order to have his needs met successfully.

Among the most crucial aspects of a school's Hidden Curriculum is the child's interaction with his teachers. Although each school has mandated policies and procedures, each individual teacher also has a unique temperament, personality, likes, dislikes, and hot buttons. With the advent of the inclusion movement, which requires children with special needs to be placed in classes of nondisabled peers to the greatest extent possible, teachers are required to make adjustments in their curricula and strategies to accommodate the unique needs of the mainstreamed special education student. It seems quite appropriate, then, that the child also attempts to accommodate the *teacher's* idiosyncratic needs and interests. For instance, if Mrs. McNamara is a stickler for punctuality and considers tardiness a sign of disinterest and disrespect, the student should make a special effort to arrive to her class on time. If Mr. Brooks considers homework to be a critical aspect of his curriculum and spends hours preparing these assignments, the child should take extra care to complete the homework accurately and thoroughly.

The special education teacher or, where appropriate, the parent should informally survey the child's classroom teachers to determine their specific requirements and idiosyncrasies. Inquire as to their feelings and opinions about tardiness, neatness, homework, importance of test performance, and so forth. Then provide the child with this information. Other students may also be valuable sources of this information, as most teachers have a reputation that includes their individual quirks and preferences. Because LD students have marked difficulty discerning patterns, they are likely unaware of these reputations and may continually and unknowingly push the teacher's hot buttons.

Consider the following about teachers and administrative structure when defining your school's Hidden Curriculum:

Teachers
- idiosyncrasies/"hot buttons"
- homework policies
- seating assignments
- interests, hobbies
- reputations
- personalities
- "turn-offs"
- grading policies

- report cards
- requesting help
- individual procedures for:
    - collecting homework
    - passing out papers
    - pencil sharpening
    - raising hands
    - lending materials
- tolerance of noise
- neatness of classroom
- amount of structure provided
- willingness to assist
- discipline policies and practices
- teaching style
- grading policies

Administrators/Support Staff
- who works for whom?
- hierarchy
- roles of secretaries and janitors
- class change policies
- roles, responsibilities, functions

Parents' Role in Uncovering the Hidden Curriculum

Parents can play an important role in assisting the child to better understand and adhere to the Hidden Curriculum at school. Walk the halls of her school to observe the Hidden Curriculum firsthand and discuss this concept with her teachers. Encourage and assist your child in complying with the cultural rituals of her classmates. Upon receiving this advice from me, a reluctant parent said, "But then my Billy will be *just like everybody else*." Exactly. Peer compliance and conformity are the keys to peer acceptance.

Needless to say, you do not wish the child to conform to the *negative* aspects of the Hidden Curriculum (e.g., gangs, bullying, drug abuse, disrespect for authority), but do not be overly concerned if your teenager adopts a style of dress or coiffure that you find unattractive. It will be temporary. Remain mindful of the sage definition of adolescence:

> *I am not what I was.*
> *I am not what I am.*
> *And I am not what I am going to be.*

If a socially challenged child recognizes and follows a current trend, it is a cause for celebration and reinforcement, not angst. His desire to be like everyone else is normal, natural, and necessary.

When attempting to identify or quantify the Hidden Curriculum of your child's school, older siblings or cousins can be of invaluable assistance. Share the previous lists with them and relate the items to their own previous experiences at the school. Be aware, however, that the Hidden Curriculum changes from year to year in many schools, particularly with regard to clothing and music. The American apparel and music industries have focused heavily on the adolescent and preadolescent markets in an effort to convince them that last year's fashions are resoundingly "out" and *must* be replaced with the "newest," "freshest," and "latest."

Become an amateur anthropologist! Walk around your child's school and note the rituals, mores, customs, and traditions. Discuss these with the child and develop ways that he can conform with these customs. Discourage him from overstepping and attempting to be "too cool." His peers will easily sense if he is trying too hard to fit in.

Among other activities that parents can try in order to enhance the child's understanding of the school's Hidden Curriculum are:

- Assist him in setting realistic and attainable social goals. His dream of being elected student body president may be unrealistic. A more reasonable goal might be that he is appointed to the layout staff of the school's newspaper. Goal setting is a difficult skill, and children with social skill deficits tend to aim too high—or too low—when setting social goals.
- Help your child to select a member of the school staff (counselor, teacher, administrator, former teacher) she trusts and

likes. Approach this person with your child and ask if he would be willing to serve as a coach or guide for your daughter as she strives to understand and comply with the school's Hidden Curriculum.

- Encourage your child to experiment with a variety of clothing styles, behaviors, and approaches. Urge her to observe and monitor the reactions that she receives from others. If a change receives positive response, continue. If her new approach is not well received, abandon it.

- Remind the child, "Birds of a feather flock together." That is, she is more likely to enjoy social success if she seeks out groups and individuals who have interests similar to hers.

- In his book *All Kinds of Minds,* Dr. Mel Levine recommends that the child maintain a "social diary" in which she records her social successes and miscues. This can be a source of valuable discussion and can assist her in identifying negative and positive patterns. ("Harry, every time you sat in the front of the class in history, Ms. Vita smiled at you and was willing to help you. When you sat in the back of the class, she ignored you and you got in trouble for talking to Zak. Maybe you should sit in the front of the class in the future.")

The Hidden Curriculum of the Home and Community

Every community and, indeed, every individual home or business possesses its own Hidden Curriculum. If you reflect upon your own environs, you will recognize the unique culture in each of the various social settings in your community.

As I reflect upon my own small Cape Cod town, I recognize that:
- The local florist shop is frequented by the owner's two elderly golden retrievers. The smaller is affectionate, but you should be wary of the larger one.
- The morning librarian is somewhat cranky and disagreeable. It's best to go there in the afternoon, when her assistant is manning the circulation desk (especially if you are returning an overdue book).

- There is no need to feed the parking meters on Thursday. That's the meter maid's day off!
- The folks in the town hall are especially helpful if you donate to their annual Christmas toy drive.
- The video store on Main Street has more dramas than comedies. If you want a good comedy, go to the store on Rockwell Street.
- The school buses invariably slow down the Maple Street traffic at 2:50 each weekday. If you need to go to the supermarket, wait until 3:30.
- The postmaster is a devoted Red Sox fan. Working the Sox into a conversation or a request will ensure you top-shelf service.
- The local hairstylist invariably runs twenty minutes behind on her appointments. If you have a 3:00 P.M. appointment, there is no need to arrive before 3:15.

If the child is able to identify and respond to the Hidden Curriculum of his school, he is better prepared to deal effectively with the Hidden Curriculum in his community.

It is important that children understand and adhere to the Hidden Curriculum as it extends beyond the school and into the community. Where do the kids hang out? What places should be avoided? What community services are available?

Parents can also make the child aware of Hidden Curriculum issues that exist in other social settings that the child will encounter. For example, Grandma Jones doesn't mind if you explore her garden, but Grandma Smith's garden is absolutely off-limits. Your local church, grocery store, dry cleaner, and florists *all* have Hidden Curricula of their own. Encourage the child to carefully observe these settings to understand the unique culture of each.

Also, assist them to look for (and respond to) the cultural mores at home: for example, filling the refrigerator water jug if you empty it; placing the television remote control on the coffee table when you are done; playing quietly on Saturday mornings because Dad works a late shift on Fridays. Because the child with learning disorders may have difficulty discerning patterns, he may be unaware of these family rituals.

RECOMMENDED RESOURCES

Get a Clue, Ellen Rosenberg (New York: Owl Books, 2001).

Jarvis Clutch—Social Spy, Mel Levine, MD (Cambridge, Mass.: Educator's Publishing Service, 2001).

Middle School: The Real Deal, Juliana Farrell (New York: HarperCollins, 2004).

The School Survival Guide for Kids with LD, Rhoda Cummings, EdD (Minneapolis, Minn.: Free Spirit Publishing, 1996).

What Does Everyone Know That I Don't Know?, Michele Novontie (Plantation, Fla.: Specialty Press, 2002).

What's Wrong with Me?, Regina Cicci (Timonium, Md.: York Press, 1999).

CHAPTER ELEVEN

Teacher-Pleasing Behaviors

Polishing the Apple

Mrs. Petrocelli turns off the ignition after she pulls into her parking space at John F. Kennedy Elementary School. She sighs deeply as she reaches for her briefcase and steps out of the car. Before she has both feet on the tarmac, Johnny runs to her. "I didn't understand last night's homework and my uncle told me that you are teaching me multiplication all wrong. He took math in college and he told me that you don't really understand math. He said that he will teach me the times tables the right way over Christmas break. Does this mean that I don't have to do my math homework during the fall?"

Mrs. Petrocelli assures Johnny that she will take his request under advisement and heads for the school entrance. In the one hundred yards to the front door, she breaks up two fights, answers four insipid questions, provides three pieces of invaluable advice, and buys two raffle tickets for the PTA's annual book drive.

She enters the office and retrieves five memos from her mailbox that had materialized there magically since she checked her mail at 8:30 last evening, when she departed the school after attending the fourth grade's production of A Midsummer Night's Dream. *The memos include instructions for the upcoming high-stakes testing, invitations to the science fair, a scolding note from the janitorial staff for failing to close her windows last night, a request from Billy's mom that he be tested for "giftedness" because he correctly answered four questions in a row while they were watching* Jeopardy *last night, and an inquiry from the principal about her "excessive request for Wite-Out and blue construction paper."*

Demoralized, she heads for her classroom, carefully circumventing the green-dyed piles of sawdust absorbing the hallway "accidents" that are by-products of the school's ongoing battle with the most recent stomach virus.

She enters her classroom, which had been leased to the local Cub Scout troop the previous evening, and begins to sweep up the scraps of felt left by their arts-and-crafts activity. She suddenly has the internal sensation that the aforementioned virus has found its latest victim when the bell rings and her students parade into her classroom. Jarvis is angry because he left his lunch on the bus. Tim is frightened because Jarvis threatened to steal his lunch. Melissa is anxious because her dog is pregnant. Oscar is worried about drama club tryouts that afternoon. Hector is elated about his dad's new job. Janie is annoyed about last night's homework. Justin is excited about his new bus driver. Marsha is confused about the upcoming fire safety assembly. And Michele wants to inquire as to why their class is not studying the Civil War, as her cousin's class is. Each one of the students clamors for Mrs. Petrocelli's attention. As the bell rings to begin the class day, she suddenly realizes that in her rush to get her own kids off to school, she mistakenly took her husband's briefcase. Her lesson plans and grading book are now on a nonstop flight to St. Louis.

She steels herself, gets her students' attention, and announces that she needs a moment to regroup and requests that they take out their social studies books and read chapter three silently.

In unison, her chorus of fourth graders chants, "B-O-R-I-N-G."

As every teacher knows, there is no such thing as a "typical day." When dealing with thirty unique and dynamic children, the variables—both positive and negative—are innumerable. The day described above is closer to typical than you might imagine.

Teaching is a lonely profession. Once that classroom door is closed, the teacher is truly on her own. Her lifeblood is the cooperation of her students. If the children are cooperative and responsive, the teacher is likely to respond in kind.

As pediatrician Mel Levine reminds us, "Childhood is political." A child's social success will be largely determined by his ability to influence those who are influential in his life. His relationships with teachers, coaches, adult relatives, and other significant grown-ups will dictate the depth and quality of his social life. By convincing these people to use their influence and power on his behalf, he can realize significant social success. He must come to recognize that adult caregivers are not the enemy and, further, that it is in his best interest to establish and maintain positive relationships with them.

One of the most effective ways to assist your child in establishing these relationships is to discuss the various behaviors that adults find distasteful or disrespectful. These are behaviors that the child should avoid (see page 362).

Unfortunately, rudeness and disrespect for authority figures are all too common in today's schools. As a result, children who are respectful and polite are noticed and appreciated by teachers! A teacher once told me, "I really like your daughter, Meggi. She was the only kid in her class who said 'Thank you' after last week's field trip to the zoo." A little graciousness can go a long way.

Dr. Alex Packer of FCD Educational Services conducted extensive surveys of teachers to identify the behaviors that they liked—and disliked—in the classroom. More than 75 percent of these teachers reported that students are more rude and disrespectful than the students of a decade ago. Unfortunately, incivility has become an integral part of the "culture" of many schools.

Among the most troubling behaviors reported are students' failure to practice basic manners (e.g., saying "Please," "Thank you") and their blatant displays of boredom and inattentiveness. Teachers, rightfully, feel that this behavior reflects a lack of respect for the instructor and the content of the lesson.

This behavior ("This is B-o-o-r-r-ing!") is quite common for children with learning problems because of their difficulty inhibiting their thoughts and feelings. Most of us have dozens of thoughts each day that we do not express verbally. ("Gee, Molly is really overdressed for this event!") We *think* it, but we don't *say* it. Children with disinhibition tend to say whatever is on their minds. Some may think this "on the mind—out the mouth" pattern is refreshingly candid, but it generally has a negative impact on the child's ability to establish and maintain positive relationships with others.

Many times a child will communicate boredom through body language, such as slouching, rolling his eyes, or heavy sighing. The child with learning disabilities often is unable to understand the nonverbal signals that he is sending. He may slouch disinterestedly in his seat during a lesson and be puzzled by the teacher's response to his behavior. "Why is she so upset?" he may ask. "I didn't say anything!"

Teachers also report that it is troubling when a child continues a behavior after he has been told to stop. The teacher, quite naturally, views this lack of compliance as disrespectful and dismissive. Unfortunately, students with learning problems often are not "one-trial learners." They may require numerous interventions and reprimands before a negative behavior is eliminated.

Another behavior cited by teachers is irresponsibility. Teachers make understandable (but often inaccurate) assumptions about a child's ability to act in a responsible and responsive manner. For example, a fifth-grade teacher will assume that her students can keep their desks neat and can clean up after themselves. For many students with learning problems, these skills are unrealistic and inconsistent. The child's noncompliance with the teacher's instructions is viewed as willful and disrespectful, although it may be neither.

Teaching Responsibility

Adults, particularly teachers, appreciate children who are responsible. These are the children who "do things right and do the right things." These children's motivation does not come from an eagerness to impress or please adults. Rather, their responsible behavior is based upon personal satisfaction, a sense of duty, and an inherent desire to complete tasks in a thorough and effective manner. They are often described as "self-motivated." Children with social skill problems rarely fit that profile.

The responsible child is less vulnerable to peer pressure, because he has a decreased need to conform in order to achieve acceptance. He is more likely to accept blame for his mistakes and have confidence in his own skills and instincts. He is able to see the logical consequences of his behavior and, as a result, is capable of making sound social decisions.

By the time a child is in elementary school, his teacher will assume that he is able to follow basic instructions, care for personal belongings, complete simple chores, and work independently. Many children with learning problems are unable to master these fundamental skills, and their performance in these areas is unpredictable and inconsistent. Once again, the child's behavior is labeled "irresponsible" or "immature," despite the fact that the behavior is directly linked to his neurological deficits.

Parents should make every effort to increase and enhance the child's responsibility and his ability to function independently. Our society places great importance upon a person's respect for the rights of others and his personal accountability. As individuals, we are all expected to meet our own needs without interfering with the needs and rights of others.

There are numerous strategies that parents and teachers can use in order to develop a child's sense of responsibility. It is important that the adult provide a positive role model for responsible, mature behavior. Be punctual. Be respectful of others. Speak in a respectful way to your children. Be polite to waiters, clerks, and other service personnel. Tip. Handle disappointment and anger appropriately. Be a good loser. Be a gracious winner. Give compliments. Keep secrets. Your child will model this behavior.

I once saw a dad stand in a cashier's line for several minutes to return a dollar that she had mistakenly given him in an earlier transaction. He had his six-year-old son with him and the boy seemed enthralled with the process. What a wonderful life lesson that child learned that morning.

You can foster a child's responsibility by promoting the traits of trust, honesty, and loyalty with him. These attributes are the hallmark of responsibility. Encourage him to take the initiative in social and academic situations by completing tasks before he is instructed to by an adult. Recognize, reinforce, and reward responsible behavior.

Parents should continually communicate the importance and benefits of responsible behavior. Avoid being preachy or judgmental, but do remind the child that when everyone carries out his duties responsibly and fully, all goes more smoothly. Emphasize teamwork and the importance of completing tasks. Talk about the value of taking the initiative by doing things *before* being asked!

An important aspect of responsibility involves a child's ability to recognize that his day-to-day performance and progress are largely within his own control. Children have a tendency to believe that something or someone else causes their behavior. They will often explain or rationalize their performance by citing the behavior of others:

> "My mother forgot to put my math book in my backpack."
> "I pushed Billy because he was walking so slowly."
> "I didn't finish raking the yard because the neighbor's dog
>   was barking so loudly that it gave me a headache."

These thought processes are damaging because they give the child the belief that he has no control over his own behavior. Children need to be continually reminded that they cannot change the behavior of others or certain circumstances, but they can and should control their own responses to them.

One of the most effective ways to teach responsibility is to *give* the child responsibility. So often parents and teachers will say, "I never give him any responsibility. He is so irresponsible." How can the child improve his responsibility skills if he is never given the opportunity to learn or practice them? Provide the child with chores and small but important jobs that he must do every day (e.g., walking the dog, feeding the cat, picking up the mail). Reinforce him when he completes the task appropriately; remind him when he does not. Provide him with opportunities to make decisions, exercise judgment, and make choices. Allow him to make—and correct—mistakes. Often parents of struggling children are reluctant to place the child in a position where he may experience a temporary failure. As a result, the child may fail to grow and learn. As the sage Chinese proverb reminds us, "With the struggle comes the strength."

Responsibility is best fostered by giving the child the opportunity to establish goals and solve problems. Parents are often overly eager to step in and rescue the child in situations wherein decisions must be made or goals must be set. These are challenging skills for many children, but they should be allowed to attempt and master these important concepts.

For example, if your child is joining a swimming team, have him name five goals or objectives that he hopes to accomplish by the end of the season. Initially, his goals may be grandiose and unattainable (e.g., "I want to be voted captain, and I want my picture in the newspaper five times"). Help him develop more reasonable and realistic goals (e.g., "I will improve my backstroke and I will be on time for every practice").

Provide the child with opportunities to develop responsibility by giving her choices and letting her make decisions: "Becky, do you want to clean your room now or wait until after supper?" Provide the child with ample opportunities to choose, decide, and pick. Reinforce the concept that their behaviors generally represent their own choices. ("I guess that you picked your grumpy mood today," "I notice that you decided not to try very hard on this assignment.") Provide the child with positive role models of responsibility by not making excuses for your own behavior. Rather than "I'm sorry I was late picking you up, but some lady in front of me was driving too slow," try "I'm sorry I was late. I should have left home earlier." Remember that responsibility is an *attitude* as well as a *skill*.

The child will need much reinforcement and encouragement as he attempts to learn responsibility. Be generous with your praise and remember to address his specific accomplishments when you praise him. ("The garage looks terrific! All the bikes are put away and the floor looks great! Terrific job!" versus "Good boy!") Offer consequences positively, not negatively. "You cannot go swimming until you clean the kitchen" is less motivating than "As soon as you finish cleaning the kitchen, you can go swimming."

Occasionally, children must experience *natural consequences* for their irresponsibility. Natural consequences are not punishments per se. Rather, they are the logical effect or impact of one's actions. If the child forgets his math book at school and he needs it for his homework, his parents should not drive him to school to retrieve the missing text. Occasionally, he should experience the natural consequence of his behavior (e.g., incomplete homework, poor grade, teacher's wrath). This will reinforce the importance and effectiveness of appropriate behavior. We are not serving our children well by continually rescuing them from the consequences of their irresponsibility. Parents often attempt to compensate for their child's lack of structure by using their own "super" structure. In the long run, this may not be in the child's best interest.

Parents often unwittingly enable their children and hinder their independence and responsibility. This occurs when a parent becomes accustomed to doing things for the child (such as making the child's bed, laying out her clothes) and works these tasks into his daily routine. The parent may fail to realize that the child has grown and developed to the point where she is now able to complete that task independently or, at least, should begin to receive instruction in that skill. One mother suddenly realized that her child's fifteen-year-old babysitter was only one year older than the child!

I recommend that parents sit down monthly and discuss the daily tasks that you perform for your child that he should be doing for himself. Recognize and celebrate the child's increased maturity and independence. Foster his growth by allowing and encouraging him to assume these tasks. A sixteen-year-old at my school took an avid interest in wood-shop projects. I asked his dad to encourage him to use their home workshop on weekends. The father informed me that his son is banned from using Dad's workshop because he once broke an expensive drill by attempting to make a hole in a concrete block. Our discussion revealed that the incident had occurred when the boy was seven years old! I reminded Dad that the statute of limitations for that infraction had long passed and encouraged him to allow the boy to have another chance. He did, and the boy gained a new hobby *and* a shared interest to enjoy with his father.

Parents often have difficulty determining how much responsibility a child is capable of handling. This can cause family conflicts, because the child is constantly asking for increased amounts of responsibility. You can resolve this dilemma by measuring and recording your child's current level of responsibility.

Complete the following Responsibility Rating by giving the appropriate number of points in each category.

Key:
Rarely	= 1 point
Once in a while	= 2 points
Usually	= 3 points
Always	= 4 points

1. Follows house rules and curfews _____
2. Is mannerly and considerate _____
3. Maintains appropriate academic performance _____
4. Completes assigned chores independently _____
5. Plans well and respects property _____

Add the scores in each individual category. Use the total score to determine whether the child's responsibilities should be increased or decreased.

If the child scores between 17 and 20 points, he is handling his current responsibilities satisfactorily and you may want to discuss and negotiate additional independence.

If the child's score is between 12 and 16, he is handling his current responsibilities well and he should be told that increased responsibility would result in increased independence.

A score below 12 shows that there is much room for improvement and that, perhaps, he already has too much responsibility! Controls need to be tightened and no new responsibilities should be added.

This informal and subjective measure can be used occasionally to evaluate the child's level of independent functioning and identify specific areas of strength and need.

• • •

If you feel that the child is now mature enough to master and use a new skill (e.g., making the bed), a structured, four-step process is recommended.

1. *Do it for him.* Make the bed for the child while he observes. Verbally explain each step in the process.

2. *Help him do it.* After he has observed the process several times, involve him in the bed-making procedure: "I put the fitted sheet on the top of the mattress and you will put it on the bottom. Then I'll put the blue pillow in the pillowcase while you put the yellow pillow in its case." As this process continues, *he* will be assisting *you* during the early stages of the procedure; as you transfer more and more steps to him, he will become the primary bed maker and *you* will be assisting *him.* Eventually, he will be completing all of the stages independently.

3. *Watch him do it.* This is the step that parents, unfortunately, often omit. Once the child has taken over the process, observe him for a few mornings as he makes the bed. Provide him with praise for the steps he has done well and offer advice, assistance, and encouragement for steps that are incorrect or inconsistent.

4. *Have him do it.* Now that he has mastered the skill, require him to make the bed daily. Avoid falling into the trap of making his bed out of habit. Now that he has mastered the skill, make certain that he uses it.

I have used this simple four-step process to teach children skills as varied as archery or shoe polishing. The difficulty of the skill and the profile of the child will dictate the length of time this process will require.

How to Improve Class Participation

Teachers also appreciate children who participate actively in class discussions. Encourage the child to make eye contact with the teacher during lessons. Many children with learning problems are reluctant to volunteer answers in class for fear that they will respond incorrectly and be embarrassed. This reluctance is understandable, but the child should still be encouraged to participate in some way.

Jackie, a former student of mine, was often reluctant to participate in class discussion in her mainstream history class. Her teacher viewed her lack of responsiveness as disinterest and lack of motivation. As the instructor told me, "Jackie needs to let me know that she is alive and at least *somewhat* interested in American history!"

I told Jackie that she was to communicate—in some way—with the teacher three times each class. She was also instructed to keep a log of the interactions and report to me daily. She made a concerted effort to "let the teacher know she was alive." Occasionally she would answer questions, when she felt confident in her responses. She filled her quota by asking for clarification during lectures, smiling at the teacher when something amusing was said, asking questions, or even requesting permission to use the restroom. After a few weeks, the teacher commended her for being so "with it," and her history grade improved markedly.

The dry or boring lectures many teachers present create a real challenge for the ADD or disorganized child. It is important for the child to recognize that the teacher has a mastery of the subject matter and the student must make a concerted effort to listen and participate. Although it is easy to become passive and disinterested in such a situation, the child must make an effort to remain involved and engaged by asking questions and participating in discussions. She should avoid clock watching, as this will only make the class seem longer and more tedious.

To help herself stay involved in a lecture, the student can make a list of several topic-related points or concepts that the teacher may discuss in class. She should listen intently to see if those points are mentioned and check them off her list. If some points are not covered, she can ask questions about them near the end of class.

How to Fix Difficult Relationships
with Teachers

Often, particularly in special education, a child may develop a crush on a teacher. The intensity of special classes, plus the complex role of advocate and guide that special education teachers play in the lives of students, can cause the child to develop inappropriate feelings toward the teacher. If your child seems to have an obsession or attraction for a teacher, counsel him that his feelings are normal but that it would be inappropriate for him to *act* on these feelings in any way. He should not tell the teacher about his feelings, but he may wish to discuss the issue with his counselor or someone else in his support system. His embarrassment may prevent him from discussing it with you. Depending on the severity of the problem, it might be appropriate for *you* to contact the teacher and share the information with her in confidence. It is in everyone's best interest that the teacher know of the child's feelings so that she can avoid saying or doing things that could be misinterpreted by the lovestruck child. A fourteen-year-old once confided in me, "I *know* that Miss Harry loves me. She touched my hand and smiled at me when she returned my math test last Tuesday!"

Unfortunately, your child will not get along with every teacher. Each child and each teacher has a separate and unique personality and temperament. It is unreasonable to believe that personality clashes will not occur on occasion. Perhaps your child's learning style is contrary to the teacher's teaching style. When a child complains about his inability to get along with a teacher, parents tend to intervene on the child's behalf and request a class change, or else instruct the child to "toughen up" because "you won't like every person that you meet in this world." Unfortunately, neither response is helpful or effective.

As a child progresses through his academic career, he will have teachers with a variety of habits, idiosyncrasies, likes, and dislikes. It is important that the child learn to adjust his behavior to accommodate these different personality types. The ability to deal effectively with a wide variety of people is a social skill that will be useful for the child throughout his life. Successful people are able to adjust their behavior in order to please their social partners.

For example, if your child's teacher is highly disorganized, the student must adjust his behavior. She must attempt to be more organized than the teacher and listen very intently during class. Highly organized teachers generally forewarn students when they are about to discuss material that is important. ("We will be discussing the succession to the presidency today, and this material is crucial to your understanding of the Constitution. The midterm exam will definitely include questions on this topic.") However, disorganized teachers seldom provide this type of structure, so the student must be extra attentive in order to recognize the important issues discussed in class.

If the child becomes lost during a disorganized lecture, she should raise her hand and politely ask for clarification or assistance. Perhaps the child should discuss her confusion with the teacher privately and ask the instructor for advice and suggestions that will assist her in following the class discussions.

When children are younger, parents must play the role of advocate or protector in student-teacher conflicts. However, as he progresses in his academic career, the child must learn to advocate for himself. The student-initiated discussions should occur as soon as possible after the difficulty occurs. Urge the child to initiate the discussion at the proper time and place and to wait until the teacher appears to be in a positive and upbeat mood. He may even want to make an appointment with the teacher. ("Excuse me, Mrs. Kennedy, but I would like to talk to you about something important. Could we meet in your classroom after lunch or just before the assembly?") This conversation is best held in a one-to-one setting.

Encourage the child to be empathetic by beginning the conversation with a recognition of the teacher's pressures and responsibilities: "Mrs. Hunt, I know that you are really busy now because the science fair is next week, but I need to talk to you about this. The other day . . ."

The child should *explain* (not *complain about*) the situation. This will make the teacher more responsive. The discussion should conclude with some sort of mutual agreement wherein both the teacher and the child are aware of their responsibilities going forward.

In order for this conversation to be successful, the student must learn how to avoid being *aggressive* and, rather, be *assertive*. Assertiveness is a useful social skill.

An assertive interaction consists of six distinct but interrelated steps.

> A = **Attention:** Get the other person's attention and gain his commitment to take your input seriously.
>
> S = **Soon, Short, and Simple:** Introduce the topic as soon as possible after the incident occurs, and explain it briefly and in simple terms.
>
> S = **Specific:** Focus on the specific behavior that bothered or offended you; do not attack or judge the offending person.
>
> E = **Effect:** Emphasize the impact that the offending behavior had on you.
>
> R = **Response:** Describe the outcome that you would prefer and expect; ask for feedback.
>
> T = **Terms:** Reach an agreement on future behavior.

A middle-school child once asked me to intervene in a situation where his math teacher would routinely read each child's test scores aloud to the class whenever she passed the completed tests back to the students. The child had a significant math disability and was understandably embarrassed by his grades. I told the child that it would be inappropriate for me to approach the teacher about this, so instead, we devised and practiced an assertiveness script that he conducted himself. The monologue was as follows:

> A = "Mrs. Boston, could I have a moment of your time to discuss something that really bothers me?"
>
> S = "It is about something that happened in our math class, third period."
>
> S = "You read my grade aloud in front of the class."
>
> E = "I was really embarrassed by that, and several of the kids hassled me about it after class."
>
> R = "I would prefer if you would give me my grade privately."

> **T** = "So if I agree to arrive at class early on the
> day after a quiz, would you be willing to give
> me my grade at that time and not make my
> grade public?"

The student delivered his script to his teacher, who was greatly impressed by his independence and maturity. She agreed to his proposal, and their relationship improved markedly. Once she was aware that her test distribution technique was a source of embarrassment for the student, she modified the approach for *all* of her pupils.

When I was a school administrator, I often advised the staff, "Don't bring me *problems,* bring me *solutions.*" That is, if you are going to come to me with a problem, also have some possible solutions that we can explore. This is sound advice for the student who is approaching a difficult teacher as well.

Other Ways to Please Teachers

I learned one of the most effective teacher-pleasing strategies when I was a graduate school instructor. One of the students in my class was an elderly nun. At the end of each class, she would pass by my desk, smile, and say, "Thank you, Rick," while all of her classmates hustled toward the door.

At the end of the semester, I approached her and told her how meaningful I found this gesture. She looked pleased but surprised. "If I dropped my pencil and you picked it up for me, I would say, 'Thank you.' Each week you taught me for three hours. Saying a simple 'thank you' was the least I could do!" I was very impressed.

Since then, I have always encouraged students to say "Thank you" to the teacher as they leave a class. This thoughtful and (unfortunately *unusual*) gesture can do much to improve a child's relationship with a teacher!

Below are several additional strategies that your child can use to improve his relationship and daily interactions with his teachers.

- Ask for feedback occasionally.

    It is appropriate and mature for the child to approach his teacher on occasion and ask for information on his progress and performance. This reflects the student's interest and motivation.

- Dress appropriately.

    As a sign of respect, the child should wear appropriate clothing and maintain proper hygiene.

- Sit in "power seats."

    Encourage the child to select a seat near the front of the classroom. This will make him more likely to pay attention and participate. Remind him to sit up straight and make eye contact with the teacher.

- Be cooperative, helpful, and positive.

    Avoid complaining and whining. Offer assistance when the teacher requests it.

- Stay busy.

    Children with learning or attentional problems are likely to get into trouble when they have nothing to do. Encourage the student to keep something in his desk that he can do when he has "downtime." He could write letters, color, do word puzzles, and so forth.

- Be social with the teacher.

    Go to class early—or remain in the room after class for a few moments—and ask the teacher questions or just make small talk. Teachers generally appreciate a child's willingness to spend nonclass time with them. This simple gesture can do a great deal to improve the child's relationship with his teacher and will make the teacher more likely to assist and work with the child.

- Volunteer!

    Teachers will often ask for student assistance with a variety of classroom tasks. Encourage your child to volunteer. His extra efforts will be noticed and appreciated.

- Don't apologize—thank.

    When a child has a problem that requires extra time and attention from the teacher, the student often apologizes. It is more effective to skip the apology but offer a generous "thank you" for the assistance.

    Instead of: "I'm sorry that I couldn't find my math homework and you had to search through my backpack," say this:

"Thanks a lot for helping me find my math homework. I really appreciate it."

- Don't complain about other teachers.

  The child places the teacher in a difficult ethical position when he chronically complains about the teacher's colleagues. If the child has a genuine concern about a teacher, it is appropriate to discuss the problem with another teacher, but chronic complaining should be avoided.

- Participate actively and constructively in class discussions.

  If the child disagrees with a comment made by the teacher or a classmate, she should criticize or correct the *idea*, not the person who presented it.

  It is also a good idea to look at and listen to the recognized speaker. If a student seated behind her is volunteering a comment, the child should turn and look at the speaker, then turn to her original position and look at the teacher as she comments on the contribution. This demonstrates that the child is engaged and interested.

  Side conversations, even those related to the subject area, should be avoided. They give the teacher the impression that the child is not fully engaged.

  The renowned Learning Center at the University of Kansas recommends that students remain mindful of the **SLANT** process during class discussions.

S	=	Sit up straight.
L	=	Lean forward.
A	=	Act interested.
N	=	Nod, smile at teacher on occasion.
T	=	Track the teacher as she moves about the room giving instructions and information.

- Before contributing a comment to a class discussion, the child should consider if the comment that he is about to make is relevant, useful, and appropriate.
- Get to know each teacher's "hot buttons."

  Each teacher has her own hot-button issues that she finds troublesome or off-putting. Mrs. Smith may be fanatical about student punctuality, but may not be particularly adamant about homework; Mr. Jones may not care about whether the student arrives to class on time, but he is a stickler for accurate and complete homework.

The child must carefully observe and monitor the teacher's behavior to determine the individual issues that are bothersome to individual teachers and should make an effort to avoid these missteps. This enables the child to be viewed as responsible and responsive.

The Parents' Role in School Social Success

It is important that parents understand and fulfill their appropriate roles in helping the child achieve social success in school. Even though the parents are not "on site" at school, there is much they can do to assist the child and his teachers in this effort.

Always remember three critical facts when interacting with the school on your child's behalf:

1. You know the child best.
2. You love the child most.
3. You have been (and will be) with him the longest.

Your perspective on your child's social performance during school hours can be invaluable for the professionals who are dealing with him. Keep in close contact with his teachers and counselors. Offer suggestions and solutions related to the youngster's school social life. Report any complaints that the child may voice regarding bullying or intimidation. Be sure to reinforce and thank teachers or coaches who assist the child in making social connections. Be positive and assertive in these communications; avoid being aggressive or argumentative.

As always, carefully observe and monitor your child's social performance in a wide variety of settings. Assess the situations in which he is successful and those in which he experiences social failure and frustration. Try to discern any patterns. Perhaps there are certain social dynamics that contribute to social success or, conversely, tend to exacerbate his social difficulties. Share this information with school personnel. For instance, "Mrs. Gilbert, I noticed that John interacts most positively when he is assigned specific tasks when doing group work. Last weekend, he was helping his grandfather and three of his cousins as they worked in the garden. John was fairly out of control. Then his grandfather asked him to lead the others in gathering the pots and stacking them. John really got to work and had a very enjoyable time with his cousins. He wasn't bossy, but he enjoyed giving instructions and suggestions to the others, and he even thanked them and congratulated them on a job well done! Maybe you could give him some defined responsibilities in classroom group work. It might help him to establish positive social relationships with his classmates."

Make a concerted effort to be cooperative with and supportive of the teacher and her efforts. Avoid criticizing the teacher in front of the child. (You would be displeased if the teacher openly reproached *you* to your child!) Complete required forms and paperwork in a timely manner and minimize the child's absences and tardiness.

If possible, parents should become involved in the school by participating on committees or volunteering at school functions and events. Most states now require schools to allow and encourage parents to play a significant role in school governance. Use this as an opportunity to help your school become more user-friendly for children with unique social and learning needs.

Parents can also contribute to the teacher-student relationship by having realistic and appropriate expectations of the teacher. Parents must come to understand that the teacher's responsibilities and duties extend beyond teaching and caring for *your* child; she must also provide services for other children. Carefully examine your expectations and ask yourself if they are reasonable and doable. This candid assessment may help you view your expectations as overly ambitious.

For example, you should insist that your child not be barred from recess or other recreational activities because of her social difficulties. It is reasonable to expect that the teacher will encourage the child to participate in these activities and that reasonable accommodations will be made to allow the child to become involved. However, it would be unreasonable to demand that such activities be individually tailored to meet your child's interest and abilities and, further, that other children be forced to interact with your child.

The parent has every right to expect that the child will not be bullied, intimidated, or harassed and that the teacher will be responsive to the child's complaints about such behavior. However, it is unreasonable to expect the teacher to create a classroom environment that totally accepts and embraces every child at all times. The teacher cannot be expected to create and establish friendships for the child. She is also ethically prevented from discussing the details of a bully's background or behavior with you.

Send positive and constructive notes to the teacher thanking her for any special time or attention that she gave the child. And always send a copy to the principal.

It is difficult for nonteachers to understand how meaningful it is to receive a positive note, e-mail, or phone call from a grateful parent. Teaching is a fairly thankless task, and teachers have no tangible vehicle to measure their own progress, performance, or impact. Attorneys can review their won-loss record; ballplayers can assess their batting statistics; waitresses can compute their daily tips. But teachers have no such measuring sticks. I know many educators—including myself—who keep a stash of heartfelt, appreciative parent notes under their blotter to give them inspiration on those inevitable "dark days" behind the teacher's desk. These small gestures of kindness and appreciation are long remembered and often result in a more positive relationship between the teacher and the child. An added bonus!

RECOMMENDED RESOURCES

Finding Help When Your Child Is Struggling in School, Lawrence J. Greene (New York: Golden Books, 2000).

The School-Savvy Parent, Rosemary Clark (Minneapolis, Minn.: Free Spirit Publishing, 2000).

PART FOUR

Social Skills in the Community

No Kid Is an Island

> "Love demands infinitely less than friendship."
> —G. J. NATHAN

CHAPTER 12

Appropriate Social Skills in Public Places

As a person goes through his day, he enters into innumerable routine "social contracts" with family members, colleagues, neighbors, and total strangers. These social contracts are unavoidable, and failure to fulfill them appropriately can result in isolation, rejection, and humiliation.

For example, when you enter a doughnut shop for your daily morning coffee, you have entered into a social contract with the strangers who are standing in line at the counter. You are expected to stand at the end of the line and wait your turn for service. If a friend accompanies you, both of you are expected to moderate the volume of your voices and discuss topics that are not highly personal or offensive. When other strangers enter the shop and form a line behind you, another social contract is entered into. You are expected to preselect your purchase, get your money ready, and make your transaction as rapidly as possible. Imagine the response of your "linemates" if you skipped ahead to the head of the line, spent an inordinate amount of time deciding on your purchase, or counted out several hundred pennies to pay for your coffee and doughnuts! You would be viewed as crude, insensitive, and unresponsive. Although the others in line are strangers whom you will probably never see again, you still have a temporary responsibility to fulfill your social contract with them.

I recall watching a fifteen-year-old student of mine purchase a candy bar from a hotel lobby vending machine. Totally oblivious of the woman impatiently waiting for her turn to use the machine, he spent a full three or four minutes making the transaction. He stood before the machine contemplating his candy choice before finally making his selection. He then spent a minute or so searching his pockets and book bag for change. Once he deposited the money, he spent another minute reconsidering his selection. When he finally pressed the button and received his candy, he stood in front of the machine while he opened and ate his treat! You can imagine the frustrated reaction of the waiting woman.

His social contract required him to make his selection and purchase quickly and efficiently, then step aside to allow the woman to use the machine. She viewed him, understandably, as rude and insensitive. In actuality, he was a sweet kid who was simply unaware of the social demands and expectations of this routine situation.

A parent of a child with social skill difficulties once told me that he had given up on attempting to integrate his child into community activities because these attempts generally caused failure and frustration for his son. "It's just not worth it!" he told me. "Anyway, Alex can get all of the socialization he needs from his family."

Unfortunately, Dad was mistaken. In order to develop socially and emotionally, a child must have successful relationships outside his family circle. No matter how loving and supportive a family is, the child needs community contacts as well. I encouraged the father to continue searching for appropriate community contacts for his son and outlined some of the benefits of extrafamilial relationships.

- The child's sense of independence and autonomy increases and improves. He comes to realize that the skills and abilities that he uses successfully at home are also effective in other settings.
- Self-esteem and self-confidence are enhanced when he earns the acceptance and approval of teammates, coaches, classmates, or colleagues.
- Social competence improves, as do his tolerance, understanding, and acceptance of others.
- The child develops skills related to teamwork, interdependence, and cooperation.

- Community activities provide an unparalleled outlet for creativity and exploration.
- The child develops a greater sense of flexibility and resilience by interacting with unfamiliar people in unfamiliar settings.

When the above-listed advantages are considered, one realizes the value in encouraging children to reach out to their community and participate in teams, clubs, and other social groups.

Integrating children with difficulties into community activities is beneficial for all involved. Many community organizations have come to realize that embracing these children has made the adult leaders more patient, creative, and understanding. In turn, the children in these programs often develop increased tolerance, acceptance, and consideration as a result of their exposure to children who struggle. The overall program improves with the presence of these children. Everyone wins!

I am reminded of a New England anecdote:

> *A group of children is waiting to enter school early one morning. A surprise snowstorm has made the front steps impassable and the janitor is shoveling the stairs as the children wait.*
>
> *A small boy in a wheelchair says, "Sir, could you please shovel the ramp so I can get in?"*
>
> *Impatiently, the janitor responds, "These kids are waiting to use the stairs. As soon as I get the steps cleared, I will shovel the ramp. You will have to wait."*
>
> *"But," said the little boy, "if you shovel off the ramp, we can all get in."*

If a program makes itself responsive to and accepting of the *special* child, it becomes more embracing of *all* children.

Public Settings and Transitions

One of the most common difficulties children with social skills deficits have (and a primary reason why they have difficulty in public settings) is an inability to deal effectively with transitions. The majority of behavioral difficulties in schools occur during transition times. Even a minor transition—moving from a math activity to the reading circle—can cause the child to become confused, anxious, and disruptive.

Transitions are difficult for children with learning problems because they have difficulty perceiving and grasping the "big picture" of social situations. When involved in a social interaction, they tend to observe and memorize the *details* of the situation, but fail to form an *overall impression* of the matter. Therefore, each social interaction seems to be a new, foreign experience in which they are unable to predict the responses of others. As a result, they become fearful and distrustful of new situations. The child's siblings eagerly await the vacation in the mountains, but he dreads it! They love Dad's spontaneous idea that the family have dinner on the roof so that they can watch the meteor shower; he finds this change quite troubling. The three most dreaded words in his vocabulary are *unknown, unexpected,* and *unpredictable.*

This difficulty with transitions can have a marked impact upon a child's ability to function in social settings. He may become overstimulated or overwhelmed when asked to deal with a novel activity in a new setting with people he does not know. As a result, his initial Boy Scout meeting or his first religious education class may be a source of great anxiety for him and can be a disastrous, ego-deflating failure.

As we have discussed, children with social skill difficulties tend to have adjustment and relationship problems in school and at home. However, they are particularly challenged when attempting to interact in public settings in the community. In fact, public settings represent something of a stacked deck for these children, for three reasons:

1. New, unique settings can create significant anxiety for these children. They have experienced difficulty in such settings before (Scout meetings, religious education classes, supermarkets), and their heightened anxiety often has a negative

impact on their behavior and their ability to interact positively with others.

2. Ironically, parents tend to be more demanding of children in public settings and expect their behavior to be calm, respectful, and nondisruptive. They actually expect the child's public behavior to be better and more consistent than their behavior at home. This is, of course, because disruptive public behavior is embarrassing to the parents, who may feel that it reflects poorly on their parental competence.

3. Generally, an excursion to a public setting has a specific—and often significant—objective and time constraint. If Mom has to stop at the grocery store to get milk for dinner on the way home from retrieving the child at soccer practice, the store visit needs to be quick and focused. There is no time allotted for the dawdling and exploring that the child might quite naturally wish to engage in there. Mom wants to buy a gallon of 2 percent milk; the child wants to play hide-and-seek behind the cereal display. Both of these objectives are understandable, but incompatible.

As human beings, we have six basic physiological needs. If these needs are unmet or if they are stifled in some way, a person can become anxious, disruptive, or perhaps become ill, or even die. These basic needs are the need to satisfy hunger, the need to satisfy thirst, the need to rest (time to rejuvenate via temporary inaction), the need for air (adequate space between you and others), the need for exploration, and the need to eliminate waste. When the child is in his home, all of these needs are readily met. He has ample food, drink, open space, bathroom facilities, and mobility at his disposal. However, when he attends his first Sunday school meeting in the church hall, his needs are not as readily met. Anxiety ensues as the child begins to focus on the unavailability of food and drink; the location of the restroom; the requirements of remaining quiet and attentive during the session. This anxiety often results in inattention or disruptive behavior. It is extraordinarily difficult for a child to focus his attention appropriately if one or more of these needs are unmet or if he is unsure how to meet them. One of the keys to improving the child's performance and interaction in novel public settings is to take measures to ensure that these needs are being met. Pack a light snack for his meeting (hunger); include a juice box (thirst); ask the adult in charge to allow your child to take a break occasionally (rest) and to not require the child to function in close quarters for extended periods of time (space); show the child the location of the restroom and ask the adult to allow the child to use a prearranged, nonverbal signal to inform the adult that he needs to use the bathroom. These relatively minor alterations can be of great reassurance to the child and may significantly enhance his ability to participate in the activity in a meaningful way.

Meeting a child's basic human needs in a new situation is one key strategy for easing transitions. Another key two-step strategy is: *Prepare the child for the situation and prepare the situation for the child.*

Suppose your child is scheduled to attend his first Scout meeting in the new church hall on Tuesday evening. On Monday evening, Dad should take him to the empty hall to acquaint him with this new environment. Once at the hall, the conversation might go like this:

> *"Todd, this is where your meeting will be tomorrow night. Let's take a look around. The boys' room is over there. They don't have paper towels, they use an electric hand dryer. Let me show you how it works.*
>
> *"On the stage, they have a projector just like ours at home. Don't touch it . . . but if the Scoutmaster asks for a volunteer to help show a video, you can tell him that you know how it works.*
>
> *"There are some flags in the corner. I know that you love flags! Let's go over and look at them and feel the fabric, but it would be good to stay away from them tomorrow night.*
>
> *"The floor here looks like it was just refinished. They probably won't let the kids play on it in boots or heavy shoes. Let's remember to wear your sneakers to the meeting."*

By conducting this brief tour, you have *prepared Todd for the situation*. He will meet new people at the Scout meeting and he will have new information to learn and master. But he will feel somewhat comfortable and relaxed in the setting because it will be familiar to him.

The second part of the formula requires the parent to *prepare the situation for the child*. Call the Scoutmaster (or baseball coach or judo instructor) and provide him with some basic information about your child and his social challenges. Be sure to provide the adult with the child's *positive* traits as well. The conversation may go like this:

> *"Coach Burns, my son, Mike, will be playing baseball with your Rangers this summer. He's a terrific kid, and his speed and agility make him a great little shortstop. He hits consistently and loves conditioning exercises. However, I also wanted you to know that Mike has great difficulty reading and will probably need some help if any reading is required. He also has some anxiety problems, and he gets very loud and hyperactive when he gets excited. We have found it useful to give him a simple hand signal of thumbs-up when he begins to escalate, and he generally calms down quickly. We really appreciate your understanding."*

This heads-up is generally appreciated by the adult in charge and will make your child's transition smoother and more positive.

A mother of a child with social problems once told me that her daughter had significant difficulty in new or unique settings. Her anxiety often caused her to be disruptive in unfamiliar surroundings. When a new mall opened in their town, Mom wisely took her daughter on a leisurely tour of it. They did not shop, and Mom explained that they would not be purchasing anything during their tour. The sole purpose of the excursion was to familiarize the girl with the setting in preparation for future shopping trips. It was an enjoyable and productive (and effective!) outing.

This mother's plan is a valuable example of a *pro*active strategy. As parents, caregivers, and teachers, we are often overly *re*active to a child's behavior. When she misbehaves or acts out at Grandma's or at the birthday party, we scold and reprimand her *after the fact*. Perhaps her behavior would have been better if we had been proactive and given her some gentle reminders *before* the activity. "Okay, Molly, we will be arriving at Grandma's house in about ten minutes. Let's remember to talk quietly during our visit, and don't forget to compliment Grandpa's garden and thank them for coming to your recital last weekend." Or, "Get in the car, Kendall, it's time for Heide's party. Now remember to use your fork when you eat and be nice to Heide's sister even though she was mean to you on the bus yesterday." Many social and behavioral crises can be averted by a little proactive action!

You will not always be there to prepare your child for unexpected transitions and situations. The child must learn to carefully observe and analyze the social settings that he enters throughout his day. He must learn to *recognize, reflect,* and *react.*

Teach the child to carefully conduct a reconnaissance mission whenever he enters a social situation. He needs to quickly consider the *people, place,* and *purposes* and be appropriately responsive to those three factors. He needs to modify his language, his behavior, and his affect depending upon the characteristics of the social environment.

For example, suppose David, a twelve-year-old, arrives home from school. He is eager to tell his older sister, Sally, about the snake that the science teacher showed to the class that day. He barges through the front door and begins searching for his sister. As he runs into the kitchen, he sees Sally, his mother, and Sally's piano teacher sitting at the kitchen table. There are several sheet-music books spread out on the table, and his mother and Sally are listening attentively to the piano teacher as she shows them various scores and musical pieces from the books.

David should immediately stop and scan the room. This *recon* mission may be quite difficult for him, as it requires him to inhibit his natural tendency to act upon his impulses, as well as his need for immediate gratification—both traits that are very common for children with social skill difficulties.

His mission is a quick but complete visual survey of the social environment in the kitchen. It is this survey that will determine his social behavior in this setting. An ineffective or incomplete survey will result in inappropriate and unresponsive social behavior. Conversely, an effective survey will ensure that David responds appropriately.

The survey should consider the three Ps of any social interaction: *p*eople, *p*lace, and *p*urpose. The *people* involved in this kitchen inter-action should provide David with significant social clues. The piano teacher comes to the house weekly, but it is quite unusual that she would be talking to both Mom and Sally; she generally conducts her lessons at the piano with Sally. The body language of the people at the table should also provide David with clues. As the piano teacher is talking, Mom and Sally are leaning forward and making direct eye contact with her. She is speaking with a serious tone and Mom and Sally are listening intently. As David enters the room, Mom looks at him and smiles, but then looks back at the teacher, who is continuing her discussion. Mom has sent a clear social signal that the conversa-tion should not be interrupted.

The *place* of the interaction also provides clues for David. It is *unusual* that the piano teacher would be in the kitchen; Mom usually uses the kitchen table for serious and important conversations. That's where the family sits when they discuss report cards, chores, or up-coming vacations. "Kitchen conversations" in David's family are im-portant and significant.

Lastly, David's recon survey should include the *purpose* of the in-teractions that he is observing. Why are these people together? What's their goal? What are they trying to accomplish? They are ob-viously selecting music for Sally's upcoming recital. They have im-portant decisions to make, and the participants are taking their respective roles quite seriously.

Once David has reviewed the social setting, he needs to *reflect*. This step in the process requires that he take a moment to analyze the data that he has gathered and to characterize and summarize the interaction. "Uh-oh! Sally is in an important meeting!"

The final step requires David to *react* and to fulfill his social con-tract. An appropriate reaction would be to quietly leave the kitchen and allow the meeting to continue uninterrupted. Perhaps before de-parting he could say, "Oops. Sorry to interrupt. I didn't realize that you were having a meeting. Sally, when you're done, could you stop by my room? I have something to tell you."

It would, of course, be inappropriate to interrupt, join, or ignore the meeting. David's social contract requires him to allow the meeting to continue and to delay or postpone *his* social agenda (the news of the snake) until a more appropriate time.

For most of us, these everyday social reactions and interactions are simple and quite natural. We conduct these recognize/reflect/react scenarios with little effort or fanfare. However, this process is extraordinarily difficult for children with attentional and learning problems. It poses a significant and ongoing challenge for them. They struggle to make and maintain social relationships with others. Their "ready-fire-aim" behavior often causes them to enter social situations inappropriately and impulsively. Again, others interpret this behavior as rude and insensitive.

Several years ago, the Riverview School community suffered a terrible loss with the death of a student's father. Marshall was a wonderful man, beloved by staff and students alike. Many of us gathered together—along with hundreds of Marshall's relatives and friends—for his burial service.

Marshall was of the Jewish faith, and two hundred mourners encircled his grave site for the final, formal ceremony. We all watched as Judy, his wife and partner for thirty years, gently placed a shovelful of earth onto his casket, which had been lowered into the grave. As she turned to hand the ceremonial shovel to Marshall's brother, two of our students broke from the crowd and ran to hug Judy.

Their behavior was well-intentioned, emotional, heartwarming, sincere . . . and very, very inappropriate. The students failed to do what their fellow mourners did. They failed to observe and perceive the dynamic ingredients of that social situation. That moment in time was clearly a *family moment,* a moment for a final farewell from the people who knew and loved Marshall best and the longest. The rest of us were relegated to bit players who were there merely to observe, not participate.

Judy is a wonderful, generous person who dearly loved and understood our students. She responded to their hugs in kind. Her grace and charm were wonderful to observe as these well-intentioned youngsters intruded on this special moment. But at that instant, I came to a new realization of the need for our students to receive additional, intense instruction in these critical areas.

As I reflect on that episode, I recognize my *own* behavior during

Marshall's final ceremony. I had never attended a Jewish burial and so I observed—and mimicked—the behaviors of others. When they stood, I stood. When they were seated, I sat. When they approached the family, I approached. We automatically use these observational strategies to navigate a new or challenging social situation. We can and must teach these skills to children who struggle socially.

Once you understand the concept of social contracts, you will have a heightened awareness of the dozens of contracts that you become involved with each day. I recently gave a presentation at a major Chicago hotel. I arose early one morning to use the eighth-floor health club. Following my workout, I boarded the elevator and pressed the button for the third floor, where my room was located. The elevator stopped on the fifth floor, and the door opened. A woman began to enter the elevator. The two of us—total strangers—were now entering into a social contract and we both assumed specific duties and responsibilities.

The woman was ending her stay at the hotel and she had two large suitcases with her. She was struggling to board the elevator with her bulky luggage. My social contract with her required me to hold the door for her by pressing the OPEN DOOR button on the control panel. I then held the door open with my foot, reached into the hallway and helped her move her luggage into the elevator car. She thanked me (*her* role in our contract) and stood near the corner of the elevator. I was standing in front of the control panel. She said, "Lobby, please." I pressed the button for that floor. Within moments, the door reopened and I left the car to go to my third-floor room. As I departed, I said, "Have a nice day." She returned the greeting.

This simple, routine interaction contains myriad examples of social contracts. Imagine if I had stood, arms folded, and watched as the door closed repeatedly on the woman while she struggled with her luggage. Imagine if I had refused to press the lobby button when she asked. Imagine if she stared icily and silently at me when I wished her well when I disembarked from the elevator. We both fulfilled our respective contracts. The interaction was simple, routine, forgettable . . . and successful.

Further analysis of this scenario illustrates additional critical concepts. Was it appropriate for the stranger to give me an instruction ("Lobby, please")? In that setting, her issuing a command was entirely appropriate. We were on an elevator and I was standing in front of the control panel. Consider my reaction, however, if I departed the elevator with her and we walked across the lobby together and she accidentally dropped her scarf, turned to me, and ordered me to pick it up. I would have been appalled. In the lobby (unlike in the elevator) I have no social contract that requires me to assist her. These social contracts are deceptively complex and intricate.

You can assist the child in improving his "social scanning skills" by using the countless social situations that we experience each day. In restaurants, malls, airports, or other public venues, assist him in observing and analyzing the social interactions of others. "Look over there, Jamal. See that young couple? Are they happy with each other or are they having an argument? How can you tell? What social clues are you observing?"

Again, you may be quite surprised at the significant difficulty that these children experience as they attempt to analyze these interactions. Their inability to read the nonverbal behaviors of others—and to determine the underlying social contracts inherent in social interactions—can cause them to react very inappropriately in social settings.

CHAPTER THIRTEEN

Meeting, Making, and Keeping Friends

Maria and Jeanne were two fourteen-year-olds who attended the residential school in Massachusetts where I served as director. They were terrific girls, and each had significant learning and language problems. The girls were roommates and shared a complex relationship. Jeanne was a gentle and generous kid admired by all for her willingness to assist others and to create harmony in our dormitories and classrooms. Maria, conversely, was very volatile and disruptive. Our staff lovingly listed her among the "high-maintenance" kids in our population. The girls' relationship was marked by inconsistency and frequent disputes, quarrels, and conflicts. Maria would generally be the spark for this friction and Jeanne would attempt to bring some peace to the valley.

Both girls were eager to maintain the friendship, but neither had an effective repertoire of social strategies to use toward that end. Maria was so desperate to keep Jeanne as her friend that she became threatened (and threatening!) whenever Jeanne spent time with others. Acting more like a jealous suitor than a friend, Maria would sabotage any of Jeanne's plans that included the other girls on their dormitory wing. Jeanne once hosted an informal party on a Friday and was hurt and disappointed when none of the girls—except Maria—arrived at her room for the festivities. She later learned that Maria had removed the others' invitations from their mailboxes to ensure that she would be the solitary guest at the event.

Maria's behavior could be viewed as cruel and willful. But it was neither. For her entire preadolescence she had longed to have a friend—a best friend—with whom she could swap clothes, share secrets, and exchange confidences. She had been unable to establish such a relationship despite sincere and concentrated effort on her part. However, at long last, she was able to form a genuine friendship with Jeanne. Her anxiety over the possibility of losing that relationship caused her to act in irrational and destructive ways. Her possessiveness and her tendency to take offense at minor slights—real or imagined—created havoc in the relationship that she so cherished. As I often advised her, she was constantly "putting out her own candle."

I well remember one particular day when the girls were sent to my office by the teacher proctoring the lunchroom. Jeanne and Maria had been involved in a loud argument, and the teacher asked that I intervene and play the role of referee, a role with which I had become quite familiar.

The two girls sat in chairs across from my desk. Arms folded and in full pout, they stared laserlike at the walls in order to avoid eye contact with me or one another.

I asked Maria about the genesis of the argument, and she began explaining her perception of the events. She loudly testified that Jeanne had promised to help her braid her hair at recess and, instead, became involved in an informal volleyball game.

Jeanne listened patiently to Maria's accusatory diatribe. After about ten minutes, during which Maria documented and catalogued Jeanne's previous slights and faults, Jeanne sighed audibly, looked at Maria and said, "Maria, it's so much work to be your friend."

From the mouths of babes! Jeanne's comment was a perfect synthesis of the difficulties that are experienced daily by children with learning disabilities. A friendship should be a pleasurable experience that provides both parties with companionship and comfort. However, the complexities of a child's learning disability and social deficits may make such relationships challenging and, in some cases, impossible.

Consider the words of Doreen Kronick, renowned learning disabilities expert from Toronto:

> *To become a friend means to become interested in, and somewhat knowledgeable about, the other person's interests; be sensitive to their needs and feelings; compromise on activities; laugh off differences; be supportive; allow the other person freedom to interact with others and spend time by themselves; be elated by their successes; share their sorrows sensitively; be able to communicate your pleasure, displeasure, and anger without such communication being destructive to either party; and to change and grow as your friend changes and grows.*
>
> *I wonder whether many learning disabled adolescents possess the sensitivity, empathy, flexibility, and maturity, and generate sufficient interest and excitement to maintain such friendships.*

Indeed, establishing and maintaining a friendship is a difficult task requiring innumerable social skills. A friendship requires equity, sharing, and mutuality that is difficult for socially disabled children to understand. Friendship can be defined as "a mutual relationship formed with affection and commitment between people who consider themselves equals."

When you were a child, you doubtless found your own friends by initiating relationships with peers who seemed to hold similar interests. Adult intervention in this process was neither expected, needed, nor welcome. However, if a child has significant social skill deficiencies, it may be necessary for the parent to play a substantial role in the friendship-making process.

How Friendships Develop

A classic UCLA study provides parents with useful information regarding the development of friendships at various ages. The information may be useful to you as you assist your child in selecting playmates. Remember that these are informal guidelines and are not designed to be comprehensive timetables. A significant amount of overlap will generally occur, and each child will have a unique pattern of development related to friendships.

Kindergarten and First Grade. Children will play with anyone. Friendships are determined largely by the frequency with which they get together. Attractiveness as a playmate is often determined by the quality and appeal of a child's toys. Allegiances and alliances are temporary and fleeting.

Second and Third Grades. Boys and girls avoid each other. Boys tend to establish rule-governed games and activities among small groups. Temporary "clubs" are formed with established (often self-appointed) leaders. Girls tend to establish small groups but are less likely to have specific activities. Friendships can be terminated for no apparent or identifiable reason or for minor slights.

Fourth Grade. Emergence of "best" friends. Small groups of boys begin to bond. Girls tend to group together based upon specific common interests or activities (e.g., ballet, choir). Friendship groups are becoming more solidly established and tend to have common interests, likes and dislikes, abilities and personalities. There is little tolerance for diversity in these areas. Reciprocity becomes important; children do favors for one another and expect favors in return. They demand absolute equality from one another: "I'll let you use my ball glove for an hour today but you have to let me use the remote control car for an hour on Wednesday."

Fifth Grade. Boy groups become more solidly established, with great emphasis on similar interests. Telephone usage and sharing of secrets becomes significant for girls. Relationships become more intimate and supportive.

Sixth Grade. Conversations become more significant for boys (previously their sole common bond was their mutual interests and activities). Girls begin to use the telephone for conversations, not information. Friendships are based on a genuine mutual understanding and affection.

It is extremely important that parents be aware of the developmental nature of children's friendships. Parents often mistakenly apply *adult* perspectives when dealing with child-to-child relationships. As grown-ups, we view friendships as solid, mutual, and fulfilling alliances that must be nurtured and preserved. Therefore, we become troubled when a child announces that he is "no longer friends with Wayne because he wouldn't give me some of his potato chips at lunch." There is no need for concern. Children's friendships are often brief, fleeting, and somewhat mercenary and materialistic. If your child chooses to terminate a friendship in response to a real or imagined slight, it does not indicate that he is disloyal or faithless. It merely reflects the normal pattern of relationships between and among children.

This research demonstrates the importance of having *same-gender* friends in childhood. Unfortunately, other children are often rejecting of girl-boy friendships during the elementary school years. Boys who play with girls are labeled "sissies"; girls who play with boys are rejected as "tomboys." Although no parent wants to foster or support these unfair and inappropriate stereotypes, you must also recognize that same-sex relationships provide the child with an opportunity to gain significant specific social skills. The child will become more comfortable with his or her sex role and these relationships will doubtless be more lasting and enduring.

Friendships are critically important in the social and emotional development of children. Those who are friendless in childhood tend to have marked difficulty establishing friendships as adults and are more likely to be poorly adjusted and unhappy. A solid childhood friendship provides each partner with an invaluable laboratory wherein she can learn to share and problem solve. It is not surprising that friendless children fail to develop the skills of compromise and sensitivity that are so important in adulthood.

Three Stages of a New Friendship

Children need to gain a better, fuller understanding of the nature of friendship. Because of the "timing and staging" difficulties (see page 346), children with limited social competence tend to view friendship as a *product,* not a *process.* They must learn the accepted steps in the development of a lasting and meaningful friendship.

Friendships generally develop in a three-step process. The sequence begins with an *exploratory phase,* in which two people begin to find commonalities in interests, skills, or backgrounds. This stage occurs at the beginning of the school year or when the child joins a club or organization. This stage can create great anxiety for the child with social skill difficulties, because he has experienced social failure and rejection in the past. Often adults will attempt to encourage the child by telling him that a "clean social slate" is a wonderful opportunity to meet new people and make new friends. This approach is rarely reassuring for the child and may only serve to increase his anxiety.

Once this initial stage is completed and the two people recognize that they have interests, skills, and backgrounds in common, the *trust stage* begins. As the two people share more time and activities with each other, a bond of trust and understanding begins to emerge.

At this point, the relationship is very fragile and can be easily terminated by jealousy, misunderstanding, possessiveness, disrespect, or other social errors. At this stage, many children with social deficiencies unwittingly sabotage potential friendships by expecting the relationship to move too quickly. This process should be gradual and measured, with each partner observing and responding to the various signals sent by the other.

During this stage, it is important that the child demonstrate genuine interest in his new friend. He should express concern, encouragement, and empathy; be upbeat and positive; be a good listener; make the partner feel important and valued; be generous.

Parents and teachers can assist at this stage by creating "work groups" that require the children to work cooperatively. These groupings can promote and solidify respect, communication, positive interaction, and sharing.

Again, these fledgling relationships can be quickly extinguished if trust is violated. Encourage the child to be honest, forthright, open, and responsive to his partner, and to be respectful of privacy and keep secrets.

If the relationship survives the perilous second stage, the pair will enter the *compatibility stage,* wherein the acceptance is solidified and the relationship matures into a lasting and mutually beneficial pairing. These relationships can withstand occasional skirmishes, disagreements, and misunderstandings because they are now stronger and more stable. The relationship is based upon a high degree of similarity in terms of interests, values, personalities, and belief systems.

How Can Parents Help?

Parents can play a critical role in helping a child develop friendship skills. Parents can select neighborhoods, schools, and community activities that will provide children with opportunities for interactions with age-appropriate peers.

Parents should also discourage children from excessive television viewing, computer usage, and other solitary activities that fail to provide them with opportunities for peer interaction. In many cases, LD children watch television in the same manner that the adult watches a fire in a fireplace: as an enjoyable activity devoid of meaning. Recent studies also indicate that much of the content of videos, television, and computer games tends to feature or glorify violence and aggression. Children with social skill deficits may come to view such behavior as appropriate.

The use of board games can be a very attractive and effective alternative to television. These activities require innumerable social skills and can provide an invaluable opportunity to learn and reinforce these skills. In order to participate fully in a board game, each participant must:

- negotiate
- take turns
- follow rules
- be gracious in defeat
- be gracious in victory
- share
- have patience
- strategize

Such activities also require and foster the academic/cognitive skills of reading, sequencing, color recognition, and so on. I remember leading an all-day bingo marathon with fifty snowbound children in New England. The social lessons learned that day were many and varied.

Assist your child in selecting some games at your local toy store. Play these games with her and teach the rules and strategies involved. Perhaps she would then be willing to invite another child to her home to play the game together.

You might be surprised at the amount of difficulty she may have learning the rules of these simple games (e.g., checkers, Parcheesi). These activities require her to simultaneously use several social and academic skills that are difficult for her. You must be patient. Avoid allowing her to modify the rules or make up the rules as she goes along. ("That move didn't count," "I get to go twice.") This pattern of rule breaking will not be accepted by her peers and will be a source of conflict when she plays with other children.

However, board games also provide a rich opportunity for the child to learn negotiating skills. The game's rules can be modified by mutual agreement (e.g., "The game table is real small, so if the dice fall off the table, the player can roll again"). But these rule modifications should be agreed upon before the game begins. A child with learning problems often has the troubling habit of trying to modify the rules as the game is in progress. Should this occur, inform her that the game will have to be discontinued if she will not adhere to the established rules.

Board games provide parents with a wonderful opportunity to give a child positive reinforcement, affection, and encouragement. Praise her when she makes a good move or demonstrates a positive social skill. Encourage her to praise your successes as well. This will serve to make her a more attractive partner to her peers and classmates. Allow her to lose a game on occasion; avoid the temptation to arrange her victory every time. "Gracious losing" is another valuable social skill.

Although sibling relationships are valuable and useful, they are not replacements for friendships between unrelated peers. Sibling relationships are compromised and complicated by the fact that both children share the same parents. Therefore, the parents are often called upon to referee disputes and solve disagreements. In a true friendship, the children must learn to settle these problems independently. Parents often find it useful to allow children to invite friends to family outings to the mall, museum, or local restaurant. This also provides the parent with a valuable opportunity to observe the child's friendship skills in action.

Try to find a family in your community that has a similar configuration to yours (children of like ages and genders). Perhaps the two families could spend social time together on barbecues or day trips. These activities can help the children initiate relationships in a very structured and supportive setting.

Beyond arranging social events for your child, you should also provide him with a solid role model for friendship. Share. Be kind and considerate. Listen. Be sensitive. Talk about *your* friends in a positive way. Give the child concrete examples of the manner in which friends should treat one another.

Helping a Child Choose a Friend

Children with social skill deficits are often desperate to establish friendships. This eagerness can cause them to make poor choices or have their feelings hurt. You can help by playing a significant role in your child's selection of friends. This may seem like an unnecessary (at best!) and inappropriate (at worst!) strategy for parents of *most* children—and it is. But, again, the child with social skills deficits may well need and benefit from this intervention. It also reflects the importance that you as the parent place upon your child's friendships and social life.

If your child has selected a friend who is a good match, congratulate him on his choice and encourage the development of the friendship by providing opportunities for the children to get together on a regular basis. If you feel that an inappropriate selection has been made, you may feel it necessary to intercede in an effort to prevent a situation wherein your child is hurt, disappointed, or victimized.

When assisting the child in the selection of a potential friend, avoid overreaching. You may be tempted to match your child with a popular, savvy classmate in the hope that the child's social acumen will rub off on your child. This is unlikely to happen. Children with learning problems do not master new skills merely by watching and replicating the skills of others. If that were the case, he would have learned those skills by watching *you* over the years! If you match your child with a classmate whose social competence is far superior to his, you run the risk of embarrassing or humiliating him.

When attempting to find a "social link" for your child, you may want to find a child who is *not* in your child's grade. Many parents find it useful to select a child who is a bit younger than the LD youngster. A younger child will probably have social skills that more closely parallel those of your child, and the age difference provides the LD child with some automatic status in the relationship.

Whenever you encounter your child's friends, talk to them in a positive, nonthreatening way. Approach the friend in an adult manner and have a meaningful discussion with him about topics of mutual interest. Don't attempt to become "one of the guys" and act in a childlike or childish manner. Use the conversation to learn more about the child's interests, background, personality, and temperament.

Child psychologist Fred Frankel posits that there are four basic traps that a child may confront when selecting a friend and establishing a relationship. The first is referred to as the "Popular Child Trap," wherein the child wishes to establish a relationship with a popular child for the sole reason that the child *is* popular. In an attempt to bask in the popular child's glory, the isolated or rejected child may wish to have the popular child as a friend. Of course, this often results in disappointment, disillusionment, and rejection for the special-needs child. Remind your child that friendships must be based upon mutual interests and complementary personalities.

A second friendship pitfall is the "One-sided Relationship." Children with social skill deficits are particularly vulnerable to this sort of connection. They are often willing to be ignored or belittled because they are so eager to have a friend. In such a relationship, one child contributes greatly to the friendship by calling, visiting, and inviting, while the second child rarely reciprocates and will participate only when alternative activities are unavailable. Research indicates that these one-sided relationships are potentially harmful to *both* children, because they can establish a pattern of dysfunctional and inappropriate "friendships."

A third trap involves the "Poorly Behaved Child." Children with learning problems often seek out misbehaving children and view them as leaders and potential friends because these children provide the child with the adventure and stimulation that they need. This child may be willing to take risks and behave in a manner that other children would not. Ironically, the behavioral traits that you find troubling about the new friend may be the exact traits that your child finds most appealing. These relationships are dysfunctional and can be damaging.

Unfortunately, many children with social skill deficits are willing to tolerate mistreatment or hassling by other children. They feel that this is the only way that they will receive attention.

I once reprimanded a group of children for hassling and belittling a classmate. The victim later told me that he regretted my intervention. "They used to make fun of me all the time," he said. "Now they ignore me. That's worse." You must reinforce the concept that every child is entitled to feel safe and secure in his own school or community.

Guiding the Choice Step by Step

Some children may need special guidance in selecting a friend. Advise the child to carefully observe the other children on the bus, at the playground, and in the neighborhood. Encourage the child to look for traits that would make a good friend: gentleness, kindness, similar interests, warm and positive personality, and so on. Discuss the idea that the *outside* of the person—size, shape, clothing, athleticism etc.—is far less important than the *inside* of the person. This search may take several days, so it is best to impose a deadline on the process: "By next Thursday, you should have selected a classmate who you feel would be a good and loyal friend."

Once your child has selected a youngster who could be a potential friend, he will need for you to coach him on the appropriate way to approach the friend. This step can be challenging for the child with a learning disorder, especially if he has a language problem. The difficulty of this task is compounded by the child's anxious fear of rejection. He will need much support and encouragement at this time. His task ahead is akin to your approaching a volatile boss for a substantial salary increase.

You may want to construct some "introduction scripts" with the child. For example, "Hi, my name is Jonathan. I notice that you walk home from school on Maple Street every day. So do I! Do you want to walk together today after school?" Encourage him to approach the child when the two of them are alone. Groups of kids can create a difficult dynamic. A private conversation is more likely to produce positive results. Be very supportive of your child during this process. He may be quite anxious and hesitant to make this big step. Tell him that his nervousness is natural and understandable.

Your child's initial overture might be spurned. Discuss this possibility with him. Assure him that some people simply don't click together and counsel him that he should not view this rejection as a personal or permanent rejection. In fact, research conducted at the renowned Ontario Institute indicates that initial attempts for a child to enter *any* group will be rejected about 60 percent of the time; even popular children are rebuffed in 30 percent of their overtures. Validate his feelings of disappointment—"I know that this must hurt, Bobby. You look pretty sad"—and then congratulate him for having the courage to make the approach. Remind him that the person who rejected his approach does not know him. Therefore, the rejection was not personal and should not be viewed that way. Encourage him to renew his search for another appropriate peer. It is simply unproductive and ineffective to merely "wait until a friend comes along." Friendship is an active process.

Talking with the Child About Friendships

Establishing and maintaining friendships is a significant aspect of social skill development. Therefore, it is crucial that parents communicate with the child regarding this important topic. Some parents feel that a child's friendships are his own personal business and, further, that the child has the right to conduct these relationships in a private, confidential manner. However, the child with social skill deficits will need the parent's ongoing guidance, advice, and counsel in order to effectively maintain these peer relationships. Because the child is unlikely to initiate these conversations, the parents must communicate that they are willing and eager to discuss this important and challenging topic.

The child may be reluctant to discuss his social problems with his parents because he may feel that he will be punished. Assure him that it is your wish and your intention to assist him in a supportive, nonjudgmental way. These conversations should be informal and positive. Avoid trying to provide instant solutions to every difficulty that the child shares. Allow him to nurture and develop his own social problem-solving skills.

It is difficult for a child to share feelings of isolation, rejection, or humiliation with parents. These situations are a source of shame and embarrassment for the child. Avoid criticizing, interrogating, or lecturing. Listen attentively, ask for clarification when it is needed, and provide him with support. Remain calm and nonjudgmental.

It is important to remember that these children are often bullied, scapegoated, and victimized. When a child informs a parent that he is being teased or ridiculed by other children, it is common for the parent to ask the child what his role in the incident was: "Billy would not have pushed you for no reason. You must have done *something* to provoke him." The sad truth is that the incident may have not been provoked at all! Kids with social skill deficits can become easy and available targets for the frustrations of other children. Don't make the unfair assumption that your child's behavior was the cause of the difficulty.

If you expect to keep channels of communication open, it is important that you consistently select a time and place for these discussions that will be both appropriate and effective. Often it is best to initiate a discussion about a difficult topic at a time when you and the child are having a good time and enjoying one another's company (e.g., walking on the beach, driving to the mall). He may be more receptive to discussing his friendship issues then, rather than in the immediate shadow of a difficult or embarrassing incident. The setting for such a discussion can also be significant. When you meet in his bedroom, he is on his turf and feels comfortable and powerful; if you wish to demonstrate your authority, you may want to conduct your meeting in your room or your home office; a meeting at a backyard picnic table promotes the idea of neutrality, openness, and responsiveness.

These conversations about your child's friendship skills are important and valuable, but they often begin disintegrating after a few minutes due to the child's language and learning problems. You can keep these conversations going by asking direct questions and occasionally *restating* or *reflecting* what the child has said. "It sounds like you were pretty upset and disappointed when Marlene and Robin went to the mall without you." Also use body language (e.g., smiling, nodding, winking, touching) to acknowledge and support the child's feelings.

These friendship discussions also provide an opportunity for the child to share his pleasure and joy at his various friendships and relationships. Provide him with plenty of praise, reinforcement, and encouragement at these times. Occasionally the child will want to discuss problems, dilemmas, or setbacks. Let him fully explain the incident or situation before you offer suggestions, opinions, or solutions. Begin by asking him how he feels about the matter and ask him to identify and analyze the *main* problem that he is facing. He will often find that the several problems that he perceives are actually the result of *one* major difficulty. Children with learning disabilities often are unable to analyze these situations and determine which problems are of the highest priority or importance. He will need guidance to focus upon the primary problem without being distracted by smaller, less crucial difficulties.

Once you have identified and isolated the chief problem, help him generate options or choices to solve the difficulty. Assist him in this process but encourage *him* to generate most of the suggestions. Once several optional responses have been generated, help him to select and implement the most appropriate and effective one.

This process will enable the child to develop his problem-solving skills and to deal more effectively with dilemmas he may face in the future. Be sure to check back with the child after he has implemented the solution. Use this opportunity to reevaluate and suggest any modifications that may be necessary.

Below is an example of a problem-solving discussion between a child and a concerned dad.

DAD: "Spencer, why are you all alone in your room on such a beautiful day? All the kids in the neighborhood are across the street in the park playing touch football. Why don't you join them? It is supposed to rain all day tomorrow and Monday. This might be your last chance to play football for awhile."

SPENCER: "They won't want me to play. They are all mad at me. Earl and Jim called me this morning and called me a jerk. Yesterday on the bus, Zack wouldn't even sit with me. I told him that I didn't care and said that he couldn't come to my birthday party sleepover next week. Roger knocked my bike over yesterday—for no reason."

DAD: "Wow, it does seem like everyone is upset with you. Why do you think they're mad?"

SPENCER: "Probably because of the sleepover. They're just jealous that we are getting a trampoline for the party."

DAD: "But, Spencer, that doesn't sound too logical. They are all invited to the sleepover. They will all have an opportunity to enjoy the tramp. Why do you think they would be mad about that?"

SPENCER: "I don't know. But, don't worry, I can fix it. I'm going to give Zack my new CD and I am going to ask Jim and Earl to come have some of Mom's cookies. Then I'm going to tell Roger that he can use my skateboard."

DAD: "Spence, you are looking at this situation as if you have four separate problems. Maybe there is one *big* problem that is causing the other three problems. I don't think that the sleepover is the difficulty. Is there anything else that could be causing this?"

SPENCER: "No, Dad. Oh yeah, and Paul is mad at me, too."

DAD: "What's up with Paul?"

SPENCER: "Well, I accidentally broke the pencil sharpener in the library the other day. I put it back together, but it still didn't work. Later on, Paul was fooling around near the bookshelves and he knocked the sharpener off the table. The librarian came over and, when she realized that the sharpener was busted, she gave Paul a detention. The other guys thought that I should tell the librarian what had happened, but I didn't because I didn't want to get in trouble."

DAD: "You know what, Spence? I will bet that is what the guys are upset about—not the sleepover."

SPENCER: "Really? You think so?"

DAD: "Yes, I do. Now how can we fix this?"

SPENCER: "I could buy a new sharpener and put it secretly back in the library. Or I could just tell the librarian what I did. Or maybe I should go to the principal."

DAD: "Well, buying a new sharpener might not help much, but you *do* need to tell someone. How do you get along with the librarian?"

SPENCER: "She really doesn't like me. I asked her for some help on my research paper last week and she barked at me. She's sort of a grouch."

DAD: "Okay, let's not start with her. You get along real well with Dr. Lindo, the principal. Why don't you go explain the situation to her?"

SPENCER: "Yeah, I'll tell her to ask the kids not to be mad at me and to come to the sleepover."

DAD: "But that's not the issue, Spence. You have to tell her about the pencil sharpener. We will put together a script tonight to help you."

SPENCER: "Okay, and then I'm going to get all my friends together and tell them that I confessed. They will be really happy."

DAD: "Do you think that you should contact your friends first? It is actually *Paul* who got hurt in the situation."

SPENCER: "You're right. I'll go tell Paul that I'm sorry and that I told the principal what really happened. Then, if Paul forgives me, we can go together to tell the other kids."

DAD: "Perfect!"

Helping with Social Crises

A parent can also play a critically positive role when a child has issues or problems related to a friendship. Many children with social skill deficits will have difficulty judging the quality of the relationships that they share with peers. They cannot distinguish the true friends from the false friends, because they tend to be trusting and a bit gullible.

There are specific traits and behaviors that our society associates with friendship. Among those traits are:

trust	compassion	shared interests
honesty	respect	common values
loyalty	consideration	consistency
kindness	sense of humor	forgiveness

There are five questions that a child should ask himself when assessing another child's potential as a friend:

1. Is this kid similar to me?
2. Does he make me feel good?
3. Can I trust him?
4. Can he help me to meet my goals in some way?
5. Is he fun to be with?

These lists may be useful for you as you help your child evaluate his relationships. Your child may find himself mourning the demise of a friendship, but upon evaluating the relationship using the criteria listed above, he may find that the relationship was *not* a good one and that its dissolution was inevitable.

The friendship traits can also be used to assist the child in evaluating his own skills as a friend to others. If he is having difficulty with a relationship, perhaps *he* is falling short in one of the categories.

Here are some other issues that may require parental intervention and advice.

> *"Mom, I know that Billy is my friend and we usually get along fine. But he's always punching me—real hard—even though I told him to stop."*

> Your child would benefit from some basic assertiveness training! This technique assists people who have difficulty communicating their feelings and standing up for themselves. Assertiveness training is a technique that can be very useful for the child who has difficulty expressing feelings, opinions, or concerns. Such a child is often bullied by peers and ignored by adults because he fails to stand up for himself.

This six-step process guides the child through expressing his concerns in a direct, assertive manner.

A = **Attention:** Be certain that you have the person's focused attention before you begin.

S = **Soon, Short, Simple:** Speak to the person soon after the incident; be brief and succinct.

S = **Specific:** Explain exactly the behavior that concerns you.

E = **Effect:** Explain the impact that the behavior has on you.

R = **Response:** Explain what you want the person to do.

T = **Terms:** Come to an agreement on each person's responsibility.

Suppose, for example, your child's friend is constantly "borrowing" and copying his homework. His assertiveness script could be similar to this:

> **A** = "Mike, could we sit down and talk about something that's been really bothering me?"
>
> **S** = "This morning on the bus you asked for my math homework again."
>
> **S** = "When you borrow my homework all the time, it really bothers me."
>
> **E** = "I get mad about it because it feels like you're taking advantage of me, and I think that it will begin to wreck our friendship."
>
> **R** = "I'd appreciate it if you would not ask me so often. Maybe we could do our math homework together."
>
> **T** = "So, it's okay to tell you no when you ask, right?"

It may take a bit of work and rehearsal for the child to master these steps, but it will be of great assistance when he is faced with peers or adults who fail to treat him with respect or are unresponsive to his needs or concerns.

> *"Dad, Sally is my good friend, but she never calls me and she is real mean to me when the other girls are around."*

Review the traits of a good friend with your daughter. It appears that Sally is sadly lacking in the loyalty, consistency, respect, and kindness categories! Remind the child that *two* people must participate in a good friendship. Also tell her that she has control over this situation. She has the power and ability to tell her "friend" that the relationship is not working effectively, or she can simply avoid Sally. Again, children with social skill deficits often have difficulty

understanding the mutuality of friendship relationships.

*"My friends are really pressuring me to do things that I
don't want to do—not take drugs or anything, but they
cut classes a lot and sometimes steal sandwiches from
the cafeteria. What should I do?"*

Several years ago, the government launched a well-
intentioned but largely ineffective antidrug campaign
that encouraged children to "Just Say No." Simply
saying the word *no* will not stop a persistent companion. Further, a simple no invites a conversation
or discussion about the issue ("Why not?" "If not
now, when?").

The word *no* should be expanded into a longer
phrase (e.g., "No, thank you," "Nope, not interested") and then the phrase should be repeated—
verbatim—in response to the inevitable follow-up
questions. It is counterproductive for the child to become embroiled in a discussion about the matter. If
he answers the questions that are presented, his response loses its impact.

For example, suppose Jack approaches Sean and asks him to go
into a store and help him steal a pair of headphones.

JACK: "Sean, you keep the clerk busy and I'll slip the headphones into my backpack."

SEAN: "No."

JACK: "Don't be a baby! You scared?"

SEAN: "I'm not scared. I'm the one who dove off the high
board last week, remember?"

JACK: "C'mon. Be a pal. I really need those headphones."

SEAN: "But you already have a pair at home. I saw them."

JACK: "Those don't work. Anyway, they're my sister's. I really need your help."

SEAN: "We might get caught."

JACK: "We won't get caught. I do this all the time. Even if the clerk does see us, we can run out the side door."

Sean's refusal would be more effective if he simply selected a phrase and repeated it over and over.

JACK: "You keep the clerk busy and I'll slip the headphones into my backpack."

SEAN: "Nope. Not interested."

JACK: "What's the matter? You scared?"

SEAN: "Nope. Not interested."

JACK: "Come on, I really need those headphones."

SEAN: "Nope. Not interested."

JACK: "We won't get caught. I promise. I do this all the time."

SEAN: "Nope. Not interested."

JACK: "*PLEASE*. I'll take a pair for you, too!"

SEAN: "Nope. Not interested."

JACK: "Aw, forget it! Let's go to the arcade."

"Dad, Sandy is supposed to be one of my best friends. But Jennifer told me that Sandy is telling everyone that I cheated on the history test last week. I didn't—really! Why would Sandy tell people such an awful thing?"

Advise your daughter that she should not automatically believe the report from Jennifer. The adolescent grapevine is noted for embellishing, modifying, and adorning the original story. Perhaps Sandy said something that was misinterpreted or miscommunicated. If Sandy is a true friend, your daughter should approach her directly—when the two of them are alone—and say, "I have heard that you told people that I cheated on the history test. You know that I didn't, and I can't believe that you would say something like that. Can you help me understand what happened?" Sandy may have a reasonable and rational explanation. Perhaps her comment was misunderstood or greatly exaggerated.

"Dad, I've got a problem. Sarah and Kristy had such a big fight and they are real mad at each other. It all started because of something that was said at Jane's birthday party last week. They both keep complaining to me about the other one. I'm really stuck in the middle. Help!"

This is a difficult problem. Many adults face a similar dilemma when friends get divorced. But, remember, nobody can *put* you in the middle unless you choose to go there. It is important to remember that you need not attend every battle to which you are invited!

Advise your child to offer two things to the combatants when one approaches her about the various offenses that the other has committed: sympathy and suggestions. An effective and appropriate response would be: "Sarah, I know that you and Kristy are really mad at each other right now, and I realize that this must be really difficult for both of you. But both of you are good friends of mine and I just don't want to get in the middle of this. I'll bet that if you two sat down and talked about this, you could fix it."

> *"Mom, last week on the field trip, Roger asked me if he could borrow ten dollars. I had the extra money that Grandma gave me for cleaning her attic and so I lent him the money. He said that he would pay me back the next day, but he hasn't."*

Advise your son that there are several reasons why one does not repay a debt. Perhaps Roger simply forgot about the loan. Therefore, your son should approach the matter diplomatically. "Roger, remember the ten bucks that you borrowed from me on the field trip? You probably forgot, but I really need it. Do you have the ten dollars with you?" If he doesn't have the cash with him, suggest an informal payment plan wherein he gives you five dollars today and five dollars next week.

Sports and Friendship

Parents will often attempt to establish an instant group of friends by having the LD child participate in sports. This should be done with extreme caution, because this well-intentioned strategy often backfires. In one of my seminars, I tell of the eighth-grade boy whose dad taught him how to wrestle in hopes that his participation on the wrestling team would enhance his social status and enable him to make friends with his teammates. The extremely unpopular boy was devastated when—after winning his first match in his home gym—he was booed loudly by his classmates. Participation on a team does not ensure instant acceptance or popularity.

Participating in sports can be hard for children with learning or attentional problems. Children with ADD are easily distracted and are often off task. Teammates are fairly intolerant of such behavior and view it as disinterest and lack of effort on the child's part. Children are generally supportive of teammates who make mistakes *if* it appears that the child is making a genuine and sincere effort. But if teammates feel that the child is not trying, they will often reject and isolate him.

At Riverview School, we offered several team sports and our teams competed with other schools. But the greatest emphasis in our physical education program was on individual recreational sports such as bowling, skiing, and golf. These activities can provide social contacts for the child when he reaches adulthood. An alumnus told me that he has many friends at the grocery store where he works because of his participation in the company bowling league. He uses this activity to establish and maintain relationships with his coworkers.

Popularity

The goal of every child is to become popular. Popularity among peers is the Holy Grail of childhood and is unattainable for some children. Sociologists posit that there are basically four types of children who walk the halls of schools today. They are:

The Rejected Child: The child who is openly spurned and bullied by other children.

The Isolated Child: The child who remains on the periphery of social situations and is uninvolved with others.

The Controversial Child: This child is in the largest classification. She has a circle of friends with whom she shares positive relationships, but she rarely reaches out beyond her group. These groupings are generally based upon similar interests, activities, geographic locales, and so forth. The chances are fairly good that you were a "controversial child" and most of your adolescent adventures featured a small, tightly knit group of friends.

The Popular Child: This child is respected, admired, and liked by all of his peers. In fact, other children like him even if they do not know him. Popular children have positive reputations. They are voted to class offices, for example, although many of the classmates who vote for them may have never met them.

For decades, psychologists have studied and monitored the children in the Rejected and Isolated groups to determine what mistakes they commonly make. However, in recent years, researchers have been studying the children in the Controversial and Popular groups in an effort to determine the skills and traits that these children use in order to achieve their social status. This trend in the research is very significant and positive, as it provides us with specific goals, strategies, and techniques that we can teach to the socially deficient child.

One of these studies included an extensive survey of two thousand preadolescents and adolescents who were asked to outline the traits that they admire and respect among their peers. Interestingly, the responses from and about girls were radically different from those relating to boys.

The first question required the children to outline the traits that they look for in a friend. The boys' responses included the following:

- Although outstanding *athletic prowess* is not required for social acceptance, adolescents are favorably impressed by peers who participate in sports. Team sports also provide innumerable opportunities for peer interaction and camaraderie.
- Teenagers respect peers who can be *trusted*. They are unimpressed with peers who consistently lie, exaggerate, or fabricate stories. Youths with social skills problems will often attempt to impress their peers by claiming that they have talents and experiences that they do not have. They need to understand that this behavior will not enhance their social status.
- Adolescents respect peers who are *responsible* and mature regarding care of materials and other property. They are unlikely, for instance, to be willing to lend their possessions (an adolescent ritual) if the other child has a reputation for losing or destroying the property of others.
- Children enjoy the company of peers who have like interests, hobbies, and passions. Some groups enjoy discussing music,

while other groups may be interested in sports. If the child wishes to break into a specific clique, he should try to become more knowledgeable about the favorite topic of the group. It is not uncommon for children with learning problems to have unique or idiosyncratic interests or hobbies (e.g., 1930s jazz, lamp-shade collections), and they may expect their peers to share their enthusiasm for these interests. They need to recognize that it is highly unlikely that this will occur, and they need to be cautious of being overly aggressive about promoting their interests with others. The child is more likely to gain friendships by expressing an interest in the passions of others rather than attempting to convert peers to *his* passions.

The survey participants were then asked to discuss the traits that they *dislike* in others. The majority of responders reported that they dislike and avoid troublemakers. They feel that you run the risk of getting in trouble often if you keep company with peers who are disruptive and disrespectful to adults. Some students with poor social skills will attempt to impress their peers by creating havoc in the classroom and confronting teachers. This generally backfires on the child and results in rejection or isolation.

The survey revealed some other traits that are off-putting to preadolescents:

- The respondents reported that they are intimidated and offended by peers who are *aggressive* in their attempts to establish relationships. At this age, children expect that peers will accept "no" as an answer and will retreat when their friendship overtures are rejected. Children with LD often have difficulty reading these social signals and may be unable to understand that the other child is uninterested in establishing or maintaining a friendship.
- Children spend a good deal of their time receiving instructions, directions, and orders from the adults in their lives. They often resent this, but they have little choice but to comply. For this reason, they are extraordinarily sensitive to being *bossed around* by peers or siblings. The constant retort is, "Hey, you're not the boss of me!" Unfortunately, children with social skill deficits

often tend to be bossy and do not recognize the negative impact that this behavior has upon peer acceptance.

The third question asked the children to list the topics that they generally talk about when they are alone with their peers. Among their responses were:

- Boys talk about girls (and vice versa). Boys report that they often speak about the relative attributes (physical and otherwise) of the girls they know in common.
- Sports is a favorite topic among boys. Conversations center on the most recent game of their favorite team and the exploits of their favorite ballplayers. If your child is not knowledgeable about sports, it might be a good idea to occasionally discuss this topic with him and give him the basic information that will provide entrée into the sports-related discussions on the bus or in the cafeteria.
- Interestingly, boys are not particularly interested in discussing personal topics such as family problems. Your son will gain very few social points by regaling his peers with stories of domestic squabbles or his deeply held fear of moths! Developmentally, boys are simply unable and unwilling to discuss highly personal or sensitive topics. Basically, they have enough of their own angst to bear and have little interest in carrying the burdens of others.

Interestingly, the responses of girls to these questions were significantly different from those of the boys. The demands, expectations, and criteria that girls hold for friendships are radically different from those held by boys.

When asked "What do girls talk about?," girls responded that "school" is a main topic of conversation. You will note that this topic did not appear on the boys' list of preferred conversation subjects. This confirms my long-held belief that girls view school as their social life. Boys, on the other hand, view school as an *interruption* of their social life.

Girls see the class day as a whirlwind of social contacts, exchanges, and interactions. Girls use school hours to talk, mingle, play, engage, share, and network. Boys experience their most meaningful contacts after school or on weekends. Girls constantly discuss the social and academic aspects of school. It is a hot and important topic for them. However, a boy who constantly talks about school—particularly during nonschool hours—is likely to be rejected by other boys.

The survey indicated that girls enjoy gossiping and discussing "private topics." For the sake of this discussion, forget the negative connotations of the word *gossip*. In our celebrity-addicted culture, gossip has come to mean the spreading of hurtful and cruel information about a person. However, gossip is actually defined merely as "talking about the lives of other people." Girls tend to do that. Boys tend not to. If three girls are close friends and two of them go to the mall together, they are likely to spend much of the afternoon talking about the absent member of the trio. ("Oh, wouldn't Annie look cute in those boots?" or "Annie would love this ice cream. Chocolate is her favorite.") If three *boys* are friends and two of them spend an afternoon together, it is unlikely that the name of the missing boy would even come up.

Girls also talk about private and confidential matters. It is widely held that girls mature psychologically faster than boys do. As preteens and adolescents, girls enjoy learning the secrets of their companions and can become quite adept at counseling and advising their friends. If a girl is experiencing trouble at home (e.g., pending parental divorce, financial problems), she will generally find no shortage of girls who want to hear the details and who stand ready to offer advice and guidance. Young girls enjoy the roles of *rescuer* and *confidante*. Conversely, boys often feel uncomfortable and ill equipped to play these roles.

When asked "What traits do you look for in a friend?," girls responded that sense of humor and friendliness were of great importance. Once again, these traits were seldom mentioned when boys were asked the same question. Girls expect and demand that other girls be friendly, congenial, welcoming, and amiable. If a girl passes a female acquaintance in the hallway without extending a smile or a greeting, her behavior is analyzed and dissected. ("Leah didn't say hello to me! Is she angry? Did I do something wrong? Does she hate me?") Boys do not require you to be friendly in order to be a friend. My brothers and I attended the same high school and passed each other innumerable times without exchanging as much as a nod of recognition. It was neither necessary nor expected.

This has significant implications for girls with social difficulties. In order to improve her social status, a girl must learn to smile, make eye contact, and greet other girls in social situations. Failure to do so can cause the girl to be branded "stuck-up" or "superior." Supporting this fact, the survey indicated that girls dislike and distrust girls who are unfriendly.

The survey indicated that girls reject and isolate girls who are unclean or unkempt. Even though they are willing to interact with girls who may be unfashionable, it is extraordinarily important that she use appropriate hygiene and self-care. Failure to do so can have a long-term detrimental impact upon the girl's social status.

Another important part of the survey asked boys and girls about the traits that they found appealing and attractive about the opposite sex. Their responses have significant implications for the adolescent or preadolescent who hopes to establish a meaningful boy-girl relationship. Both genders responded that physical attractiveness was important, but it was not the top criterion for either gender.

Boys noted that they wanted a girl who was "loyal" and "confidential." This doubtless reflects the fact that boys do not feel comfortable discussing their home and school problems with their male friends, so they want someone in their life with whom they can share their secrets without being concerned that the confidante will share the information with others. Girls spend innumerable hours trying to look good for potential boyfriends, but in reality, boys often want a girlfriend with whom they can converse and share.

Girls stated that their ideal boyfriend is one who is "sweet," "thoughtful," and "gentle." Boys continually attempt to impress girls with their athletic prowess, physical strength, and manliness. Advise the boy that girls are more impressed with sensitivity and sincerity.

Boy-Girl Relationships and Dating

I was counseling a thirteen-year-old boy who desperately wanted to impress a thirteen-year-old girl in his class. His lack of social perception presented a considerable obstacle. He would meet her at the bus stop each day and attempt to impress her by throwing rocks at the distant stop sign, or grabbing her in a headlock and tossing her to the ground. I counseled him that these feats of strength were not likely to stir her. I advised him to be more gentle and thoughtful with her.

One day, I asked him how his relationship was progressing. "Pretty good," he replied with a smile. "I think she likes me. Last week I gave her a penguin keychain at lunch. I told her, 'You once told me that you thought penguins were cute. I saw this keychain at the drugstore yesterday and I thought of you. I hope that you like it!'"

Home run!! He *listened to her,* he *remembered what she said,* and he *thought of her.* It is not surprising that she was becoming attracted to him.

Among the greatest challenges faced by any preadolescent is the painful initial foray into relationships with members of the opposite sex. This can be a particularly difficult process for the child with learning problems and social deficiencies.

As human beings, we develop in several areas: physical, cognitive, sexual, social. The child with LD may be developing very appropriately in the area of sexuality and, as a result, has all the needs, urges, and curiosities of his classmates. However, his social skills may be significantly deficient. As a result, the child may attempt to satisfy his normal sexuality needs by utilizing his poorly developed social skills. The result can be disastrous and humiliating. Children with social deficiencies often have difficulty dealing with the timing and staging of relationships. They may view a relationship as a *product* rather than a *process.* As a result, they may move a relationship too quickly and ignore the step-by-step process that is required and expected. I well recall the following exchange that I had with a smitten sixteen-year-old girl at my school.

> SANDY: "Mr. Lavoie, my dorm counselor won't give me permission to go to the boys' dorm to see my boyfriend. You guys don't understand. Brian and I really love each other. We are going to get married right after graduation. We are going to buy a cocker spaniel and name her Magoo. We will have three

daughters. He likes the name Britney for a girl, but I think it's dumb. But we really, *really* love each other and we really, *really* need to spend time together. Can I *please* go to the boys' dorm for the afternoon?"

MR. LAVOIE: "Well, we can certainly discuss it. I didn't know that you had such a serious relationship with one of the boys. Is it Brian Mitchell or Brian Southwick?"

SANDY: "I'm not sure of his last name, but he has reddish hair and wears glasses—I think."

In the words of Jim Morrison, "Hello, I love you, won't you tell me your name?"

When attempting to initiate and establish a relationship with a member of the opposite sex, the child must be advised to pace and plan his initial approaches. If he comes on too strong or, conversely, if he waits passively in the hopes that *she* will notice *him*, he is unlikely to achieve his goal.

Below is some advice for a child who is attempting to be noticed by a prospective girlfriend/boyfriend.

1. Pay attention to her.

    By smiling, saying hello, asking questions, or showing an interest, the child is letting her know that he is interested in establishing a relationship and, further, that he is a desirable and thoughtful partner.

2. Spend time with her.

    Recommend that the child telephone the prospective partner or walk her to class. Seek her out at social events (e.g., dances, ball games, assemblies) and sit with her.

3. Be respectful and mannerly.

    At these early stages of a relationship, it is particularly important to be polite (e.g., say please, thank you) and respon-

sive. If she looks sad, ask her if she is okay. If he looks puzzled, ask him if you can help. Remember to always speak
kindly of her, whether she is around or not!

4. Be thoughtful.

   Write her a note or give her a flower. Give her a small gift
   that is related to a previous conversation. ("I bought you this
   picture of the Statue of Liberty because you told me that your
   grandfather lives near there. When I saw it in the store, I
   thought of you.")

5. Use the grapevine!

   Ask *your* friends to tell *her* friends that you are interested.
   That's the way teenage communication works! Or you can be
   more direct by telling her—at the right time and in the right
   place—that you are interested. Tell her you enjoy being with
   her.

Parents often ask at what age it is appropriate to begin dating.
There is no one answer to that question. The child should begin dating when he is ready physically, socially, and emotionally. The dating
experience will be unsuccessful if it is initiated in response to peer—
or parental—pressure. In some communities, dating rituals begin at
thirteen or fourteen, while in other communities serious dating is
postponed until later. Your child may need guidance regarding his
readiness to enter the dating arena.

Encourage the child to begin his partner search in the most obvious places—his neighborhood, church, school, and community.
Forewarn him of the dangers of seeking partners on the Internet,
through classified ads, or similar avenues. There are significant risks
involved when a child attempts to establish a relationship with a person that she does not know well. A chance meeting at the mall or a
video store is seldom a solid foundation on which to begin a relationship. Remind the child *never* to accept rides from strangers and
strongly encourage that the first date be in a public place.

Because of the language problems that accompany learning disabilities, your child may have difficulty initiating or maintaining a

conversation. Of course, conversations are a significantly important step in the early stages of the dating ritual.

Below are some suggestions that will be helpful for the child whose conversational skills may be problematic as he or she attempts to initiate a boy-girl relationship.

1. *Talk about someone whom you both know.* But don't be mean or gossipy! Talk about a classmate's new car or the class officer elections.

2. *Talk about your family.* Tell her about your sister's recent acceptance at college or the latest adventure of your family pet.

3. *Talk about current movies or TV shows.* This is a great way to start a conversation. Talk about a movie you recently saw or the latest episode of a favorite television show.

4. *Talk about school.* Ask how she is doing on the long-term science project or how she liked the recent assembly.

5. *Talk about current events or issues that affect you both.* Talk about an article that you read in the newspaper, or ask her if she had a difficult time with her driver's test.

6. *Share your opinion.* Talk about an upcoming sporting event or school election and share your thoughts.

Parents should remember that dating mores and customs have changed substantially since the 1960s and 1970s. Although it continues to be inappropriate for a girl to be overly aggressive when seeking a boyfriend, it is now quite acceptable for a girl to be assertive and to ask a boy to accompany her to a social engagement. It is also increasingly common to share the cost of a date. However, the boy is generally expected to pay for the first date. It is also generally accepted that the boy will pick the girl up at her home for the initial date.

Reputation

Reputation is a crucial element of a child's social profile. Once a child develops a reputation among his peers—particularly a *negative* reputation—it becomes his indelible label. Unlike most adults, children are relatively inflexible and unforgiving in regard to interpersonal relationships. Once they brand a peer as a "loser" or a "nerd," they tend to interpret and evaluate all of their interactions with that child through that "filter." The child's positive behaviors are ignored, while his mistakes and miscues are viewed as evidence that the loser label is accurate and fitting.

As the University of North Carolina's Dr. Mel Levine explains, this is due to the fact that school-age children tend to take a *dispositional* view of others. That is, they assign a certain label to a person ("My English teacher is a jerk," "Michael is fun," "My neighbor is mean") and they seldom depart from that evaluation. If the English teacher helps the student with a project, the child attaches deceptive or duplicitous motives to the behavior: "Oh, he was just trying to show how cool and smart he is." These children are unwilling and unable to modify or adjust their attitude toward another person, even in the face of clear evidence that they may have been incorrect in their initial assessment.

Adults tend to take a *situational* view of other people, wherein they judge others based on their behavior in various settings and circumstances. "Joe can be a real jerk sometimes, but he was really helpful last night when my car wouldn't start," or "I hate going out to dinner with Russ. He *never* picks up a check. But, boy, does that guy know his baseball!" School-age children are generally unable to take a situational view of people in their social world.

I remember walking down the main street of our town with our then sixteen-year-old son, Kitt. We passed a neighborhood boy, Justin, and I wished him a good day, but Kitt was stonily silent. I asked him why he did not speak to Justin. Kitt responded that Justin "was a jerk" because he stole Kitt's lunch once—in second grade. In the world of childhood, the statute of limitations on a baloney and cheese sandwich is obviously a decade or more. The judgments that children make about one another are often rigid and irreversible.

Because children understand well the concept of "reputation," they become very protective of their own social standing. They are careful to say and do the "right" thing at the "right" time. They develop and foster an image that will ensure acceptance and popularity. Unfortunately, children with learning problems are often unaware of these peer-imposed norms and, as a result, continually make social faux pas that create and foster a negative reputation.

Teachers must be particularly aware of the impact of reputation on a child. I often remind elementary school teachers that in a typical neighborhood school, the children in fourth grade are, in effect, a *family*. They have attended school as a unit for the past four years and will be together as a group for several more years as their academic career progresses. The fourth-grade teacher is, basically, a visitor who is involved with the family for 180 days. The class's rejection of Alex is based upon four years of his disruptive behavior and—perhaps—their being punished for his mistakes. Rather than fostering and propagating Alex's negative reputation, a teacher should try to highlight and use his strengths to modify and improve his classmates' opinion of him. By teaching Alex some appropriate peer-pleasing behaviors, a teacher may be able to adjust the label that his classmates have affixed—and he has earned—over the years.

Teachers and parents can help a child to improve his reputation by helping him to determine which settings or activities are most troublesome for him. If he identifies recess as the source of most of his peer conflicts, encourage him to temporarily avoid this activity or plan a more low-key role during recess times. This may blunt the peer's belief that "Billy *always* spoils our recess!"

As Billy gradually reenters the recess activity, provide him with ample guidance, coaching, and supervision. Mom may want to accompany him to the classmate's birthday party; the Scout leader or teacher may want to "shadow" him as he reintegrates into the activities that had been troubling for him.

Often, a child will attempt to buy his way out of a poor reputation by giving toys or money to his peers. This approach seldom works effectively and can be converted to extortion by bullying or aggressive classmates. If a child begins stealing cash from home or if toys or other possessions are inexplicably missing, you may want to investigate this. Your child may have become the victim of this damaging cycle of "buying friends."

The most effective strategy for improving a child's reputation and enhancing his popularity is for the adult to demonstrate genuine public acceptance and affection for the rejected child. Spotlight and celebrate his hidden talents. Discover his skills and feature them in your curriculum. Allow and encourage him to become the class expert in some activity or project. When you demonstrate your approval of the child, his classmates may be intrigued and want to get to know him better and occasionally involve him in their activities.

Maintaining Friendships

The world of friendship is often alien to children who are socially incompetent. They have little knowledge of the dynamics of this crucial relationship. As a result, they may not even understand the *definition* of friendship. I recall a child who was consistently ignored by his classmates telling me that he had "lots and lots" of friends and even listing several by name. When I inquired about the definition of a friend, he replied, "A friend is someone who doesn't pick on you."

Children with social skill deficits need to recognize that there are several levels of friendship, which reflect the intensity of that relationship. The initial level is that of an *acquaintance*. People in this group include individuals with whom you have brief encounters on an occasional basis. This group may include classmates, fellow bus riders, the clerk at the video store, or the waitress at the coffee shop. It is inaccurate to view these people as friends, because the relationship includes none of the mutuality and sharing that characterizes true friendship. The child must realize that it would be inappropriate, for example, to tell an acquaintance a family secret, ask him for money, or invite him to go on vacation with your family. Those activities are only appropriate for people that share a true friendship.

The second level of relationship is that of *companion*. This relationship is deeper than that of an acquaintance, but does not meet the criteria of genuine friendship. A companion is a person with whom you spend a significant amount of time. Examples of companions include teammates, members of church groups, or neighbors.

This relationship has a *common interest or activity* as its focus. You interact fairly intensely with the person during this activity (e.g., bus ride, basketball practice, play rehearsal), but you interact minimally at other times. In fact, you need not even *like* a person in order for him to qualify as a companion.

The third level is a *genuine friendship*. Unlike the previous two levels, this friendship involves intimacy, caring, and—most important—reciprocity. Two children who have formed a genuine friendship are willing to make sacrifices for one another. They share possessions and confide in one another. They are able to take one another's perspective on issues and they take great comfort and joy in this relationship.

More Friendship Pitfalls

Socially incompetent children encounter numerous pitfalls as they attempt to establish and maintain their friendships. It is necessary that parents, caregivers, and—most important—the child be aware of these obstacles and avoid them.

Among the most common mistakes is one that I discuss in my workshops. I refer to this miscue as "putting out the candle." This occurs when the child, in his desperation to maintain a friendship, will actually destroy it by being overly possessive, jealous, or demanding. The child fears that his friend will form relationships with others and that he will become again the odd man out. To prevent this, the child demands exclusivity in the relationship and becomes angry and jealous when his friend enjoys the company of another. Eventually, the friend tires of this behavior and discontinues the friendship. The child's behavior has backfired and has caused his worst fear to be realized.

The child must learn to give his friends some space and should not be fearful or threatened because the friend keeps company with another. An important part of friendship is allowing the other person to be independent and unique. Use examples of your own relationships to illustrate this concept to the child.

A second error occurs when the child fails to recognize the mutuality of the relationship. Friendship is a two-way street. Each partner must make withdrawals *and* deposits in order for the friendship to grow and develop. Children often destroy friendships by expecting and demanding encouragement, support, assistance, and sensitivity from their partner, but they are unable or unwilling to give these in equal measure. These one-sided relationships are rarely lasting and can become dysfunctional and inappropriate. Friends must share the burden equally.

Children with social skill problems often use the withdrawal of friendship as a threat or a bargaining chip. ("If you won't lend me your basketball, I won't be your friend anymore!") These constant threats have a negative effect upon a relationship, as they reflect a lack of respect for the other child and for the friendship itself. This behavior soon becomes tiring and the relationship begins to deteriorate. Friends don't threaten friends.

Another mine in the friendship minefield involves the child's selfish use of the relationship for personal gain. The child may view his friends as his own private source from which to borrow money, sports equipment, videos, and so forth. ("Come on, give it to me. Be a friend!") Some children will also select a friend for the wrong reasons. They may attempt, for example, to establish a friendship with a high-status child in order to boost their own popularity. A child with a reputation of "using his friends" becomes an unappealing candidate for friendship. Loyalty is a valued trait among children.

In order for friendships to grow and develop, they must be nurtured by genuine sensitivity. Some children believe that "friends can say *anything* to each other," and this candor can easily become hurtful and destructive. Friends need our sensitivity, understanding, and empathy. Friendship is not a license for cruelty. Children who are verbally impulsive are at great risk for offending others unintentionally. I recall hearing this exchange between two girls who shared a wonderful friendship—and an impulse-control problem.

PAULA: "Nancy, Nancy! I couldn't wait to tell you! *I'm going to the prom!*"

NANCY: "What?!? Someone invited *you* to the prom?"

Game over. Friendship ended.

This exchange is a good example of the egocentrism that often characterizes the social profiles of children with social skill deficits. Children who are highly egocentric tend to view the world through their eyes only and have marked difficulty assuming the point of view of others. This inability to adopt the perspective of their peers often causes them to say or do things that are viewed as selfish or insensitive. In an extreme example, when I was the director of a residential school for children with learning problems, one of the boys was seriously injured in an accident. An announcement about the accident was made to the student body and, within moments, a boy excitedly approached me and said, "If Bobby dies, can I be the one who lowers the flag to half-mast? I learned how to do it in Scout camp last summer!" The boy, a sweet and sensitive youngster, was simply unable to view the situation from the perspective of others.

Dr. Robert Selman, of Harvard University's Graduate School of Education, posits that there is a predictable progression to a child's ability to take the perspective of others. Children with social skill deficits often have delays or obstacles in these developmental sequences.

Level 0 (ages three to seven)
- The child is unable to realize that another person may interpret the same social situation in a different way. "Grandma is mean. She got mad at me just because I wanted to talk to her during church services."
- The child may have difficulty interpreting behavior as being intentional or unintentional. "He broke my toy on purpose!"
- Relationships are based exclusively on proximity and availability of toys. "Christian is my friend. He lives next door and has two tricycles. He lets me use one."
- Adults are needed in order to initiate and maintain these primitive friendships.

Level 1 (ages four to nine)
- The child begins to recognize and acknowledge the feelings and viewpoints of others. "Benjy gets mad when I jump on his trampoline with my shoes on."

- True friendships begin to form based on mutual interests. "I like Jimmy. He collects baseball cards, too."
- The child begins to understand the unique needs and skills of his friends. "Janey is *so* good at swimming. She's going to help me learn to jump off the diving board."

Level 2 (ages six to twelve)

- The child begins to understand how he and his actions are viewed by others. "Mikey thought I was a jerk when I told him that I lost his CD."
- True cooperation, give-and-take, and compromise begin to occur. "I don't want to watch TV, but Mike said that if I watch his favorite program, he will shoot hoops with me later."
- Relationships are *very* fragile; small slights or offenses can still end the relationship.

Level 3 (ages nine to fifteen)

- Friendships become a source of intimacy and mutual support. "I was really mad at school today, but I felt better after I talked to Tom."
- Personal problems may be shared.
- Minor skirmishes or disagreements do not signal the end of a relationship; both sides assume that the friendship will continue. "Jeanne was so mean to me today about my new haircut. I'll tell her that she hurt my feelings when she picks me up for the bus tomorrow."
- Close, exclusive, two-person cliques characterized by possessiveness and jealousy are formed.

Level 4 (fifteen to adult)

- Relationships become solid and mutually beneficial.
- Both parties recognize the need for other relationships within the social setting; possessiveness decreases.
- It is very common to have many friendships at various levels of intensity.

Again, many children with social skill problems fail to develop their friendships skills along a parallel course with their peers. Conflicts are frequent and intense. Imagine the conflict when a child at Level 2 attempts to form a relationship with a classmate who is functioning at Level 4.

Specific Social Skills Necessary
for Successful Friendships

Mel Levine, founder of All Kinds of Minds and author of *A Mind at a Time,* has identified and quantified the several social competencies that a child needs to master if he is to initiate and maintain friendships. When these critical skills are considered, it becomes understandable how children with learning disorders can find the social arena to be such a significant and frustrating challenge. Most children with social deficits are experiencing difficulty in several of these areas. Which ones present specific challenges for *your* child?

Relevance: The ability to read a social situation and adjust behavior appropriately.

Parents often report that their socially deficient children are noted for saying or doing the wrong thing at the wrong time. This is due to the child's inability to accurately "read a room" and determine the social ambience of a setting or situation. For example, suppose a group of students are joking and talking as they sit at a cafeteria table. They are discussing the torrential rains of the past few days, and one jokes that they ought to start building an ark in their industrial arts class and begin collecting pairs of animals from the zoo. The socially deficient child fails to understand the jocular nature of the conversation and argues that it would be impossible to build a boat that large because the semester ends in ten days. His inability to contribute in a relevant manner causes him to be rejected or isolated from the others.

Affective matching: The ability to understand, reinforce, and replicate the current feelings or emotions of a peer.

This skill is closely related to relevance. Often, a child is unable to accurately discern the emotional states of those in his environment. As a result, the child's behavior fails to match their behavior. He may laugh loudly at a solemn event or may appear sad and troubled during a joyous occasion.

I recall receiving extraordinarily good news during a telephone call one day while at school. I began excitedly searching the campus for my wife to share this news with her. One of the teachers told me that she was in the dining hall. I rushed into the empty hall and saw her sitting at a table with two colleagues. Janet and one of the teachers sat on either side of a third teacher, who had obviously been crying. The three sat closely together. Janet had her arm around the shoulder of the crying teacher and was speaking to her softly.

Immediately, I recognized that a problem of some sort had occurred and, further, that this was neither the time nor the place to share my good news. Rather, I joined the group and inquired as to the nature of the problem and offered any assistance that I could. I had read the emotional tone of the room and adjusted my affect to match theirs.

Children with social skill deficiencies often lack the social savvy or insight to identify the social tone of a situation and, therefore, tend to act inappropriately.

Timing and Staging: *The ability to pace relationships appropriately.*

As mentioned previously, children dislike and distrust peers who are overly aggressive in their attempts to establish relationships. Children with social skill problems often fail to recognize that there exists an established sequence of steps in initiating a friendship. As a result, the child comes on too strong in his initial attempts and the connection is never made. Again, these children view friendships as a *product,* not a process.

Suppose a new boy moves into the neighborhood. The socially competent boy who lives next door may wait until the new boy is in the driveway, then ride by on his bicycle. He will introduce himself and ask a few relevant questions. He will end the brief exchange by suggesting that the two go to the local mall together some indefinite time in the future. This is a very appropriate initial gambit.

However, the socially deficient child—oblivious of timing and staging—will approach the situation much differently. He may run excitedly to his new neighbor's house and bang on the door. His first exchange with the new boy will include the suggestions that they become best friends, sleep over at each other's homes on the upcoming weekend, borrow each other's bikes, and serve as ushers in each other's weddings! The new boy is overwhelmed by this aggressive social assault and avoids his neighbor for the foreseeable future. Your child will need significant guidance and assistance to understand the appropriate timing and staging of peer relationships.

Social Memory: *The recall and use of prior interactive experiences.*

One of the primary characteristics of the socially deficient child is his tendency to repeat the same social mistakes. A mother once wearily told me, "He keeps doing the same inappropriate things over and over. He just doesn't learn!" She was correct.

Children with learning disabilities often have significant memory deficits and a tendency to forget past incidents. As a result, they do not learn from their mistakes and have minimal "accumulated social wisdom." They approach each social situation as if they have never experienced that situation—or anything similar—in the past. Whenever your child is entering a novel or unique situation, remind him of times in which he was in a similar situation and discuss or analyze the behaviors that were successful in the previous setting. You might say, "This is the first time that you have ever been to a synagogue, Sean, but remember when we went to that big church with Grandma in Boston? I want you to be quiet and not talk during the prayers, just like you did with Grandma."

Social Prediction: *The ability to predict the consequences of social behavior.*

A common but largely ineffective comment made by parents in response to a child's social errors is, "What did you *think* would happen when you said [or did] that?" Therein lies the problem. These children are often *unable* to predict the social consequences of their behavior by foreseeing the responses of others to their actions. As a result, they have few social strategies available when

attempting to ingratiate or impress others. They may develop a repertoire of ultimately unsuccessful behaviors (e.g., making strange
noises, attempting to scare others) that they feel will improve their
social standing.

Recuperative Strategies: *The ability to compensate for social errors.*

One of the most challenging and difficult of all the social skills is
the ability to rebound from a social error, assess the damage, and repair it. This task is difficult for adults who possess well-developed social skills, so you can imagine how challenging it is for the child with
social deficiencies.

When the child makes an embarrassing or hurtful social error, he
often responds by merely avoiding the offended party. He has no
strategies to deal with his miscue and may even try to bribe the victim of his faux pas by offering a reward if the error will be forgiven.
Again, it is important to remember that the task of repairing a damaged relationship is difficult and complex. Consider the last time that
you were in a position to fix a broken relationship. It wasn't easy. As a
child increases the frequency of his social interactions, he will simultaneously increase the frequency of his social errors.

The child who has difficulty with recuperative strategies will
often have difficulty understanding and utilizing the basic strategies
for apologizing. There are some widely accepted guidelines that must
be followed when a person attempts to apologize to another.

Janet Giler, a California family therapist, recommends this seven-
step process in making a sincere apology:

1. Admit the mistake: "I know that I was wrong when I embarrassed
you in front of your date last night. I shouldn't have talked about your
old girlfriend in front of her."

2. Explain why it occurred: "I had a lousy day at school yesterday
and was in a bad mood. It made me angry to see you two enjoying
yourselves and I really responded inappropriately."

3. Acknowledge hurt feelings: "I realize that you must have been
embarrassed, and Sally was obviously angry and upset about what I
said."

4. *Apologize*: "I am truly sorry that I hurt your feelings and ruined your evening."

5. *Affirm the relationship*: "You are a great brother and have helped me a lot. I don't want you to be mad at me."

6. *Offer to correct the error*: "Is there anything I can do to fix this? Want me to apologize to Sally?"

7. *Commit to not make the same mistake again*: "From now on, I won't hang around you guys so much when Sally comes over and I'll be sure to watch what I say!"

This conversation should be held in a serious tone of voice and with eye contact. The child should be cautious in Step 2 to avoid flimsy, unrelated excuses or rationalizations. Acknowledging that he was in a bad mood is not sufficient reason for his behavior. If the person accepts the apology, the child should thank him.

Awareness of Image: To present oneself as a socially acceptable person; also, to recognize the level of status that you currently hold.

A socially competent child will constantly monitor his social environment and adjust his behavior, language, mode of dress, and so forth, to conform favorably to his peers. This degree of conformity is particularly important for the adolescent. Many children with social skill deficits have difficulty understanding and adhering to these social mores (see "Mastering the Hidden Curriculum of School," Chapter 10). They also may view themselves as higher on the social ladder than they actually are. This can result in unsuccessful and hurtful attempts to break into cliques that are beyond their social status and skills. A former student of mine had an older brother who was extraordinarily athletic and popular. His teammates and friends were attentive and kind to the younger brother. Their kindness was a reflection of their affection and respect for the older brother but not rooted in any genuine feeling for the younger sibling. However, the younger boy felt that the popular boys were his "good friends." He was troubled to find that their kindnesses and attention ended when the older brother graduated from their high school. The younger boy made several rebuffed attempts to hang out with the older, more mature group, and his feelings were deeply hurt as a result.

Feedback Cues: Sensitivity to positive and negative feedback during interactions.

When involved in conversations or interactions with others, it is important that a child monitor, understand, and respond to the verbal and nonverbal feedback cues that she is given. For example, if she makes a comment that has offended the person to whom she is speaking, she must take steps to repair the situation. The ability to read and respond to these cues is critically important to social success.

How to Improve Friendship Skills

As you work with your child to improve her social and interactional skills, attempt to determine which of the above-listed areas are the most difficult and challenging for her. By determining which specific skill sets she lacks, you will be able to better focus and concentrate your instruction and intervention.

Dr. Levine, in his innovative book *Jarvis Clutch, Social Spy,* offers strategies or approaches that parents can use in order to improve the social competence of the child who struggles with establishing and maintaining friendships.

Goal Setting: Assist the child in establishing realistic, attainable social goals and the strategies to meet those goals. The objectives may be, for example, to make three phone calls to friends every week or to have two playdates each week. Setting these goals means the social activities are far more likely to be completed. In the sage words of management genius W. Edwards Deming, "That which gets measured gets done."

Counseling/Coaching: Make sure the child establishes a relationship with a trustworthy adult who can provide ongoing social coaching. A parent can play this role, but some children may feel more comfortable confiding in a person who is a bit more detached from home life (e.g., uncle, clergy, older cousin, neighbor).

Modeling: Encourage the child to carefully observe the other children in his environment. What do the kids wear? How do they talk? How do they act? Assist the child in replicating some of these successful strategies.

Experimenting: Assist the child in reinventing himself on occasion. Try different ways of dressing, talking, or acting. Help him to evaluate the effectiveness of these changes by observing how his peers respond.

Interest Sharing: Children (and adults!) are naturally attracted to peers who have interests and affinities similar to theirs. Encourage the child to develop interests, collections, and so forth, and to seek out children whose interests mirror theirs.

Self-Coaching: Although it is useful and effective to have a social coach, it is not possible for the coach to accompany the child throughout the day, offering counsel and advice for every social situation. Therefore, the child must learn to monitor her own behavior and provide herself with advice when she is faced with a challenging social situation. By using this *self-talk* (e.g., "You're being too bossy" or "Jump into the conversation someplace"), she will make fewer social errors and will be more likely to respond appropriately.

Confiding: In addition to an adult coach, it is beneficial to have a peer or sibling who will provide the child with advice, feedback, and assistance on social situations. Often, a peer will have a better understanding of the social scene than the adult coach.

Record Keeping: Many children benefit from maintaining a *social journal* wherein they record the various social interactions that they faced that day. Dr. Levine suggests that the child should also rate (on a scale of 1 to 10) his reaction to the situations.

Using Your Strengths: The child should be urged to use his affinities and talents to make social inroads. Most children with learning problems have areas of specialized knowledge and experience.

Developing a Support System

As human beings, we rely on support from others in the various environments where we live, work, and play. Some people provide us with *emotional* support by boosting and fostering our self-esteem. For example, a coworker who cheers you on at the company softball game could be said to provide you with emotional support. But he is not necessarily your friend.

A second type of support we receive daily from others is *informational* support. This type of support provides us with the data or information that we need in order to solve problems. The librarian at your town library or a research intern at your company may provide you with this information. But she is not necessarily your friend.

Instrumental support is a third type of assistance we receive daily. This support comes from people who provide us with the resources that we need to complete our tasks at work and home. You receive instrumental support from your local grocer and the information technology folks at your office. But these people are not necessarily your friends.

The final type of support is referred to as *social companionship*. People who provide you with this type of support generally share activities with you and may provide you with encouragement and support as needed. You may receive social companionship from a tennis partner or a person in your car pool. Again, those who provide this sort of support are *not* necessarily your friends. A friend is a person who provides you with all four types of support: *emotional, informational, instrumental,* and *companionship.*

Children with social competence difficulties are often confused by this concept of a social support system. On my desk, I have a Rolodex that contains hundreds of business cards from professionals with whom I have interacted over the years. I will often tell my students that that Rolodex represents my *support system.* Not every person listed is a friend of mine. Some of them provide me with instrumental or informational support, while others may provide emotional support or companionship. Only my friends provide me with all four types of support.

As I tell my students, there are two things that you must do to make your support system function effectively. First, you must know which type of support each person in the system provides. It would be useless to contact your tech support staff if you were having difficulty starting your car, as it would be pointless to call your auto mechanic if your computer was denying you access to the Internet.

Second, to ensure that your support system remains in working order, you must be mindful of your responsibility to contribute to the system by reciprocating, praising, encouraging, and thanking those who support you. You cannot simply make withdrawals on this system; you must make some deposits as well. This reciprocation is particularly important for those individuals who provide you with emotional support and companionship. Failure to reciprocate may cause the person to withhold his support.

None of us could function successfully or effectively without an intact support system. Children, too, need a variety of support from key peers and adults in their lives.

Parents can help children develop friendship skills by maintaining a strong family network in which the child has the opportunity to encounter a variety of people of different ages, genders, interests, and backgrounds. This exposure will enable the child to enhance his flexibility in social situations.

Afterword

As you work to improve and enhance a child's friendship skills, you should know about some unique and valuable research completed in 2003 by the Frostig Center of California. This pioneering organization conducted extensive surveys and interviews with adults who have had lifelong struggles with learning, attentional, and social problems. However, the subjects of this research were selected because they had achieved a good deal of success in their social and occupational lives. The research was designed to isolate and identify the specific behaviors, traits, and attitudes that contributed to that success. There is great wisdom in this approach. By identifying the traits of successful adults with learning problems, we can more effectively plan and sequence our social skill instruction for children who are rejected and isolated by their classmates. These traits appear to be the vehicles by which the surveyed adults achieved success, stability, and fulfillment in their lives.

Primary among the traits identified by this survey was *self-awareness*. These adults have a clear and thorough understanding of their strengths, weaknesses, needs, and abilities. They are aware of their specific academic and social problems and the impact that these difficulties have upon their daily lives. However, they also recognize and use their strengths and view themselves as competent and confident people. They do not *deny* their difficulties, but neither do they use their problems as an excuse for failure, lack of effort, or lack of progress. They are able to explain their difficulties to others (self-advocacy) and can match their talents and limitations to appropriate vocational and social choices and decisions.

The second trait is referred to as *proactivity*. This refers to the positive and definitive steps the person takes to achieve his social or vocational goals. These successful adults are able and willing to make decisions and take control of their actions and their lives. They accept successes graciously and are not defeated or depressed when they fail at a task. They seek and follow the advice of others, but they are largely independent in the important decisions of their lives.

A third important trait is *perseverance*. These successful adults were goal directed and did not surrender in the face of obstacles or adversity. They adhered to the ancient Japanese proverb: "Fall down nine times; get up ten times." Interestingly, however, these adults were also able to recognize when it *was* time to quit. They recognized their limitations and were willing to modify or adjust their goals if failure seemed inevitable. When they failed at a project or task, they were able to recover quickly and did not fixate or ruminate on the failure.

These adults were also very adept at *goal setting*. Their goals were specific and achievable, but the adults were also willing to be flexible and adjust their goals if circumstances warranted. Their goals involved all aspects of their lives, including education, employment, and social life. The goals were accompanied by specific strategies to achieve them. These goals were often reviewed and modified in response to various circumstances or situations.

Each of the surveyed adults reported that he had developed a strong *support system*. This system consisted of friends, relatives, and acquaintances that he could call upon to provide assistance, support, guidance, or mentoring. The successful adults not only drew support from these individuals but also contributed to the relationship, by providing support and expressing genuine gratitude for assistance that was provided.

Effective emotional coping strategies were also common among these adults. They were able to recognize stressors and had specific and effective strategies to deal with emotional upsets. They were able to plan their activities in a way that prevented emotional problems and frustrations.

In order to help a child improve and enhance his social status and become a more attractive social partner, help him to develop the traits and strategies listed in the Frostig research.

RECOMMENDED RESOURCES

Best Friends, Worst Enemies, Michael Thompson, PhD (New York: Ballantine Books, 2001).

The Friendship Factor, Kenneth H. Rubin, PhD (New York: Viking Press, 2000).

Good Friends Are Hard to Find, Fred Frankel, PhD (Los Angeles: Perspective Publishing, 2000).

Conclusion

Children spend six hours each day in the classroom. Most schools are in session for 180 days each year. This translates to 1,080 hours per year that a child spends in school, and accounts for less than 20 percent of a child's waking hours. The remaining 80 percent of his time is spent on school buses, playgrounds, ball fields, in church pews, restaurants, movie theaters, at birthday parties, and at home.

For the child with a learning disability, the in-class hours present significant challenges and obstacles. His learning problems cause him to process, receive, understand, and express language differently, and the classroom is a source of failure and frustration. But what about the remaining 80 percent of the child's waking time? Are his recreational and social activities also impacted by his learning and language disabilities? The answer is a resounding *yes*. The child who is unable to comprehend the story's plot in his literature class will *also* have difficulty following the sequential steps necessary to make his bed or steal second base. The girl who cannot remember the state capitals in her social studies class will *also* be unable to remember that Grandma's black dog can go outside, but the white one should never leave the house unless he's on a leash. The child whose notebook and locker are overflowing with old tests, candy wrappers, elderly sandwiches, class notes, unsent Christmas cards, bowling score sheets, and unsigned permission slips will *also* have considerable difficulty maintaining an orderly bedroom or cleaning up Dad's workshop after finishing a project. The boy who takes two weeks to decide which project to enter in the science fair will *also* be unable to decide if he should attend Little League tryouts.

Learning disabilities and attentional problems are pervasive. They have an impact upon every moment of the child's day. Even if a child is enjoying significant success in an individualized, responsive academic program, he might be having significant difficulty in his social life outside the classroom walls. The rejection and isolation that he experiences are extraordinarily painful and can have a negative impact upon the child's self-esteem and mental health.

The greatest impact of these social skills deficits is on the child's inability to establish and maintain friendships. Life without friends is a lonely and barren existence. Friends share. Friends care. Friends believe. Friends trust. Friends protect. Friends advise. Friends commit. Friends nurture. Friends love.

What is a life without friendship? Many ancient societies have recognized the devastating consequences of being friendless. The Lakota Sioux, the Australian Aborigines, the Pennsylvania Amish, and the ancient Romans were very diverse cultures that had little in common. However, there was one form of punishment that they *did* share. If a member of these communities committed a major or serious crime and was found to be guilty of the offense, he was sentenced to banishment. He was forced to move his family and belongings to the outskirts of town and was unable to enter the village for any reason. Although the offender would be protected by the townspeople if attacked by external enemies, he was not welcome to participate in the social life of the community.

However, if the elders felt that banishment was not a severe enough punishment for the crime, the offender received a harsher sentence: shunning. This punishment required the criminal to remain in the community and to attend social functions and events. However, he was banned from speaking to anyone, and community members were forbidden to converse with him. The elders felt that shunning was among the most severe and devastating reprisals that a community could exact. Archives from these cultures indicate that many people who were shunned developed severe mental health problems and self-destructive behaviors. A Pennsylvania prosecutor once filed a suit against an Amish community for its use of shunning, and a court in that commonwealth determined that shunning met the criteria for "cruel and unusual punishment" under the guidelines in the United States Constitution.

Many children with learning and language problems are shunned in their own schools and neighborhoods every day. Because of their atypical and at times disruptive behaviors, they are unable to develop meaningful and lasting relationships with their peers. To complicate and worsen matters, they are often rejected, isolated, and misunderstood by the adults in their lives—even the ones charged with their care.

These children can and must be helped. Research, strategies, methods, and programs do exist to provide these youngsters with the guidance and counsel that they need in order to enjoy social success. But there are no easy answers. The solutions involve intense observation, careful planning, sensitive advising, and painstaking follow-through. The effort is worth it, because the *kids* are worth it.

A colleague of mine once conducted an informal seminar with a dozen preadolescents who were experiencing academic and social problems. He asked them the "magic wand" question. "Suppose," he began, "that I were to give you a magic wand and you could eliminate *one* of your problems. Would you choose to eliminate your academic difficulties and get better grades? Or would you choose to eliminate your *social skill* problems and have more friends?"

When the votes were tallied, the students voted to abolish their social skill deficits—by a margin of 12 to 0!

Appendix

Top Twenty Manners
That Adults Appreciate

1. consistently saying "Please," "Thank you," "You're welcome," and "Excuse me"
2. writing thank-you notes
3. making eye contact
4. cleaning up after yourself
5. showing respect for adults
6. not interrupting
7. treating people the way that you would like to be treated
8. using appropriate table manners
9. having a firm handshake
10. demonstrating compassion and sympathy toward others
11. opening doors and offering a seat to others
12. responding appropriately when spoken to
13. listening attentively when others are speaking
14. showing consideration and respect for guests
15. respecting the property of others
16. respecting the privacy of others
17. using good telephone manners
18. returning things that are borrowed
19. thinking before speaking
20. apologizing—sincerely—when a mistake is made

Top Ten Behaviors
That Annoy Adults

1. littering
2. spitting, burping, belching
3. walking in large groups in public
4. rowdiness at movies, ballgames
5. inappropriate public displays of affection
6. pushing, shoving, cutting in line
7. talking back
8. intolerance, prejudice
9. embarrassing or insulting others
10. using obscene language

Top Twenty Table Manners

1. Place your napkin on your lap as soon as you are seated. If you leave the table at any time during the meal, place your napkin on your chair. Never sneeze or blow your nose into your napkin. One hand should remain in your lap as you eat.
2. Never reach in front of someone to retrieve the salt shaker or gravy boat, even if the object is within your reach. Ask that it be passed to you.
3. It is okay to ask for a second helping. Precede the request with a compliment. "That salad was delicious. Could I have a bit more?"
4. Don't talk with your mouth full. If someone asks you a question and your mouth is filled with food, put one finger in the air and continue to chew. This will signal your dining partner to wait for a moment for an answer.
5. Bread or rolls should not be eaten whole! Break off a bite-size piece, butter it if you prefer, and eat it.

6. If a bite of food is unexpectedly hot or spicy, take a few sips of water. Fanning your open mouth is inappropriate.

7. "Elbows off the table" is an appropriate rule. However, once the dishes have been cleared and the family is conversing, elbows on the table are okay.

8. When asked to pass the salt or pepper, always pass both shakers together. When passing a pitcher or gravy boat, always turn it so that the other person can grasp the handle.

9. Always turn away from the table to sneeze, cough, or yawn.

10. If you find a seed, pit, or bone in your food when chewing, remove it from your mouth with a fork or spoon.

11. When eating meat, cut and eat one piece at a time. Never cut up the entire piece of meat and then begin eating it.

12. When eating long pasta, twirl only a few strands at a time using your fork and spoon. Cut off any trailing pieces and return them to your plate using your fork.

13. Have appropriate posture at the table. It actually helps you to digest your food better!

14. Drink any liquid by sipping, not gulping. Milk mustaches are not cute after age four.

15. Eating food off another's plate is not mannerly or hygienic.

16. An ice cream dessert should be eaten with a spoon. Use a fork for cake or pie.

17. When you are finished eating, ask permission to leave the table.

18. Do not begin eating until everyone is seated.

19. Never complain about the food.

20. Conversations and discussions should be appropriate and include everyone at the table.

Top Fifteen Rules for Participating
Positively in Sports or Games

1. Encourage and congratulate teammates.
2. Appropriately comfort and encourage teammates when mistakes or errors are made.
3. Smile, laugh during the game.
4. Positively offer suggestions or assistance.
5. Compliment good plays by teammates and opponents.
6. Congratulate winners; comfort, encourage losers.
7. Shake hands and make eye contact.
8. Be good-humored and appropriately self-deprecating when you make a mistake or error; no sulking or overreacting.
9. Cheer enthusiastically for *all* teammates.
10. Play the entire game; no quitting!
11. Balance enthusiasm with appropriate demeanor and behavior.
12. Joke without being hurtful or exclusionary.
13. End the game positively by saying good-bye and commenting favorably on the game: "That was fun! What a close game! See you on the bus tomorrow. Bye!"
14. De-escalate conflicts or disagreements through compromise.
15. Follow the rules and be willing to modify them when appropriate. "You are leading 14 to 0. How about if your best three batters hit left-handed for a few innings?"

Top Ten Tips for Buying, Giving, and Accepting Gifts

When buying . . .

1. Remove the price tag, but try not to damage the gift when you do so.
2. If you don't know how to wrap, ask someone to teach you. It's a valuable skill. If you really can't wrap, use a gift bag or aluminum foil. But do not give an unwrapped gift or one in a plain brown bag. Tacky!
3. Include a card. Buy one or make one, but include one inside or taped to the outside of the package.

When giving . . .

4. Be confident and positive when presenting a gift to someone.
   - *Do say,* "Happy Birthday," "Happy Hanukkah," "Merry Christmas," "I hope that you like it," "When I saw it in the store, I thought of you."
   - *Don't say,* "I couldn't spend very much," "I didn't know what to get you," "You probably already have one of these," "You probably won't like this."
5. Remember the STPT of gift giving. Alex Packer, in his invaluable book *How Rude!,* provides a useful formula for choosing and purchasing gifts:
   - **Selection:** What is the relationship between the gift and the recipient? Is it appropriate? Inappropriate? A Smashing Pumpkins CD for Grandma, a Shakespeare collection for a four-year-old, a motorcycle helmet for someone who doesn't own a motorcycle, a box of candy for your aunt who owns a candy store, a Britney Spears poster for your minister—bad choices.

- **Timing:** Give a gift on or before the special day, if possible. That demonstrates your thoughtfulness.
- **Proportion:** What is the relationship between the giver and recipient? How much time and money should a gift cost? Too much? Not enough?
- **Taste:** A gift should never be offensive or insulting; joke gifts can backfire. Giving a bald-joke book to your hairless uncle might not be too cool if Uncle Danny is in a bad mood when he receives it! Gift giving is an opportunity to be nice and kind.

When accepting . . .

6. Some appropriate things to say when you open a gift include:
   - "Thank you so much," "It will look great in my room," "I know that I will enjoy reading/using/wearing it," "It will keep me nice and warm."

7. Some impolite things to say when you open a gift:
   - "How much did it cost?" "Not another sweater/wallet/watch?!" "Why did you get me this?" Even if you are disappointed with a gift, remember: It is never appropriate to hurt another person's feelings.

8. Write thank-you notes. Don't think of this as a chore. Rather, view it as an opportunity to make the giver feel good. It is not required that you write a thank-you note to a person you have already thanked verbally, but it is not a bad idea. It is impossible to over-thank! Write a note as soon as possible after you receive the gift. Again, this demonstrates your thoughtfulness and good manners. Write by hand, if possible.

Although it is okay to write a thank-you note on
the computer, it is best to do it in your own
handwriting. If you do use a computer, make
sure that you sign it by hand. Don't begin the
note with "Thank you for . . ." Give some news
first. For example:

> *Dear Grandpa,*
> *We had a great time at your house last week*
> *and the plane ride home was fun. I never flew*
> *on a small plane before. The pilot showed me*
> *the cockpit. I wanted to thank you for the great*
> *computer game you gave me. . . .*

- Always mention the specific gift that you are
  acknowledging. Example: "I really love the
  Civil War CD-ROM that you gave me for
  Christmas," or "All of my friends love the
  snowflake sweater that you gave me." Avoid:
  "Thanks for the gift. It was neat."
- If someone gives you money, use the thank-
  you note to tell the person how you will spend
  it. Example: "I will use the money to buy a
  new baseball glove." Or "I will save the money
  for our March trip to Disney World."

9. It is appropriate to return a gift to the store if
   you already have an identical one (e.g., CD,
   book) or if it doesn't fit (e.g., sweater, gloves,
   dress).
10. It is best not to tell the giver that you returned
    it unless she asks.
    - If she asks, then say something like, "I really
      loved the CD. In fact, I liked it *so* much that
      my friend gave me the same CD for my birth-
      day last month. So I returned yours and got
      the new U2 CD. It is great!"

Top Ten Tips for Internet Usage

1. Never share your password with anyone for any reason.
2. Never give personal information (e.g., address, phone number) to anyone in a chat room.
3. Inform an adult if you ever receive an e-mail that is improper, threatening, or indecent.
4. Most of the information on the Internet is protected by copyright; don't copy or use it without permission.
5. Before you enter an online chat room, read several of the incoming messages to be sure that your message is appropriate and on topic.
6. Be careful of your wording in e-mail messages. Because your message is not accompanied by facial expressions or tone of voice, your message and your intent may be misinterpreted.
7. Don't believe everything that you read. Remember that some information on the Internet may be incorrect, false, and unproven.
8. Never say anything in an e-mail that you would not say to a person face-to-face. The anonymous and detached nature of e-mail can cause people to communicate in an inappropriate way.
9. Avoid forwarding or responding to chain letters of any sort. Most people do not appreciate being included on such lists. Chains are often methods for unscrupulous individuals to create massive mailing lists.
10. Many communities report that students are using e-mail to spread hurtful rumors about classmates. With one keystroke, a child can destroy the reputation of another. It is inappropriate, cruel, and unfair to participate in such activities.

Top Twenty Behaviors That Parents Should Avoid in Order to Present Positive Role Models to Their Child

1. failure to return items that you borrow
2. failure to be punctual
3. failure to do chores or pick up after yourself
4. failure to treat others with respect
5. failure to apologize when appropriate
6. tendency to complain or whine about work
7. tendency to spend money recklessly or frivolously
8. tendency to use vulgar, sexist, or racist language
9. failure to take responsibility
10. tendency to lie or exaggerate
11. inability to make or adhere to decisions
12. failure to use good table manners, or reserving manners for special occasions only
13. tendency to be rude or overly aggressive when driving or playing games or sports
14. failure to use appropriate conversational manners (e.g., interrupting, failing to listen)
15. tendency to be overly critical or to participate in malicious gossip
16. failure to listen politely
17. failure to keep promises or commitments
18. failure to ask permission before borrowing something of the child's
19. failure to respect property of others
20. failure to provide praise and reinforcement to others

Top Fifteen Appropriate Behaviors at Sporting Events (as a Spectator or a Player)

As a spectator

1. Never use obscene language or harass the players, coaches, or officials in any way.
2. Applaud outstanding plays by *either* team.
3. If a player is injured, quietly wait until he is treated by the coaches or medical personnel. When the player leaves the field or assumes his position, applaud.
4. Respect the decisions of the officials.
5. Respect your fellow spectators by using noise-makers, props, signs, and umbrellas appropriately. They came to watch the *game,* not to watch you!
6. Be attentive and appropriately solemn during the playing of the national anthem.

As a player

7. Play by the rules.
8. Never argue with officials or coaches. If there is a disputed call, let the coaches discuss it with the referees.
9. Control your temper! Tantrums, breaking or throwing equipment, or arguing with teammates or opponents are *not* acceptable.
10. Be a good sport! Congratulate other players (teammates or opponents!) for good play.
11. Don't show off!
12. Cooperate with teammates and coaches.
13. Be a gracious winner; don't brag or make fun of opponents.
14. Be a gracious loser; don't complain, make excuses, or blame others for the loss.
15. Try hard. You owe it to your teammates.

Rules for Challenging, Unusual Social Events

1. At a funeral
   - Dress conservatively.
   - Sign the guest book.
   - Be observant and respectful.
   - Say something to the bereaved.
   - Write a note after the service.

2. Visiting the sick
   - Call ahead.
   - Leave the hospital room when the nurse enters.
   - Bring a small gift.
   - Be upbeat.

3. On a bus
   - Let people off before you get on.
   - Have your fare ready.
   - One seat per customer; put your book bag on the floor or on your lap.
   - Thank the driver.

4. At the movies
   - Avoid sitting directly in front of someone.
   - If you need to leave, say "excuse me" and keep your body facing the screen as you leave the row.
   - No talking during the movie.
   - Keep your feet and knees off the seat in front of you.
   - Take your trash with you.

5. On a plane
   - Before boarding, gather all the material you will need during the flight and remove it from your carry-on bag.
   - Recline your seat slowly.
   - If you are in an aisle seat and the person next to you needs to get up, stand and go into the aisle to let him pass.

- Don't stay in the bathroom longer than necessary.
- Lower your window shade if there is a movie.
- Entertain yourself by reading, doing puzzles, or sleeping. Don't expect your seatmate to entertain you.
- Never joke about bombs or hijacking on the plane or in the airport. Security personnel take this *very* seriously.

6. At a concert
   - Be sure to let your parents know where you are.
   - Go with a friend and stay together even when you go to the bathroom. Hold hands if you have to.
   - As soon as you arrive, look for the exits.
   - If someone makes you feel uncomfortable, contact a security guard.
   - Never accept food or drink from someone you don't know.

Ten Pieces of Advice to Offer Children in Solving a Child-Child Conflict

1. Make a plan. (What is my position? What is *his* position? What will make us both happy?)
2. Don't use threats or insults.
3. Stick to one topic; don't introduce past disagreements or problems.
4. Be direct in stating what you need and feel.
5. Don't exaggerate, lecture, be sarcastic, or put words in his mouth.
6. Pick the appropriate time and place to have the discussion.
7. Observe and respond to the other person's body language.

8. Use "I" messages. ("I was unhappy that you didn't invite me" versus "You're a jerk for not inviting me.")

9. Acknowledge and accept your role in the problem.

10. Restate and acknowledge the other person's feelings. ("It must have made you angry when I said that. . . .")

Index